Why?
On Suffering, Guilt, and God

WHY?

ON SUFFERING, GUILT, AND GOD

A. van de Beek

Translated by John Vriend

WILLIAM B. EERDMANS PUBLISHING COMPANY
GRAND RAPIDS, MICHIGAN

Copyright © 1990 by Wm. B. Eerdmans Publishing Co.
255 Jefferson Ave. S.E., Grand Rapids, Mich. 49503

Printed in the United States of America

Library of Congress Cataloging-in-Publication Data

Beek, A. van de.
  [Waarom? over lijden, schuld en God. English]
  Why? on suffering, sin, and God / A. van de Beek; translated by
John Vriend.
     p.   cm.
  Translation of: Waarom? over lijden, schuld en God.
  ISBN 0-8028-0427-6
  1. Theodicy. I. Title.
BT160.B37313   1990
231'.8—dc20   90-35599
                                                      CIP

CONTENTS

FOREWORD

THIS BOOK IS AN ATTEMPT TO GIVE ITS READER ACCESS TO THE EXTREMELY difficult issues of suffering, guilt, and divine government. In making this attempt we shall not (assuming it were possible) investigate all the literature concerning these issues. Our goal is rather to think through these issues independently—via a different approach to and a fresh ordering of the data—in order to point out a way in which we can live with God's relationship to suffering and sin. This means at the same time that we will find a way in which we can "live with" God. The history of the human race is a history of suffering and sin in which the question why? arises all the time. If one cannot relate to God regarding this question, which characterizes human existence, one may well ask whether one can relate to God at all.

That is not to say that the question will be answered here. Rather, the object of our reflection will be the way in which we deal with this question and the way in which, with this question in our heart and head, we relate to and journey with God. If we journey with God, it is with the living God—with him who is making his history with us. The conclusion of this book, accordingly, will reflect that theme.

The book is intended for all who are theologically interested, not just for those who are professional theologians. Where for the undergirding of the line of thought a somewhat more specialized expansion is needed, it is provided, wherever possible, in fine print. For the sake of readability the number of references and footnotes has been kept down to a minimum.

I

INTRODUCTION

1. APOLOGY

THIS BOOK IS THE PRODUCT OF FURTHER REFLECTION ON MY IDEAS ABOUT the Trinity, as I articulated them in my dissertation on the human person of Christ.[1] In light of the idea of the mutability and history of God it seemed possible to me to make headway on the problem of suffering and sin in relation to the will and action of God.

The purpose of pursuing the line of thought in this direction hardly needs an explanation. The questions of suffering and sin, after all, perpetually engage human beings. The question of suffering comes most to the fore, but I am not sure whether beneath the waves of this sea the issue of guilt does not play a larger role. In any case, as a question that is always in the foreground and hence explicit, the problem of suffering predominates. Anyone who has spent a few years in the pastorate knows that innumerable people are weighed down by grief, loneliness, dread, and other forms of suffering, whatever they are called. One may well ask oneself whether there are people who do not have such feelings, given the degree that most are continually weighed down by them.

In addition, the circle of one's own immediate experience is invaded by a flood of information from all parts of the world in which suffering is predominant. Some people no longer want to look at televi-

---

1. Abraham van de Beek, *De menselijke persoon van Christus. Een onderzoek aangaande de gedachte van de anhypostasie van de menselijke natuur van Christus* (Nijkerk, 1980).

sion programs depicting war or starvation, unable to tolerate them anymore. In the face of this excess of suffering they are overcome by feelings of powerlessness. But also, if one seals oneself off from all this information, anxiety continues to build up. The attempt to drown out feelings does not help; they continue to gnaw at one's vitals. Accordingly, where the preacher keeps track of the experiences of the pastor and in his sermons speaks of suffering, he invariably finds a willing audience. A sermon on suffering appeals to people. Suffering is a problem to them, and a sermon on it is a sermon on them.

Now the church has always seen suffering in relation to God. The question is this: what role does God play in the experiences of suffering? The church through history has attempted to answer this question. We, for our part, must try, at the end of the twentieth century, to find our own way in this complex of problems. The community of faith knows it is called to go its way both with God and with the experience of suffering. And it knows that in one way or another the two are interrelated. This book is an attempt to help the community of faith to travel this road. It seeks to help in the search for the way in which God and suffering—and in the background, sin and evil—are related.

In attempting to find a way in this complex of problems we subject ourselves to certain criteria. We want to deal with the questions within the context of the Christian faith.

Anyone wanting to speak about God can do this only within the horizon of faith. To step outside that horizon is to step outside one's relationship with God, where one observes that nothing can be said about God, and accordingly, nothing can be said about God's relationship to suffering. That does not mean that faith is a subjective option. It is a response to authoritative revelation.[2] In the Christian faith authoritative revelation is inseparably bound up with Jesus Christ.

Primarily this means that we are bound by the sources of the Christian tradition, of which Jesus Christ is the center. To become detached from those sources is to become detached from the Christian community. Christian faith cannot do without Jesus Christ, or else it ceases to be Christian faith. And Jesus Christ can never be viewed apart from the tradition in which he stood and from the witness of the people around him who recognized in him the revelation of God—that is, apart from the Old and the New Testament. Here we find the critical norm to which in our thinking, whatever our further orientation may be, we need

---

2. Hendrikus Berkhof, *Christian Faith* (Grand Rapids: Eerdmans, 1979), pp. 46-47. See also Abraham van de Beek, *God Kennen—met God leven* (Nijkerk, 1982), pp. 5-9.

to subject ourselves. What we are told in the writings of the Old and the New Testament is decisive. It sets the tone for everything we want to say about God and about suffering, though this does not mean that everything in these writings is on the same wavelength. On the contrary, confronting us in the pages of these books of many centuries is a broad and colorful array of testimonies. But this does not alter the fact that for us these multicolored writings are witnesses to the truth of God as articulated by Israel, the apostles, and evangelists. We have no better criterion than the Bible. Therefore, for us these words of men fulfil the function of the Word of God.

To say that the Bible is the decisive criterion for what we say on a given subject does not mean that it is enough for us simply to repeat what the Bible says. Prophets and apostles, wise men and evangelists, always voiced their thoughts in a specific situation. Today we are living in another situation, in which we shall have to formulate anew the relationship between God and suffering as it relates to our situation. Hence we must operate with a second criterion, the human situation of the contemporary world. What we say about God and suffering will have to do justice to the experiences of our time, the thought patterns of our century, our culture, and our language. Unless we do this we shall be speaking in a vacuum and our words will not register. Unless they relate to the experiences and understanding of our own generation, our words no longer relate to God and suffering, for that suffering is a part of our experience and understanding. Our experience of suffering and the way we think and talk about it have to be included. The entire contemporary world, television and the daily paper, literature and philosophy, everything people think and experience—it all conspires to critique the Christian confession.

Fortunately, we do not have to start from scratch. We do not have to face the confrontation with the issues of God and suffering for the first time, not even in the second half of the twentieth century. We may build on the work of others. Having ourselves been shaped by the tradition, we cannot act otherwise. For that reason too, the history of dogma and ideas is a criterion for what we say in the present. What theologians and philosophers before us have experienced, digested, and said may and must be implicated in our own reflections, just as it is woven into our experience. We are children of the history that lies behind us. From the earliest written sources to the most recent literature, words about God and suffering are in excess. It is not possible, of course, to consider it all in this book; no human being can possibly survey it all. But we may and must, as far as we can, make grateful use of it.

As our final criterion, we may also mention the intrinsic consistency of the line of reasoning. It would seem self-evident that the movement of the argument in a given book should be consistent. But with this subject consistency is not entirely possible. The line of reasoning will not be without seams or even cracks. By saying this I am already saying now that this book does not offer *the* solution to the problems posed. If it had been possible to describe with continuity the relationship between God and suffering, we would have landed either in absolute monism or in absolute dualism. In absolute monism history is a duplicate of God's will and action: nothing escapes this *one* source of power. In that context divine command and human responsibility lose their meaning. If we want to be consistent, we have to say that in absolute monism the creation cannot even exist, because alongside and in the one source of power there is no room for multiplicity and hence for history. Absolute idealism carries within it the seed of its own destruction.

Hendrikus Berkhof says that to some ears the confession that God is the creator sounds blasphemous.[3]

In the final analysis, dualism and monism are contagious. Since in monism nothing can exist outside of the one self-sufficient and unchanging being, creation has to be denied. Accordingly, the world of perishable and changeable things becomes the world of nonbeing, the world of illusion. In his *Republic* (IV), Plato's thought tends in this direction. In dualism, God from the beginning encounters the negative world of matter (or however it may be described). One finds extreme dualistic tendencies in Gnosticism. A somewhat different, more theistic type of dualism occurs in Parseeism, with its conflict beween Ormazd and Ahriman. Whether one views the world as illusion, in contrast with true imperishable being, or as negative, because it is bound up with non-divine and non-divinely-willed matter, in practice will not make much difference. In neither case is earthly existence essential.

In absolute dualism God has nothing to do with evil. Evil comes from the other side, and God encounters and combats it. God is present only where the good is. But if that is the case, one may well ask where in this world God *is* present. After all, the world is permeated by suffering and sin. If God has nothing to do with suffering and sin, then with what in this world *is* he involved? In the dualistic framework we keep God pure. He keeps his hands clean. But we stay out in the cold. We have to manage without a God who holds the world in his hands, because otherwise those hands might get dirty. In the final analysis we have to manage without God, or perhaps worse, with a God who

3. Berkhof, *Christian Faith,* p. 149.

disaffirms us in our deepest experiences. Consequently, we may well ask whether such a God can still be our God.

If we do not wish to take either the road of absolute monism or that of absolute dualism, we have no alternative but to acknowledge in advance that the discontinuities in our thinking will remain. This book will show a lack of consistency, just as the world shows a lack of consistency, and as the relationship between God and his world shows a lack of consistency. As I begin to write this book, I am aware that in the end I will not have solved the problem I have set myself to address. I even have the feeling that the issues at stake are too big to write about. But if for that reason I should now decide not to write the book, the question would still persist, not only within myself but also in all those others who are confronted by suffering, and who cannot manage without a God who is fundamentally involved in this world because they know God speaks to them. In short, this book intends to make a contribution in the common struggle to fathom our human situation with God; in other words, a contribution in the common struggle to know God as the God of *this* world—*our* world.

2. OMNIPOTENCE

THE QUESTIONS CONCERNING THE RELATIONSHIP BETWEEN GOD AND suffering arise from two assumptions: the assumptions that God is almighty, and that he is good. If God is almighty, everything happens as he wills it to happen. If people have unpleasant experiences, they nevertheless occur in accord with the will of God. For if God had not willed them, they could not have occurred. On the other hand, however, people also want to cling to the goodness of God. But if God is good, how is it possible for such nasty things to happen? That would not be a problem, of course, if God were not also powerful. In that case, God would not want the nasty things to happen either, but he simply could not do anything about them. However, if God is powerful, he would be able to do something about bad things. But they happen, which raises the question of whether God is good.

Both divine omnipotence and divine goodness are fundamental to Christian theology. The idea that God is almighty is widely accepted, and awareness of his omnipotence is universal. One finds it not only within the orbit of the Christian church, but also among people who either have said farewell to the church or have only very indirect ties with the Christian tradition. Even if people no longer believe in God, the concept they have of God, the feeling associated with the word "God," is that of omnipotence.

Jürgen Moltmann points out that ultimately atheism even presupposes an all-controlling God, but one who is now indicted, cursed, repudiated. The God behind this world has to be monstrous. "These blasphemies are fundamentally provocations of God, for there is something that the atheist fears over and above all torments. That is the indifference of God and his final retreat from the world of men."[4] In atheism as well as theism, conclusions are drawn from the world to the power behind it. The theist speaks of the Almighty, the All-Good; the atheist of the nothingness which manifests itself in the chaos of this world.

Actually, the experience of God as an experience of omnipotence is not limited to the Christian tradition. We also find it, for example, in Judaism and in Islam. Wherever the concept of God is monotheistic, the connection with omnipotence arises, as it were, automatically. The concept of God, after all, implies a contrast with that which is earthly, limited, and created. God transcends everything. It is probably the case that for most people the phrase "God is almighty" is no more than a tautology, a sentence in which the predicate adds nothing to the subject; in other words, a sentence in which the predicate is already implied in the subject. For most people, at least in the Western world, the word "omnipotence" adds nothing to what has already been said by the word "God." As far as these people are concerned, the word "almighty" could as well be deleted from the Apostles' Creed; nothing would change. Even without the word, God is understood as omnipotent. *If* God exists, he is omnipotent; otherwise he is not God. From its very beginning the church confessed that God is the almighty. To be sure, the word "almighty" is rare in the New Testament, but the idea is continually present. One only has to call to mind a metaphor like that of the potter and the clay (Rom. 9) to see how Paul could speak of God's power. At an early stage already the word "almighty" was incorporated into the creeds. Both the Apostles' and the Nicene Creed attribute to God, besides the predicates "Father" and "Creator," the epithet "almighty."

In the course of the history of the church the omnipotence of God remained virtually a fundamental given. One of the better known formulations occurs in the Heidelberg Catechism, Lord's Day 10, question and

---

4. Jürgen Moltmann, *The Crucified God: The Cross of Christ As the Foundation and Criticism of Christian Theology* (New York: Harper & Row, 1974), p. 221.

answer 27. The answer to the question: "What do you understand by the providence of God?" reads:

> Providence is
>> the almighty and ever present power of God
>>> by which he upholds, as with his hand,
>>>> heaven
>>>> and earth
>>>> and all creatures,
>>> and so rules them that
>>>> leaf and blade,
>>>> rain and drought,
>>>> fruitful and lean years,
>>>> food and drink,
>>>> health and sickness,
>>>> prosperity and poverty—
>>> all things, in fact, come to us
>>>> not by chance
>>>> but from his fatherly hand.

According to this confession everything that happens happens by the will of God: not only joyful things like health, herb, and grass, refreshing rain and warming sun, but also sickness, inundating rains, and searing drought.

Generations of Protestants have grown up with the Heidelberg Catechism, and with the thoughts of Lord's Day 10. The sense that all things are governed by God is deep-rooted, fundamental in the life of a Protestant. We hear echoes of it in numerous well-known psalms and hymns.

> I know that the Lord is almighty,
>> Supreme in dominion is He,
> Performing His will and good pleasure
>> In heaven and in earth and the sea. (Ps. 135)

"We praise, we worship Thee, we trust, / And give Thee thanks forever, O Father for thy rule is just, / And wise and changes never; / Thy hand almighty o'er us reigns, Thou doest what Thy will ordains, / 'Tis well for us Thou rulest."

It would be very easy to add other examples. For that matter this sense of security in, and dependence on, almighty God is not only found among Protestants; it is also present in Catholic circles. There it is much

7

expressed not so much in song as in remarks made in passing: "Just leave it to the good Lord."

Berkhof prefers the term "superior power" *(overmacht)* to "omnipotence." "Superior power" is more dynamic than "omnipotence." Also, Berkhof describes this superior power dialectically as "defenseless superior power" *(weerloze overmacht)*. Still, in Berkhof the all-dominant power of God is decisive. He *can* be the defenseless one because history will not in any case pass out of his control. "And so he has involved himself in a history with us in which, for the sake of the genuineness of this covenant partnership, he hides his superior power and manifests it in his defenselessness, to give us the room we need to become ourselves; but in that defenselessness he maintains his superior power to keep us from choosing eternally against him and therewith against ourselves."[5] Although the defenseless but superior God, in a dynamic process of interaction, may perhaps conquer human beings more psychically than physically, his power is no less decisive.

Because in Protestant circles the formulation of Lord's Day 10 of the Heidelberg Catechism can be considered classic for understanding the omnipotence of God, it is not surprising that it is the first subject of criticism. This criticism has been brought to sharp expression in Martin Hart's *A Flight of Curlews*.[6] He says that if it is true that God causes all things, health as well as sickness, to come to us out of his hand, then God is also behind the cancer that is killing his mother. God wanted this suffering, this demolition of a human being. He even caused it. The elders who come to visit her confirm it: this is the will of God. However, Martin Hart cannot believe in this God anymore. He declines to let this God be his God. Lord's Day 10 of the Catechism appears in print on the title page of his book—nailed to a pillory. Consequently, *A Flight of Curlews* is an impassioned protest against the confession that an almighty God causes all things to come to us out of his hand.

A Flight of Curlews has become a bestseller. Much has been said and written about it. People resonate to the theme of the book, epitomized in the episode of the elder's visit. People who are excited about this book see a problem with a church which expects you to confess a God who is the cause of everything. People of the second half of the twentieth century have trouble with that. A rational, just, and ethically acceptable rule by an omnipotent God is something they can no longer "place." Some still struggle with it. Many have simply "tuned out." Because it

---

5. Berkhof, *Christian Faith*, p. 139.
6. Martin Hart, J. W. Arriens, trans., *A Flight of Curlews* (London: Allison & Busby, 1986). The Dutch title is *Een vlucht regenwulpen* (Amsterdam, 1979).

does not make sense to them, the idea of omnipotence is no longer an option to them; nor, therefore, is the idea of God, for traditionally the two concepts go together. Many have renounced God. Obviously, considering the popularity of *A Flight of Curlews,* commitment to God has waned. God and his relationship to suffering continue to intrigue many people. But for those who have not sworn off God, the problem is all the more acute. In our world, how do you deal with the government of God?

I have the impression that in our day the whole issue has become much more difficult than it was in earlier days. In the eighteenth century people could still sing lustily about the goodness of God. Today that raises huge questions. There are several reasons for this:

a. The experiences of the Second World War. God after Auschwitz—is that still an option? The gruesome reality of the systematic murder of millions of innocent people has produced a shock which has by no means been "processed" yet. Rather, the horror of the concentration camps of Germany has been reinforced by all the horrors which followed: in Korea, in Vietnam, in continuing oppression and violence in all parts of the world. Can we still call a world in which such things are possible a world that is under the rule of an omnipotent God? And if it be a world under the rule of God, can we still call such a God our Father and acknowledge him as Lord? Must we not break all our ties with him?

b. The worldwide scope of the suffering. As a result of modern means of communication we daily face a barrage of information about suffering and injustice that is more than we can grasp. Misery stares at us from earth's remotest corners. Suffering is not a moment's ripple in an otherwise placid pool; the whole world is a churning sea of suffering. It is not an incidental feature here and now, nor just an occasional blow I absorb in an otherwise peaceful life; it is everywhere and the world is full of blows. Suffering is not an incident somewhere in the world; the world as such has become a suffering world.

c. A reaction to the Enlightenment. In the eighteenth century people could still view the world as a well-ordered system with the Supreme Being at the top. The cosmos was systematic and cohesive. But since then it has proven to be chaotic, and the thinking of mankind has become fragmented. We can no longer "place" an all-embracing Supreme Being who is the point at which all the laws and rules in nature, ethics, psychology, and all the other spheres of life are coordinated.

d. In our culture there is no room for the supernatural. We are immersed in the tangible and visible. We live in a world of causal connections. There is no room for a power or an influence outside of the power of direct causality or what is empirically verifiable.

9

Specifically, the German theologian Rudolf Bultmann has addressed himself to this complex of problems (see esp. his essay "New Testament and Mythology: The Problem of Demythologizing the New Testament Proclamation") in *New Testament and Mythology*. Twentieth-century man lives with the results of the natural sciences and can no longer believe in the intervention of a supernatural being in the natural order. In the new world image modern science has given us supernatural powers no longer have a place.

Karl Jaspers has pointed out that Bultmann overestimates the possibilities of science, which neither claims to nor does furnish a world image or life-view. It is no more than a block of provisional practical knowledge.[7] The provisional character of scientific knowledge has been even more forcefully highlighted by Karl Popper, in *Conjectures and Refutations. The Growth of Scientific Knowledge*. Now while it may be true that Jaspers and Poppers are correct from the perspective of the theory of science, the scientific method, in which the world is conceived as a causally closed system, in practice does function as a life-view and makes no distinction between atheism in methodology and atheism in life-orientation. At least in the foreground forces other than the measurable and observable data of the world play no role. Behind these data there is undoubtedly a world of experience, a world of myth, and a world of faith, which continue to propel history. Faith furnishes "the courage to be" (Paul Tillich). However, for most people this faith is not the consciousness of an omnipotent, intervening God, but a nameless substratum of desires and ideals which, to be sure, propel the observable and measurable world of twentieth-century man, but which rarely rise to the surface where they can be communicated. One can even say that modern science, precisely in its limited and provisional character, could only arise and flourish within a worldview in which only the objectifiable is primary.

e. Developments in scientific technology. Man has acquired the power to control things and can manage life himself. Unless God clearly manifests himself as the one who can manage other things, including that which we cannot, his presence no longer has any meaning. What can be achieved in the world we ourselves have to achieve, and beyond that nothing is achievable. Of God you do not notice a thing—except chaos.

f. The increased awareness of the importance of life on earth. Partly as a result of increased prosperity life on earth is no longer merely a brief passage preceding one's real, eternal existence in heaven. The earth and our life on it have become important. Consequently, the problem of suffering becomes much more acute, because suffering has become more intense. You can no longer dismiss it by saying, "It is only temporal. Soon we will be in heaven and all is forgotten." This temporal life itself is now so important.

7. Karl Jaspers and Rudolf Bultmann, *Die Frage, Der Entmythologisierung* (München: R. Piper & Co. Verlag, 1954), pp. 9-46.

g. The increased "maturity" of man. People have learned to protest against authority. Authority is no longer automatically accepted, but must prove itself as benevolent. This change, which has now been going on for centuries, especially since the Renaissance, affects authority in the state, in the church, in education, and in the home. It would be strange if it did not also apply to God. God's authority has to be acceptable. God too needs a societal base of support. In contemporary society, and (because the church is a fellowship of contemporary people) also in the contemporary church, authority for its own sake, omnipotence as such, is not possible.

This list of influences is not complete; only a number of noteworthy phenomena have been cited. Nor do all the different influences operate in the same direction. Some reinforce each other; others are in opposition. However, as the result now of one movement and then of another, by one influence operating here and another there, the total effect is that people of the second half of the twentieth century have an extraordinary amount of trouble with faith in an omnipotent God who governs all things.

On the other hand, we must observe that at best the difference between this and earlier centuries can only be one of degree. Otherwise this entire issue would be new, which is certainly not the case. In earlier centuries people also had trouble with God's rule. One only needs to read Psalm 73, the book of Job, or the Greek tragedies. The synagogue has linked Psalm 42 with the beginning of the book of Exodus: to the drowning of one's children in the Nile one can only react with the cry of godforsakenness. After the destruction of Jerusalem in 586 B.C. and A.D. 70, as well as during the pogroms of 1940 to 1945, people have responded with the indictment, "My way is hid from the Lord, and my right is disregarded by my God" (Isa. 40:27). And the people in the fourteenth century who saw masses of their fellow countrymen fall victim to the bubonic plague also experienced their world as totally miserable.

The circumstances in which for centuries people have had difficulty acknowledging the rule of God cannot alter the fact, however, that today we are still stuck—and stuck badly—with the problem of evil. To the suffering of centuries has been added the suffering of *this* century. The problem has just continued to grow. On top of all the painful experiences of people of past generations have come our own experiences. Against the background of all these other tales of woe we must now somehow come to terms with the suffering of this century, as well as our own personal suffering.

*   *   *

IF IN THIS CONTEXT THE CONCEPT "OMNIPOTENCE" PLAYS A LARGE ROLE, IT is important to take a closer look at its meaning. One can explain the formula "God is almighty" in two ways: (1) God can manage all things; (2) God can do anything. With a view to this ambiguity a distinction was made in the Middle Ages between *potentia ordinata* and *potentia absoluta*. The first is the power of God as it accords with his will. What God wills happens. If it is God's will to create, a creation comes into being. Because God willed this world it has become what it is. Whether God could have created another world is not the issue. We have to deal with *this* world which God has willed. In this existing, God-willed situation, no power can counter his power. Nothing is equal to his will; all things are subordinate to him. *Potentia ordinata* represents what we mean by saying, "God can manage all things." The problem which occupies us in this book then becomes the question whether God cannot manage suffering, sin, and injustice. Or do we have to say, "He does not want to overcome these forces; they are taken up in his will and hence in his *potentia ordinata*"?

The *potentia absoluta* is the power of God whereby he can do all things, even what he has not willed. God could just as well have created another world. Whatever one might possibly conceive, God can do it. And what we cannot conceive God is able to do, for he can conceive it.[8]

In the Middle Ages, in order to avoid logical problems, certain matters had been excluded from the *potentia absoluta*. Given a consistent *potentia absoluta* position, one might for example arrive at the remarkable question: "Can God make a stone he himself cannot lift?" If God cannot, he is not omnipotent; if he can, he is stuck with a stone he cannot lift and is not omnipotent either. The conclusion would have to be that absolute omnipotence is impossible. Now such an example seems foolish, out of keeping with the seriousness of the subject. It is, however, the picture many people have of God's omnipotence and one which causes them to abandon his omnipotence. In the years of my pastoral ministry the question was put to me in all seriousness by people who were no longer able to believe in God. Of course, the source of the trouble lay not in the example but in the problem it illustrated: Is the notion of the om-

8. In an editorial note in Thomas Aquinas, *Summa Theologica* (Taurini, 1938), qu. 25, 5, pp. 187, note 1, we read: "Potentia absoluta vocatur qua secundum se considerata Deus potest quidquid possibile est, aut nullam contradictionem involvit. Potentia autem ordinata aut ordinaria dicitur qua operatur secundum ordinem lege aliqua praefixum, suaeque voluntatis imperio constitutum." (English: " 'Potentia absoluta' is [called] that by which, considered in itself, God is able to do whatever is possible or involves no contradiction. 'Potentia ordinata' or 'ordinaria,' however, is [called] that by which he works according to the order pre-established by some law, and constituted by the authority of his own will.")

nipotence of God correct? Can an omnipotent God even exist? And if he is not omnipotent, he is not God!

We only have to formulate the question in a slightly different way to be face-to-face with the issue under discussion: Can God make a world he himself cannot manage? Is it possible that the omnipotent God created a world which is not subject to his will? Apparently the answer is yes, for such a world exists. But if the world is not obedient to his will, can God still be considered omnipotent? Limiting ourselves to the *potentia ordinata*, we have to ask, Given the existing situation, can God really manage it? In my opinion, pastorally that is the most pressing question. Is the world not slipping out of God's hand? Is he in control of my situation? Still, we must not stop too soon; we also must involve the *potentia absoluta* in the problem. Could God really not have created another world? Could he not in the beginning have created a perfect earth of peace and justice? The concept of absolute omnipotence implies that God indeed could have but did not. Consequently, for us the question remains: *Why* did not God do things differently? Why is there so much suffering and injustice, if God could have acted differently?

Thomas Aquinas answers the question concerning the *potentia absoluta* affirmatively: Therefore God can do what he does not ("Ergo Deus potest facere quod non facit").[9] However, this power must never be viewed apart from his foreknowledge and foreordination. But this only makes the problem bigger: if God knows in advance what is going to happen and incorporates this knowledge in his decision (whereas his power as *potentia absoluta* is not subject to it), large questions arise concerning the decisions of the divine will. He knew what would happen; he could have made another choice, but he did not. Even with the restriction that the *potentia absoluta* may not lead to logical contradictions, the high Scholasticism of the Middle Ages, rejecting voluntarism along with the primacy of the will, leads to a God who is logical, to be sure, but one at the same time very remote from his people who suffer in the world he has made.

If we view God as absolutely omnipotent, he becomes a dark enigma (certainly if we drop the medieval restrictions). His omnipotence is at odds with itself. Omnipotence clashes with omnipotence in him, and it seems absurd to confess God as the absolutely omnipotent being. However, we must not too quickly shrink from this absurdity. Does this absurdity possibly correspond with the absurdity of the suffering present in a world which is God's world? Does it correspond perhaps with the absurdity of a God with a history and a God who is triune? Philosophical constructions may seem mere sport (*Spielerei*). They may seem

9. Aquinas, *Summa Theologica* I, Q.25, 5.

disrespectful and insufficient. They may also help to put in words the colorful riches of God's encounter with human beings and thus help us to understand God better. If, after all, the world belongs to God, our thinking is included in it and we must do our very utmost to find a way to journey with God.

3. GOODNESS

THE GOODNESS OF GOD, IN CONTRAST TO HIS OMNIPOTENCE, HAS NOT BEEN taken up in the early Christian creeds. To explain this fact one might advance that goodness is already conveyed by calling God "Father." That, however, is only partly true. Apart from goodness, the concept "Father" also connotes other motifs, as for example "authority." Then one may just as well argue that the power of God is already included in the word "Father." Hence the meaning of the statement "I believe in God the Father" does not coincide with that of the sentence "God is good." The same applies to the predicate "Creator."

Admittedly, in later theology it is explicitly said that God is good. One encounters "goodness" in official church creeds and in the most important works of dogmatic theology, in the early church, the Middle Ages, as well as in the period of the Reformation, and in recent literature. In almost all dogmatic works the goodness of God is a fixed part of the doctrine of the attributes of God.

The *Belgic Confession* mentions the goodness of God alongside of other attributes like wisdom and omnipotence. From the mass of dogmatic literature we shall cite only a few examples: Augustine, *Soliloquia* I, 1, 6: God is "summum bonum"; "amabilem se fecit; bonum amando, nos meliores efficimur" (In *Psalmos* 144, 1). In his *Summa Theologica*, Thomas devotes a separate *questio* to the goodness of God (I, 6); further on also there is repeated reference in the *Summa* to the *bonitas Dei*. Calvin says, "Now we hear the same powers enumerated there that we have noted as shining in heaven and earth: kindness, goodness, mercy, justice, judgment, and truth."[10] Heppe writes: In the love of God "is manifested the 'goodness of God,' according to which God is in and for Himself 'supremely good' and towards creation 'beneficient.'"[11] Karl Barth makes the goodness of God the

10. John Calvin, *Institutes of the Christian Religion* (Philadelphia: Westminster Press, 1960), I, 10, 2.

11. Heinrich Heppe, *Reformed Dogmatics*, G. T. Thomson, trans. (London: George Allen & Unwin, 1950), pp. 95-96.

foundation of his doctrine of God by describing the being of God as "the one who loves in freedom."[12]

Still, one cannot regard the omission of the goodness of God from the early creeds as accidental. Moltmann has set forth the extent to which, in the early church, attributes of the Roman emperor were transferred to God and to Christ.[13] Even if on this point his views require some refinements, what remains intact is that the belief that God's power was over the powers of the world was the core of what the early church confessed concerning God. God was mighty, mightier than all earthly rulers and especially mightier than death. According to Moltmann, the early church's longing for victory over death led to its viewing God as the unmoved ruler.[14]

Even though the goodness of God has for centuries been viewed as a necessary attribute of God, or even as his supreme attribute—the expression of his very being—in the minds of many people the notion persists that omnipotence is a more essential attribute of God than his goodness. For many people a God who does not control all things and is not invincible cannot *be*. Either God is omnipotent or he is not God—even if he were not good. Even if God should act capriciously and prove himself an arbitrary tyrant, he could still—to them—be God. To be sure, he would then be a God who inspired dread, but he would be God nevertheless. But with goodness the case is different. A God who, though perfectly good, is not powerful and cannot cope with things, who is overwhelmed by the powers of his world, is much harder to place than a God characterized by tyrannical caprice. In the eyes of many, a powerless God cannot exist, even if he were perfectly good. The sentence "God is good" is much less a tautology than "God is omnipotent." This means that many people cannot concur with the conclusion of Thomas Aquinas: "Goodness should be associated above all with God."[15] To their minds, omnipotence occupies that position; if need be, God's goodness can be discarded.

Now the goodness of God is a complex matter. Goodness requires a norm. A thing is good because it satisfies a norm, a standard by which good and evil are judged. The goodness of a thing or a person can therefore be established by reference to something else that serves as criterion. For example, for human goodness one can pose as norm the

12. Karl Barth, *Church Dogmatics*, II, 1, 28 (Edinburgh: T. & T. Clark, 1975), p. 257.
13. Jürgen Moltmann, "Gottesoffenbarung und Wahrheitsfrage," in *Parrhesia, Karl Barth zum achtigsten Geburtstag* (Zürich, 1966), pp. 149-72, esp. pp. 151-53.
14. Moltmann, *The Crucified God*, p. 214.
15. *Summa Theologica*, Q. 6, 1 (Blackfriars edition).

common interest over private interest. A thing is good if it serves the common interest and bad if, though it possibly serves my private interest, it injures the community. In this case, the community is considered more important than the individual and the interest of the community is the norm for good and evil. Another criterion could be self-sacrifice. Do I opt for my own advantage or do I consider the other more important than myself? The good person sacrifices himself (herself) for the other; the bad person takes advantage of the other. In this case, the well-being of the other is the standard by which I am judged. Though one could mention other criteria, the point is that there is a criterion, a norm above us, to which we are subject in making our evaluations. As a rule, for believers in God, the divine command, however different the understanding, will be the final norm. God himself is the authority by whom our goodness or "badness" is measured.

According to classical theology, the norms of good and evil are derived from the will of God. "The good" is not something that stands by itself, but that which conforms to the will of God. "Good" is what God wills. By saying that, one at the same time says that God cannot will evil. The moment God wills anything it is good. After all, his will is normative, the highest ethical authority. What moral authority could there be—apart from God's own will—by which the goodness of God could be measured? Accordingly, we would be able to solve the problem of the omnipotence and the goodness of God by saying that all things that happen are expressions of the will of God. That follows from his omnipotence. But then all things are good, for if all things are or occur by virtue of his will they cannot be evil. If we call them evil, we are mistaken. We have forgotten the norm, namely, that God so willed it.

In some passages of Augustine one gets the impression that he wants to take this road. "He is good for he is God."[16] "It is by him [the Holy Spirit] that we see whatever we see to be good in any degree, since it is from him who doth not exist in any particular degree but who simply is what he is."[17] Because God is the only source and also the highest will, everything that is is good. Nothing is evil, for nothing that exists does so outside of the will of God. However, I think that at such moments—in other passages he definitely shows he does know of evil in the world—Augustine has in mind especially the evil which people suffer and not so much the evil dealt with in the subject of ethics. We should bear suffering with joy, and in any case, with patience, because it comes to us out of God's hand. When he deals with the evil deeds people commit, Augustine presumably

---

16. Augustine, *The Confessions of St. Augustine,* Bk. 13, ch. 19.
17. Ibid., ch. 31 (cf. Christian Parma, *Pronoia und Providentia: Der Vorsehungsbegriff Plotinus und Augustins* [Leiden: Brill, 1971]).

follows another line of thought which fails to resolve how that evil can exist. Still, in the case of a deep thinker like Augustine, we must not exclude the possibility that he in fact viewed the entire world—not only together with its suffering but also with its injustice—as a world willed by God and therefore as a good world, a perspective sharply opposed to the Manichean tendencies of his day.

Logically, it is possible to solve the problem in that manner. Then the whole world is good, the outflow of God's will. I would even say that it is not only a logical solution but can be an existential experience, a moment of mystical ecstasy in which one accepts God, the world, and oneself, to the utmost. This total acceptance is no dull resignation; it is intense joy over the whole of existence as divinely willed reality. This world is accepted by God because he has willed it as it is. This form of dealing with evil can thus serve as a base for projecting the theme of reconciliation back into all eternity. If reconciliation is all-embracing, it embraces also the times, and the world—with all that is, was, and will be—is reconciled and willed from all eternity. It is elect in the manner of double predestination: even in its reprobation it is divinely willed and therefore good.

Meanwhile, in practice life is more complicated, even in the Old and New Testament. In the first place, not everything in the Bible is called "good." People turn out not to be what God has intended. There is disobedience and evil. In Scripture the simplicity of absolutely accepting everything that happens in time and space as the result of the good will of God is broken by human sin, of a God who is angry because people do not conform to his will.

In the second place, the goodness of God is no empty concept. His goodness is full of content: full of love, mercy, compassion, grace, and all those other things which indicate that God does not will suffering and sin, but saves people who are threatened by them. That is how the goodness of God is understood in the Old and the New Testament, and the church also has correctly interpreted it in this fashion: as goodness which does not will injustice and oppression and, even more, as goodness which saves people and has compassion on them. Even the dogmatics of scholasticism regarded the love he expressed in grace, mercy, patience, long-suffering, and forgiveness as the essence of the goodness of God.[18] All these concepts indicate that God has a relationship with people. In that relationship human feelings count. The goodness of God does not exist in isolation, but is bound to the experience of people. The mercy extended to the heartbroken is experienced as salvation. The

18. Heppe, *Reformed Dogmatics*, p. 96.

human face God encounters, the human face marked by suffering and strained by fear, is the norm by which God's goodness allows itself to be measured. To manifest his goodness, God has "encamped" himself among suffering, sin-broken people. If in their suffering people are not allowed to look for mercy, then God's goodness has become empty. Such an empty form of goodness, however, is not the goodness of the God of Israel, the God of Jesus Christ, who in the human face of his Son made his goodness replete with compassion and forgiveness. Ever since Jesus Christ has come into the world, the goodness of God can never again be viewed apart from him in whom God so loved the world that he gave his only Son. In Christ, God in goodness and with his entire being has turned to the cries and tears of the wretched.

4. SUFFERING AND SIN

ON GOD'S SIDE, THE PROBLEM OF HIS RELATIONSHIP TO EVIL CONSISTS IN THE relationship between his omnipotence and his goodness. On the side of evil there are two aspects: evil on the one hand assuming the form of suffering, and on the other that of sin. Suffering is the evil we experience, the evil that comes over us, not sought out but endured. Suffering is *passio,* in which human beings are first of all passive, those in whom suffering is realized. To be sure, one can become active in resisting or processing suffering, but this activity is secondary to the experience of suffering coming over us.

Concretely, what is the evil that comes in the form of suffering? I believe that we must include every unpleasant experience and situation which is experienced by people (and animals and possibly also plants[19]). It is whatever violates the wholeness of life, and wherever peace (in the absolute sense) is violated. Suffering occurred in the concentration camps. Suffering occurs where people die of hunger, or are wasted by debilitating illness, where animals are tortured. Suffering occurs where people are forced, helplessly, to watch the suffering of others; it occurs in the sense of powerlessness with which prisoners see their fellow prisoners being executed; it throbs in the powerlessness with which

---

19. Recent investigations have demonstrated that plants react to harmful stimuli, a fact which can be observed by the changes in electrical tension. The fact that these reactions are not manifested in a way that humans immediately recognize does not mean it is not a comparable experience.

people watch a loved one die of a deadly disease. But suffering is also present where a child cuts his knees. The latter, too, is suffering; it gives a person an unpleasant, possibly even an unhappy, feeling. We have to be extremely careful in order not to trivialize suffering, even seemingly small-scale suffering.

For in the first place it is not possible to measure the painful experience of another person by the degree of its visibility. Then we would fall into the error that accounts for extra suffering—on top of the pain already borne—by those who have an ailment that is not immediately noticeable. They continually have the feeling that their suffering is taken less seriously than that of others. "If only I had a broken leg, people would sympathize." One person may feel more unhappy on a visit to a dentist than another on her way to a surgeon. Still more unhappy may be the one who cannot point to any cause for his insecurity, his feelings of restlessness and fear, which nevertheless prevent him from fully living. In the second place, even in the case of minor pain, no matter how small, the question comes up as to the sense of it. In it, too, evil is manifest. Why can evil break into God's good creation? Every disturbance of peace is a pointer to the fact that this world is a broken world. Hence every wound people incur raises the entire complex of questions relating to suffering. Even if but one child in the whole world were to experience one day of sorrow, we would still have to ask ourselves how God could possibly allow this day of suffering in the life of this child; then, through this one child and this one day, the question of God's goodness and omnipotence, and of human suffering, would forever stand before the world in all its starkness.

This is not to say that all suffering is the same, as if it does not matter whether someone experiences a concentration camp or a fall from a bicycle. Suffering is present in both cases, but the extent to which it manifests itself is infinitely different. In a skin injury we may perhaps, upon reflection, discover the "why?" of suffering, but in the darkness of Auschwitz this question is so overwhelming that we can hardly cope with it anymore. Stupefied by the manifestation(s) of evil, we can hardly approach God anymore because we can no longer look him straight in the face. Either we despise a God who allows such things, or we despise him even more because he cannot prevent such things. In many daily situations of distress we can speak with God, seeking help or comfort, but after the horror of the Holocaust we do not know what to do with God anymore. Afraid to hear that God abandons people, we are even more afraid to hear that he cannot cope with evil. Even a person who did not experience the camp or who was born after the war despairs of coming before God with these things. It will be a long time before this wound has healed in the soul of mankind and the people of Europe will again recognize their God—even though our world does struggle to recover from the years 1940-1945.

In addition to suffering, evil also takes the form of sin. In this active form of evil people do not undergo but commit it. Here man is the cause. Here the question of divine government assumes an even sharper profile than in the case of suffering. In the case of suffering, one can, for example, refer to its pedagogical value, but in the case of sin there is no possibility of escape. Why did God permit—or perhaps even will—that human beings should be sinful? How could he create beings who were able to commit the horrors humans have perpetrated? Actually, the question concerning the possibility of sin is the last question in the complex of questions concerning the relationship between God and evil. It is the question to which all the others can be traced. In the case of this question it is most evident that we cannot find a solution in the form of a consistent line of thought. When he came to this question, Barth correctly said that we face an unfathomable mystery.[20] And when, in his discussion of "God and Nothingness,"[21] Barth proposes to analyze this mystery, we discover on every page that he is not succeeding, just as no one else ever succeeded in answering the final "why?" In the end we get no further than a description of the situation, leaving to God the mystery of his being and turning to the face of God in his history with people, the face which in the final analysis is the face of Jesus Christ. For if we venture to occupy ourselves with the questions which relate to God's action in a suffering world, it is only because we already know from the start that he is the God of Jesus Christ. It is only together with this God that one can risk inquiring into the "why?" Solely on the basis of the covenant, within the security of his love, dare we ask this Father about his "management." We ask him because he is most important to us, because we cannot ignore him, because it is impossible for us to be indifferent to him, and we cannot be content not to know him. At the same time, however, we know that we only dare ask these questions in the knowledge that, essentially, we already know him as the one who loves us and *knows* us. If we want to fight through the question of the "why?" to the very bottom, the way is that of the child, not of the proud titan.

Suffering and sin are two forms of evil. In saying this we cannot regard the two in total isolation from each other. We may distinguish between suffered evil and ethical evil, but we cannot separate them. In the first place, both are manifestations of the one dark power which

20. Barth, *Church Dogmatics* III, 3, 50, pp. 289ff.
21. Ibid., pp. 289-368.

threatens the world. By sin the door of the world was opened to all sorts of misery. Or should we say, because the door of the world was somehow open to evil, sin and all other misery entered it? In the second place, the flip side of evil done is always evil suffered. The sin of one person is the misery of the other. The injustice of the oppressors is the misery of the oppressed. Not every form of suffering can be directly attributed to sin, but every sin does call forth suffering, either in the victim or in the doer. In the third place, to commit sin is itself a form of suffering. It is a matter of being driven by a force we do not control. It is a question whether people suffer more from the consequences of others' sins than from sin itself. For through sin a breakdown occurs in human dignity, with all the attendant conscious or unconscious feelings of frustration and inferiority. It ends in powerlessness and guilt and from there it proceeds in a cycle of new injustice and new guilt. To commit injustice is to be imprisoned in this vicious circle which ultimately demonizes the doer and destroys him in his deepest self. Socially and existentially the sinner comes down in the world. When the Christian church confesses that all are sinners, the question is not whether a person has come down in the world but in what way, both socially and existentially, a person lives in that condition.

In the fourth place, we must ask whether suffering is in fact always so passive and only endured. Is it not true that people sometimes seek out suffering in a masochistic attempt to escape from their loneliness and feelings of inferiority? People may actively inflict suffering upon themselves. They may even pursue that course to the point where they choose the way of self-destruction as the ultimate confirmation of themselves as suffering beings. In suicide, as an act of violence or as chronic self-annihilation, suffering and sin are inseparably intertwined, and we are confronted on an extreme scale with the absurdity of a broken humanity. In the fifth place, we can characterize suffering as judgment upon sin. In that connection, the idea is that sin must be punished. Sin cannot remain without penalty. And finally, suffering can be viewed from the angle of one's being trained in righteousness. By suffering, a person is purged and becomes a more worthy human being. In the following chapters these aspects of the relationship between sin and suffering will be developed.

5. Approaches and Elaborations

ONE CAN APPROACH THE PROBLEM OF THE RELATIONSHIP BETWEEN GOD and evil in different ways. One can start either with the omnipotence of

God or the goodness of God. If one opts for an approach based on omnipotence, one assumes that God controls all things. All things come from the hand of God. It is a monistic point of departure. The question becomes this: "Given the evil in the world and given the omnipotence of God, how can God still be good?" One then arrives at a position needing to defend the proposition that God is good. Consequently, the goodness of God continually interferes in a system which one seeks to build on a foundation of omnipotence. On that basis one runs the risk of merely providing space for the goodness of God to the degree that it does not really disturb the system; in other words, one proceeds to restrict the goodness of God in favor of omnipotence-based conclusions.

If one chooses for an approach based on the goodness of God, one assumes that God is absolute love, full of compassion and grace. The question then becomes this: "Given the evil in the world and given the goodness of God, how can God nevertheless be omnipotent?" One must then defend God's power, with the risk that, though one conceives of God as absolutely good, one also has a powerless God, outside of whose will and domain other powers exercise dominion. A consistent and systematic reflection on God's relationship to the world on the basis of God's goodness leads to dualism.

In opting for one or the other of the two starting points one has in fact already made a choice for the decisive shifts which follow. Still, one has to start somewhere. If one refuses to make a choice, one has to take both roads. That I have attempted to do in the following chapters. First I have taken the access road of absolute omnipotence: evil comes forth from the hand of God. After that I start anew and take the access road of God's goodness: God does not want evil and opposes it. The point is, one cannot do both at the same time. One has to start with one of the two approaches. If I choose to begin with omnipotence, it is because this access road is usually taken in the history of dogma. But one could just as well start with the other. The reason for my using the words "access road" is to indicate that the problem cannot be resolved within a one-sided system, but that it lies smack in the middle in the field of tension between the two.

On both of these access roads we find a variety of elaborations, conceptual models in which the attempt is made, and is ever again to be made, to come to terms with God's relationship to evil. We aim successively to discuss these elaborations or models. In doing so one model will have more appeal to us than the other. Some will exert a special attraction, others will have a repellent effect. Individual reactions also will differ. What appeals to one person may repel another. To one person resignation is a blessing; to another even the word is an abomination. To one a suffering God is a comfort; to another it means total collapse. We must be careful not to charge another person too quickly with heresy over the choice of the alternate model, but trust that it equally concerns and involves the multi-colored mystery of God and his world; possibly it can speak as authentically (and as contritely!) about God. This also implies an invitation to the reader—if you are repelled by one of the following models, please keep on reading. You will possibly recognize something of yourself in a given construction. And if nothing there elicits your interest, you will in any case hear the voice of another who will speak to you about his struggle with God over the suffering of the world.

In the last part of the book, after an analysis of the different models, some sort of evaluation will be necessary. A choice will have to be made. The analysis must serve to prepare for decisions about the way we need to go; about the way in which we ought to speak about God; or more modestly, it must help us find a passable road and suggest ways in which we can acknowledge God in an authentic manner.

From the above it will be clear that I myself have little inclination to make a choice from the different existing models. In all of them are glimpses of the way God deals with people, because in all of them are hints of how people relate to God. In the last chapter our concern will be to indicate a framework in which the different models can be fitted. That framework is the history God makes with people, the history he himself began and was able to begin because he is the living God. Only within that history do alternate models gain their meaning and place, and one will not exclude another.

II

GOD AS THE SOURCE OF ALL THINGS

IN THIS CHAPTER WE SHALL DEAL WITH THE DIFFERENT POSSIBLE SCENARIOS if we start with the omnipotence of God. Here the idea is that everything that happens is subject to God's will or, to put it more strongly, that all things come from his hand, not only joys but also suffering. It is the starting point we find in the classic formulations of Lord's Day 10 of the *Heidelberg Catechism*, a starting point which continually calls forth this question: But, then, is God still good? If God lets me be sick, how does that square with his love? If, by the will of God, people die of misery, or perish under injustice and oppression, how can one still speak of God's compassion? We shall start with one of the best-known solutions, the idea that God does it for pedagogical reasons.

6. THE DISCIPLINING FATHER

ONE OF THE IMAGES IN WHICH THE BELIEVER'S RELATIONSHIP TO GOD IS expressed is that of a child. Lord's Days 9 and 10 of the Heidelberg Catechism are based on this image. It is God's *fatherly* hand from which all things come to us. In the New Testament the image of being a child ("sonship") plays an important role. Just think of Romans 8: we have received the Spirit of "sonship" and cry "Father" with the word of childlike trust ("Abba"). There is a relationship of love and devotion.

Also, there is the hope of an inheritance: eternal life. Aware that we are God's children, we receive encouragement in suffering (vs. 18).

However, children do not always have a positive experience with that relationship. After all, fatherhood implies upbringing, and upbringing, punishment. The image we encounter in Hebrews 12 is God as the disciplining Father. In the process of being brought up children also get to hear the word "no," and when disobedient they receive punishment. Punishment is necessary with an eye to their future. In Hebrews 12, the saying, "For the Lord disciplines him whom he loves" is applied to God as Father and believers as his children.

The saying, "He who loves his son chastises him," despite frequent assumptions, is not a Bible text. In the Authorized or King James version, Proverbs 3:12 reads: "For whom the Lord loveth he correcteth; even as a father the son in whom he delighteth." In Hebrews 12:6 this text is taken over in a somewhat modified form: "For whom the Lord loveth he chasteneth, and scourgeth every son whom he receiveth." (The Septuagint already has the modified version.) In verse 7 this conclusion is drawn: if then we are chastised, we are sons. (On the subject of God disciplining out of love, see also Deut. 8:5 and Rev. 3:19.) So the idea expressed by the saying is certainly not alien to certain books of the Bible, but an explicit text is lacking. The nearest approach to it is Proverbs 13:24: "He who spares the rod hates his son, but he who loves him is diligent to discipline him."

By itself, the word *paideuein* in Hebrews 12:6 need not mean "to chastise." It may refer to any form of nurture. But, in light of the *parallelismus membrorum* adopted from the Septuagint, the first half of the verse must be interpreted by *mastigein* employed in the second member. In the later Jewish literature the theme of God's discipline is regularly used to interpret the suffering of Israel or of the righteous (Bertram, *op. cit.*, pp. 606, 610). The unambiguous conclusion of the letter to the Hebrews (suffering points to sonship) is not always drawn. There is also a sense that suffering is ambivalent; it can mean both judgment and discipline and the sufferers may be both the ungodly and the righteous.[1]

It is clear from the letter to the Hebrews that the people addressed in it had not only to listen to words of rebuke, but to endure heavy blows. Their chastisement does not consist in apostolic admonition or in prophetic rebuke; they suffer concrete oppression. And the author interprets this oppression as the striking hand of God.

When God strikes his children, his aim is to bring them to, or to keep them on, the right track. He disciplines us for our good that we may share his holiness (12:10). In the upbringing of children the purpose of

---

1. Gerhard Kittel, ed., *Theological Dictionary of the New Testament*, vol. 5 (Grand Rapids: Eerdmans, 1967), pp. 603ff.

every disciplinary measure is that they shall take the right course. The purpose of the suffering we experience at God's hand is that we shall go his way, the way of sanctification. We are inclined to leave that way. When everything goes well we easily forget God. In time of prosperity we have much less interest in God and tend to forget our neighbor. However, in that situation God does not leave us to our own devices or abandon us on our self-chosen road. For that very reason we are buffeted. As a result of this chastisement, we again discover our own vulnerability and dependence. Through the suffering which overwhelms us we become aware that we cannot find our own way. Then we suddenly discover how we did in fact go our own way and how much we in fact need God and our neighbor.

The idea that God lets people suffer to keep them close to himself is a view one also can find in the church today. "Once there is another war, the churches will fill up again," it is said. (In another war will there be people left to fill the churches? one asks.) It is in fact the case that in crisis situations people are frequently more open to the faith. The old routines no longer work. One is forced to think about and experience the limits of one's own possibilities, possibly even the limits of one's own existence. Such a situation cries out to a person to ask who he is; what is the meaning of one's life? The pastor's experience is that, compared to the healthy, hospital patients are often more open to questions of faith now that they find themselves in situations of dependence. They are continually faced with the limitations of life, at a time when they are removed from their familiar surroundings. In such a situation a person may begin to search for a foothold—which may take the form of reaching for the hand of God. When one is thrown back on the final questions of life, she comes closer to God. The truth that in extremity people learn to pray is confirmed over and over.

The folk wisdom of church people, however, goes beyond this. The continuation of it is "And when their situation changes for the better, they forget all about it again." This also proves to be true. When the war was over, the churches emptied even faster than they had filled. After release from the hospital, when the minister visits them at home, people's openness to questions about God is suddenly gone. Often one even encounters resistance to such questions—as if people want to forget that moment of weakness in the hospital as soon as possible. The intense search for God and for fellowship with him which gives a person courage in the period of crisis is over, and one returns to the old ways of regular church attendance and routine prayers.

Now it is indeed possible that the moment of reflection did not amount to anything. The possibility exists that the search was not for the living God, but only for some support in a precarious situation. Still, we must not be too critical of it. If as the church of Christ we confess that he is the source of our lives, the ground of our existence, then in the human search for a final foothold, no matter how ephemeral, we may experience something of the eager longing of his world for his presence. For through him and unto him all things were created (Col. 1:16). All things are directed toward him. Recognizing that, we may see in the human search a glimmer of this directedness toward Christ. In this connection we cannot set limits, determining for example how intense must be the search, or how long-lasting the perceptible effect, in the lives of people. Where would we draw the line on the scale of intensity, and what is the standard for its duration? Precisely those who sense what it is to be children of God realize how little even the deepest intensity means and how quickly the most intense experience can change into its opposite. It is not the seeking of the seekers, but the grace of him who seeks the lost (who, remarkably enough, sometimes also undertake to search!) by which people are saved.

There is another aspect to the search for God in time of extremity and the return to shallowness when cares are past. We are looking at this dual phenomenon in the framework of the father-child relationship. In that framework it is understandable that in time of distress the child seeks the protective hand of the father, but that in times of calm the child is barely conscious of this hand. More often than not, children are absorbed in their games. They are busily involved with each other or with their toys. At those times they do not think at all of the protection they need; still less do they consciously seek it. Not until a danger threatens or something happens—a big dog appears on the scene or the child falls off his bike—do they come running and cry for their dad (or more often for their mom). At that moment they realize their need for a protective or comforting hand. Children who continually feel the need for that protection or comfort are not happy children. As a parent you know that that protection and comfort is much more necessary than your children suspect, but how unfortunate is the child who feels so threatened that he himself knows this.

God's children are also children absorbed in their games, busily involved with each other or the world around them. Not until the time of distress is upon them do they realize how badly they need the protection and comfort of their heavenly Father. He is continually aware of how threatening the world is in which we live. If *we* always had to know, we would die of fear and grief. Fortunately, God often lets us play. He understands how deeply absorbed we are. He who pities those who fear him, as a father pities his children, knows our frame; he knows what he can expect of his creatures (Ps. 103:14). And when "worse comes to worse" he is there as our protector and comforter.

Still, the life of a child cannot simply proceed undisturbed. The child must grow toward maturity, toward personal and corporate responsibility. That is a process via problems, suffering, and the working through of many a "no." The palm tree grows under pressure. Without this pressure children become spoiled. In the alternation of relaxation and pressure God goes his way with his children: in that pattern he goes *their* way with them. The experience of life people have is often experience of suffering. By it they are cleansed and refined. Mature people, people who radiate the power of the Spirit, are usually people who are "acquainted with grief." They know of disappointment and frustration. Suffering has been imprinted in their lives. In that connection, what weighs heaviest is not always the concrete facts everyone can see. The suffering which a person bears in the quiet of her own heart may hurt far more than the wounds which are visible to all. The uncertainty that marks a person's secret struggles with God, which is known only to God and to this one person, and of which at best a loved one or a friend has some inkling, has a greater maturing effect than clearly demonstrable disappointment. By suffering, especially suffering in secret, people mature—they learn to accept; they live, not in mindless resignation from which all hope has been drained, but in a hope that bears all things. They also understand the relativity of our ideals and of human suffering. They know what it means to learn by suffering what really has value. In the experience of suffering, what finally remains is the relationship with Jesus Christ who chose the road of suffering, who knew the joy which lay before him (Heb. 12:2) and so persevered. Growing alongside of others in the acceptance of suffering we grow alongside of others in hope. Concern for the world is not lessened by the prospect of joy. The mature Christian does not exhaust himself renouncing the world, any more than Christ sought to renounce the world. On the contrary, on the basis of the prospect of joy we can take upon ourselves responsibility for the world without succumbing under its weight. We need not run from the suffering of the world; we can actually take it to heart. And the more the suffering of the world penetrates our hearts, the more we experience that through this suffering God will let us be his children. For this new suffering which we admit to our hearts again purifies and refines our life. The more we take upon ourselves the burden of this world's suffering, the more we mature in leaning on him who is the Lord of the world.

He became the Lord of the world, received the name that is above every name, because he was willing to take the suffering of the world upon himself. He was prepared to go the slave's path of obedience to the point of death. By this draconian discipline he became the Lord before whom every knee shall bow (Phil. 2:6-11). He attained joy, who took the suffering of the whole world upon his neck, bearing the cross for all people. That is what furnishes hope to the world. The person who learns to read the experiences of the world's suffering in the lives of the children of God grows in this hope. He has within him the mind which was also in Christ Jesus (Phil. 2:5).

Before we continue, however, we must also consider the other side of the idea that suffering brings us closer to God. "In extremity people learn to pray," we are told. But in extremity people also learn to curse. Suffering can so embitter people that they can no longer believe in God. Or if they still believe in God, they can only spit in the face of the God who did it to them. This God can no longer be their God, and certainly not their Father. Chastisement for pedagogical reasons is a risky business. By it you can permanently alienate a child. For God also it is a risky business to chastise people. Suffering does not always have a positive effect on people, certainly not in the short term. Suffering in the world and in the lives of people cuts too deep for us to capture it only in the idea that it yields a cry for greater closeness with God. It is not necessarily so; it is only a possibility. In this section we shall discuss it.

In the context of the idea that suffering comes from God and that God is our Father, suffering has a nurturing function—God lets us suffer, himself striking us in order that we may live a sanctified life. Suffering can be experienced as a comfort because in our suffering God is at work with us, concerned with us. He evidently finds us worth the trouble of striking. He feels responsible for us. That is the line of thought followed in Hebrews 12: "It is for discipline that you have to endure. God is treating you as sons; for what son is there whom his father does not discipline? If you are left without discipline, in which all have participated, then you are illegitimate children and not sons" (vv. 7, 8). When the children of others behave in a way of which we cannot approve, we do not proceed to punish them. That is the responsibility of their own parents. We have to keep our hands off. But it is different in the case of our own children. Our children are precious to us. We want to give them a direction in life which will enable them to live happily as responsible and mature people. That is also how, according to Hebrews 12, we may regard God's action. When God strikes us, the reason is that he feels responsible for us as our Father; he wants to put us on the road of mature sanctification. But when we are no longer being chastised, we would have to conclude that God is no longer interested in or involved with us. Evidently God does not find us worth the trouble of getting his hands dirty. He is apparently not our Father, for what real father is there who leaves his children to fend completely for themselves?

The greater a person's sense of guilt before God, the more clearly the thrust of this idea will come home to him. It even happens that people who live with a deep sense of sin become fearful when all goes well. "Has God possibly written us off?" "Has the measure of my sinfulness become such that God says, 'You are on your own. I wash my hands of it'?" A silent God can be worse than a chastising God. In the experience of chastisement there is renewed contact, from which it becomes clear that reconciliation is possible. The fact that God takes the trouble to strike us shows he thinks there is a future for the relationship. Behind this idea, therefore, lies a very deep sense of being a child of God. Based on this awareness is a sense of need, even necessity, to experience the correcting hand of God. For where there is sin, there is need for reconciliation. Where people have strayed (and who does not stray?), correction is needed. Only then do you know that God is still there for you, and that you are still there for God.

Yet this does not detract from reconciliation in Christ, but rather confirms it. Received in him as children of God and adopted into the fellowship of reconciliation, we have also been adopted into the fellowship of his suffering. Suffering reconfirms in us the fact of fellowship with the Suffering One. Jesus is the Son, says the letter to the Hebrews. As Son he suffered (5:8). If now we too are sons, it is inevitable that we will also suffer. As Son, Jesus is the pioneer and leader (12:2) of those who through him are God's children. He has taken the cross upon himself, despising the shame. If the pioneer has taken this road, then also those who follow him will travel this road of the cross and of shame. If we refuse to travel this road, we do not follow him and he is not our leader. Then we are not sons who are traveling the road of the Son. The Son of God is the suffering Son. People who are God's children follow him. And they suffer. Thus, if we experience suffering, we may know ourselves confirmed as children of God and in fellowship with the Son, Jesus Christ.

Meanwhile, the idea of fellowship with Christ provides an extra dimension to the pedagogical value of suffering. Our first association with this was that to put us on the right track God has to chastise us. By this he puts us or holds us on the path of obedience. In that case chastisement is the pedagogical punishment of sin. In Hebrews 5:8, however, we are told: "Although he was a Son, he learned obedience through what he suffered." So Jesus also needed suffering to learn obedience. From this one might infer that Hebrews does not recognize the sinlessness of Jesus, which is not at all the case. In 4:15 it is expressly

31

stated that Jesus did not sin. He experienced temptation outside the domain where sin rules, but remained free from it. He is the high priest who is "holy, blameless, unstained, separated from sinners, exalted above the heavens" (7:26), and the sacrifice without blemish (9:14). Precisely for that reason he is of such inestimable value for people. Still, he had to learn obedience. What can this mean ("to learn obedience") if it is not "to unlearn the way of disobedience"? Apparently it means learning to accept the will and the way of God. It is that which is sometimes called "to become of one will with God." In 5:7 there is mention of "prayers and supplications, with loud cries and tears, to him who was able to save him from death." This brings to mind the story which the synoptic gospels tell of Jesus' struggle in Gethsemane (Matt. 26:36-46; Mark 14:32-34; Luke 22:39-46). There too the reference is to the way of obedience validated in the endurance of suffering—"Your will be done." It is only in the way of suffering that one proves himself—can prove himself—obedient. Only in suffering unto death do we see that obedience is not an empty phrase, but submission to the end. Suffering taught the Son submission. It is a course of struggle and tears. Thus the Christian follows the Son Jesus Christ, in obedience receiving "sonship" through struggle and tears. It is in suffering which we learn to accept as the way of God that we prove to be his children, one with Jesus Christ who also wanted to travel the road of obedience.

Thinking about suffering in this way, we might get the idea that we should be delighted with the suffering we experience. In the final analysis, this conclusion is correct. In the Pauline literature we repeatedly encounter expressions where the apostle says that he rejoices in his suffering (e.g., Rom. 5:3; 2 Cor. 12:9ff.; Col. 1:24). In admonitory passages believers are exhorted to rejoice in their afflictions (Phil. 4:4ff.; 1 Thess. 5:16) and Paul boasts of their steadfastness in suffering (2 Thess. 1:4). For in suffering believers experience the most intense fellowship with the Lord and hence also the most intense hope: if we share in his suffering, that is, "in order that we may also be glorified with him" (cf. Rom. 8:17; 2 Cor. 1:5).

In practice, meanwhile, this level is not easily reached. True, in the history of the church people have looked forward with joy in the Lord to the experience of suffering. Christians have at times even sought out suffering. In the early church some believers presented themselves as candidates for martyrdom. But most of the church fathers thought that inappropriate. Suffering is far too deep a matter that we should seek it. If we take martyrdom upon ourselves we no longer realize what it means to be crossbearers. We fail to realize how severely Jesus suffered under the cross, a way he was prepared to go but did not desire to go. In

Gethsemane he begged to be spared the experience. The church, in its imitation of Christ, usually took the opposite approach to suffering from that of the seekers of martyrdom. Suffering is rather a source of grief than of joy. The letter to the Hebrews very soberly observes, "For the moment all discipline seems painful rather than pleasant" (12:11); it is the experience of the child. At the time when the child is punished, the experience is not very nice at all. That is also the experience of the children of God. If by suffering God indeed teaches us righteousness (12:11), that is a hard thing to swallow. How can suffering ever become a source of joy? Only a masochist can think that way. And even then the joy is mingled with a fear that is deeper than the joy.

Unwanted suffering evokes resistance. People do not easily allow something unwanted to be imposed on them, especially not suffering. Add to this that often the meaning of suffering is totally unclear. It is the very same thing with the child punished by its father. Often the child does not understand why it was not allowed to do what it did. Why did my parent respond so harshly? Why is father so unreasonable? Indeed, sometimes fathers are harsh, and frequently parents make demands that are completely unreasonable. They often make mistakes in the upbringing of their children. With God, however, it is different. As parents we do the best we can, to be sure; but God, says Hebrews, "disciplines us for our good that we may share his holiness." God is not a misguided parent. When *he* disciplines it is really for the best. In God's case we cannot dismiss the training methods he adopts by speaking of unreasonableness and harshness. His actions are meaningful and in our interest, even in the suffering that comes over us, or better, which he brings to us.

That does not alter the fact, however, that as a rule we find it hard to grasp its meaning. Often the suffering believer does not in the least understand why God lets him suffer, still less why the world is full of suffering. The "whys" of people accumulate, headed by the "whys" of those who believe that God guides our lives as a merciful Father. People rise up in rebellion against God. Though a person does not just let suffering come over her, she has to accept it—it comes over you. It is hard to put into words the kind of feelings it evokes toward God. They are the feelings of the child who loves the father and at the same time detests him; feelings that oppose each other and make one powerless; a mingling of impotent fury and impotent hope, of longing and rejection. In that frame of mind people may curse God while at the same time crying out to him. In that condition you can say: "As far as I am concerned I have had enough; I no longer want to live this way; I no longer want to live with You in this fashion." And at the same time you

33

can say: "Out of the depths I cry to thee, O Lord! Lord, hear my voice!" (Ps. 130:1, 2). There is a confusion of contradictory feelings until peace breaks through, sometimes gradually as the suffering is "worked through," at other times by a sudden victory by which people can be present to God again. That is the way of Dietrich Bonhoeffer, and of his *Letters and Papers from Prison*, the way of the suffering believer in every age. It is the way of Jesus of Nazareth, who after his agonizing struggle in Gethsemane says: "Rise, let us be going; see, my betrayer is at hand" (Matt. 26:46), and who takes the road that leads to his death. If we are one with Christ on the road of his suffering, we will also be one with him on the road of his struggle to accept suffering as children and to go the way of the Father. If we have difficulty accepting suffering, that need not surprise, still less worry us. It should rather have to concern us if we had no trouble with it and could accept it without any problem. If we could, would we still be one with the Lord? If he had trouble with it, should we not also have trouble with it? He went the way of suffering "with loud cries and tears," offering up "prayers and supplications" (Heb. 5:7). He dreaded the suffering to the point of sweating blood (Luke 22:44). Then what can we expect of ourselves other than loud cries and tears, prayers and supplications? If we do not sweat blood from fear, it is only because we do not yet bear the suffering the way Jesus bore it. Because Jesus had so much difficulty accepting suffering, he also understands what suffering means for us. "For we have not a high priest who is unable to sympathize with our weaknesses, but one who in every respect has been tempted as we are, yet without sinning" (Heb. 4:15). "For because he himself has suffered and been tempted, he is able to help those who are tempted" (Heb. 2:18). Jesus, who himself experienced temptation through intense struggle, knows what we experience in temptation. He understands our inner rebellion. He empathizes with our feelings of impotence. Our "why?" may echo his "why?" on the cross (Matt. 27:46). Jesus the Son knows what it means to be Son of God and to have to learn obedience by the way of suffering. To arrive at genuine submission and surrender, therefore, is a laborious process. It is like the procession of Echternach: three paces forward and two backward. And in a new experience of suffering we have to go through the same process of rebellion and surrender before we can say, "It is good for me that I was afflicted" (Ps. 119:71).

Accordingly, if we understand suffering as the loving chastisement of the Lord, this theological construct does not eliminate every problem in advance. It is not simply a call for resignation. For then suffering would no longer be suffering. It is rather a road you can travel—just try to live with God and suffer in this way. And if you take that road, you will discover sooner or later that in suffering God enriches your life. But much earlier on this road you will already have met him who also as Son went the way of suffering, so that as child of God, through rebellion and surrender, you go your way following him.

*   *   *

SO FAR WE HAVE TALKED ABOUT THE PURPOSE OF SUFFERING, ABOUT THE children of God, and about Jesus, the suffering Son. We also have to speak, however, about the Father. Ostensibly it may seem harsh that God lets his children suffer. Even if it is for the sake of future righteousness, how can God do this? Then is he not a harsh God whose principle is "the end justifies the means"?

This question, too, we must view within the framework with which we have been working, that of the father-child relationship. If God lets us suffer, he does this as a loving father. It is not a cold mechanism that is applied to us; God's compassion is a component in it, which means that God himself also suffers in my experience of suffering. The father who punishes his son has trouble doing that. He feels the blows in his own soul. To discipline your children is not pleasant; it touches you at a deep level. In Jeremiah the Lord says about Israel:

> Is Ephraim my dear son?
>   Is he my darling child?
> For as often as I speak against him,
>   I do remember him still.
> Therefore my heart yearns for him;
>   I will surely have mercy on him, says the Lord. (Jer. 31:20)

Having to punish his people has deeply affected God. So when people suffer as a result of his chastisement, God is moved, precisely because he is our Father. In his book *The Crucified God*, Moltmann has written very movingly about the Father's suffering in the suffering of the Son.[2] In the suffering which Jesus endured in keeping with the will of God, the Father also suffered. But if the Father suffered along with the suffering Son, then he also suffers when his other children suffer. In our suffering the Father is deeply and painfully involved. When we experience suffering as the chastising hand of the heavenly Father, we should associate it not with a harsh and unmoved God, but with a merciful Love who in our suffering experiences that suffering in his own heart.

2. Moltmann, *The Crucified God*, p. 243.

Now what is the scope and reach of the confession: "In suffering we encounter the love of the Father"? One might say that this can only be true for the believer, and not universally true. It says something about my relationship to God, but it is not a statement about God himself. I experience *my* suffering as given me by a loving Father. In a Dutch church periodical, C. Bezemer has written of Lord's Day 10 of the Heidelberg Catechism: "We hear the speech of the believer.... It is not the intent of this Lord's Day to furnish an adequate explanation for the way things in life go as they do and to use the Lord God as the keystone for this explanation."[3] Accordingly, says Bezemer, as a believer one can only speak for oneself as one states that all things come to us from God's fatherly hand. Now this personal relatedness is undoubtedly the central fact in the confession of God as Father who acts for our good. The reference is to God as Father, as the Father of his children who are united with him in Jesus Christ. So everything points to the fact that what we have here is the believing confession of the Christian, a confession in which Christians are rooted as they live their lives and by which they are encouraged. From this one could, therefore, infer that this confession lacks universal validity: it is only true in faith, not factual. It is even less true for people who themselves do not experience suffering that way.

Still, in drawing such lines of demarcation we have to be careful. In the first place, for the believer this confession is not just an idea with which he comforts himself. For him it is the way things are. That God is our Father may be a metaphor, but it says something about the reality of the relationship between God and man. God really relates to the believer as a father to his children. In that confession the believer therefore not only articulates the experience of his faith but also speaks about the reality on which his faith is based and from which his experience flows.

The concept of "reality" may create misunderstanding because of the different forms which reality takes. Physical reality, for example, is not the same as religious reality, though the two are definitely related. On the concept of reality, see T. J. van Bavel's book, where he remarks: "By reality we mean ... that it refers to something that is 'different' from the subject. This 'something' can, of course, also be 'someone.' In any case the reference is to something given to the subject or thrown into his lap: the presence of something or someone other than himself. By saying this we recognize that the world outside of ourselves cannot simply be traced to our own creativity."[4]

---

3. Cornelius Bezemer, "Zondag 10 van de Heidelberger Catechismus," in *Hervormd Weekblad* 92 (1981), 4604, p. 1.
4. Tarcisius Jan van Bavel, *Meedenken met Edward Schillebeeckx* (Bloemendaal, 1983), pp. 188ff.

In the second place, the suffering of Jesus as the Son embraces more than only the people who assent to it. Just as his rule is all-embracing and his Lordship worldwide, so also is his suffering all-embracing, including the suffering of the whole world. That a large part of the world has trouble with that idea is another matter. Actually, what child of God does not have difficulty experiencing suffering as suffering in fellowship with Christ? Though one person has even more difficulty with it than another, and many cannot see it at all, this does not mean that it does not apply to all. The church would only be able to relinquish that position if it also relinquished the position that Christ is Lord of the world, not just of the church. In the suffering of innumerable unnamed people who disappear into the mass cemeteries of the world we encounter the suffering of their Lord. The cry of the blood of wretches mercilessly sent to their death calls out for the blood of the Savior of the world. In his sonship, which could only be suffering sonship, the suffering of all is included; it can never again be conceived apart from the relationship between the Father and the Son, and so not apart from the father-child relationship between God and his people.

In the third place, the God whom we in Christ call Father is also Creator of the world. The church is not a segment of new reality with a God of its own, in a world which beyond that has nothing to do with the church and its God. The God whom the church confesses as its Father is none other than the God by whom and in whom people live and move (Acts 17:28). He is the Father of the world, though surely in a way other than for the church; but he is not another Father. When in the second century Marcion posited the latter, the church forcefully repudiated his position. It was one of the church's most far-reaching decisions. The Father of Jesus Christ, whom we acknowledge as Father, is the Creator of the world. He is the God of common reality, which therefore is never common in the sense of neutral. It is the creation of God. He is the Father of all human beings and all are his concern. If we acknowledge that God is the Father of believers, and I know that the discipline present in my suffering is of concern to him, then would not the suffering of all those other people be of concern to him? Would we not even suspect that to the degree the discipline does not bring people close to God, it concerns God even more? In the prophets God laments Israel's impenitence. It makes him suffer because his people harden themselves under the blows they experience. But precisely as the prophets speak of the impenitence of Israel, are not all the nations in view, just as the salvation of Israel issues in blessing for all nations? The sufferings the people of God endure as chastisement can never be isolated from the nations, unless one is also willing to exclude the nations from salvation. And in the New

Testament the boundaries have been opened up completely: salvation is intended for all. However great the tension may be—between Israel and the nations, between the church and the world, between redemption and experience, between salvation and existence—if we cease to acknowledge the world as divinely created in its totality, and dichotomize the confession of God the Creator and that of God the Father, the church becomes a self-willed pious club which no longer helps to bear the tensions of the world—God's world and therefore our world.

7. THE STRANGE WAYS OF GOD

IN THE LAST PART OF GENESIS ONE FINDS THE STORY OF JOSEPH. JOSEPH IS HIS father Jacob's favorite son, hated by his brothers because of this favoritism, and for dreams in which all the members of his family bow down to him. Joseph's untroubled life comes to an end, however, when his brothers sell him into slavery in Egypt. Despite a prosperous career as a slave (to the extent one can call a slave prosperous) Joseph, though innocent, lands in jail. There he gets to know Pharaoh's butler and baker, also in detention. He interprets their dreams, the reason why later, because no one is able to interpret the dreams of Pharaoh, he is brought before the king. When Joseph proves able to interpret the king's dreams and advises him to take measures against a threatening famine, he is given the task of implementing those measures, and to that end crowned as viceroy. With the famine looming, the surrounding nations are able to take advantage of the accumulated stores of grain. Jacob and his family are also saved from starvation. So, in a roundabout way, Joseph's going to Egypt serves to save the lives of members of his family and of many others as well. Moreover, the dreams of his youth are fulfilled. What seemed evil yielded blessing.

Genesis 45:5ff. tells us how Joseph "worked through" his bitter experiences. When his brothers are upset at the discovery that the king on whom they are dependent is their brother, the one they themselves once sold into slavery, his response is: "And now do not be distressed, or angry with yourselves, because you sold me here; for God sent me before you to preserve life" (45:5). True, the brothers were filled with hatred when they sold Joseph, but God used Joseph's "career" to bring about rescue. The real subject of Joseph's going to Egypt is God, not the brothers: "So it was not you who sent me here, but God," Joseph says to his brothers (45:8). It was God's purpose in the famine that was to come to save Jacob and his clan as well as many others. To reach that goal God began to take measures early. He saw to it that Joseph arrived in Egypt in order there to lay the groundwork for the salvation of Jacob and his family. God reached that goal via the brothers and the unreliable wife of Potiphar. "And God sent me before you to preserve for you a remnant on earth, and to keep alive for you many survivors" (v. 7). With everything that befell Joseph God has his purpose: the salvation of people.

This does not alter the fact that this purpose was realized via the suffering of a man. Joseph's experiences are especially bitter; and in the heart of everyone who hears the story, certainly in the region where it happened, it calls forth intense feelings. To a free-ranging nomad, slavery in a foreign land is a fate almost worse than death. Apart from the familiar protective environment of the clan, the nomad is at the mercy of anyone who meets him. As slave he is at the mercy of the man who purchases him. He may do well as slave, as Joseph did in the house of Potiphar, but at any moment it may become starkly clear that he is a slave, defenseless against the will of a master who can suddenly imprison him, guilty or not. And in ancient times, to be incarcerated was to be buried alive. Prison was a dungeon in which you lived in your dirt, shared your space with vermin, ran the chance of being forgotten, and where for a minor infraction of the rules you might see your life shrink to nothingness.

I deliberately recited the Joseph story at some length. It reminds us of the countless individuals who find themselves at the mercy of those in power, of the countless people who are placed in dentention without trial. It reminds us of the many who were dispatched to faraway places, delivered up to the whims of whoever was in charge. It calls to mind the people who disappeared because oppressors no longer wanted to hear their voices. When Joseph had to travel the road of suffering, that was not just a little setback he had to work through in order to reach a higher goal; time and again it was the road of hopelessness. It was a road to oblivion, physical and spiritual ruin; even the hope that the butler would rescue him from oblivion proved to be empty (Gen. 40:23).

However, the way of suffering leads to the salvation of Egypt, Jacob, and others. Therefore Joseph learns to interpret his experience as salutary. It was God's way. It was meant for evil, and in his suffering Joseph experienced it as such; but God made all things turn out for good. Thus, strangely, God had gone his way. Whereas people meant evil, God proves to have used their evil intent for his saving purpose. Whereas people saw disaster come over them, God used it for salvation. This tenor pervades the Joseph story, and this is how Israel read it in the Torah. The way of Joseph is the way of Israel and of the righteous Israelites. Though

Israel and the righteous may suffer, it is the way of God to prepare salvation for Israel and many others. Via his non-zero status as a slave and his living burial in a dungeon, Joseph becomes the ruler of Egypt, father to Pharaoh (45:8). God so led circumstances that the greatest power on earth becomes subject to Joseph. Similarly, the way of Israel, "imprisoned" and delivered up to the whims of the powers of the day, is the way to salvation and rule over all nations.

The idea that God uses suffering and even involves the evil plans of people to attain a higher goal can often be found in the church. People who have passed through suffering not infrequently, after the passage of time, remark that it was good for them to have been so afflicted. A factor in this is not only that through suffering they gained a new spiritual maturity but also that they admit they would never have reached this new and favorable situation if earlier they had not gone through a valley; and if at the time they had had a choice they would not have taken the road which led to the happiness of the present. It is a good thing that at that time God placed them on this course; now, to their surprise, they have to say in retrospect that the road they had not wished to travel proved the best. They now view this road as God's guidance.

In the classic Reformed formulary for baptism, we read that God will avert all evil or turn it to our profit. God does not always avert the evil. Sometimes he himself brings suffering upon us. But the confession expressed in the baptism formulary is that *when* God brings evil upon us he does it for our good. Out of the evil that comes over us God lets us experience the good. The formulary puts this idea in the context of the father-child relationship. It might belong there, but because there are also other aspects to it, we are here considering separately God's bringing good out of evil. There is the aspect of the absolute power of God to guide everything in accordance with his will. There is in particular the aspect of God's transcendence because God's purpose is realized via a chain of ordinary earthly causality. God does not directly intervene. In view of the attitude of Jacob and Joseph we do not exactly need a supernatural explanation to understand the hatred of the brothers. Nor is a scene like that of Potiphar's wife and Joseph unique in the annals of world history. Nor is it inexplicable that the butler forgets Joseph upon his return to Pharaoh's court and with his detention behind him. That is how things go in the world, and psychology can explain them. Still, Joseph sees this whole history as God's way and, following him, numerous believers see their journey through suffering to happiness as God's way. However transcendent God is, he is continually present. Accordingly, it would perhaps be better to speak here of God's hiddenness rather than of his transcendence. In his hiddenness, however, he is continually present, acting via people. Even when, as in the book of Esther, his name is not mentioned, he is the acting subject throughout the whole history. The hiddenness of God is an essential aspect of the idea we are considering. Throughout the entire Joseph history God is not noticeably present. Noticeable only are the brothers, the wife of Potiphar, the forgetful butler, the desperate Pharaoh. Therefore the acknowledgment that the road traveled was the way of God was an acknowledgment in retrospect. In the believer's confession that is usually how God's leading plays a role: in retrospect there emerges the insight that this road was the right road and therefore the way of God, who knows better than we what is good for us. The theme is, Later you will understand.

Associated with the hiddenness of God is the acknowledgment that God's leading is not generally provable. A person can praise God and consider himself fortunate because God at one time led him into a dark valley and yet the outcome was favorable, but another person will attribute it to a high degree of luck that after all the problems the person experienced the end result was so good. In that case Joseph had an incredible amount of good luck. Or in another case people see no connection whatever between the suffering and the good things which came after. The latter could just as well have come without the former. If someone applies for a job and someone else gets it, that is a disappointment. Later on an opening occurs in a much better position and he does get it. Then the person involved can thank God that the first application was denied and that the disappointment led to a better job. But who can guarantee that the new job opening would not have occurred in any case or that if by way of the earlier job opening the person would not have landed a still better position if it had gone through? For the believer the guidance of God may be very concrete and unassailably real; for the outsider it need not be so at all. This brings us to another aspect of the hiddenness of God: to the believer himself the recognition of God's leading may be questionable. One moment he clearly sees God's hand in what happened; the next it seems unreal. For us who believe in the absolute guidance of God in our lives, doubts may arise whether a given situation was actually for good and whether the interpretation applied to it was not wishful thinking to strip the suffering of its meaninglessness. If one can fit the experience of suffering into a plan of salvation or even God's plan of salvation, the experience loses its absurdity. To put it more strongly, if one can view the vicissitudes of life as the underside of God's embroidery by which he creates his splendid kingdom, then it loses its arbitrary senselessness. For some, God's leading is not a question—they are utterly convinced of it. For others God's leading is not a question either—they think it is pious self-deception. For many the issue is one of continued back-and-forth questioning: sometimes they think they have a firm grip on the thread, then it lets go and proves to be or seems to be a loose end. Still, they continue to search; because their lives do not make sense unless they can experience and confess God's involvement in it.

In this line of thought, a third aspect of the hiddenness of God in this line of thought is that the person who later acknowledges God's leading does not usually see that leading during the experience of suffering itself. God is the apparent absentee. On the basis of the father-child relationship one may, to be sure, have problems with God's pedagogical methods, protest against them, and even doubt the relationship, but God is still the present God. But when the reference is to the hidden leading of God as we are now discussing it, God is not reachable. The loneliness is greater. Meaninglessness is not just crouching at the door; it has invaded the house. When we thought we needed him to rescue us immediately, he seemed to us to remain in his ivory tower. Only afterwards does it become clear that God was there and that he had come into our home along with the senseless suffering.

Nevertheless, despite God's hiddenness and the challenge to the confession of his leading, people do again and again take courage at the thought that it was good for them to have been led through the valley. Over and over they interpret their lives in the light of Joseph and of Israel. In light of that encouragement they dare to journey into the future and to sing:

> Never mind about tomorrow
> I am led by God's own hand,
> Lift my eyes in spite of sorrow
> To the unfamiliar land.

Now the basis of the belief in God's leading is not the experience that a situation initially experienced as negative turned out to have a positive sequel. Rather, the reverse is the case: on the basis of the belief in God's leading the road traveled is interpreted as God's road. The possibility of linking concrete suffering with concrete happiness confirms this belief, makes reality transparent, and causes people to acknowledge God's presence. At the root of the struggle to recognize the hand of God is the belief that his hand is recognizable, and accordingly, that the hand of God leads history. This belief is opposed to the idea that the experiences of life are coincidences or the product of fate. Life in its totality is in God's hand and he has in view the well-being of humans. Evil is subject to God, not in the sense that God fights for people by combatting evil and overcoming it, but in the sense that God uses evil for his own ends. Evil has no real power, only the relative independence that is given it by God. The ungodly person, the oppressor, or the slanderer does what he does not under his own auspices, but because God uses him as an instrument in his service.

This idea, while applicable to the lives of individuals, also applies to all of world history. World history is God's work and moves to its goal in accordance with his plan. It is written by "the finger of God." Amidst the political and military confusion of the world God sits enthroned above the nations and directs them in accordance with his will. Where people in power pursue their own interests, they unconsciously and involuntarily serve God's interests. Where they are out to maintain and enlarge their power, they are actually pawns in God's mighty plan of salvation to the greater glory of his name. According to the prophet Isaiah, the Persian king Cyrus forged his political and military plans to liberate Israel (Isa. 44:28; 45:1-5). God used him to bring Israel back to the country he had promised them. He says of Cyrus: "he is my shepherd, and he shall fulfil all my purpose" (Isa. 44:28). Cyrus is God's servant without knowing it and without knowing Israel's God (Isa. 45:4f.). But Nebuchadnezzar is equally God's servant for the purpose of punishing Israel (Jer. 25:9). In a world of chaos, violence, and suffering, God goes his sovereign way. He makes everything serviceable to his future. What Isaiah and Jeremiah say of Cyrus and Nebuchadnezzar can also be applied to rulers and nations of later times. It also applies to the powerful of today. For the power of God has not decreased. Americans and Russians in their pursuit of power are merely servants of the Lord. The English, the French, the Germans, the Chinese, and the Japanese were and are means in his hand.

Now one can believingly confess this, but things become considerably more difficult if one asks himself how this is to be made concrete. How, then, is the way of God to be recognized in the history of the nations? As long as we stay on the terrain of Scripture, we can feel sure of ourselves. Nebuchadnezzar served to punish Israel and Cyrus to liberate it. The interpretation of history by the prophets bears the stamp of the divine Word. But the moment we cross the boundaries of the Old and the New Testament, it becomes more difficult to speak about the way of God. Was the victory of emperor Constantine over Maxentius in A.D. 312 a victory for the coming kingdom of God? Or was the church being tested to see whether, when it was tempted to seize power, it would remain in the grace of God? "In hoc signo vinces" ("In this sign you will conquer"). But a victory in the sign of the cross is no guarantee that the Crucified will be served by it.

43

As we approach our own times, it becomes even more difficult to interpret history as scripted by God's hand. What must we do with the Second World War? How can one say that Hitler was God's servant? Did the immense suffering of the camps and the gas chambers possibly serve to give Israel a new place among the nations and to make the Christian world aware of the hatred which a history of centuries had built up against the firstborn of the peoples of God? Did Vietnam serve to make America and its allies conscious of the limits of power? And has Afghanistan taught Russia the same lesson? And if they teach it (do the powerful ever really learn that lesson?) was it God's intent to make this point with Vietnam and Afghanistan? By comparison with the immense suffering involved, the solution seems so pale. It does not seem to us to do justice to the rivers of blood that have been shed. What remains is too insignificant to justify the suffering.

It is hard to interpret history as God's script. In the soil of the belief that God leads the history of the world and of individuals, the "whys" grow in abundance. If indeed God led the history of the thirties and the forties, why did he let Hitler do as he pleased? If God leads the history of people, why did a young family lose a father? To the list of whys every one of us can add his own. Sometimes these whys are world-embracing; sometimes they are limited to an incident in the life of an individual. But they all carry within them the cry for someone to give meaning to history before the face of God. In the pastorate it is sometimes said, You must not ask "why?" but "what for?" Now the "what for?" may be implied in the "why?" "Why?" is more inclusive; it is related both to causes and to ends. If one restricts himself to "what for?" one separates the matter from the past, from the things done which cannot be undone.

One especially detaches the matter from the issue of guilt. In many "whys" there is a guilt component. Suffering is made worse by the fear that something in our own past is the cause of suffering. If we exclude the issue of guilt by limiting the question to the "what for?", that removes some of the pain. The desperation of guilt yields to the search for the purpose. Now one can certainly advise someone else not to ask "why?" but "what for?", but if that person's suffering is existentially bound up with the dread of guilt, that advice does not touch the real problem. Only when people are free in their relationship to God and the barriers of fear and guilt are gone can they think about the purpose God has in mind with the suffering. This is perhaps one of the reasons why we find it so hard to interpret recent history: our feelings of guilt prevent us from looking ahead to the purpose of our suffering.

Added to this is the fact that the answer to the question "to what end?" can be as obscure as the one to the question "why?" It is often not possible to follow the thread of history. Often the meaning of a concrete event is completely undiscoverable. This does not alter the fact, however, that the moment one begins to ask "what for?" one believes there is a possible meaning. Regardless, God is behind every event. The meaning may not be clear to us, but it does exist. It is against this background of belief in meaning, the specificity of which eludes us, that we must regard many Christian hymns. They often imply that the thread of history cannot be followed, neither in the present nor into the future. The uncertainty of the future is aggravated by the impossibility of interpreting the present. Still, the present and the future are still meaningful, for both are led by God. It is for that reason that songs like "He Leadeth Me" and "When Through the Deep Waters I Call Thee to Go" are sung with such zest. People generally find it hard to live with chaos. Christians who believe that God wills the order of salvation and not chaos find it even harder. Amid the chaos of the world the questioning heart finds rest in God not as wishful thinking but in recognition of God's way in the life of Joseph and of Israel. Of the past people confess that what God has done he has done well; and with confidence they look forward to the future, "for by his hand He leadeth me." That is not an illusion, but deep trust in the God of Israel.

Despite the biblical grounds for the notion that "with a crooked stick God can strike a straight blow," we are still stuck with a number of problems. In the first place, this notion has a confirming effect with respect to history. If history is God's script, one easily accepts an uncritical attitude regarding it. As things have gone, so God wanted them; and so we have status quo. Therefore, what people have done (or, more precisely, left undone) bears the stamp of divine approval. Here I am not yet speaking of the relationship between the will of God and human responsibility. That problem arises in all kinds of ways and is therefore not specific for the model under discussion here. The issue here is not the responsibility of humans, but the question whether history has always followed the right track. In the course of centuries, have the switches always been set correctly? Are there no events or tendencies which to the end continue to resist being interpreted as meaningful? In other words, the idea of God's hidden leading in every event ends in an optimistic view of history. It also ends in an optimistic view of the life of every individual. It is the position of Hegelian idealism. Does this view do justice to a world which groans under the weight of injustice and suffering? Can one still fit the beastly circus of St. John's Apocalypse into the framework of God's leading? Should one not rather see God as the opposer of the beasts from the abyss?

A second question is this: why is the detour of suffering necessary? To come back to the Joseph story, if God wanted Joseph to be "prime minister" of Egypt, could he not have arranged this in another way? After all, is he not the one who leads history? Could not Joseph have interpreted those dreams as a free man? Did he have to go to jail for that purpose, when in fact he was already a slave? These questions seem speculative, and may even sound irreverent. But they must be posed. For if one wants to find comfort in the mysterious leading of a God who turns evil into good, and who amidst the seemingly evil can therefore be acknowledged as merciful and gracious, then one must be certain that his goodness and mercy are real. If we go in search of the meaning of suffering, then our search should show that this course of suffering was necessary to reach the desired result and was not just an arbitrary option. It is already clear that apart from the ultimately free choice of God no absolute construal of meaning is possible. It would, after all, restrict God's freedom. The idea of the hidden leading of God never takes us further than the claim that, via the causal laws of the earth, God executes his will. But the determination of the course of causality is completely up to him, a confirmation once more that the recognition of God's course in the chain of events is not the source of the belief in God's leading, but an outflow of it.

A related question is this: If God governs the world, why did there have to be a famine in Egypt? God used Joseph's suffering to prevent greater misfortune. In that connection we have to ask not only whether all the painful steps in Joseph's experience of suffering were really necessary but also whether the famine itself was really necessary. Or is that an apriority? Is it perhaps the case that all of God's mysterious ways of preventing greater misfortune are really only necessary because misfortune already exists?

A final remark: if we confess the mysterious ways of God and regard suffering as a way to good fortune, is it possible also to reverse the thesis and say that from good fortune follows new suffering? The marvelous rescue of Jacob and his family resulted in Israel's coming to live in Egypt, which in turn issued in forced labor and the murder of newborn children. Cyrus's victory brought Israel not freedom, but Persian rule, with its alternation between good governors and bad ones along with their respective interest groups. Today's happiness not infrequently proves to result in tomorrow's despair. Again, Hegelian idealism can furnish the solution: every synthesis calls forth a new antithesis until the all-inclusive goal of history has been reached. But that line of thought somehow seems to me too shallow. It takes no account of failures, or the fact that evil is *evil*, which is the basic problem in the approach which attributes evil to the detour a merciful God has to make to realize the good.

A moment ago we said that if assigning meaning to suffering is to be thorough, it must not only say that via suffering good fortune came about, but also that this good fortune could only have come about by way of this suffering. Now, to be sure, because of God's freedom no final answer can be given to that question, but we can come up with a number of intermediate answers. In the first place, the joy of the positive is greater against the dark backdrop of the negative. Often it is only after the loss that we realize what it was that we possessed. Think of the childless marriages mentioned in the Bible: Abraham and Sarah, Elkanah and Hannah, Zechariah and Elizabeth. Their long wait made the joy of parenthood all the greater. One component in these stories is that, as a result of the long period of waiting and the fruitless prayers, the beneficent action (precisely where salvation was concerned), really does prove to be a gift of God. The joy and the songs of praise arise from the period of waiting and from the realization of the impossible possibility. Not only have the childless couples of all times experienced that the joy was all the greater for their having to wait, but in all sorts of other situations one can have the same experience. For all kinds of reasons, great and small, people have said afterward, "It is good that I have been afflicted."

A second answer is that we have to postpone a complete understanding of the meaning of suffering till later. To a person in despair one can say, "Someday you will understand." And, indeed, sometimes that happens, but certainly not always. It is also possible that one totally fails to understand the meaning of a given instance of suffering; and even if one begins to understand it, many questions still remain. Hence, one has to postpone the "someday" to eternity. Not until then will we understand the way of God. At best we now partly understand the way of God, but in heaven all enigmas will be solved. Then the problem of a necessary meaning and of the freedom of God will also be solved. For now we are in the world, not completely one with God, and the necessity we imagine is ours, not God's. If we are able to see a necessary reason why God takes us on a given road of suffering, we may be imposing an external necessity upon him. But in eternity we will know as we are known (1 Cor. 13:12); then our knowledge will be knowledge in God, so that it accords with the logic of God's will. Then the necessity of our thought is nothing other than God's will.

To this claim one can link the idea that all suffering is meaningful as preparation for heaven. Our future is in heaven. There prevails the greatest happiness, and the highest goal. The road to it is a process of dying to what is earthly. How can one better learn to die to the earthly than by experiencing that earth offers but little joy and that even its joys pale rapidly in the shrouds of sorrow. All the suffering of the world makes us seek God and brings us closer to a joy that is imperishable.

This idea is diametrically opposed to the tenor of our century, and to the mainstream of its theology, by which many eyes have been opened to the value of this earth and this life as the scene of God's action. God has given the earth for humans to live in and that is their destiny. But this view cannot do justice to the fact that our earthly thinking is a process of thinking along with God, and not just an exercise in futility. Still, it carries strong biblical undertones from within the Johannine and Pauline literature. We must ask ourselves whether, following the present preoccupation with man on earth and the earth as the dwelling place of man, there will not be and needs to be fresh attention devoted to man as destined for heaven and to the glory coming after the beauty and the splendor of the earth recede. In the light of the heaven which awaits us, the contours of the suffering of the world lose their sharpness. They then are seen in the context of perseverance: hang in there a bit longer; soon it will be over. That is how Paul speaks in Romans 8: "the sufferings of this present time are not worth comparing with the glory that is to be revealed to us" (v. 18). Longing for heaven may soon be expressed as longing for life after death, and an earth-centered theology may just as well be succeeded by a concrete eschatology with a prospect of an apocalyptic ending of the world to the sound of trumpets and with the Lord coming down on the clouds of heaven. It should not surprise us if within the Christian community the ethic of social and political involvement will not in the near future make way for asceticism.

In the course of the history of the church various tendencies have been manifest. Initially there was a tendency to view suffering in the light of the Lord's imminent return. Earthly existence was of this aeon. This did not, to be sure, always lead to asceticism (Col. 2:16ff.; 1 Tim. 5:23), but it did lead to great restraint with regard to earthly existence (1 Tim. 6:7ff.; Luke 12:32ff.; James 5:1ff.). Everything had to serve the aeon to come. When the eschaton failed to materialize the emphasis was shifted to eternal life. Communion with Christ yielded *athanasia* and the Eucharist became *pharmakon athanasias* ("the medicine of immortality," Ignatius *Ad Ephes.* 20, 2). In the Constantinean age stress was laid on the extension of God's rule into the world, although critical voices like that of Augustine in *De Civitate Dei* continued to be heard. In the Middle Ages, particularly the late Middle Ages, one sees various tendencies run through each other. On the one hand, there is the political power of the church with its matching theology; on the other, the monastic ideal of poverty and a strong sense of the transience of earthly life; alongside were the "enthusiastic" groups, like that of Joachim de Fiore, who expected the imminent arrival of the eschaton. The history of the

Anabaptists shows how the divine kingdom and worldly power may be interwoven. In more recent times there has been a divergence between a practical Christianity increasingly occupied with the control and subjugation of the earth and its possibilities, and the faith that was oriented to life after death and the inner life of the soul. In the nineteenth century world domination and pious meditation about heaven sometimes went hand in hand. Not until the present century, especially after the Second World War, did attention for the world come into its own, also in theology. It is striking that in this connection nineteenth century movements with a pietistic coloring played a pioneering role. Think of the mission societies, Heldring, and the Blumhardts. Meanwhile, the high point of this earth-oriented theology seems to be past. Besides politics Dorothee Sölle has discovered mysticism in *Death by Bread Alone. Texts and Reflections on Religious Experience*. The political involvement of Christians often seems to limit itself to the one apocalyptic issue of nuclear weapons. Hand in hand with a no-nonsense position in politics, there seems in the church to be a drawing back upon what many say is the real concern of the church, the eternal salvation of the soul. Apparently, in the tension between the eschaton, eternal life, and life in earthly structures, it is extraordinarily difficult to do justice to all three.

Several times we designated the road through suffering to glory as the way of Joseph and of Israel. We might have added, "and of its Messiah." I intentionally refrained from this in order not too quickly to resolve christologically the tension described and the questions they evoke. This is all the more valid because often the line of thought is not framed in christological language. When people talk about God's leading, it is usually not rooted in the way of Christ, but in a general concept of omnipotence and protection. However, we cannot abstract the way of God from the way of Jesus Christ, and we must therefore place everything we have said in that light. The way through suffering to joy is the way of the Lord. In the gospels we repeatedly read that the Christ *had to* suffer and be raised on the third day (Matt. 16:21; Mark 8:31; Luke 9:22; 24:46). Proceeding from the Scriptures, Jesus himself called his disciples' attention to the fact that the Messiah had to take this road, and after the Resurrection he referred back to it. Accordingly, the early Christian church viewed the way of Jesus as necessary. But why "necessary"? One can interpret it by saying that he who knows the Torah and the prophets has to know that this was to be the way of the Messiah. Just consider it: that is how it went with Israel, King David, and the prophets. One finds this pattern in the psalms. The righteous go the way of suffering, but God does not let his Holy One see corruption (Ps. 16:10; Acts 2:27). If we now focus on the one righteous man, the Messiah, can we expect anything else? Who of the prophets had not been persecuted? Would the Prophet of all prophets then remain exempt? Will not his suffering be the sum of all suffering? But then will not God's deliverance also culminate in him? One who knows the Old Testament can know that that is how Christ will fare.

Still, this does not yet do sufficient justice to the "must" of the Messiah. It is not only the "must" of human experience, of the wisdom of life, but also and particularly a divine "must." If it is the way of Israel, of the prophets, and of the righteous, it is apparently the way intended by God. God evidently brings his people to joy by way of suffering. Thus, according to the Scriptures (which are God's own speech) the Messiah of God must also suffer, die, and rise again. In this connection the history of Gethsemane is illustrative (Matt. 26:36-46). Jesus prays that the cup may pass from him. It is God's will, however, that Jesus shall suffer and die. The way of suffering to glory is the way of Israel's God himself. To him, it is the essential way of dealing with the world. There is no other way. Life can become imperishable only through death. The way of joy is the way of the cross.

If that is the way of God, of his Messiah, of his people, of David, of Joseph, of Israel (both as patriarch and as people), then that is also how the way of his church must be. The fellowship of believers bears the cross of Christ behind him. We cannot expect anything other than that suffering will be our portion in this life. This puts in another light the idea that God's ways are mysterious. If Christ is the wisdom of God, and our wisdom must and may be measured by his, it is no longer strange that God allows us to suffer for a higher purpose; it is rather self-evident. Now this purpose or goal may in the first place be the kingdom of God, but that does not exclude the course of world history or the life stories of individuals; it includes them. For by way of these histories God brings people to his kingdom. Regardless of how precisely the meaning of world events must be construed and described—and it may often not be clear at all—the fact that it exists as a divine "must" for Christ is clear. If the process of world events should no longer be subject to the divine "must," it would no longer be subject to the Messiah. Then the world would no longer be the world of Jesus Christ and Jesus Christ would no longer be the Messiah of the world. If in his life the necessity of passing through suffering and death existed, then it also exists for the world of which he is the firstborn and head. By our saying and believing that, suffering becomes a sign of hope.

Let us continue for a moment to reflect on the goal Jesus achieved by undergoing suffering. We start by saying that by it he achieved something for himself. By being obedient until death he received the name that is above every name, and every knee in heaven and on earth must bow before him (Phil. 2:6-11). When God lets Jesus go the way of death, God also exalts him. It was God's plan that the Christ should suffer; but the same texts which voice the necessity of suffering also consistently mention in the same breath the necessity of resurrection. The Christ must suffer and rise again on the third day. On this road of suffering the goal is not lost from view. Hebrews 12:2 goes even further: for the joy set before him Christ endured the cross and despised the shame. When he took the cross upon himself, Jesus already had the exaltation in view. Because he knew of the joy which was to come, he found the cross bearable. By his suffering with loud cries and tears, Jesus reached the objective of being seated at the right hand of God. It is well to take a look at this nuance in the suffering of Christ. There is in the church a tendency to talk about suffering in a masochistic way, as though it were an end in itself. In that line of thought self-sacrifice is the Christian's goal; self-interest is opposed to the interest of the other. Self-interest, asking what advantage your self-sacrifice will bring you—all this is tainted language in the church. But a text like Hebrews 12:2 shows us that self-interest and the interest of another need not be mutually exclusive, but can be compatible; also, that the goal you must reach may well be factored into the sacrifice you must make. When the Christian church endures suffering, it is not for the sake of the suffering as such, but because it is the road to the joy that awaits it. On account of that goal the church must persevere and, according to Hebrews, persevere a bit longer. The suffering God brings is also suffering for one's own good: for Jesus, the session on the throne of God; for Joseph, the session on the throne of Pharaoh; for David, the session on the throne of Israel. It is not disgraceful for a Christian to inquire about the goal of suffering, to inquire also what you yourself will gain from it. For that matter, what else should we expect from the God for whom people are not cannon fodder in the conduct of his war, nor the refuse of history for the greater glory of his name—but a people whom he loves and remembers, whom he regards as so precious that he calls them by name that they may live. Humans do not have to sacrifice themselves masochistically. They have value which may take the form of self-esteem and even self-interest. We do not have to sacrifice ourselves to a greater degree than Jesus did.

In a work of Christian theology, the idea that the suffering of Christ was aimed at more than his own glory requires no argument: he suffered and died for the sake of others. For *their* glory he entered death. In the church that language is more familiar than language that he entered death for his own glory. But the two are inseparably connected. Our joy can never be real if it is definitely at the expense of another. For that reason we now stop to consider the other-directed side of Jesus' suffering. He did it for others. The suffering of the One is meaningful for the salvation of the many. In that regard Jesus does not stand alone. He stands alone and is unique in that he effected the absolute decisions concerning suffering and glory. He is the head; others are incorporated in him. That is irreversible. But if humanity is indeed incorporated in him, his way will be recognizable in others. The suffering of the One is meaningful for the salvation of others. This also implies that the suffering of one person is meaningful for the salvation of another. We return to the Joseph story. Through slavery and prison Joseph achieved the salvation of many. People who live as followers of Christ need not in our time be excluded from this suffering for the other. In that connection we do not always have to think of spectacular things. The sickness which brings one person to a hospital may be the cause of salvation for a fellow patient. The death of a bishop at the hands of an assassin may level the road of freedom for many of his people.

Joseph underwent suffering against his will. In no way did he assent to the way he was of service to the salvation of others. God sent him to Egypt, as he later says, but he himself was only the passive object of this action. The sick person also undergoes ailment against his will. He probably did not prefer the hospital—with what is entailed—over his own health. People undergo much suffering willy-nilly, even if later it turns out that God used it for the well-being of others. In the case of Jesus that is different. He consciously took upon himself the way of suffering for others. He humbled himself (Phil. 2:7), opting for the way which led to death for the sake of the lives of the many. A priest in Latin America who champions the cause of his people at the very least has to expect that he will have to suffer for it. But he opts for the risk of suffering for the sake of others. Here too, the choice is not for suffering as such. The issue is a choice for salvation. But if the salvation of the other can only be achieved by my suffering, then that suffering is included in my choice. That is what happens in the case of Latin American priests who open their mouths. That is the story in the lives of all the Christians who championed justice and love in every age. That is how it was for Jesus Christ. He too did not want to suffer, but he opted for suffering to bring salvation to others. In the case of Jesus, suffering for the sake of salvation achieved results. It achieved results in the life of Joseph. It has been fruitful in the lives of many. This means that to assume the burden of suffering is not meaningless. If God uses suffering to achieve salvation, that suffering is worthwhile. If in this manner we work out the thought that sometimes God works in mysterious ways with people, that idea does not lead to passive resignation in suffering but serves as a powerful incentive for action. If we dare to risk suffering, it is not meaningless but positively redemptive.

Sölle has said that the belief that God leads history, even in its suffering, has made Christianity masochistic and passive.[5] We cannot deny that this belief has often had this effect. But passivity is not automatically assumed with God's leading of history. It is only the case if we assume that divine initiative and human initiative are mutually exclusive, which is by no means the case. If we assume that man can think and will along with God and that God even works via our thinking and willing,[6] then we can seek salvation and, if necessary, to that end take the way of suffering upon us. John B. Cobb is even of the opinion that the risk of suffering is necessary for anything ever to be achieved. Without the possibility and reality of suffering no creation is possible. When God opted for creation, he opted for the possibility of failure. But God opted for it in order to reach the higher goal of a more richly profiled reality, one that is beyond the "filled" emptiness of nothingness.[7]

It is worthwhile to run risks, for suffering is not fruitless. We must of course keep in view the question of whether the suffering we opt for will serve the goal we want to reach. Unfortunately, we cannot always tell in advance. It is not always clear in advance whether God will use our suffering for the objective we are shooting for or for something else. Sometimes God will even have to hold us back from the senseless suffering we think we should undertake. In the book of Exodus we encounter the moving story of Moses, who for Israel's sake offers to have his name blotted out of God's book (Exod. 32:32). He wants to take upon himself the darkness of being outside the covenant relationship with God in order that God may uphold his covenant with Israel. He is prepared to sacrifice himself for Israel and for the name of God. But God rejects the offer (v. 33) for the possibility of continuing the covenant and God's own mercy. Our choice to sacrifice ourselves for the sake of others may be unnecessary because it does not lead to the desired goal or because there is another, shorter way. Our knowledge is limited, certainly where the mysterious ways of God are concerned. But that limited knowledge need not stand in the way of taking the risk that we are not serving the goal we are aiming for because even then, in our blind gropings, we may confess that God makes all things, even our miscalculations, work together for good for those who love him (Rom. 8:28).

This section is perhaps less coherent than the preceding one. I am aware as I write that the line of thought zigzags a bit from time to time—certainly in the first part—if we do not see God's leading in

5. Sölle, *Suffering*, trans. Everett R. Kalin (Philadelphia: Fortress Press, 1975), pp. 17-30.

6. Augustine, *De Gratia et Libero Arbitrio*, chap. 41-43.

7. John B. Cobb, Jr., and David Ray Griffin, *Process Theology: An Introductory Exposition* (Philadelphia: Westminster Press, 1976), pp. 69-75.

christological perspective. One reason for this, I think, is that the idea under discussion here is not easy to assimilate. It takes effort to believe that God is scripting your own life story, especially if you know how easy it is to deceive yourself. It takes even greater effort to believe that God is scripting world history. But that the idea takes effort does not mean it is less true. We should rather suspect the opposite: it is intrinsic to the theme that it takes effort. After all, God's way proceeds through the depths of hiddenness.

8. SUFFERING AS JUDGMENT UPON SIN

ONE CAN ALSO VIEW THE SUFFERING PEOPLE EXPERIENCE AS PUNISHMENT of the sin they have committed. People do wrong things and have wrong attitudes. God, a judging God who does not ignore sin, responds to this by punishing them. He is a judging God who does not ignore sin. This view is akin to the pedagogical aspect of suffering, the biggest difference being that the pedagogical model is future-oriented. If one thinks of suffering as being for our good, then the decisive moment for which suffering is necessary lies in the future. In thinking about suffering as punishment, the reference is to the past. The decisive moment which effects the suffering lies behind us. Suffering is not the road *to* something, but the consequence *of* something.

Currently it is not in vogue to regard suffering as judgment upon sin. It does not very well fit the image which contemporary man has of himself and of God. It is too reminiscent of a vengeful or a childish God seeking to get even. It also focuses too much on people's culpability. People have little tolerance for being considered guilty of anything. It does not fit in with their sense of autonomy. This does not mean that at the bottom of our hearts there is not a heavy weight of guilt. Precisely our vulnerability when it comes to sin or guilt is a sign that we may be almost choking in either. But we have the hardest time acknowledging it: we are more inclined to speak about fate than about guilt, about powerlessness than about sin. Regarding the suffering of the people entrusted to his care, a pastor will almost always think twice before saying, "This is God's judgment on sin." If he does say it, the members of his church will probably feel worse. In the ears of many people, the statement that they have to suffer because God punishes them for their evil deeds sounds more like blasphemy than a confession.

Still, if we scrutinize the biblical data, this idea has much support.

The Old Testament is full of stories of divine punishment, starting with the first sin. Because they have eaten of the forbidden fruit, Adam and Eve are expelled from paradise and must die. That is the paradigm of sin and suffering. The consequence of sin is the loss of paradise and ultimately death. This basic pattern takes shape in ever new forms. In the days of Noah, God considers the godless situation and decides to destroy the whole of mankind, except for one family. "So the Lord said, 'I will blot out man whom I have created from the face of the ground, man and beast and creeping things and birds of the air, for I am sorry that I have made them'" (Gen. 6:7). There is nothing in that statement that is pedagogical. It is not for the good of mankind. On account of their sins, God decides he no longer wants humans.

Nor does this pattern change after God has chosen Israel as his special covenant people. Then too the connection between sin and punishment remains. When in the wilderness Israel complains about a lack of water and decent food, God's response is not, according to Numbers 21:6, water from a rock and sustenance from the sky, but the permission of poisonous snakes to wreak havoc among the people. The number of examples can easily be multiplied: during the wilderness journey (Korah, in Num. 16); in the period of the entry (Achan, in Josh. 7); in the time of the judges; in the history of the kings (the census, 2 Sam. 24); Ahab and Elijah (1 Kings 17). Furthermore, the prophets keep speaking of the judgment that will befall Israel on account of its sins. The very first prophets whose message we have available to us in writing (Hosea and Amos) are primarily the prophets of misfortune, the misfortune which will come as divine punishment on Israel's sin. But a late book like Daniel also views the suffering Israel underwent before and after 586 B.C. in the context of guilt. "We have sinned and done wrong and acted wickedly and rebelled, turning aside from thy commandments and ordinances. . . . Therefore the Lord has kept ready the calamity and has brought it upon us; for the Lord our God is righteous in all the works which he has done, and we have not obeyed his voice" (Dan. 9:5, 14). Over and over what the stories of primeval history so graphically depict is realized anew: God comes down to the people, and looks at what they are doing. The Lord came down to see what the people had built (Gen. 11:5); God saw the earth and behold it was corrupt (Gen. 6:12); he calls the man he is looking for and says "where are you?" (Gen. 3:9); and each time God pronounces judgment. God "visits" people. He conducts a visitation. The Old Testament employs the word *paqad*: to visit, to inspect, to afflict. It is to conduct an active visitation with a view to establishing order. Thus, for a godless world and for sinful Israel, God's visits turn into visitations, a source of misfortune, famine, contagious diseases; of defeat, destruction, drowning, or being swallowed alive by the earth. In the twentieth century we may have problems with a punishing God; by far the larger part of the Old Testament apparently does not. Sin and punishment are inseparably connected and for that reason sin and suffering, guilt and misfortune, are also inseparably connected.

Now one can say, "That is the Old Testament. There God indeed is a punishing God who brings suffering upon people on account of their sins. But in the New Testament things are very different. In the New Testament we meet God as the loving, forgiving God in Christ." Undoubtedly there is a distinction between the Old and the New Testament. In Christ there occurs a genuinely new action of God. But that event cannot be described as it was above. In the first place, the Old Testament also knows God as the forgiving God. In between acts of punishment and interwoven with judgment there is grace, intercession, reconciliation, sacrifice, and forgiveness. "Who is a God like thee, pardoning iniquity?" is Micah's cry of confession (Mic. 7:18). And a many-voiced chorus of prophets and poets chime in with him. Conversely, the New Testament also knows of suffering as judgment upon sin. When King Herod makes an oration in which he blusteringly puts on display his power as a ruler, the measure of his sin is filled up and divine judgment strikes him down; even before his death the worms consume him (Acts 12:20-23). The death of a cruel tyrant may still seem within the pattern of the expected; not so the judgment over Ananias and Sapphira. Certainly they had been deceptive, but to be immediately condemned to death—even for Sapphira who came looking for her husband—seems very harsh to us indeed. But that *was* the sentence. They die as punishment upon their sin. But there is more. Especially in the later epistles, when false teachers heighten the tensions in the churches, there also repeatedly occurs the threat that if they persist in their errors, they will not escape from their judgment. He who spurns Christ will receive a heavier punishment than he who violates the law in the Old Testament (Heb. 10:28-29). Because God has come nearer to people than ever before, the punishment will also be the greater. He who abandons the way of Christ and indulges in libertinism will certainly receive the reward of unrighteousness (2 Pet. 2:13). The judgments of ancient time are a sign of the greater judgments which will befall the despisers of God in Christ, says the writer of Jude. In the New Testament grace is conditioned by eschatological fulfillment, but so is judgment. Accordingly, the Old and the New Testament know of suffering, death, and misfortune as judgment upon sin and disobedience.

Now the punishment of sin does not stand by itself. It cannot be abstracted from the covenant which God has graciously made with people. On the contrary, punishment of sin has its place precisely within the framework of covenant. Punishment is judgment upon covenant breaking. This comes out most clearly in the book of Deuteronomy. There it is repeated over and over that if the people keep the covenant, they may expect peace and prosperity; but if they become unfaithful to the God of the covenant they will experience every kind of misfortune. This line of thought culminates in chapters 27 and 28, the official formulation of blessing and curse. Parts of these texts at some time possibly played a role at the religious festivals of Israel in the mountains around Shechem.[8] In any case, the author of Deuteronomy regards them as conditions of the covenant between God and Israel, as the rules of a contract. Both parties promise to keep these rules, and assent to the sanctions against unfaithfulness. From this viewpoint one can even say that when God punishes Israel for her sins, it is not a contradiction of God's covenant faithfulness but an outflow of it: because God adheres to the covenant, he also adheres to its sanctions. Therefore judgment upon Israel is totally just. In other texts detailing the making of covenant, one can also find such formulations concerning the conditions people must fulfil. If they do not, they may not expect the blessing of the Lord; on the contrary, he will cause disasters to come over them. "If they violate my statutes and do not keep my commandments, then I will punish their transgression with the rod and their iniquity with scourges" (Ps. 89:31, 32).

Accordingly, the close connection between sin and suffering has its place within the framework of the covenant. If in Christian theology we want to give shape to a doctrine of covenant, then we shall have to find a place in it for sin and punishment. In our reflection on infant baptism, however much attention we pay to God's promises and faithfulness despite human unfaithfulness, we shall never be able to abstract them from the responsibility we bear as covenant partners. Since within God's covenant with Israel unfaithfulness toward God entailed concrete punishments as consequence, we cannot exclude these consequences from baptism as a covenant sacrament—nor, for that matter, from the Lord's Supper as sacrament of the covenant (Luke 22:20). If members of the church of Christ share in covenant fellowship with the God of Israel, we obligate ourselves to be willing on our part to undergo the consequences of unfaithfulness in judgment, punishment, and suffering. To belong to the church of Christ is a sacred matter; and though unfaithful-

---

8. See Martin Noth, *Geschichte Israels* (Gottingen: Vanden Hoeck & Ruprecht, 1963[5]), pp. 83-104; see also Noth, *Das dritte Buch Mose, Leviticus* (Gottingen: Vanden Hoeck & Ruprecht, 1962), pp. 171-73.

ness within it may not always be punished with death as in the case of Ananias and Sapphira, God can also punish it today. To many people this may be an insuperable stumbling block; in biblical-theological terms it can certainly not be excluded, but on the contrary is to be expected. For not a few people in the twentieth-century Christian church, it is a concept that continues to be a part of their religious world. It could be that they have their eyes open while others have them shut. In any case they can look back upon a wealth of tradition within Israel and within the church.

The idea of the punishment of sin was most determinative for the life of the church in the Middle Ages. Already in Augustine a deep penitential consciousness is manifest; according to tradition he had the psalms of penitence by his deathbed. In the late Middle Ages the theory of penitence developed into a complete system of sins and penalties. God was regarded as the righteous judge. The justice of God was viewed as his punitive justice. It is his *iustitia*, in the sense of the penal code. Punishment is in proportion to sin. In this manner the justice of God becomes something threatening to people, who continually feel guilty and hence continually fear punishment. God's justice is the justice of the law, a threat to people in the way a police officer is to a thief.

In her book *Suffering*, Sölle states that until now the official doctrine of the church has served especially to produce this image of the justice of God. By contrast, in Christian devotional literature we tend rather to find the love of God which seeks the lost, although it is a qualified love.[9] The established church proclaimed God's authority as judge and kept people under tutelage. God was a threatening God, allied with the institutional church, and people were best off if they suppressed themselves or kept silent, in order not to bring the punishment of God upon themselves. According to Sölle, Calvin especially cultivated this image of God.[10]

This view of Sölle is one-sided. In its official pronouncements the church has spoken about forgiveness and grace. And in Calvin the love of God is stronger than his judgment. Though popular revivalists at times eagerly employed the horrors of hell to move people to faith, it is not true that in the church's tradition love and justice were always opposed. Luther's discovery that the justice of God was his saving justice (Ps. 71:2: "In thy righteousness deliver me and rescue me") has been too important for this to be totally obscured. Over and over in Protestant circles the idea revived that the justice and faithfulness of God belong together and form the basis of forgiveness (1 John 1:9). All this does not alter the fact, however, that the mainstream of the church's life, especially in the Calvinist tradition, took another direction, one that was more akin to the medieval concepts of the justice of God. A precedent was set by the Heidelberg Catechism,

9. Sölle, *Suffering*, pp. 24, 25.
10. Ibid., p. 23.

Question 11: "But is not God also merciful?" To which the answer reads: "God is certainly merciful but he is also just." Here the justice of God is opposed to his mercy. On the basis of that justice man must expect to be punished. The mercy consists in the fact that there is a vicar or mediator, but mercy cannot invalidate the judicial principle that sin must be punished. In the Roman Catholic tradition people proceeded from the same principle. Only they had not only the compensation of the vicarious work of Christ, but also that of the saints and their own good works.

In the Middle Ages a distinction was made between temporal and eternal punishments, a distinction which recurs in the *Heidelberg Catechism* (Answer 10). Eternal punishment is the punishment of hell, the irrevocable verdict of unending lostness, pictured in the imagery of fire and torment. On the back wall of the cathedral at Albi is a painting which depicts the torments of the lost—naturally it hangs on the west side of the church where the laity are, to serve as "a book" to warn them away from sin. The Middle Ages displayed a profusion of such scenes. The heavenly judge will render judgment, and whoever by the rules in force (which were the rules of the church) deserved judgment was bound to receive it on the *Dies Irae* (Day of Wrath).

Today the church no longer universally accepts as self-evident the idea of eternal punishment. The existence of hell is denied or, more often, deemed irrelevant for our faith, which is assumed to focus on our actions in history, and not on our eternal destiny. To others hell is as self-evident as the supermarket on the corner. Both positions raise questions. On the one hand, hell is never self-evident. When we speak of it, we are speaking of a *mysterium tremendum.* Compared to many more recent sources, the Bible is remarkably restrained when it comes to representations of hell (as it is, for that matter, when it comes to representations of heaven). Sober words about weeping and gnashing of teeth, and even the idea of a pool of fire and brimstone, cannot be compared with the tormenting devils of medieval paintings. When reference is made to hell, it is on the periphery of the message, as an extreme possibility. Front and center is salvation, life in Christ. Some passages, specifically in the Pauline literature, speak so emphatically of the all-inclusiveness of the work of Christ that hardly any room is left for another possibility. All that is in heaven and earth is gathered into one in Christ (Eph. 1:10; cf. Col. 1:20). In the New Testament hell only makes its appearance where salvation is denied.

Before the face of God in Jesus Christ we can only speak with diffidence about eternal punishment, about definitively excluded possibilities. As we live on the basis of his compassion, eternal judgment seems to us an impossibility; however, in the Scriptures it recurrently rises to the surface as the stark contrast to the way into life. On the basis of God's works in Jesus Christ hell may seem an impossibility; but according to the message of the early church it is a very real possibility. We must also take these data from Scripture seriously, even though they confront us with a terrifying enigma. Apparently God can bring people into a definitive state of suffering by comparison with which all conceivable earthly suffering pales into nothingness. Death is not only sung about as overcome in the risen Christ (1 Cor. 15:55), but it is also the door to the second death (Rev. 21:8). Besides the data of Scripture, another reason to speak about hell as a serious possibility is the sobering truth of human beings' opposition to God. If people definitively reject God, if they reject him also as the gracious God in Jesus Christ, one must not force them against their own deliberate choice to belong to him. It seems God himself does not impose himself on them, but respects this ultimate human decision. One cannot and may not box people about the ears with "hell and damnation"; the subject is too "dreadful" for that; but in awed respect before the judgment of God we do have to and may speak about hell and damnation. Fortunately we do not always have to speak about it.

In view of the relationship between covenant and punishment of sin one will have to say that punishment as eternal punishment primarily threatens the innermost circle of the covenant. If we view Jesus Christ in the inmost circle, the one possessing the most intimate covenant relationship with God, then hell primarily strikes him. It is not without reason that the church confesses that Jesus Christ descended into hell. When people go to hell, they there encounter the Other who went before them for the purpose of deliverance. In this manner 1 Peter 3:19, the New Testament text about the descent into hell, stands in a totally new light. In this way one can also arrive at the idea of hell as a transitional phase. It is real; as real as was the suffering of Jesus Christ; but it is not the end, anymore than the gospels (which are the church's kerygma) end in the cross. Not even the Gospel of John, where the cross is so climactic, ends with it. So we can also understand that people—Origen is an example—arrive at the restoration of all things, the *apokatastasis panton,* in which even the devil, as God's creature, is still saved. The idea of Jesus' descent into hell shows us very graphically that hell as eternal judgment is not an independent, tensionless, theological datum. At the same time certain texts, specifically Matthew, Revelation, and the later letters, keep us from smoothing everything down to the level of a universal atonement in which there is no room for a "no" from God.

Besides eternal punishment, traditional doctrine knew of temporal punishments. Included were all the punishments one underwent during this life, but also the punishments of purgatory. A church member who died not having done sufficient penance suffered purgatory as a temporal punishment in order to make up for it and to be purified for heaven. Protestant churches repudiated the doctrine of purgatory. It was too much tied up with the sale of indulgences, masses for the soul, and the church's power of absolution. In addition, scriptural proof for it was lacking. In recent years Hendrikus Berkhof has expressed the idea that hell as a form of purification will be a provisional—hence a temporary—stage.[11] In any case, the doctrine of purgatory did not deny the seriousness of judgment as punishment, and at the same time it did justice to the superior power of grace—in Catholic tradition as this applies to people within the church, and in Berkhof in a world-embracing perspective. To say this is to indicate that the problem of purgatory is a derived or secondary problem. It is a theological construct intended to relieve problems raised by the idea of the eternal lostness of man (Berkhof) or of the baptized (Catholic tradition). If one acknowledges hell as an extreme possibility, then a solution in the direction of purgatory is not necessary, certainly not if one also acknowledges the falling away of baptized or professing members (Heb. 6:3).

However, questions also remain if we acknowledge that judgment may issue in either of two directions. What, for example, is the situation of the redeemed and the lost within their own categories? One person has suffered more in this life than another. We all arrive with empty hands, but the hands of some are emptier than others. The hands of some are marked by the callouses of deeds of love and the scars of suffering under the cross. Similar differences exist among the lost. In order to do justice to these differences, could one not conceive a sort of vestibule, a time of suffering and works of love? A better idea than this construct (which has no support in Scripture) is to think of different degrees of glory and lostness. The fact that John and James were denied the privilege of sitting on either side of the Son of Man (Mark 10:35-40) does not mean that such places of honor do not exist in heaven. When it comes to judgment, the one who knew the master's will and did not do it receives a more severe beating than the one who did not know it (Luke 12:47ff.).

Both eternal and temporal punishment in the form of a sentence of purification lie in the future. For the living, both constitute as yet only possibilities—conceived either as real or as unreal. For that reason a discussion of it usually has a somewhat speculative character. It is usually more a word of warning than of explication. Accordingly, it usually has no direct existential impact on people's lives: it remains a possibility next to other open possibilities, and for most people who

11. Berkhof, *Christian Faith*, pp. 535-37.

believe in an eternal judgment the possibility of eternal peace is more real than that of eternal punishment. For Christians heaven is nearer than hell, a sense that changes if the thought of eternal punishment is applied to a specific person in one's own environment. In the case of purgatory the situation is somewhat simpler, for purgatory is a limited punishment in expectation of heaven; but when it comes to hell the discussion requires more care. One would certainly want to see certain persons punished. For many Europeans and virtually all Jews, it would be unbearable if Hitler should have a place in heaven.

Still, one should be very careful with this idea. In the first place, it is not up to us to judge. If God wants to distribute eternal punishments, he will do it himself. We do not have to, not even in the case of Hitler. Moreover, this pattern of thought tends quickly to degenerate into the exclusion of others on the basis of personal rancor or one's own negative experiences. If one believes in the reality of eternal punishment, at the same time he cannot condemn anyone to it. This applies all the more in a situation in which we are confronted with people who have lost a loved one. There it is impossible and forbidden for one to render a verdict himself. In part of the church an awesome fear exists of the possibility that a loved one was eternally lost. From the preceding discussion it will be clear that I do not in the least regard this as a relic from the Middle Ages, but that it proceeds from a way of relating to Scripture in which an attempt is made to take all the data seriously, including what shocks us. It is also based on a sense of the value every individual has in making his decisions. The Christian church cannot do without fear of judgment. When the possibility of eternal judgment comes so close that a deceased loved one might be subject to it, clearly this possibility is a frightening abyss. We might wish to bridge this abyss, repair the disruption which it produces in our thinking, but we never quite succeed. However much the overwhelming presence and power of God's grace in Christ overcomes the powers of darkness, as long as the *apokatastasis panton* (the restoration of all things) is not the sure foundation of Christian belief, an open hell will continue to stare us in the face.

Till now the movement of our thinking was from sin to punishment. Sin may be followed by punishment. But the problem becomes more difficult if the order is reversed, so that in the case of a concrete instance of suffering the question is posed whether it constitutes punishment of sin. As pastor I have been asked by the mother of a child who was terminally ill: "Does he have to suffer this because I have done wrong?" One's first reaction as a pastor is to deny it—the example of John 9 comes to mind. When Jesus and his disciples encounter a man born blind, the disciples ask, "Rabbi, who sinned, this man or his parents, that he was born blind?" (9:2). For them it is certain that blindness is a penalty for sin. In this case the problem is that the man was *born* blind. Accordingly, his handicap cannot be the response to a sin committed earlier. Is it possibly a punishment of the parents for a wrong done by them that they now have a handicapped child? Jesus rejects the question. The underlying assumption that blindness is a penalty for sin is already mistaken. "It was not that this man sinned, or his parents, but that the works of God might be made manifest in him" (9:3). Hence one cannot logically argue back from suffering to sin. In the same situation one can even offer the reverse argument on the basis of 1 Kings 14. When the child of Jeroboam I dies young, it is to preserve the boy from the total judgment that is to come over all of Jeroboam's children. Abijah is the only one of these children who will come to the grave "because in him there is found something pleasing to the Lord" (v. 13). To save the boy from having to experience all the suffering that was to come, God caused him to die young. "Whom the gods love dies young" (Menander). This apparently applies also to the God of Israel. Herein lies a possibility for consolation. The curse of the closed circle which assumes that this concrete instance of suffering is the inevitable consequence of sin must be broken. Should the examples cited not be adequate, the entire book of Job is there to teach us that suffering may be caused by things very different from the sin of the sufferer.

Sometimes, however, the relationship to a concrete sin does exist. But the examples of Abijah, the man born blind, and Job show that one should not too quickly posit a causal relationship—and certainly not a self-evident causal relationship—between suffering and sin. But they do not exclude the possibility that in other situations such a relationship does exist. Sometimes that is clearly demonstrable. If, despite numerous warnings, a drunk person drives a car and wraps it around a tree, the suffering he must then endure is undeniably a consequence of sin. In that case there is a causal connection. The connection is not indirect—via God who causes a seemingly unconnected punishment to follow a given act—but recognizably direct. Only the interpretation of suffering as *punishment* points to a judgment which transcends the chain of causality. Otherwise one could at best speak of "consequence." We could also say that we do not view the action of God as intervening in the causality of the world, but as a framework of interpretation, as an attempt to give meaning to causality.

In those cases where sin and suffering are so clearly connected that one can speak of consequences, it is best to link comfort with forgiveness. If we only address ourselves to the suffering, we are neglecting the real source of pain. Only in the forgiveness of sin does a person find the deliverance which can be the basis for enduring and processing the suffering. That is also true if the other does not himself acknowledge his guilt. Guilt is more than a feeling of guilt. If the feeling of guilt is not present (or is perhaps not expressed because the guilt itself is too big to accept), it is incorrect to ignore the guilt, say, from a fear of offending the other. In that case one fails to do justice to the other because one does not accept him (or her) as an adult person who is responsible. Only in the act of accepting responsibility and hence in the assumption of guilt can there be the openness which shapes the wholeness of a human being. Otherwise, though bone fractures may heal, human life worthy of the name remains broken.

To be sure, an outsider cannot always clearly discern the causal connection. But this does not mean the same applies to the sufferer. Not everything is or needs to be in the open. One must be very careful when speaking of sin and punishment and use those words only in case of a clear relationship between sin and suffering. What is hidden from the outsider may, however, be clear to the sufferer himself. For that reason, too quick a reference to the man born blind may prematurely close off the matter. Behind the sufferer's question—whether the suffering is perhaps his own fault—may be an attempt to confess a sin which stands in the way of accepting comfort. If the other person indicates that he wants to talk about it, we must allow him the opportunity and thus be instrumental in his deliverance from guilt. If we ourselves land in a situation where we clearly recognize our suffering as a consequence of our sin, it is essential to confess it, first before God but then also before another human being. Not that the sin must be put on public display, or trumpeted from the housetop; rather, it may be confided to one person we can trust and who is prepared to be privy to our secret and carry it with him in the forgiveness of God. Sometimes the connection between suffering and sin may be even more deeply hidden, so that even the sufferer has no inkling of it. At the same time, however, a deep sense of guilt may be present as the cause of suffering. If this sense only arises from the general rule that suffering is punishment, then, as we saw earlier, that has to be corrected. If one is dealing with an intuitive awareness of connections which cannot be explained, it is important in any case to put into words the source of the sense of guilt, even when its relationship to suffering cannot be made fully clear. There may be hidden links which escape us, even though we are very deeply involved. In this case, forgiveness is more important than analysis.

Meanwhile, we have again come close to the position that in an indirect way suffering follows as God's judgment upon sin, although there is no direct causal connection. If the connection between suffering and sin is discernible, though only in an intuitive non-objectifiable way, then we can do something with it. If the connection is in no way visible, not even in the heart of the sufferer, we cannot say anything about it. Then the suffering may also be punishment of sin, though we do not know it, and can do nothing with it. Since suffering is not always the consequence of sin, it is correct in that situation to say nothing about the relationship between sin and suffering. If one does introduce this model, one is speaking of an unknown sin which possibly does not exist and can therefore not be discussed or forgiven. That is the last thing one should do to a fellow human being or to oneself.

Suffering is not necessarily the consequence of sin, but it can be. That is the conclusion of the first part of this section, which dealt with the issue on the individual level. But how do things stand collectively? In my opinion, there is no essential difference, because sin is rarely purely individual: sin is against oneself and against God. For that matter, it is "trans-individual," for sin vis-à-vis God is sin vis-à-vis Christ, the person who has brought the new humanity to light in wholeness. Virtually without exception, sin is also against others. It is the awareness of this fact which as a rule gives guilt its sharpness. Imagine the grief one has caused others: parents, husband or wife, children, friends. Accordingly, forgiveness of wrongs done is primarily forgiveness by those who have had to suffer the result of the wrongs I have done.

The Bible repeatedly refers to common suffering as a result of one person's sin. In the second commandment of the decalogue one reads of "the Lord your God . . . visiting the iniquity of the fathers upon the children to the third and the fourth generation of those who hate me" (Exod. 20:5). Presumably, the reference is primarily to the consequences which the actions of one person have on another. In the ancient Orient, "the third and fourth generation" describes the fundamental social unit: the extended family consisting of grandparents, parents and children, sometimes together with the great grandfather. Especially the father is decisively important for all. When he goes wrong, his action immediately affects the whole family. When he introduces images of gods, the whole family is involved. When he squanders the family's belongings, they are squandered for all. The sin of one affects all, to the third and fourth generation. In our culture, which rarely has extended families, a dynamic equivalent translation of the second commandment would refer to the second and third generation (parents and children, possibly together with the grandparents in some parts of the country). The sin of the parents directly affects the children. The father who becomes an invalid as a result of drunkenness causes the children to suffer. They bear the consequences of his sin.

However, as soon as this reality becomes an excuse for children to avoid being active in "the way of righteousness," because they are blocked by their ungodly fathers, the childrens' reasoning becomes a smokescreen. The prophet Ezekiel explodes at those who think they can do nothing about the bad situation of Israel because of the sins of the fathers (Ezek. 18). With a new beginning of justice and well-doing, it is possible to break the cycle of sin and punishment. As human beings we are not doomed to powerlessness by what has gone before.

There is still another dimension of meaning in Exodus 20:5: people are not regarded as individuals but as a fellowship. If in this collectivity one person goes wrong, the whole group is guilty. There is a clear example of this in Joshua 7 and 8. One Israelite, a man called Achan, has stolen some of "the devoted things" of Jericho. As a result all Israel is guilty. The consequence is defeat in battle; thirty-six men perish (Josh. 7:5). Sometimes the relationship between the sin of the individual and the misfortune that strikes the group is directly demonstrable. In the case of Achan this is not so. In our own situation we sometimes suspect a relationship between the sin of an individual and the suffering of a group in a way which cannot be directly explained. Even more than in the case of the suffering of the individual we must be on our guard here. All too quickly the tensions evoked by suffering in the group are charged to one of them. It is all too easy to look for a scapegoat. Extreme caution is in order before we trace the problems of a group to one individual, even when that individual acknowledges the misfortune is his fault. It is very well possible that the fault is his, but equally the fault of others, possibly even more the fault of others; that in fact a faulty collective attitude has become explicit only in that one person. Often it is the most open people, or the people at the bottom of a group, who become its victims. Essential to thinking in collective terms is that both suffering and sin are communal. The sinner, in fact, is merely a sign of collective sinfulness. Every Israelite could have been Achan. Therefore, collectively they are at fault. This reality is fundamentally developed by Paul in the first chapters of Romans. "Therefore you have no excuse, O man, whoever you are" (Rom. 2:1). One person can be the direct cause of suffering because one person can become the exponent of collective sin. Viewed in this light, the death of Hitler possibly becomes a commonplace "solution" which distracts attention away from the real problems of Western culture. By the disappearance of the one in whom all sins were bunched together, many sins—of oppression, the pride of achievement, superiority, and the bottled up drive toward emancipation on account of which the West is on the brink of exploding—are released for a moment, but not banished. Accordingly, the dividing line between the expelled tyrant and the glorified martyr is very thin.

Sometimes, amidst collective guilt, it is possible to find an exponent in whom everything is concentrated: the symptom-bearer, whose expulsion to hell as the scapegoat offers a moment's relief. The curse has been removed from the camp. Achan has been killed; Hitler is gone. Suffering makes room for new hope. However, it is not always possible to find such a clear exponent. Only then does the collectivity of guilt really stand out. Perhaps then it is also possible to find a more basic solution to the problem. If today the world suffers poverty and hunger, it is the collective fault of rich and poor countries. An isolated individual is powerless to bring about real change, but that is not to say that one is without blame. For in that case others would have more blame than I do, whereas in fact the fault and the blame belong to everyone. We together are to blame for the suffering of all, for the poverty of the oppressed and the frenetic frustration of the rich. We may try to single out a few as really responsible, say, the bosses of multinationals. They are also to blame, but by singling them out as solely to blame, we are denying the essence of the problem. The solution does not lie in purging a few scapegoats. It lies rather in the downfall of the suffering righteous one who is willing to bear the iniquity of all in the place of all. The history of Jesus Christ teaches us that salvation comes not from the death of Judas but from the cross of Christ. The definitive solution lies in the moment when all human beings, in imitation of the Lord, are willing to be the suffering righteous, to be accounted sinners, to forgive one another and in that forgiveness to serve one another. This is not pie-in-the-sky piety: it must be given shape in economic and social structures. Only then can we stop looking for scapegoats. Only then the curse of sin and its consequences, in which the world already now bears God's judgment, is broken. For in a world in which people learn to think collectively, the suffering of one person is a pointer to my sin.

Actually, we are not permitted to make this connection in every instance in which misfortunes strike the world. That would create a collective burden that, like an individual one, is not bearable. Much misfortune in the world cannot in any way be directly correlated with human wrongdoing. If we nevertheless blame people for it, we are saddling them with guilt that cannot be demonstrated. And inexpressible guilt is unpardonable guilt. Accordingly, on the collective level we must only see the relationship between sin and suffering where it is concretely demonstrable.

Now we can take one step further and expand the collective to include all of humanity in all of its history. In other words, is the suffering of the world not the punishment of the sin of mankind as an absolute collective? Or are suffering and death not the consequence of the original sin of Adam? Here again we can start in the realm of consequences: sin was the Trojan horse. Because man sinned, the door was opened to the powers of darkness to manifest themselves in the world in all sorts of ways. They were the cause of new sin and new guilt. They caused suffering, fear, and death. In this manner, individual suffering can in no way be linked with individual sin. The suffering of the individual is produced by the powers of the darkness which entered as a result of the sin of all. The suffering individual is not more guilty than others, as Jesus said on the occasion of the murder of certain Galileans by Herod: "Do you think that these Galileans were worse sinners than all the other Galileans, because they suffered thus? I tell you, No; but unless you repent you will all likewise perish" (Luke 13:2, 3).

In the context of this section we are considering suffering as punishment by God precisely when there is a demonstrable causal relationship between sin and suffering. If now we know ourselves bound together with all human beings in an absolute collectivity, every experience of suffering is traceable to a collective guilt which is punished by God in the individual's suffering, a part of universal suffering. Now the punishment of sin is at the same time the expiation of sin. Once the punishment has been borne, the guilt has been blotted out. The practice of criminal law shows that no punishment can totally remove the sin, nor can a jail term make the thief a good man. Forgiveness is more powerful than punishment. Still, punishment serves to make expiation: guilt is cancelled. By punishment the sin has been placed in another light. If now the individual bears suffering as judgment upon collective sin, then he does it for others. The sin of the world now stands in another light as a result of my suffering. Therefore, in my suffering I share in the suffering of Christ. There is no suffering in the world that is not bound up with the suffering of Christ. Accordingly, there can be no suffering which in Christ would have no consequences before God. If God brings suffering upon people, it creates obligations for him.

In the case of individual suffering, we noted that its interpretation as punishment of sin is a possibility, but not the only conceivable one. In the case of common suffering and common guilt one might suppose that it *is* the only possibility. Especially Romans 5 seems to point in that direction—as though death as the ultimate exponent of suffering is exclusively the consequence of sin. Still, here too we must refrain from drawing premature conclusions. Death is also the consequence of sin. Sin and death, guilt and suffering, are related right down to Adam. But the sin of mankind is not the only source of suffering. The metaphysical powers of darkness both transcend and precede humanity. Especially the book of Job teaches us to look beyond the immanent creational connection between sin and punishment. The New Testament is as clear on this point; in the letter to the Ephesians the author refers to transcendent powers which attack the church (Eph. 6:12). The existence of the world of darkness, to which sin and death belong, is antecedent to the existence of the world of mankind, of Adam.

*   *   *

GOD PUNISHES SIN THROUGH THE CONSEQUENCES OF MEN'S DEEDS. IN addition, we saw in Scripture that certain punishments stand in no causal relationship to sin, like the defeat of Israel at Ai or the death of Jeroboam's son. And in our own times we can sometimes sense something of a divine punishment in which God makes no use of earthly causality. However, interpreting it is a precarious matter and only somewhat manageable on the individual level: I experience my suffering as punishment of a sin I have committed, and this experience prompts me to confess the sin and to receive forgiveness. In Scripture, however, punishments also occur by divine intervention on a collective level. That punishment assumes various forms. The punishment for numbering the people was a contagious disease (2 Sam. 24:15); the punishment for Korah's rebellion was that the earth crust opened and swallowed the rebels (Num. 16:31-33); the penalty for Ahab's Baal worship was a famine (1 Kings 17:1); the penalty for consulting an alien god by Ahaziah's servants was fire descending from heaven (2 Kings 1:10). It is a precarious matter in the twentieth century to interpret collective disasters as divine punishment upon collective sin. An earthquake is a collective disaster, but what does it punish? Who can tell as long as there is no prophet to announce the judgment beforehand? Only in a remote and derivative way can disasters prompt us to reflect on our godforsaken situation and to repent. And every disaster, wherever in the world it occurs, calls out to all. For the victims of an earthquake in Agadir and the victims of a flood in Bangladesh are not greater sinners than we are.

Besides the direct punishments of God (fire from heaven) and the judgments that come via secondary causes, there also are divine punishments of sin through human agency. Human beings may be called by God to punish sin. When at Mt. Sinai Israel made the golden calf, the members of the tribe of Levi were instructed to act, sword in hand, against their brothers (Exod. 32:27). Admittedly, Achan was found by divine judgment to be the guilty one, but his sentence is carried out by men (Josh. 7:25). Exodus, Leviticus, and Deuteronomy are full of instructions to people to put away the evil person from among them. Accordingly, people are instruments in the hands of God. Man is God's partner,

69

by his name carrying out the divine sentence. Primarily this is a task for the government. A divinely given charge always has to do with calling. If the government is no longer the authority called by God, the practice of punishing people loses its legitimacy. For that purpose a social contract is not a sufficient basis. All human beings together do not have the right to break the life of another human being, whether by the death penalty or a prison sentence which can have an effect on a person's future worse than death. Legitimacy for punishing people can only be rooted in the faith that God wants to punish sin. If God does not punish sin, there is no reason for man to do it. But God does punish sin and also calls people to act to this end in his name.

Also in this regard it is not merely a privilege to be elect. Imagine being called to take up the sword against your brothers. Imagine being called to sentence another person to a jail term when you are aware of your own moral deficiencies. Imagine being a judge. Although you know yourself to be a sinner, you are called nevertheless to pronounce a judgment over another human being. It is a terrifying thing to put people on the relentless road of a judicial sentence. This fear has been stylized in the formal rules of criminal law. It is the only way a judge can maintain his mental health and at the same time avoid judicial error. Only a system of law formulated collectively and developed over the course of history is bearable for human beings. Accordingly, things become dramatic when justice begins to stumble in the streets. When the government no longer fulfils its divinely appointed task of punishing injustice, but perverts justice into injustice, the individual may be called to reestablish justice. In the name of God he must then execute the punishment of the unrighteous. It is a dramatic turn of events which no one can elect or appropriate to himself. Too often people have taken the law into their own hands. Too many people think that, given their situation, the time for that is ripe. Too many usurpers have exchanged injustice for even greater injustice. Not everyone is fit to wear the prophetic mantle of Elijah. It only fits the person who was called by God against his own will. And the person who has to wear this mantle had better remember the fate of the prophets: how many of them have not been killed and stoned? To be called outside of the established order of authority means one must himself endure the suffering and bear the responsibility to the end. The worst punishment is for the called person himself. There is nothing heroic about it. It is pure misery. Accordingly, the person who is really called will choose this road only because he cannot do otherwise, acting against his own preferences, thus to be sacrificed on the altar of the rights of others.

From the task of man to punish the guilty in the name of God the necessity of punishment emerges. In the preceding discussion we already saw a number of times that punishment has a positive function. There is, first of all, the psychological significance of punishment. Guilt calls for recognition; punishment is a means to that end. In the section about the chastising father we already noted how intensely liberating punishment can be. We saw above that suffering also serves the function of compensating, at least partly, for sin. This is especially true for voluntary suffering assumed for the purpose of relieving the suffering of others.

In the second place, punishment is necessary for the sake of cleansing of the earth. The earth has been polluted by evil. When the unrighteous aggrandize themselves, the world is no longer recognizable as the world of the righteous God of Israel. In the story of Achan, it is precisely the example of the curse in the camp which illustrates the pollution of all by the one polluting source. Therefore it has to be removed. Accordingly, punishment is at the same time deliverance. The punishment of the unjust oppressor is the liberation of the oppressed righteous. In the Old Testament the word "paqad" (to visit) therefore has a double meaning: on the one hand, it is the visitation of sin and punishment of the ungodly, and on the other it is a visitation of the faithful toward their salvation. In Zechariah 10:3 one finds the two meanings in one verse: "My anger is hot against the shepherds, and I will punish *(paqad)* the leaders (he-goats); for the Lord of hosts cares for *(paqad)* his flock, the house of Judah, and will make them like his proud steed in battle." Compare Psalm 72: when the king brings the justice of God on earth, the oppressors are crushed and the poor delivered.

In the third place, punishment is necessary for the sake of God's name. For the sake of the holy name of God, injustice cannot remain unrequited. That is the truth of the sentence in the classic Reformed formulary for communion, which states "that the wrath of God against sin is so great that He, rather than to leave it unpunished, has punished it in His beloved Son, Jesus Christ." If God left injustice in its place then the Judge of all the earth would not do right (Gen. 18:25), anymore than if he should kill the righteous along with the ungodly. For the righteous and the ungodly are not the same.

For the rest, the recompense of the righteous of which the Bible also speaks balances the punishment of the ungodly. God blesses the Egyptian midwives Shiphrah and Puah for their "white lies" on behalf of the children of the Israelites (Exod. 1:20ff.). God blesses believing Abraham (Gal. 3:9). Also, today blessing is the experience of people who walk with God. In the churches we meet the people who bring forth fruit in old age and are ever "full of sap and green" (Ps. 92:14), surrounded by good fortune and blessing, living on the basis of the faithfulness of the Lord.

It is more often the case, however, that we see the Lord blessing the deceptive Jacob. Sometimes it takes a very long time before the ungodly receives his punishment and the righteous experiences deliverance and blessing. Very often they die before that which is crooked has been straightened out. Jeremiah complains: "Why does the way of the wicked prosper? Why do all who are treacherous thrive?" (12:1). And the saints beneath the altar continually cry out: "How long before thou wilt avenge our blood?" (Rev. 6:10). They are waiting for the moment when things will be straightened out on earth. If there is not a definitive judgment in the end, a *final* judgment, the Judge of all the earth will not have done right; then his name is nowhere and the earth remains polluted. Also, there is then no real forgiveness and for all eternity people remain stuck with their guilt.

If there is no final decision in which things are straightened out, history remains without purpose or meaning. If things are really rectified, justice will also have to be done to those who died in skewed relationships, to millions who were murdered and oppressed, to the innumerable unrighteous who died in glory. Without a resurrection from the dead, a final judgment is meaningless. Without a resurrection from the dead a future world will continue to confirm the skewed relationship of the past. A kingdom of righteousness founded on multitudes of lost and enslaved people, who are written off as the refuse of history, just cannot be. The history of God's world has no rubbish bin—certainly not a rubbish bin in which the righteous disappear.

A fundamental consideration of this subject can be found in Wolfhart Pannenberg.[12] Pannenberg proceeds from the assumption that history derives its meaning from the future, a future which incorporates all that has gone before. Absolute meaning can only be found in an all-embracing conception of history, in which the fragmentation of death has been overcome.

We must comment further on one aspect of suffering as divine punishment. Until now we have focused in particular on issues of justice: the consequences God wills and justifies; the righteous judgments executed by God or in his name which make straight that which is crooked. But in Scripture the punishment of God sometimes also has very different, much more emotional aspects. Then the focus is not so much on God's justice as on his wrath. When a penalty is imposed by a judge, there is always a certain emotional detachment. One complies with the

---

12. Wolfhart Pannenberg, *Grundfragen systematischen theologie,* vol. 2 (Gottingen: Vanden Hoeck & Ruprecht, 1980), pp. 66-79.

legal rules by which the judge is bound. That is also the case when the law is covenant law established by God himself. In the case of wrath, however, there is no such emotional detachment. In that case God is involved with all "the fibers of his being," and his wrath is overwhelming. It is the wrath of thunder and lightning (Ps. 18:8-16); it is a blast from his nostrils. The Hebrew word for "wrath" is the same as the word for "nose." Wrath is fury's raging, because the measure of iniquity has become full. Words like "anger" and "fury" also convey the intense emotional involvement. Sometimes the wrath of God is the fury of affronted majesty. He is the Holy One, whose holiness shines even more brightly in Christ than it did in Moses (Heb. 12:18-25). Accordingly, the writer of Hebrews warns Christians not to grow slack in the service of God. "For our God is a consuming fire" (Heb. 12:29). "It is a fearful thing to fall into the hands of the living God" (Heb. 10:31). In other passages wrath is more that of wounded love. God has given everything to Israel. He has led them from Egypt but "their heart was lifted up; therefore they forgot me. So I will be to them like a lion, like a leopard I will lurk beside the way" (Hos. 13:6, 7).

In Scripture God is not always the sweetly loving, tolerant God. He is not even always the reliable Judge. Sometimes God is a fierce Fury before whom human beings can only tremble. God can be so terrifying that people cry out to the mountains: "Fall on us and hide us from the face of him who is seated on the throne, and from the wrath of the Lamb" (Rev. 6:16). God is not always "the good Lord," and in our day it is well for us to realize that. Primarily, the image of a loving, forbearing God is correct, but God will not be toyed with. Generally, wrath stored up for a long time turns into wrath that cannot be stopped. We must guard against having too simple and too sweet an image of God. He too easily becomes a sentimental figure, as innocuous as he is good. But a goody-goody God can easily be ignored. A really loving God is very different. If we treat the loving God as though he were "nice," the moment may come that his measure is full and he no longer puts up with it. God is no wimp.

Religious pedagogy is rife with warnings against depicting God as an ogre, a warning that is warranted. God is not the quiet secret agent who is always watching you. Essentially, a child may and should feel safe with God. But if God becomes the all-approving "good Lord," he cannot also be a source of trust to a child. He must also be the God who has to be taken seriously. Only a God who does not swallow every-thing—both what others do to me and what I do to others—is able to win trust and is worthy of it. This also applies to adults. For them too a God who lets matters be as they are is worthless. And even if people should opt for such a God, and consequently adopt a neutral pose toward obedience and righteousness because God would not be heard from in any case, that is not yet to say that God is that way. God is not as we would like him to be but as he really is and has proven himself to be: a God who is not mocked (Gal. 6:7). For the people of God there is no time when they have more reason to fear the wrath of God than when their awareness of it has ebbed away. In our day God has hidden himself. We are living with the sense of an absent God. But he is the present Absentee. If we call for the revelation of his presence, for a sign of life, for a day in which he is on the scene and does justice, we may well consider that the day could be darkness and not light (Amos 5:18). The day of God's revelation is the day of his wrath, the *dies irae,* as John Newton knew ("Day of Judgment! Day of Wonders").

Only after having said all this, amidst fears of judgment upon our unfaithfulness, amidst despair over the hopelessness of our situation, may we say that "he will not always chide, nor will he keep his anger for ever. He does not deal with us according to our sins, nor requite us according to our iniquities" (Ps. 103:9-10). If God did do this, then our situation would be hopeless indeed. If in his love God did let himself be finally discouraged by our unfaithfulness, then we would be hopelessly lost. But God returns. He is God and not man (Hos. 11:9). He cannot be angry forever. Wrath is not the final component in the justice of God; his justice is bound up with faithfulness. "He is faithful and just and will forgive our sins and cleanse us from all unrighteousness" (1 John 1:9). The justice of God consists in his continuing trustworthiness and faithfulness to the covenant he initiated. He remains faithful even when we are faithless. He cannot deny himself (2 Tim. 2:13). God does not allow our sin to cancel out his covenant justice. He does not let our untrustworthiness undo his trustworthiness. But things do go to the brink, embattled as his steadfastness is by wrath, judgment, and anger. It is only because he is God and not man, the Holy One, the Wholly Other, that things turn out well. It is the miracle of the God who so loved the world that he gave his only Son (John 3:16). God's holiness is manifest in his liberating action in Jesus Christ on behalf of a lost world. In that he is manifest as the Wholly Other; but the fact that things go to the brink of darkness and through the darkness is evident in Gethsemane and on the cross: "My God, my God, why have you forsaken me?" (Matt. 27:46). The song concerning the *Dies Irae* knows the *mysterium tremendum* of God's judgment.

> Hark! the trumpet's awful sound
> Louder than a thousand thunders,

74

Shakes the vast creation round.
How the summons / Will the sinner's heart confound!

But precisely in this song, in the midst of dread, there is a moving sense of God's grace.

See the Judge, our nature wearing,
Clothed in majesty divine;
You who long for his appearing
Then shall say, This God is mine!
Gracious Savior,
Own me in that day as Thine.

That which is true to the point that we must be afraid of eternal condemnation also applies to the punishment we undergo on earth. In some experiences of suffering the connection with sin is clear. Sometimes it is suspected. As a rule, a direct relationship can not be absolutely established. But if our suffering involves punishment of sin, we can only, in the style of John Newton, ask for mercy. We can only utter the prayer that ultimately the punishment is not the expression of the fury of an affronted God but the love of the Father who, however affronted, cannot finally let go of his child. As a father takes his child into his loving arms, God has compassion on the human being who has been broken under judgment. In the loving embrace of the Father the brokenhearted are healed.

9. BEHIND SUFFERING AND SIN

IN THE PRECEDING SECTIONS, IN ORDER TO GIVE EXPRESSION AND FORM TO the idea that suffering comes from the hand of God, we have set forth different possibilities. All things come from him: sickness, cares, disasters, and grief. He lets these things happen to us, in order to discipline us, to save us from worse experiences, or to punish us for wrongs we have done. All these models presuppose that the world is imperfect. God chastises, as a father does his children when they go wrong. God takes us into dark valleys to shield us from a darkness which is greater still. God punishes us because we sinned. Accordingly, in all these models evil is assumed. *Given* a sinful and broken world, God disciplines or punishes us. But we must ask: If God is the almighty, how is it possible that this assumed evil is there? If God governs all things, how then can we still sin? How then can there be a threatening darkness? Once evil is present we can conceive models of how in that situation God deals with people, but where does evil come from? For this problem we may refer to Adam's fall in paradise, the point at which "things got out of hand." All sins follow in the wake of original sin, but this does not really help us understand. In the first place, Adam is the collective head: reference to him only means that sin is an archetypal human datum in which all of humanity is involved. As a result of the collective character of evil, the problem only gets bigger: where does the commonality of sin come from? In the second place, we can simply ask: How then could Adam sin? If God is omnipotent and wills the good, if Adam is his creature, how can things then still go wrong?

We can extend the chain. Adam attributes the blame to Eve, "the woman whom thou gavest to be with me" (Gen. 3:12). But that does not help us out of the impasse either. For Eve also was subject to God's omnipotence. She is the woman God gave. Eve, in turn, moves the cause even further away, to the serpent. Perhaps here is the solution: that evil arises from the power of darkness, that this belongs to the devil, to Satan, of whom the serpent is the symbol. In the next chapter we shall deal at greater length with Satan as an anti-god power. In the present context, however, this idea does not help us. For at this juncture we are dealing with the idea that God has absolute power. If he is the almighty, Satan also is subject to him. Then the question becomes, in the creation of the omnipotent God, how there can be a Satan. Can he be more than the watchdog, or possibly the bloodhound, of God? So the problem remains: Where does evil come from?

This is a most difficult juncture. Accordingly, we could say that this is where we stop. Here we are at the outermost limits of what we can and ought to say. Evil is present; it is a reality with which we have to deal, and if we want to penetrate it further we come to a terrain that is inaccessible to man, not only because it is impossible to move there, but also because it is impermissible to proceed. This fear of being involved in things which do not concern us is not new. Already in the second century Irenaeus warned against *curiositas,* and in the history of Christian theology his warning has often been repeated. We must not "curiously pry into"[13] but trust. Luther's reply to the question what God did before he created the world is famous: "He created a hell for curious people." What we cannot know, nor need to know, we must leave in the hand of God. We must not violate his secret. We must let God be God

---

13. *Canons of Dort* III-IV, Art. 7.

and not attempt to penetrate the mystery of eternity where a human being can only perish. One who would look God squarely in the face to fathom the depths of his being will die (Exod. 33:20).

Accordingly, we must pause before we go on. It is fitting to be quiet for a moment, perhaps even for a long moment, before we pursue our present line of thought. The pause to be quiet before the deep mystery of God must be antecedent to all further words. Any theological pronouncement can only come after the silence of reverence. The terrain we are now entering is holy ground par excellence. Between the previous sections and what follows, there is again a silence pregnant with reverence.

Barth speaks about the unbridgeable gap between God and nothingness. Still we have to speak of God's relation to it, since also in our theologizing we cannot totally withdraw from nothingness. But we can only speak of it in brokenness. "Here if anywhere theology as the subjective reproduction of objective reality ought not to impose or simulate a system."[14] This does not alter the fact that he devotes a hundred pages to the nothingness that God did not will but that still exists. For the fact that we can only speak in brokenness about God's relation to nothingness "does not mean . . . that we ought not to proceed here and everywhere with the greatest intellectual probity and with rigorous logic and objectivity."[15] Not that Barth resolves the problem, but then who does overcome the tension attendant on evil?

After the quiet pause of reverence we enter the sanctuary. We need not remain silent, and for these reasons, in order of increasing importance.

1. The question where evil comes from continues to assert itself. We may even say that though we may not pose it the question is there and comes up over and over. Our intellect forces us to order things, including our thoughts about God. That is also good. We may and must speak about him in orderly fashion. Our entire theological enterprise rests on that foundation. It is also our mandate. We must serve God with our whole selves, including our minds (Matt. 22:37). We must not exclude our thinking, for that too is God-related, even when the human urge to penetrate to the level of the final truths confronts us with questions which frighten us.

2. Our relationship to God is of so much weight that he continues to hold our interest to the very end. We want to know who he is. If he is the beloved, the most beloved, it is intolerable that his deepest being should be for us a dark secret. Fortunately we need not always get to the bottom of a love relationship. That would be overreaching ourselves.

14. Barth, *Church Dogmatics* III, 3, 50, p. 294.
15. Ibid., p. 295.

Even in a relationship between human partners the final questions need not always be posed. But fundamentally there must not be any closed doors. True, we need not always enter the innermost part of a sanctuary. The doors cannot always be open, because that would constitute the profanation of miracle. But at moments of deepest intimacy we may go to the bottom of each other's hearts, in order after that to pursue life again with questions and secrets. If God is the most beloved being, we cannot and may not refrain from seeking his inmost heart and secret for a moment. In that process we run the risk of profaning that which is sacred. But if from fear we should be silent before this mystery, we would fail to do justice to the miracle of his love; the fear is that we would come upon a layer of reality we could not handle. And in that case there would no longer be a basis of trust between him and us. Genuine faith has the confidence that it can handle what emerges into the light as a dark secret from the life of the other—from the heart of God, who is our God.

3. In the Old and the New Testament also are texts which posit deeper relationships between God and evil than the pedagogical and the punitive. Admittedly, the passages in which that happens are much fewer in number. They occur at moments of extreme tension, when the final questions in God's relationship to Israel, to the church, or to the world are raised. It is where, in their relationship to God, people are thrown back upon their last defenses, when faith in God stands or falls with their ability to process these questions. The final questions arise when the faithfulness and integrity of God are in question.

4. Because God has revealed himself completely in Christ we need no longer hold back before some final divine secret. In suffering and on the cross Christ shared in God's final secret and we may share in *his* secret. "For all that I have heard from my Father I have made known to you" (John 15:15). In him the mystery is a revealed mystery (Eph. 1:9). Moses must still veil his face (Exod. 34:33), but we are at liberty to contemplate the full revelation of God (2 Cor. 3:12-18). Not everything is as yet fully clear: we are the people of God in transit. We still see in a mirror dimly, writes Paul, to the same church to which he wrote that the veil over the face of God has been taken away (1 Cor. 13:12; 2 Cor. 3:16). Yet we believe that behind the God who revealed himself in Christ there is not still another God, a God of a deep dark secret. God has become known to us to the very bottom of his heart. What still remains obscure to us are not the dark mysteries of God's being, but rather the little secrets which belong to a strong father-child relationship. They are the surprises of salvation which God still has in store for those who love him (1 Cor. 2:9). It is not the hiddenness of the unknown God. The resurrection of Christ has made the unknown God known to us (Acts 17:31).

Accordingly, in the following sections we shall pursue further the line of God's omnipotence. All things come from his hand. But in that connection we now no longer have the option of referring to something else, to antecedent sin or to protection for the future. We are now dealing with the absolute relationship existing between God and evil, in which both suffering and sin are included. In essence then, it no longer matters with which evil one starts out, whether it is the most minuscule disappointment or worldwide misfortune. For both are directly connected with God. In neither case can one relativize it (that is, posit a relationship with something else by which the evil is reduced). In every form of evil there is an immediate connection with God.

10. Providence

IN THIS SECTION THE CORE OF THINKING IN TERMS OF GOD'S OMNIPOTENCE emerges: all things come from the hand of God. We must not begin to explain, to look for causes or motivations, but all things happen as they happen because God willed them so. It is the theology of Lord's Day 10 of the *Heidelberg Catechism*. That Lord's Day reveals the influence of John Calvin. Calvin emphasized the power of God, operating on the principle that all things proceed from God. God has created all things in accordance with his will. This applies not just to the beginning of creation, but continuously to the maintenance of the world.[16] All that exists has been willed by God, down to the smallest being that exists and the smallest event in history.[17] Calvin denies any such thing as chance. An event we might call "accidental" or a chance concurrence of circumstances in reality is not accidental, but divinely willed and governed. Events are not subject to chance but to providence, God's providence. That is true of pleasant events and of those that seem evil. In this connection Calvin himself goes back to Augustine, who also gave providence much prominence. Calvin even refines and accentuates Augustine's theology at this point.

The chapters on providence in the *Institutes* (I, 16-18) do not stand alone in Calvin's theology. They rather constitute the foundation of his thought. In his writings the omnipotence and glory of God are either explicitly or implicitly continually

16. Calvin, *Institutes* I, 16, 1.
17. Ibid.

present. (On providence in Augustine, see the work of Parma, *Pronoia und Providentia,* cited earlier.) Calvin especially follows the later Augustine, who increasingly distanced himself from the early dualistic features he brought with him from his Manichean past. Approvingly, Calvin cites Augustine's criticism of his own earlier writings in which, by the standard of his later views, he spoke all too easily of "fate" and "fortune" (*Retractiones* I, 1, cited by Calvin, *Institutes* I, 16, 9).

A heavy emphasis on God's providence has the advantage that in all the changes of life there is still always certainty. When we allow all the events and things that surround us to affect us deeply, chaos threatens. We do not know what to do with the countless experiences of our daily life. They seem absolutely senseless; they confuse us, and if they are too overwhelming they make us despair. Amidst this chaos it is a great comfort to be able to say that all things are in God's hand. He governs all things and nothing happens by chance. If you look at the underside of a piece of embroidery—to cite a familiar example—all you see is a chaotic tangle of threads. But looking at it from above you are impressed by the beauty of its pattern. If we look at the events of the world from the underside, we cannot discover any pattern; it is a chaotic tangle in which the connecting threads crisscross each other. But viewing it from the top, the Creator delights in the beauty of his handiwork. Now we look at things from the underside, but some day we shall view the beauty of the history of the world, either looking over God's shoulder with him, or vice versa. Then our own chaotic history also will prove to be full of beauty as the work of God's hands. Accordingly, faith in divine providence has primarily to do with comfort. It provides a center of security amidst the events of life we do not know how to process. When the experiences of our lives are so many loose ends blowing in the storm, we know that at bottom they are anchored firmly in the wisdom of God's government.

In light of the security this furnishes people, one can also understand their resistance to the idea that God does not will evil or suffering, and that he fights alongside of us against the forces of chaos. For then God is co-involved in our struggle; there is a power not subject to his power, one which he may perhaps be able to subdue but which is not a priori dependent on him. But on that view, in the will of God the absolute grounding of the world, together with everything that happens in it in the will of God has been given up. This brings an uncertainty in which God, rather than curbing the unrest of my life, is himself involved in it; yet actually he should be the rock on whom, in all my unrest, I can build.

Thus the first reason for saying that all things are governed by God is a pastoral one. In theology that is not an unimportant motive, for theology is related to the faith-life of people. Theology, as the doctrine of people's faith, the systematization of what they confess, has no choice but to give much weight to pastoral motives. People have their own way of confessing and living as believers. At the same time, however, theology is critical reflection on the faith and confession of believing people. People may entertain wrong or one-sided notions. No one has a complete overview of the totality of God's works outward toward the world. Accordingly, the need is constant for critical distance from the pastoral needs of believers and hence also from one's own pastoral needs which are parallel to, different from, or perhaps even opposite from those of others. For that reason systematic theology, in interaction with the pastorate, is always in search of other motives.

A second motive could perhaps be that the world in which we live—culture and history—demands such a formulation. However, that is certainly not the case here. If we look at the world, we do not see it asking for the thesis that all things come from the hand of an omnipotent God. History seems totally capricious, prey to the powers of man and the play of natural forces. Certainly, if anyone should be responsible for world events at all, he has lost control on a grand scale—unless God is a giant who wildly and blindly hurls around large blocks of stone, causing their fragments to fill the air. That picture does not, however, fit an omnipotent God. We are talking about omnipotent *government*. And where there is government, one looks for order. But it is precisely this order that is lacking on the world scene. The only order that is visible is the "order" of chaos. The chaotic character of the world, the absence of order, is precisely the reason, the most important reason, for people's inability to believe in an omnipotent divine government. The reasoning that "if you look around you, common sense tells you . . . ," a reasoning that is otherwise so important and makes for strong theories, is useless when it concerns divine government. Empirical observation seems to furnish no verification; rather, it seems to pose the opposite. Why then, if the world in which we live so powerfully undermines the pastoral needs of human beings, do we still hold to the confession that the world is led by the hand of God?

The *Belgic Confession*, article 2, proceeds from the idea that God's government in nature and history furnishes an opportunity for us to get to know God. This notion is further developed in Heppe's *Reformed Dogmatics*. According to him, on the basis of this knowledge it is even possible for man to "enter into living fellowship with God as with his God and Lord."[18] Calvin in the *Institutes* knows only of an innate sense of deity which, however, is so fractured by the Fall that

18. Heppe, *Reformed Dogmatics*, p. 54.

it remains fruitless (I, 4, 1). Paul Tillich has demonstrated that though from within the finite structure of the world one can infer the question of God, the conclusion that God exists does not logically follow from it. Proofs for God's existence are not arguments, but analysis.[19] Being poses the question of God; but though the structure of a possible answer is implied in the question, the answer itself comes to us in the revelation in Jesus Christ.[20]

An important reason for endorsing the idea of providence is the philosophical "god concept" most people have. After the Greek philosophers, God was the One. He is the ultimate cause, the all-encompassing power. Behind the multiplicity of the world lies the unity of God. Though in the different philosophical systems it is developed in different ways, the idea is always that God is the "absolutely One." Especially in Augustine the perfect oneness of God as the supreme and absolute source of all things forms an important motif for his reflections on God's omnipotence. When in the later history of theology Aristotle replaces Plato as *the* philosopher, the relationship between the governing God and the process of world events becomes even more definite. In a system influenced by Plato, the world always retains something of an adumbration and hence of a distortion of the one divine being. But Aristotelian conceptions provide a more direct link with God. God is the first cause of all that is. Though he operates via earthly causes, *he* is the driving power. The laws of causality are the laws of *secondary* causes. Above and behind them is God, the first cause. Although in the period of the Reformation important influences of a different kind play a role, and especially biblical-theological data prompt different emphases, the basic pattern remains the same: God is the one source of all that happens. In this connection, the influences of Augustine and hence a Platonic structure predominates; in Lutheran theology and in Calvinism the structures of Aristotelian philosophy tend to stand out. The culmination of this trend occurs in the Protestantism of the eighteenth century in which God is "the Supreme Being" or "the Most High Majesty."

It is striking that in this view God is so often denominated impersonally. He is *the* One, *the* Supreme Being. He is not so much a personal, deciding God but a general principle. He is the highest being, instead of a living, willing, acting God. This is corrected again by the idea that God is the projection into infinity of an earthly power. If an earthly king—in the eighteenth century usually an absolute monarch—was powerful, more powerful than all his subjects, then as king of kings God is more

19. Paul Tillich, *Systematic Theology*, vol. 1 (Welwyn, Eng.: Nisbet & Co., 1964), pp. 227-33.
20. Ibid., vol. 2, pp. 136-38.

powerful than all earthly kings. He is the super-king. He is the Supreme Majesty. This extension of earthly power into heavenly proportions is not bound up with the philosophy of Plato or Aristotle. Nor did it just arise in the Constantinian Christianity of the fourth century. It was not only then that God received the face of the Roman emperor. Accents may have shifted, but in theology the idea that God is the super-emperor is much older. The idea that God is the infinite possessor of power is a feature of virtually all conceptions of God in all cultures and religions. The word "God" is charged to the limit with this concept of om-nipotence; behind all powers stands the power which is higher than them all; it is the power which embraces them all: *omni*-potence.

Nor have the books of the Old and the New Testament escaped this tendency. God is the highest Lord: the *Adon.* He is even the *Baal,* and not until faith in the God of Israel was threatened by waves of syncretism did the word "Baal" become tainted. The Greek translators of the Old Testament could find no better word for the name of God than *kurios,* the Lord. In the New Testament *kurios* again turns up as a title of majesty for Christ. He is the King of kings and Lord of lords (Rev. 19:16). Over and over divinity is defined by conceiving a power greater than all earthly powers.

Accordingly, two lines of thought run to God as the Most High, one with a dynamic aspect in which God is the driving power of events, the being which embraces all things, the ground and meaning of all exis-tence, including neuter and impersonal—and another with a static aspect in which God is the greatest potentate to whose will we all, even the highest earthly powers, are subject. In practice the two lines are virtually always connected. God is the all-inclusive force as well as the all-inclusive power. Only then is he really all-inclusive, and then is there no longer any possibility of escape. If God were only the all-inclusive power, the absolute monarch, there is still a possibility of resistance—resistance he can indeed strike down—but resistance nevertheless. But if at the same time he is the driving force from which all things derive, including rebellion, things get much more difficult. Often, however, the concept of the highest power already automatically includes the idea that the will of God is so strong that all things must obey him from the start. Conversely, if God is only the driving force but not the deciding will, the problem has lost its sting. For then one has only made a statement about the possibility of existence, the possibility of a historical process, but nothing about a governing will. If God is the One, then, though he is the driving force of all things, the manner of actualization has been left completely open. If actualization results, though it proceeds from him, it proceeds not from his will, but from his might. In other words, in the first case God's power is critical: he makes his demands as ruler, but resistance is possible. In the second case God is not critical: the reality of the world is the realization of his being. The combination of the two produces a God-concept which is as solid and immovable as a rock, and probably the most prevalent concept of God. The word "God" stands for this massive notion of God; he is the driving force in whom the critical detachment of his will has been incorporated in advance. That is the God of the classic theology of Heppe: "God is (1) an independent being, (2) upon whom all things depend, (3) who governs all others."[21] That is God as Hart pictures him when he prefaces his *A Flight of Curlews* with Lord's Day 10 of the Heidelberg Catechism.

One can say this image is a caricature which people have made of God. It is the God of the philosophers or the God of the rulers, but not the God of the Scriptures, not the God of Jesus Christ. At first sight that observation seems liberating. Barth has taught us that for a correct view of God we must not resort to our God images but to Christ. A liberating aspect of this was that by saying this one could escape the dilemma of empirical verification vs. the God image one held. Still, in that manner we run into a number of insuperable difficulties. In the first place, Barth himself cannot escape the practice of operating with the image of the omnipotent God, precisely in the context of divine government and evil. What God wills is always effective; even "what He does not will, is potent."[22] Also, God's "no" calls something into being. More important, however, is that the function which the word "God" has in theology (and that in every theology) determines that this image will be used. If "God" evokes the idea of absolute power and might, the implication is that when we are talking about absolute power and might we are talking about God. If I use the word "God," I cannot escape having this in mind. And even if I did not, the person who heard me use the word would have the association. When the authors of the Old Testament call the God of Israel *El* or *Elohim*, the Hebrew words in the Old Testament translated by "God," the entire content of the words *El* and *Elohim* comes along with them. It is said: Baal is not *Elohim*, but the Lord, for Baal does not give fire, but the Lord; and Baal does not give rain, but the Lord (1 Kings 18). Associated with *Elohim* is the idea of rule by fire and rain. He who can do that is the true God. Accordingly, "God" is not an empty concept, but one filled with power and dominion. Hence when we talk about God we are talking about the mighty God. This image may subsequently be

21. Heppe, *Reformed Dogmatics*, p. 52 (slightly altered from the translation by G. T. Thomson—Trans.).
22. Barth, *Church Dogmatics*, III, 3, 50, p. 352.

corrected in all sorts of ways, but the correction occurs against the background of the original God image. If we have a different God image, we must do a lot of talking each time to make that plain. But even in the case of the seemingly most divergent models, the basis proves to be this God image. When Moltmann speaks of "the crucified God," the suffering of God is interesting because it is the suffering of the powerful God. God continues to have the last word about the reality of the world and the ethical choices of human beings—only it is a different last word.

It is the nuances which make theology interesting. The fundamental pattern is the same everywhere: God has the last word. It is the name of the God which decides the religion one holds to, not the model of the God concept. What is the name of the God (the almighty) whom you serve and what has he done? That is the relevant question; not, is your God powerful or not? For if he is not powerful he is no God. The most urgent question of twentieth century Christianity is this: did God lose control of the situation in Auschwitz? Were there powers there stronger than he? Was he the powerless one who perished with his people? In that case God has been judged. Then he is not the sovereign power to whom the world is subject, and we shall do well to subject ourselves to the powers that were stronger than he—the powers of darkness, the power of the Superman, of *Blut und Boden*—and worship them as the true God. As yet the powers have not won a final victory over God, but they have made great gains. And after the Second World War no kingdom of peace and justice has arrived on earth to restore the disfigured face of God; rather, injustice and violence continue. Either God must be able to cope with this situation we see on our television screens or he is not God anymore. Then only the question remains whether we shall end up in a godless world in which chaos prevails because no power is on top, or in a world in which another God—whatever his face or name— holds omnipotent sway. If God wants to preserve his deity, he will have to demonstrate his omnipotence, albeit by way of saving a world in ruins. Or should we say precisely by saving a world in ruins? For the glorified Christ is the crucified one. God's power is so great that he saves one doomed to death and already has glory in view on the downward road to death. But without the resurrection the cross would have been a failure. Without the glory, Christ would not be the Son. God can let things go a long ways in and with the world he created in his Son; but without a last saving deed planned in advance in the world's passion history Easter will not be confirmed. Then the deity of God and Christ have passed away. There is much stretch in God's omnipotence, and the more elastic it is the greater his superiority will prove to be; but things cannot be stretched endlessly without a final deed of glorification.

In Christian theology the final criterion will ever have to be found in the Bible. When the image of God on the one hand and empirical reality on the other are so far apart as to be contradictory, and when at the same time there is a pastoral urge to confess God as the almighty, it becomes all the more important to look at the data of the Old and the New Testament. In the first place, as we saw earlier, by using the same words as surrounding religions, Scripture adopts the main pattern of their god concept. The acts of the history of this God confirm his divinity. He is *Elohim*, like the *Elohim* of the Semitic peoples, like Chemosh and Dagon. He is *Theos*, like Zeus and Hermes. He belongs to the same category. But within this category he outshines them all. By comparison with him all "almightinesses" prove to be relative, subject to his omnipotence. He is the God of gods (Ps. 50:1; Josh. 22:22). And *because* the one God of Israel is enthroned above all gods they lose their divinity. In their own territory they may be strong, but in the context of nations and gods they are subject to Israel's God. The different books of the Old Testament do not all speak the same language when it comes to the relationship between God and the gods. Sometimes every nation has its own God, including Israel. "For what great nation is there that has a god so near to it as the Lord our God is to us whenever we call upon him?" (Deut. 4:7). But though he is but one among all the gods of the nations, for Israel he is mightier than them all. Sometimes he is the highest God among the gods, the one to whom they are all subject and to whom they are accountable. God is the head of the gods (Ps. 82). Sometimes the gods are contemptuously described as "vain things" (1 Sam. 12:21; 2 Kings 17:15). The gods of the nations have not been able to save their servants for they were no gods (2 Kings 19:18; Isa. 37:19). Deutero-Isaiah goes furthest: the gods are no more than images of wood or stone. In a sarcastic parody he depicts the senselessness of serving idols (Isa. 44:6-20; cf. Ps. 115). The New Testament is more homogeneous in confessing that there is *one* God, the God of Israel who in Jesus Christ reveals himself as the God of all. In this manner the New Testament ties in with the severe monotheistic tendencies of Judaism, consistently extending the lines drawn in Deutero-Isaiah. In the cultural climate of Hellenism it was also natural to speak of one God as the Most High. The different gods of the nations are merely manifestations of different aspects or only different names for the one God. Paul does speak of the god of this age (2 Cor. 4:4). And though for Christians there is but one God, there are many so-called gods who are real as "gods" and "lords" (1 Cor. 8:4-6). However, they are that only insofar as people serve them, not in reality ("by nature," Gal. 4:8). But whatever the relationship beween God and the gods may be, whatever ontological status they may have, elevated above them all is the God of Israel. He is the really ultimate power and therefore the only true God.

*   *   *

THE BIBLE WRITERS NOT ONLY ADOPT THE WORD "GOD" AND HENCE THE concept of "God," however; they themselves also explicitly use the method of extrapolating from earthly power. He is the King of kings. In the case of the expression "the God of gods," one might even call the credo of Israel an extrapolation from the credos of the nations. The god-image of the nations serves as a model for speaking and thinking about God in Israel.

It is harder to find the philosophical image of God in Scripture. First to come to mind in this connection is, of course, wisdom literature. But in the book of Proverbs God is the one who issues the commandments rather than the source of all being. Typical for this is that in Proverbs the name "the Lord" is used, not the word "God." This is different in Ecclesiastes. That book is most in tune with the Greek philosophy of the Hellenistic period. God gives power to eat and to drink (5:18), or withholds it (6:2). Whatever God does endures forever (3:14). What people think and do proceeds from God without their being aware of it (3:10ff.). At death the spirit returns to God (12:7). Also, the book of Job is based on the conviction that God is the decisive power behind world events, even though he can delegate that power to others. Psalm 104 is fascinating: when God sends forth his Spirit things are created; when he hides his face they die (29, 30). The divine presence calls things into being; it is the ground of the possibility of their existence. In the absence of it, or as a result of the disappearance of it, life cannot be realized. There is here no hint of conflict with suffering and death. The roaring lion (v. 21) and the laboring man (v. 23), life and the cessation of it (for that is what death is here), all belong to the movement of things and events that proceeds from God for his personal delight (v. 26). When the last verse says: "Let sinners be consumed from the earth, and let the wicked be no more!" (v. 35), one gets the impression of a transition to another world of thought. There, all of a sudden, God's judicial power is introduced into a song that deals with the creative dynamics of the Spirit of God. But for the author of Psalm 104 the two go together.

The two are much more interwoven in Psalm 33 where words about the God who calls things into being are linked to the interventions of the heavenly ruler. "By the word of the Lord the heavens were made, and all their host by the breath of his mouth" (v. 6); ". . . he spoke and it came to be; he commanded, and it stood forth" (v. 9); "he fashions the hearts of all" (v. 15). Everything comes forth from God. At the same time, however, he is the mighty one who keeps a critical eye on everything. He fashions the hearts of men, but at the same time observes their deeds (v. 15). From where he sits in heaven he looks out on all the inhabitants of the earth (v. 14). He brings the counsel of the nations to nought (v. 10). All things are subject to him; the aspect of the judicial moment as well as the total flow of events, the thread and meaning of history, are both present. Both come together in the counsel of God "which stands for ever, the thoughts of his heart to all generations" (v. 11).

Also in the New Testament there are texts which point to God as the source and essence of all things. Whereas in John 1 one can still think of the creating Word of God by which all things were called into being, and not of the pre-existence of the eternal Logos (although it seems to me impossible that in the Hellenistic world in which John's gospel functioned this aspect did not also play a role), Acts 17 can hardly be heard other than against the Greek background. On the Areopagus, addressing Greek philosophers and citing their own poet Aratus, Paul says: "We are his offspring; in him we live and move and have our being" (17:28). There too, just as in Psalm 33, we see the link between God as a force in creation of whom and by whom all things exist, and God as a critical judge (vv. 30ff.). In the epistles too one can find texts which point to God and even to Christ as the ground of existence (e.g. Eph. 1:10; Col. 1:17).

After this general sketch the question arises whether it is at all fleshed out pastorally. Do the above considerations perhaps only form a general framework in which the Bible writers lived, one which in certain phrases they also used to describe the greatness of God, some-times even in a missionary context? Or is the fact that all things come from the hand of God also fleshed out concretely when it concerns the pastoral situation of the suffering human being, the suffering people of God, or suffering humanity? The intent of Lord's Day 10 of the Heidel-berg Catechism is pastoral. The entire Catechism is intended to show that the doctrine of the faith is comforting. Looking at the texts cited under Lord's Day 10 we find Matthew 10:29, the familiar verse about the sparrows. It is often said, "No sparrow falls to the ground without the will of your heavenly Father." The message is then that God leads all things; not even a sparrow falls to the ground against his will; could anything then happen to you if God, the heavenly Father, does not want it to happen? But that is not what the (Greek) text says. "The will of" is a fictitious augmentation, added against the background of the image of the all-governing God. The text says only: "And not one of them will fall to the ground without your Father." Exegetically one then has two choices. One can translate "without the will of your Father," but also "apart from the presence of the Father"—without him being there. God is present; but we are not told how he is present. He can be present as fellow-sufferer, or as fellow-fighter, or as the governor. Still, from the perspective of the whole of biblical theology, and from within the whole of the theology of Matthew's gospel, it is plausible to say not only that events do not occur outside the domain of God's presence, but also that they do not occur outside the domain of his power. Consider for example the texts from the Sermon on the Mount which admonish us not to be anxious over food and clothing (Matt. 6:25-34). But even then a difference remains between the positive ("God willed that a sparrow should fall—and therefore it fell") and the critical ("in relation to this event God will if necessary demonstrate his power and fight against the forces of death").

In a large number of texts the presence of God as the God of might must, in any case, be interpreted in the second sense. He is not present only as one who quietly waits for things to happen, nor even as one who suffers with the earthly sufferer, but as one who applies his power to combat and to overcome misfortune. God is the mighty One who comes to liberate his people. The prophets are full of such promises—not only in the salvation prophecies in which Israel is promised salvation from its enemies, but also in many prophecies of judgment. For judgment upon the ungodly, the exploiters, and the deceivers is salvation for the poor and the deceived. It is encouragement in anticipation of God's mighty liberation. Isaiah 40 is characteristic. Israel is in exile and has given up hope. Its people think God has abandoned them, that nothing can be done against the power of the nations. The Gentiles have won. In that situation the prophet speaks of the power of God before whom all nations are no more than a drop from a bucket, the dust on the scales (v. 15). God will save his people—so splendidly that they will mount up with wings like eagles (v. 31). Thus, the mighty presence of God primarily has to be interpreted in its pastoral application. When people are desperate, have lost or are in danger of losing their courage, the prophet points to God for whom no situation is hopeless. When a situation is structurally bad, and not just thought to be bad in a moment of discouragement, the mighty God is there to redeem it. That is also the message of the familiar words of Isaiah 55:8, 9:

> For my thoughts are not your thoughts,
>   neither are your ways my ways, says the Lord.
> For as the heavens are higher than the earth,
>   so are my ways higher than your ways
> and my thoughts than your thoughts.

Often this text is used to express the non-transparency of God's government: you cannot understand God anyway; you must resign yourself to your suffering. But this is the opposite of what the prophet intends. Israel had resigned itself to its situation: "There is nothing more to be done anyway; there is no way back. The best thing for us to do is to build a future in Babylon." Over against this the prophet declares in the name of God: "Those may be your thoughts, but I have something else in mind. I am thinking of liberation and return and I do see a way back to Jerusalem. My thoughts are not your thoughts and my ways are not your ways." In their seemingly hopeless situation the Israelites need not in spiritual paralysis resign themselves to their fate, but may act and proceed in the name of their mighty God. The pastoral message of Isaiah 55 is that in their suffering people must not let themselves undergo everything in a despondent frame of mind but, because God is mighty to liberate them, may actively pursue a future of hope. Accordingly, in this case suffering is not a God-willed lot you have to accept, but something he has not willed and will overcome. It is better therefore not to speak of omnipotence but of superior power, as Berkhof does.[23] Sometimes this power assumes the form of defenseless superiority. However, that is not its primary and certainly not its only form. The primary form is that of the majestic glory in which God rules. He is the God before whom the mountains melt like wax (Ps. 97:5), and when he arises the wicked also perish like wax (Ps. 68:2). Even before his angel the Roman guards became like dead men (Matt. 28:4). Superior power means that God is stronger than the powers which threaten people. Omnipotence means that all things come from the hand of God. Whereas the superior power of God can be found in many biblical writings, the question is whether that is also true of omnipotence.

To begin with, we could perhaps call omnipotence an inference from God's superior power. If God is superior in power, he is that not only at a certain moment, but always. He rules from everlasting to everlasting. The superior power of God extends backwards and forwards in time as far as we can think. By taking one more step one can say that God's superior power is preexistent: from all eternity God is the mighty one. Creation itself already came forth from the word of his power. The power of God is antecedent to the world. Once we have arrived at this point it is hard to conceive of any obstacle to also calling God "omnipotent." The entire process of world events, from its very first beginning to its ultimate end, is subject to his power. From beginning to end the history of the world is encompassed by God's superior power.

23. Berkhof, *Christian Faith*, p. 133.

It is not a power which only asserts itself at some point in history. In that case it would still be limited, temporally limited, superiority. But God's superior power is unlimited superiority which embraces everything. That is not another power than omnipotence.

Still, in contemporary theology there is a reluctance to draw this conclusion. In this connection the over-specific exegesis of Matthew 10:29 is used as an argument to show that the Bible does not teach that the will of God is behind the entire process of world events. That, however, is a misunderstanding. The fact that this is not taught in Matthew 10 or Isaiah 55 does not mean it is not taught elsewhere. Nor am I thinking in the first place of texts in which God is literally called "the Almighty." The words used in the original do not automatically imply the traditional concept of omnipotence. They do refer to the great power of God, his superiority over all other powers in heaven and on earth, but they do not self-evidently imply that all things must be attributed to his will.

In the Old Testament "the Almighty" is the translation of *Shaddai*. The meaning of this word is not clear. The translation "the Almighty" came to us via the Greek of the Septuagint: *pantokrator*. But it is very much a question whether *Shaddai* had the same meaning as *pantokrator*. In any case, the translation is too uncertain to serve as a foundation for a doctrine of the attributes of God. In the Septuagint, for that matter, the two words are not completely equivalent. *Shaddai* is sometimes also translated by *ho theos sou*, "your God" (e.g., in Gen. 17:1). On the other hand, *pantokrator* is also the translation of *sebaotōt*: the Lord "of hosts." Its meaning is not completely clear either, though the word *sabaā'* (army) shows that in any case it has to do with power.

In the New Testament *pantokrator* occurs in 2 Corinthians 6:18 and in nine instances in Revelation. All these texts occur in a context which has Old Testament features. The term conveys an impression which has no specific New Testament coloring. The reference is probably more to superior power than to omnipotence. "The reference is not so much to God's activity in creation as to His supremacy over all things. The description is static rather than dynamic. Hence it has only a loose connection with the dogmatic concept of the divine omnipotence, which is usually linked with the omnicausality of God."[24] In a period of persecution the Christian church would pose the superior power of God against the Roman emperor. Still we have to take account of the fact that the increasing use of this word coincides with a growing sense of the totality of God's power, just as in Deutero-Isaiah the thought of God's superior power tends in the direction of omnipotence. One must remember that in Revelation world events are planned in heaven, that the vision begins with the image of the Creator, and that the book of history is in the hands of Christ. The word occurs with great frequency in Christian literature in the post-New Testament period.

24. Kittel, *TDNT*, vol. 3, p. 915.

An increasing sense of the omnipotence of the God who directs all processes may also emerge in the suddenly frequent use (from the end of the first century) of *despotes*. In the New Testament God is only rarely referred to as *despotes*. But already 1 Clemens uses the word frequently. *Despotes* is the master who has absolute—if necessary, arbitrary—power.

If we are looking in the Bible for support of the idea that God is not only he who overcomes all powers but also he who initiates all processes, we turn in the first place to the above-mentioned texts in the psalms and to wisdom literature. God governs destiny and directs the human heart. What he wills happens, and it endures forever. If contemporary theology has problems with the classic doctrine of omnipotence, that is not because of biblical data but in consequence of the shocking experiences of this century which could no longer be squared with God's omnipotence. Reflection on these experiences has led to renewed study of the Bible in which justice could be done to other emphases and texts read in a new light. It is true that as a result the confession of God's power acquired new nuances, but one goes too far if he dismisses omnipotence itself as an unbiblical datum. The concept is explicitly present in the writings of wise men and poets and blossoms in the message of prophets and apostles.

Now it is easier to picture the idea that all good things come forth from the hand of God than that all evil things do. Few believers would have difficulty singing Psalm 136:

> Each creature's need He doth supply,
> His grace abideth ever;
> Give thanks to God, enthroned on high,
> Whose mercy faileth never.

We also pray that God may give us our daily bread. He gives us a mouth to speak, ears to hear, and eyes to see (Exod. 4:11). He provides the rain which causes the crops to grow (1 Kings 18). He protects us from evil—the reason why we pray that he will not lead us into temptation. Our life, our happiness, our prosperity all come from the hand of God. Still, even in this connection problems emerge. In the dry summer of 1988 many North American churches organized prayer services for rain. For some this was a sign of faith and hope; others had difficulty with it. Is it proper to pray directly to God for a change in the weather? Also, the rather poor attendance at some services on regular days of prayer or thanksgiving (at least where they are still held) indicates that the awareness that all blessing comes from above is not very strong. There are many reasons for this. Undoubtedly the most important is that we attribute such things as rain or drought to natural processes which go their own autonomous way, and not to an all-governing God. We are so used to thinking in terms of low pressure and high pressure areas—our speech and our hearing about the weather is so thoroughly framed by that context that God no longer has any role in it. What we assume about the weather applies equally to our health, our jobs, and all the other areas of our life.

A second reason why we have difficulty attributing everything to God lies in the problems associated with answer to prayer. Does prayer really change anything? Can you tell that after God has heard the prayer he causes things to take a different turn? Elijah prayed and there was no rain; he prayed again and it rained (James 5:17, 18). Also, prayers for dry weather in the rainy spring of 1983 (the Netherlands) were answered. Dry weather came. But the drought was more than the farmers wanted. To the best of my knowledge no new prayer services were then organized to pray for rain. After the prayer services for dry weather, was that too precarious? More important is the fact that to my knowledge no services of thanksgiving were held when the rain finally stopped, which in the seventeenth century was still done. In 1653, after prayer services were held following a long period of drought, when rain fell again, there were services of thanksgiving. If that was not done in 1983, then in those places where people did have prayer services, was there really a deep sense that all things come from God? The big question is whether the dry weather would have come without the prayer services. And what if the rain had continued throughout the summer, so that the entire harvest had rotted in the fields? The person who believes that all things come from the hand of God will say that God's counsel is higher than our wills and that one always has to say "Your will be done." But doubts remain. It does not always seem fair to blame the person who prayed by saying that he prayed wrongly (James 4:3).

In the third place, the prosperity of the last several decades has given people a feeling of independence. Man himself controls all things, if not in his actions then certainly in his thinking. And the things we do not yet control are not, in principle, beyond our reach. In the future we also expect to control them. The extent to which people ask, "Do you still believe in God?"—to that extent there is the associated idea that in the future man will be able to control everything. As though God and man were merely competitors.

While the idea that the good comes from the hand of God by itself already raises problems, things get vastly more difficult if we bring to mind the implication—that evil also comes from the hand of God. If

93

blessings are a gift from him, we must also attribute setbacks to God. That is no more than consistent, and then we are in the thick of the big problem. Can you attribute to God the lack of food, aphasia, deafness, blindness, sickness, the totally devastating storm? In this respect Calvin is very consistent. "Suppose a man falls among thieves, or wild beasts; is shipwrecked at sea by a sudden gale; is killed by a falling house or tree. Suppose another man wandering through the desert finds help in his straits; having been tossed by the waves, reaches harbor; miraculously escapes death by a finger's breadth. Carnal reason ascribes all such happenings, whether prosperous or adverse, to fortune. But anyone who has been taught by Christ's lips that all the hairs of his head are numbered [Matt. 10:30] will look farther afield for a cause, and will consider that all events are governed by God's secret plan."[25] If you walk into the street and a car skids into a wall right next to where you are, you must not say, "I was lucky" but "God so willed it." But that also applies to the other situation in which you have gone one step further and the car slams *you* against the wall. Then you must not say (if you can still talk), "I was unlucky to get into the car's way," but "God so willed it." Sickness, disasters, hunger, handicaps—they all come from the hand of God. But also the things people do to each other—murder, torture, abuse—"God has so willed it." Undoubtedly in the ears of many people this sounds horrible, even blasphemous. How can a person attribute such things to God?

Still, we must guard here, as earlier when we spoke of the wrath of God, against having too "pious" a view of God. God can be fierce and capricious. Certain texts in Scripture go very far in attributing to God all kinds of evils that strike people. According to Exodus 11:4, God not only enables people to see but he also makes them blind, deaf, and dumb. We are not of course concerned only with "proof texts" (the gathering up of loose texts—though this is not always illegitimate, for example, in wisdom literature) but with the function texts have in their contexts. In Amos 3:6 we read: "Does evil befall a city unless the Lord has done it?" Here the reference is primarily to the evil which strikes Samaria. The disasters which strike this city are not accidental. They are God's judgments. This evil, in its full impact, has been effected by him. But Amos can only say that if he assumes that the experiences of good and evil, of blessing and misfortune, are all to be attributed to God's action. Amos interprets this evil as judgment. Because God rules, and disasters strike the city, Israel must reconsider its relationship to God.

Isaiah 40 to 46 speaks convincingly of the superior power of God,

25. Calvin, *Institutes* I, 16, 2.

by comparison with which all gods are as nothing, no more than wood and stone (43:9-20). From the beginning God was the mighty one (43:1), and his power does not weaken (40:28). God, the ruler of history, also governs people. Even kings are no more than instruments in his hand. Cyrus is his servant, not because Cyrus has declared himself a confessing adherent of Israel's religion but because in his imperialistic plans Cyrus unwittingly carries out the will of the God of Israel. The nations may devise plans, but the Lord executes his own plan. In that regard this passage constitutes an extensive prophecy concerning what is also expressed in Psalm 33. In addition, Isaiah says that *all* that happens happens because God creates it. Not only the liberation but also the misfortune. "I am the Lord and there is no other. I form life and create darkness, I make weal and create woe, I am the Lord who do all these things" (45:6, 7). Just as Israel's return under Cyrus is the work of God, so, in judgment, was the exile. From the hand of the Lord the people has received double for all her sins (40:2).

Already Proto-Isaiah was of the opinion that the nations which devastated Israel only carried out what the Lord wanted. Assyria was the rod of his anger (10:5). God sent him to take spoil and to plunder (10:6). Because the king of Assyria does not realize that God is using him, and believes he is able to choose his own way, he will himself also be punished (10:12-14). In 10:15 the relation between God and the nations is succinctly depicted: "Shall the axe vaunt itself over him who hews with it, or the saw magnify itself against him who wields it? As if a rod should wield him who lifts it, or as if a staff should lift him who is not wood!" What is true of Assyria also applies to Babylonia. The Babylonian conquerors who go around murdering and plundering and destroy Jerusalem are the "consecrated ones" under the Lord's command (13:3). The course of history is therefore the course chosen by God in which all the powers are merely instruments for the realization of his plans. "For the Lord of hosts has purposed, and who will annul it? His hand is stretched out, and who will turn it back?" (14:27). That applies to all nations (14:26).

While the prophets deal especially with the history of Israel and the nations, the book of Job focuses on individual suffering. In the framework narrative Satan receives God's permission to strike Job with all kinds of suffering. Although God does not himself directly inflict suffering on Job, he does decide the length to which Satan may go (2:6). At the very least God is co-responsible, not to say finally responsible, for the decision to make Job suffer. Things are decided in heaven, and earth can only undergo them. That point is not in dispute in the dialogues: God brings suffering upon Job. On that point Job and his friends are agreed. The question is whether he does it in love and wisdom (5:8-27), or even because now it is evident who Job in his rebellion really is (15:2-35), as the friends think; or whether it is totally non-intelligible (28:12ff.) or even unjust (27:2), as Job himself charges.

Also, the New Testament knows of human suffering originating with God. The man born blind was born blind for the purpose of glorifying God's works (John 9:3). Paul speaks of a sharp thorn in his flesh, a messenger of Satan to harass him (2 Cor. 12:7). But this thorn in the flesh was given him by God.

Some authors go even further. They also attribute sin to the will of God. In 2 Samuel 24:1 we read: "Again the anger of the Lord was kindled against Israel, and he incited David against them, saying, "Go, number Israel and Judah." Because God is angry and wants to strike out at Israel, he himself provides the occasion: the census. To the author of the books of Chronicles this apparently went too far; he wrote it was Satan who incited David (1 Chron. 21:1). Other authors agree that Satan was the instigator of evil, but view him as an instrument in the hand of God, as we noted in the case of Job and Paul.

The conclusion of Isaiah 63 is very moving: "O Lord, why dost thou make us err from thy ways and harden our heart, so that we fear thee not?" (v. 17). Israel has had to process all sorts of disasters. Prophets have repeatedly charged that it was their own fault. However, the author of Isaiah 63 positions himself on the side of the people. If God is the powerful one (Deutero-Isaiah) and governs all things and has demonstrated this in the history of Israel (63:11-14), why then does he allow Israel to sin over and over? Why does he cause them to err in order then to punish them? Thus the entire doom-filled burden, all that has gone on in Israel in the way of sin and judgment, is laid on God. By formulating it thus the prophet enters upon the road taken by the Messiah: "My God, my God, why hast thou forsaken me?" (Matt. 27:46). In this lament the absurdity of all the laments of Israel is gathered up—the "why?" concerning the way of darkness on which God leads his people. Jesus prayed he would not have to take it: "My Father, if it be possible, let this cup pass from me" (Matt. 26:39). It was in God's hand to let him take it or not; but the Father let him. It is the strangeness of the God who gave up his own Son (Rom. 8:32). In Greek the word for "giving up" also means "to betray." That betrayal can be heard in Jesus' lament: "Why hast thou forsaken me?" It is also conveyed in the words "why dost thou make us err from thy ways?" of Isaiah 63:17. He from whom you expect your final salvation, on whom you count, leaves you in the lurch.

By comparison the poet of Psalm 103 sees God as being closer to man. For him man is dust, like a flower of the field. These words belong to the same tradition as Deutero-Isaiah (40:6) and the creation story of Genesis 2 (v. 7). God made man of the dust of the earth. Man is therefore a finite being. But God knows this. He knows our frame (Ps. 103:14). We are what we are because of God. However, he does not use this position in order to punish us in judgment but to show his steadfast love from everlasting to everlasting upon those who fear him (v. 17). Meanwhile, we have returned to our starting point. Our whole life and the entire history of the world was begun by God, willed and led by God, and is therefore also known by God.

We are led by God and without him we can neither stir nor move—not even the superpowers of the world—anymore than a saw can move without the hand of him who pulls it. We are led on the road of joy and the road of sorrow, on days when thorns turn into cypresses and briers become myrtles (Isa. 55:13), and on days when we feel the thorn in the flesh; days when an angel of God is sent to set us free and days when a messenger of Satan comes to buffet us. This gives us enormous certainty. Nothing can happen without the will of God, however strange the way may seem. However much dictators and tyrants, presidents and party leaders, generals and industrial magnates may flaunt their power, they are only instruments in the hands of almighty God.

Now we are not at the very beginning of history. God *has* done certain things. If there ever was a *potentia absoluta* of God, it no longer exists. God has accomplished things which have resulted in knowledge of himself. Though free in his choices and though he decides about everything, he has bound himself to certain deeds. The omnipotence of God is the omnipotence of his own will. What is most important for us to know about his will he has already made known to us: he wills to receive us as his children in Christ. He wants to be our Father. The almighty God directs the nations as he pleases, but he does it as he who has chosen us in Christ. We have the omnipotent God as our ally. This does not mean that he enters into an alliance with us to carry out our designs. On the contrary, we are totally dependent on him. We are placed on the road to carry out his plans, even when they run counter to our feelings and desires. He is the shepherd, and we are the sheep of his pasture (Ps. 79:13). But he is the good Shepherd, the faithful Father. He is the God who loves us in Christ. Accordingly, a world governed by God is a safe world in which to live. The omnipotent God loves me and in love leads my life. That is the confession of Lord's Day 10. He who leads my life from beginning to end, with all my experiences, joy and grief, health and sickness, rain and drought, prosperity and setbacks, is no other than he who in Christ has given me life. My earthly life is included in the eternal life of the risen Lord. From this confession arise the hymns

97

of trust and surrender, which many Christians love to sing. I deliberately refrained from calling them "hymns of resignation," because the inspiration of these hymns is security and rest, rest that is charged with joy and confidence, rather than acquiescence which is full of resignation. It is the claim of confidence even in the face of great danger. The security which faith in the omnipotence of God affords people is voiced especially in the words of Christian hymns. Only song can encompass tension to the point of including death. For that purpose the assertions of prose fall short. This indicates that surrender to the omnipotence of God does not always occur smoothly. Often a long history of struggle is needed before one comes to terms with God's almighty will. It is not simple to become, as a traditional expression has it, "of one will with God." Sometimes a person succeeds, other times not. Or better, sometimes one receives surrender as a gift but cannot hold on to it. The moment one wants to assert control over it, it slips away from one's heart.

However much faith in divine providence may be a rock of security for many Christians, this does not alter the fact that we are still stuck with several big questions. First of all, there is the question concerning the meaning of suffering and behind that the question concerning the meaning of sin. The question of Isaiah 63:17 ("O Lord, why dost thou make us err from thy ways?") has not yet been answered. In the second place there is the question of the possibility of unbelief. If all things are governed by the will of God, does that apply also to the choice for or against the Christian faith? We here encounter the problem of election. The same tradition of Augustine and Calvin which so strongly champions the doctrine of divine omnipotence also produced the doctrine of double predestination, a doctrine which teaches that God elects some people to eternal life and others to eternal damnation. How does that teaching fit into the background of a God who is present in all things? How can that God reject people? The same question comes at us from another viewpoint: how is it with those who do not acknowledge the omnipotent God as their Father? Does he not also relate to them as Father? In the next section we shall say somewhat more about these two questions.

At this point our concern is with another question: if everything is led by God, then what about the autonomy of nature and human freedom of choice? We have already noted that man's coming of age and technical expertise, plus his knowledge of the processes of nature, tend to undercut faith in providence. This view is based, however, on the assumption that what is done by man cannot at the same time be done by God, and that if rain is the product of a low pressure area it cannot come from God. But this assumption is wrong. God's working is not restricted to his direct interventions. I would not say that these interventions cannot happen, but they are unusual. Even when they occur, natural processes are as much as possible left unviolated. As a rule, however, God's working is entirely indirect. One does not see him, but he is present everywhere. God and his world are not in competition with each other. One cannot add God and man as though they worked alongside of each other, but when God works he works via human beings and natural processes. When God provides rain, he does so via clouds and low pressure areas. Rain does fall from heaven in two ways. Still it is the same rain. God does not stand outside his own world as one who pushes things here or there with effects in the direction of man. God is *in* the world; or better, the world is in him. He is the sustaining ground of our reality. He is the power and energy of our existence who pervades the whole of creation. In him we live and move, for we are his offspring (Acts 17:28). When we breathe we do it with the breath he blew into Adam's nostrils. When the creation is freed from chaos it is because God's Spirit moved over the face of the waters (Gen. 1:2). It is the dynamic Spirit of God who penetrates and pervades everything. This means we can only speak about providence in a pneumatological perspective, and when we do, it cannot be with a doctrine of the Holy Spirit that is an appendix to the actual doctrine of God. Pneumatology is the actual doctrine of God. No proper doctrine of God is possible apart from the doctrine of the Holy Spirit and the Trinity. If we speak of providence without remembering that in his relation to the world God is present as Spirit, faith in providence in fact becomes a rock-hard stumbling block. Monotheism without Trinity leaves no room for humans, unless it be room at the expense of God. But by speaking about the Spirit providence gets a different face. It is the living dynamics of the divine breath in the world by which we live and move and will and act. When God takes away his Spirit, everything grinds to a halt.

All this also applies to the human will. Human beings can only exercise will because God's life animates his will. Augustine especially developed this idea, proceeding from the assumption of a psychologically free will. Viewed psychologically, the human will is free. When I make a choice, I experience the fact that I am choosing. But why do I choose? In my choices am I conditioned by sociological, pedagogical, genetic, or other factors? Undoubtedly they play a role, but they are not finally decisive. Moreover, it does not help much to refer to such influences for the purpose of defending the freedom of the will. If I should attempt to combat providence in the interest of the freedom of the will, I am not benefited if I immediately sell out this freedom to sociological or pedagogical factors. In any case, the human will is never totally subject to them. There is a domain of personal freedom in which I make my own choices. But why do I choose as I do? Because this choice happened to arise in my mind. To the extent that the spontaneous thoughts of a human being are not prompted by external factors they are completely fortuitous. Even if I choose to reject a spontaneous thought, the new choice again arises from a void. If we stop at the freedom of human choice, we are left with a completely fortuitous cascade of thoughts and are the prey of chance. In other words, psychology ends with an open question; it has no answer to the question whether our thoughts come to us from elsewhere, and even less to the question whence they come. Accordingly, man is either controlled by fate or total necessity, *anangkè,* or by fortune, *tuche,* total caprice.

Providence, according to Augustine, means that neither chance nor fate determines our will, but the living God. It is the divine Spirit who introduces coherence into our life. It is the Spirit of the same God who called us into being. He whose breath is in our nostrils is he who is the "breath" of our thoughts. Therefore divine providence does not deprive us of our freedom. On the contrary, because it frees us from chance and fate, it is the only guarantee of our freedom. Our will is structured because the one will of the one God animates ("blows through") it. Our entire existence and the whole world is pervaded by that one and the same Spirit. It is no accident that the theologians who most stress providence are the theologians of the Holy Spirit. Because many forget this and people do not think in trinitarian terms, providence becomes a leaden burden; the truth is it offers us the space that liberates: it is the Holy Spirit who pervades our life, who is inseparably bound up with it, who knows us better than, and before, we know ourselves. If God is the all-pervasive and the all-sustaining force of the world, that is not to say he is totally absorbed by it. Rather, the world is taken up in the divine presence; it is sustained by him. One may not reverse the order of this proposition.

The idea that where God in his actions goes beyond the existing orders he at the same time as much as possible acts in continuity with them, so that miracles (better, "signs") do not needlessly disturb nature, can be found especially in Gijsbert D. J. Dingemans.[26] The idea that one may not "add up" God and man is clearly set forth in Piet J. A. M. Schoonenberg's *Hij is een God van mensen: Twee theologische studies.* From another perspective this complex of themes has been treated by Tillich's first volume of *Systematic Theology,* especially in the chapter "Being and the question of God." According to Tillich, God is not the first cause;

---

26. Gijsbert D. J. Dingemans, *Wetmatigheid en worden: een hermeneulisch-theologische studie over de verhouding van geloof en natuurwetenschappen* (Gravenhage: Boekencentrum, 1974), pp. 140ff.

he is not a reality outside of our reality, but "the ground of being" or even "being itself." He is the one who takes the loose ends of the analysis of reality which always yields open questions and ties them together, so forming the world into a meaningful whole. Therefore he is also "the answer to the question implied in being."[27]

Calvin continues to build on this idea. In reference to belief in the omnipotence of God one could say: "It does not matter then what I do; my life is determined at every step in any case. I do not have to be careful when I cross the street, because if God wills that I shall not have an accident I will not have an accident; and if God does will it, I will not be able to escape it." The same objection against belief in providence was already made in Calvin's day. But he rejects it. It is shortsightedness not to look beyond an initial spontaneous glance. For God also gave you brains. Your reflections on whether or not to cross the street also come from him. He has given you eyes for the purpose of seeing the dangers. Also, the reckless decision to cross the street without looking is rooted in God's working. All our reflections come from him and are determined by him.

We find ourselves on the line of thought followed in Isaiah 10:15: The king of Assyria is like a saw in the hand of God, but he does not know it. He thinks he himself dreams up and executes his war plans.

In the Middle Ages this thought was given expression in the idea of *concursus*. This notion was developed especially in Lutheran theology. *Concursus* means that God and world operate concurrently. Concurrence is the opposite of rivalry or competition. In the case of competition one cannot do what the other is doing. In the case of concurrence the one always does what the other does. The course of natural and psychological processes runs parallel to the course of the willing and working of God.

Linked with the preceding question is the issue whether in this belief in providence one is not actually saying the same thing that was said in the old belief in fate. If everything is determined by God, what difference does it make whether you say "God" or "fate?" What is the difference between God and fate? What difference does it make whether you say, "God has decided it thus" or "that's just (his) fate"? Is there really any difference between "you have to entrust yourself to God's guidance" and "you can't fight fate"? Calvin rejects this identification. To be sure, there are similarities, he says, but the words "fortune" and "fate" are so burdened with negative feelings that he prefers not to use

27. Tillich, *Systematic Theology*, vol. 1, p. 181.

them. For him the central difference between the notion of fate and belief in providence is that in the case of fate everything runs along fixed pre-programmed lines. Everything has been put into the computer and only needs to come out, whereas in the case of providence it is the continuing personal presence of God which accompanies and leads you at every step. You are not strapped into a roller coaster that has been set in motion and whizzes along its pre-programmed course, but are sitting in a baby carriage which is pushed by your father, the one who loves you and who is with you every moment.

Calvin is correct in saying that a life under the continuing care of God is something different from a destiny that is fixed already from the very beginning. God is not only present at the beginning; he is there at every step. But then—to stay with the image—how can it possibly be that in God's baby carriage people die as a result of exploding hand grenades, or that a child sitting in the back of mother's bicycle is crushed to death by a truck? Believing in God's providence we still have a lot to fight through with him before we can say, "Let him watch; let him control; all is wisdom what he does."

A final question is whether in this way God and history are not so absorbed into each other that all differentiation is lost. History and salvation history then coincide. At best the history of salvation is part of general history, a segment of the whole which then consists of the history of salvation and the history of calamity. But then salvation history does not stand in a critical relationship to general history. Both issue from the one counsel of God. All that really exists is the history of the divine counsel, the history in which the eternal counsel of God is realized and takes shape. God, then, may not be identical with fate; he *is* the extrapolation into eternity of cosmic process. In essence God and history then coincide. For God cannot be critical of a history he himself has directed and produced. At first blush one might suspect that this option would lead to a conservative viewpoint: history is God's history and therefore do not tamper with it. The existence of the poor and the rich is simply a given. One must not resist this for God has willed it so. Thus faith in divine providence has not infrequently been used to maintain existing power structures. The outcome of history is sanctioned, and one has no warrant for breaking down the divinely established order. If you are born a poor man you will remain a poor man all your life. If God has you born as a nickel, you must not try to become a quarter. That would be titanic arrogance.

To draw this conclusion from belief in divine providence, however, is premature. It constitutes misuse of it in the interest of those in power. Faith in divine providence indeed acknowledges that the course of history as it flowed till now was the will of God. But that is not to say that God wants to perpetuate the existing state of affairs forever. There have been plenty of radical shifts in history; they are divinely willed shifts. A consistent faith in divine providence not only sees the status quo as having come from the hand of God, but also revolution, whether that be the rebellion against a Spanish king in the Netherlands in the sixteenth century or the American Revolution of 1776. In the direction of the course of history, including its shifts, God involved human beings: Moses, David, Jehu, but also the king of Assyria, Nebuchadnezzar as well as Cyrus, William of Orange, George Washington, Napoleon, and Karl Marx. Why should it not be true to say of Marx that "he is my servant" for the liberation of so many oppressed people? Who knows whether God is not planning a shift in history in which he wants to involve us? This he will do via our own wills, via our own choices, in which we decide that change is necessary. If we look at the immense problems of the world, we can only lose heart. We feel powerless in the face of the powerful, as well as in front of open or hidden power structures. But if we realize that it is not the powerful and the power structures which rule the world but God, we take heart. Change is possible. When God works we are stimulated, not paralyzed. If God wills a thing, *we* are able to do it. Our willing is sustained by his willing. "Work out your own salvation with fear and trembling; for God is at work in you, both to will and to work for his good pleasure," writes Paul to the Philippians (2:12f.). Because God initiates the willing and the doing we can also will and act. And salvation is not only the salvation of the soul but the salvation of the entire human being God created, together with the whole world he made. Wherever God is at work, there salvation and renewal are possible. And he works everywhere. Accordingly, the idea of divine omnipotence does not have a conservative effect as far as the future is concerned. That is the case only if we regard God and man as rivals, a view which is incompatible with a doctrine of omnipotence. In regard to the past this doctrine does, however, have a confirming effect. The past is unquestionably the way of God. A big problem thus confronts us: in the past did God never will anything other than what happened? From within the message of Jesus Christ as Lord of the world is there no continuing criticism, not only of all the lords of the future and the present, but also of the lords of the past? Christology is the great troublemaker in the domain of omnipotence beliefs. That is not to say we should renounce belief in omnnipotence. After everything that has been said that would hardly be possible. It does mean we must place the omnipotence of God in the contexts in which it belongs. That is what we shall attempt to do in the final chapter of this book.

11. GOD AS POTTER

IN THIS CHAPTER, IN WHICH WE ADDRESS THE ISSUE OF GOD AND EVIL ON the basis of God's omnipotence, we must discuss one more model. In the preceding section a number of questions surfaced which are so fundamental that it is good for us to treat them separately. Those questions are:

1. Why does the omnipotent God let humans suffer and sin? "O Lord, why dost thou make us err from thy ways?" (Isa. 63:17). Why this process in which God lets people sin in order subsequently to punish them? Why is there suffering if one cannot relate it to punishment?

2. How does this connect with faith and unbelief? Was it also God's will that some people should remain unbelieving? Has God willed that some people should perish? If God directs history, must we say that they were even destined to be lost? Both questions come together in the image of the potter. I have hesitated whether to regard it as a separate model or merely as a nuance of divine providence. However, the image is so much more radical that it can no longer be subsumed under providence. In the case of providence the primary idea is that of well-ordered government in which all events meaningfully are conjoined. History is the grand plan of God from which there is no deviation and whose final destination, which is positive, is in God's hands. Inherent in the image of the potter is a strong element of capriciousness: there is no rule to be discerned in history, no answer to the ultimate "whys." It may seem we are now back at the idea that in the face of the final "whys" we must maintain a reverent silence because the origin of good and evil is above our heads and we therefore face the prohibition of *curiositas*. That, however, is not the case. We have in the meantime gone past this prohibition (we were allowed and able to go past it) and have said that evil also comes from the hand of God. If everything comes from the hand of God, then we want to think this through to the end. Even the sinful deeds of humans come from him. Therefore, the question of how to construe evil has become much more far-reaching. It is the question concerning God's being, which cognitively is to risk "biting off more than you can chew."

The answer to the two questions is very simple in this framework: "Because God has so willed it." God has so decided it, period. It sounds like the answer of an authoritarian father who, when a child asks, "Why do I have to do this?" says, "Because I say so." In an infinite sense, God assumes this authoritarian stance with regard to human beings. Things happen, including the things which affect the foundations of our existence, because he wills them. It is the image of God which Sölle calls "Byzantine,"[28] the image of the Byzantine emperor who had absolute power over the life and death of people. It is the God of Jesus Christ with the face of a Roman emperor. The corresponding biblical image is that of the potter, one even more radical than that of the authoritarian father or the absolute ruler. The most authoritarian father is still brought up short by the stubbornness of his child, and the power of the absolute ruler encounters the limits of what the popular will will bear. That is what absolute rulers and dictators have learned. But in the hands of a potter clay is totally moldable. It cannot talk back. It does not even sulk as it yields to pressure from the hand of its master. It is simply shaped into the vessel the potter wants.

The image of the potter occurs in all three parts of the book of Isaiah (29:16; 45:9; 64:8), in Jeremiah 18, and in Romans 9:21. The least radical text is Jeremiah 18:1-11. God is not pleased with Israel, so he will send them into exile. To demonstrate that God has that freedom Jeremiah has to go to a potter. This potter is just working on a vessel which, however, turns out badly. He again kneads the clay into a lump—by which the vessel is destroyed—and makes a new vessel. Just as a potter is free to knead a failed vessel back into a lump and to make a new one, so also God is free to let Israel fail and perish, and to start afresh. In this image we encounter, in the first place, a reason for destruction, namely, the sin of Israel. In this respect the image would rather seem to belong to the model of the judge. The special nuance of Jeremiah 18 is that God has complete freedom to do with Israel what he wants. One could say the reference is more to a failure than to sin: God's product, Israel, is a failure; not, Israel is punished because of its own failure. The whole of Jeremiah 18 is clearly controlled, however, by the theme of Israel's sin and guilt, which is also evident in the verses where the image of the potter is interpreted. There is mention of repentance from evil (v. 8); of doing what is evil in the sight of God; of not listening to the voice of God (v. 10).

Therefore we would be putting too much weight on the imagery if we merely viewed the sin of Israel as a failure in the work of God. The intent of the image is sufficiently reproduced by saying that God is justified in letting Israel go down to ruin; even more, that this action is self-evident and natural, just as it is completely natural for a potter to put a failed vessel back on his wheel. In the second place, we note that the clay is used again for the second vessel. That could be an indication that God will use Israel again in making a new covenant. Although this

---

28. Dorothee Sölle, *Leiden*, p. 30. In the English translation, *Suffering*, p. 20, this expression has been lost. —Trans.

application of the metaphor is not explicitly present in Jeremiah 18, this idea must be borne in mind, considering that elsewhere (31:31-34) Jeremiah does employ the theme of the old and the new covenant. With the same people, the sons of Israel, God makes a new covenant. Accordingly, at the base of discontinuity there is continuity: everything is again made new, but for the same partners. Hence in Jeremiah the point is not that from the start God decides and regulates everything as he pleases. Indeed, the reference is to God's freedom, but it is freedom in relation to the covenant with Israel. He is free to annul a broken covenant and to establish a new one.

The point of Isaiah 29:16 is a different one. Here certain Israelites say, "We can do as we please; who will notice it?" In response, the prophet says that that notion is as strange as for clay to be boss over the potter. The clay does not see the potter, but the potter certainly sees the clay. Israel does not understand God's secret, but God does understand the secret of Israel, the people he has made. The reference is not so much to God's freedom as to his superiority over his people. God is inescapable. The prophet does not have in mind God's covenant relationship to Israel but rather his relationship to people in their earthliness and smallness. In the later texts in Isaiah this line of thought comes clearly to the forefront. God is the one who has complete control over people. He directs their lives, their history, at every step. Isaiah 63 has stated: "O Lord, why dost thou make us err from thy ways?" Isaiah 64 follows through on this thought and shows in verse 8 what great weight is attributed to God's initiative in Israel's actions. "Thou art our Father; we are the clay, and thou art our potter; we are all the work of thy hand." What humans are and do is done by God. Their sins also come from his initiative. The iniquities are the means by which God lets Israel perish (64:7). Like a potter, God molds his people into his workmanship, the purpose of which is not clear to the product. And like a potter he will soon create a new heaven and a new earth (65:17).

This brings to mind Genesis 2. There the potter is not mentioned, to be sure, but the idea is the same: God takes clay and forms man. Man, then, is the work of his hands. And his life is the breath of God. Eve is also the work of God's hands. The difference between Isaiah 64 and Genesis 2 is that in Genesis God is the beginning of human existence, whereas in Isaiah God also forms the deeds of humans. Both lines of thought are woven together in Isaiah 45. God in freedom creates the existence of his people and no one can ask him to give an account of his product. "Woe to him who strives with his Maker, an earthen vessel with the potter! Does the clay say to him who fashions it, " 'What are you making?' " (45:9). God has made heaven and earth (v. 12). He rules over all. He also rules the future of Israel. He is free to reject them on account of their sins, but equally free to save them in his mercy. If God saves Israel, no one can ask him: "Why doest thou this?" For he is in charge of all things. It is an act of God's unfathomable freedom to elect Israel. This idea forms the basis of the classic Christian doctrine of election. The point of entry is the liberating good pleasure of God. Without any reasons based in man, without owing an account to humans, God has chosen humans in order to save them. My salvation is not based in my works or in my faith, for how uncertain it would then be; my salvation is only based in the electing will of God who is able in freedom to do with me what he wants. The fact that I am a believer is the work of God's Spirit who irresistibly causes me to believe.

However, as we reflect on this confession, the question concerning the position of the non-elect arises. What is the situation of those in whom the Spirit of God, basing himself on God's election, does not irresistibly work faith? Extending the lines of Isaiah 45, we arrive at the thought that that too has been willed by God. All things are in his hand. He leads nations and people to direct the process of world events in accordance with his will. In freedom he elects his people; in freedom he uses the kings of the nations as his instruments and in freedom he subsequently discards them. Still, the idea that God creates people or nations in order to reject them does not occur in the Isaian literature.

We do, however, find it in the final potter text: Romans 9:20, 21. There Paul says that a potter makes different vessels, some for honorable, and some for everyday, use. God makes some vessels for glory as vessels of mercy, others into vessels of wrath intended for destruction, destined only for breaking. In this connection Paul refers to Pharaoh (v. 17). Pharaoh served to reveal God's glory, raised up by God for that purpose. God intentionally allowed Pharaoh to harden himself, thus allowing his people to suffer the plagues, in order to make the liberation of Israel all the more glorious. That already was the view of the author of Exodus (9:16). For Israel that was a way they could process the events around the Exodus. God has everything in his hands. He even had Pharaoh in his hand. When Pharaoh said "no," that was because God intended him to say "no." God even hardened Pharaoh's heart. Thirteen times the Exodus story reports this. If as a result Israel had to suffer and the suffering was prolonged, that was not meaningless, but for the greater glory of God (14:4, 17, 18). Exodus views the hardening of Pharaoh from the perspective of the superiority displayed in God's liberation of Israel. Pharaoh only serves as an instrument with which to establish the name of the God of Israel forever.

In the letter to the Romans Paul's position is much more difficult than that of the author of Exodus. For now the reference is not to the hardening of Pharaoh but to that of Israel. Paul is in a tight spot between the election of Gentiles by faith in Christ and the rejection of Israel. The election of the Gentiles is God's good pleasure, owing to his grace alone. That is the theme he has developed in the preceding chapters. But how then is one to understand the position of Israel? Did God then reject his people? (Rom. 11:1). Because with all the fibers of his being Paul is bound up both with believing Gentiles and with Israel, a much more thoughtful and objective answer is needed. First Paul says that God is free to reject. He is free, after Israel has rendered service as an object for menial use, to reject his people. Some objects serve to be forever an ornament *(doxa)*; others serve for a period of time as kitchen utensils to make things clean. But then they are discarded. The potter can make both from the same lump of clay. The purpose they serve depends completely on his will. People are created from the same clay. God can cause them to be born from the same ancestor. But the purpose people serve depends exclusively on the will of God who made them. Some serve as everlasting ornaments *(doxa)* in the glory *(doxa)* of God. Others serve for a period of time to prepare that glory and are then discarded. They are cloths for polishing the brass and can then be thrown away as refuse. No redress is possible. God is free to make us what we are (9:20ff.).

It is in this line of thought that the teaching of double predestination is rooted. There is an election to eternal life and an election to eternal destruction. In chapters 9 to 11 of Romans Paul also takes another line. After speaking of the potter he again poses the question: "Has God rejected his people?" and says, "By no means" (11:1). He supports this argument with his own election. He too is an Israelite, yet is a believer in Christ. Hence within Israel there is a distinction between the elect and the non-elect. And just as in the days of Elijah, the chosen remnant is the true Israel (11:2-5).

In Galatians the idea is that believers are the true Israel. The church supplants the old covenant people. Biological lineage is not decisive, but the posture of faith in the footsteps of Abraham is (Gal. 3:9). In Romans Paul is more positive about Israel as a biological unit. There the true Israel consists of believing Israelites; they are the representative remnant. Gentile Christians are grafted in as alien branches (Rom. 11:17).

The idea that the remnant which is saved represents the true Israel also fits into the classic doctrine of double predestination. In the second half of Romans 11, Paul again struggles with the question of Israel's position. It is evident he cannot believe that God will forsake Israel, stemming as it does from the root of Abraham. Then it can only be that, though for a time God rejects them for the sake of others, it is not in order to let them fall (v. 11). Accordingly, their rejection was no election unto death. Meanwhile, it is a question whether Paul would employ the same language if he were speaking about Cain, Ishmael or Esau, and especially Pharaoh. We must keep a close eye on the course of the argument in these chapters. God is free, to elect or to reject. If therefore Israel is lost on account of being rejected, no one can say to God, "Now what doest thou?" At the same time, as he continues to write and pursue his thought, Paul cannot imagine that God would *actually and in fact* forsake his people. That can definitely not be the case. However, if God saves them, it is not for any external reason whatever. Also, the salvation of Israel is solely the result of the free election of God, who is not bound to reject his people on account of their iniquity. It is the freedom of the potter to use an everyday utensil as an ornament. If he does not, who can object? If he does, it is his good pleasure. Paul cannot imagine, however, that in the end Israel would not serve in the kingdom of God as an ornament (for *doxa*). It is the same line of thought which is followed when with a view to the superiority and freedom of God, one totally assents to the double election; at the same time, living with the God who in Christ saves people, one cannot imagine that God would let anyone perish. Accordingly, Romans 11, while it does not rob the teaching of double predestination of its core, shows that God's action can never be viewed apart from what he did in the calling of Abraham and the resurrection of Christ.

In his conflict with Pelagians, Augustine extensively developed the doctrine of double predestination. Although in orthodox circles it was usually formally recognized, it never did become popular in the church. In the ninth century Gottschalk, a monk from Fulda, was a forceful advocate. He was condemned at synods at Mainz (848) and Quiercy (849). The synod of Quiercy (853) declared that God predestined people to life, but knowing the lost in advance (*praescivit*), he predestined them to punishment (*praedestinatio ad poenam*) (Denzinger 621). In Calvinistic theology the line of Augustine was resumed. In Calvin election is bound up with the way of the Spirit in the hearts of people. God has the initiative in our faith-history, but that initiative, though founded in the eternal counsel of God, is contemporary with that history. Accordingly, Calvin can also speak about degrees in election: there are differences within the elect people between one person and another, differences which emerge in the course of God's dealing with the covenant people (*Institutes* III, 21, 6). In the Canons of Dort (1619) the issue has become more static. The focus has shifted from the way of the Spirit with people to preexistent eternity where everything was fixed. The pneumato-logical context had to yield to the once-for-allness of the decree. The Canons, accordingly, reject the idea that there are various kinds of election (I, 8; rejection of errors I, 2). Election and reprobation are unequivocally and forever fixed in advance. Still, also in the Canons, election and reprobation are not in equilibrium: the number of times election is mentioned far exceeds that of reprobation. In a later period, in hyper-Calvinistic circles, the emphasis shifted in favor of reprobation and the door of election was left less and less open.

In the context of this section, the discussion held in Dort about infra- and supralapsarianism is important. This discussion could only arise in a climate in which the omnipotence of God was central. All things come from God: even our eternal weal or woe is determined by him. The question was, did God first decide to save people or to reject them; and did he, on that basis, decide to let them fall, in order to be able to save or to condemn them (supralapsarian: the decree of election precedes that of the Fall), or did God decide to let people fall and on that basis decide to save them or to let them remain in their fall? (infralapsarian: the decree of election follows and is dependent on the decree of the Fall). At Dort no decision was made one way or another. Opinions were divided. Many were afraid of the attempt to penetrate God's mystery. Among infralapsarians, moreover, there was the additional concern that people would attribute evil to God and he would become the cause of sin.

Within the model under discussion here, supralapsarianism is the most consistent. From eternity all things have been willed by God. He has unequivocally determined our goal and our path. To that end sin is merely a means. God is free to let us err from his ways to the end that we shall be lost. We could therefore say, what people do and effect is precisely what God wills; can you then still speak of human guilt? Or is God actually the guilty one? Not only was there anxiety about these consequences at Dort, but Calvin too wrestled with the issue. Still, within the position of absolute omnipotence, this problem certainly need not be unresolvable. In the first place, in the case of God you cannot speak of guilt because he is a law unto himself and owes no one an accounting, as Calvin already remarks (*Institutes* III, 23, 2). In the second place, also in this regard, God and man are not in competition. If God wills that a human being shall do a culpable deed he will do it. This does not exonerate a person; on the contrary, it makes him guilty precisely because God has called this deed culpable. Accordingly, the ultimate implication of divine omnipotence is the supralapsarian view of election: from all eternity God has decided over man's weal or woe and therefore he lets man sin. Infralapsarianism still attempts to create some space in the unbroken line of God's will, while supralapsarianism consistently builds upon his absolute omnipotence.

In the Netherlands a shift occurred in the discussion of election as a result of a conflict in a number of independent Reformed churches. This conflict, which in 1953 led to a split, centered in the views of Dr. Cornelius Steenblok, who denied that the offer of grace was extended to all; according to him, it was extended only to the elect. Christ did not die for all, but only for the elect. Although in Steenblok the emphasis lay in an extreme viewpoint and he linked to it far-reaching consequences for preaching, this viewpoint as such was not new. Gottschalk had already written in his *Libellies ad Hrabanum* that Christ did not die for the non-elect. Friedrich Loofs thinks he can find impulses in the direction of this idea already in Augustine.[29]

Therefore, like all good things, evil, judgment, disaster, and lost-ness have all been willed by God. God even allows man to sin. God has even willed hell as the ultimate expression of his eternal rejection. Barth especially has taken up arms against this view. He sums up the entire complex of the powers of darkness, the devil, hell, and sin, under the concept of "nothingness." Barth strongly asserts the position that God has not willed this "nothingness." Nothingness is that which has not been created or chosen and which therefore has no substance or being or reality and never will have. Nothingness is the impossible possibility. It is the possibility God has not willed; it is the divinely repudiated possibility. It is the road he passed by, deliberately passed by. Nothing-ness is that against which God in all eternity said "no," and to which he will in all eternity continue to say "no."

This idea has been set forth at length in Barth (*Church Dogmatics* III, 3, § 50: *God and Nothingness*, pp. 289-368. Also the exegesis of Genesis 1:2 in III, 1, § 41, pp. 101-10 deals with this theme). The waters over which the wind blows are chaos. This is not the primeval substance, or an anti-divine, demonic reality, but the possibility that God did not choose for the world. God chose for the world as it is: the creation as house for the covenant, "the external basis of the covenant."[30] All other possibilities he rejected. They fall under his "no."

Accordingly, nothingness is that which is inimical to the creation as willed by God, and hence inimical to the covenant of God which is the "internal basis of creation." Now this goes further than the concept of sin. It is an evil power, a third power outside of God and the world. It is the reality of the devil, of hell, of chaos. It is the power which sin calls forth and which ends in death. Death is the absolute ruin of creation, the disappearance of that which God willed into being.

The reader must be aware that "nothingness" must not be equated with the non-existent. The latter is that which is not there, absent. Nothingness, on the other hand, is that which is vain, devoid of sub-stance, that which God has repudiated, that which is not, but which still asserts its impossible presence. The influence of nothingness in humans is too real for us to dismiss it as that which does not exist. It is so real, after all, that Jesus had to become man on account of it. God himself had

29. Friedrich Loofs, *Leitfaden zum Studium der Dogmengeschichte*, vol. 1 (Tübingen, 1959[6]), p. 373.
30. Barth, *Church Dogmatics* IV, 1, 41, pp. 94ff.

to take measures to control nothingness. "That which confronts God in this way, and is seriously treated by him, is surely not nothing or non-existent."[31] Nor is nothingness to be equated with what is not the other—merely delimitation and hence a lack—because then one could conceive of nothingness as the empty space outside the universe. But delimitation belongs to the distinction of things, also between God and man. Delimitation exists between the world and God. But that is not nothingness, absolute evil. Boundaries have been established by God and are essential to his creative action in which he calls a thing into being outside of himself, and because it is essential to God's creative action, it is also essential to the covenant and to the grace to which creation tends.

Barth does not deal with the question how there can be something outside of God as the Absolute One. Creation and covenant—that is the reality of the history of God with which theology occupies itself. And because they exist as willed by God, they are not evil, not nothingness. With respect to creation, that also means that nothingness is not simply the shadow side of the goodness of creation—the depth which gives the greater prominence to height, decline over against growth, resistance over against development, a brake on progression. The shadow side belongs to the essence of creation and constitutes a part of it. Height and depth, growth and decrease, development and resistance, progression and curbs, all belong to the good creation of God. The shadow side is inherent in creation. It is willed, hence instituted, by God. In his exegesis of Genesis 1:3 concerning the creation of light and darkness, Barth illustrates this point by saying that the night has been instituted by God. God also created the night: he willed the darkness; darkness is not nothing, merely the absence of light; nor is it nothingness itself, but it has its own substance as willed by God. The night proclaims the glory of God.[32]

Why cannot the shadow side of creation be nothingness? First of all, because this would dishonor God. Then we would be attributing evil to the Creator as its cause—as if God himself had made creation evil. And that notion is absolutely incorrect. For God has willed creation to have both light and darkness. God entered a covenant both with the light and the darkness. Both light and darkness have been accepted by him in Jesus Christ. "We cannot ignore the fact that in Jesus Christ God has again and expressly claimed the whole of creation as His work, adopting and as it were taking it to heart in both its positive and negative aspects."[33] If on this basis one has to acknowledge that God has made all things good,

31. Barth, *Church Dogmatics* III, 3, 50, p. 349.
32. Barth, *Church Dogmatics* III, 1, 41, pp. 117-33.
33. Ibid., III, 3, 50, p. 301.

even the shadows of the night, then one cannot maintain the obvious prejudice that this is where one must look for nothingness. Another argument is that one disguises the actual nothingness if one equates it with darkness, the negative side of creation. Then one pretends that nothingness is part of the way things are. The case is then that the world is not perfect. Because that is the way it is, one is also inclined to accept it. But by this approach one weakens the absolute evil of nothingness and one can no longer with a good conscience work at Christian theology, not a theology which acknowledges the deity of God in Jesus Christ, in whom the absolute and definitive "no" over nothingness has been pronounced.

Accordingly, nothingness is that which is in no way willed by God, that which is devoid of substance. This thought seems to be diametrically opposed to the view sketched at the beginning of this section, that all things come from the hand of God. Good things, creation and covenant, have been willed by God; they come from his hand. But evil things, nothingness and sin, do not come from his hand because he never willed them. Still, the issue in Barth is more complicated than one would at first think. For nothingness does exist. The devil exists and death is real. "There is real evil and real death and real sin."[34] How must we interpret the reality of evil? What is the nature of "exists" in the sentence: "nothingness exists"? It is a peculiar mode of existence, a special kind of existence. It is not the being and reality of creation. Still, it finds its ontic nexus in God's "yes" to creation. For God's electing action also entails rejection. God's action is holy, charged with contrast to that which is unholy. When God pursues his holy will to the end, it always occurs in opposition to the possibilities that have been rejected. Nothingness consists in resistance to God. Nothingness is that by which the positive presence of God assumes form as pure grace. It gives election its profile. In that way it exists. It is precisely as that which has been rejected that it gives profile to God's action. It is not just there, an accident, but exists as willed by God in its negation. For that reason too evil is not a counter-god, an evil deity, over against the good God of Jesus Christ. Evil does not derive its existence from an absolutely other source as counter-pole vis-à-vis God. Nothingness "exists" in its peculiar mode of being as an outflow of God's negative choice. Belonging to God's election in grace is reprobation as an effective act. Also, reprobation calls forth things, but they are called forth in order not to be. On his left hand, God also does nothing for nothing, without its being effective. "His rejection, opposition, negation and dismissal are powerful and effective like all His works because they, too, are grounded in Himself, in the freedom and wisdom

34. Ibid., p. 310.

of His election."[35] Nothingness lives by the fact that also that which God does not will is always effective.

In Barth's exposition of nothingness, the immense tension surrounding the issues of God's goodness and omnipotence comes fundamentally to light. He gropes for words to identify the mystery, but the words fall short and continually contradict each other. Barth himself already said that theology here encounters its limits. Insoluble discontinuities remain; Barth solves them dialectically. Always, if one says one thing, one also has to say the other. One continues to oscillate between the different positions, positions which by themselves are not acceptable. I personally prefer another method over the dialectical, but that is a subject for the last chapter. Here I will content myself by saying that even Barth, who has with such power set forth the superiority and presence of God in Christ, cannot avoid positing a connection between God and evil. Nothingness may arise from God's "no," but for all that it is a reality which disrupts and disorganizes the world. Though it be an alien work (opus alienum) of God, it remains a work of God. It may be a work that proceeds from the left hand of God, but it still proceeds from the hand of God, for God's left hand is also the hand of God. This does not alter the fact that Barth's primary position is that evil has not been willed by God or incorporated in the way of his election. We must not attribute nothingness to the will of God, any more than sin, death, and suffering.

In this history of the church, the great counter-pole of Barth's view is that of Augustine. According to Augustine, the choice of God to allow people to perish and not to save them by his irresistible grace lies entirely within God's freedom. Both theologians place the emphasis on God's freedom, but for Barth God is "the one who loves in freedom."[36] Augustine also leaves room for God to freely choose for reprobation. From eternity God has predestined some people to the condition of lostness. "He just predestined [them] to punishment."[37] They are "predestined to death,"[38] "for eternal ruin,"[39] "to go into the eternal fire with the Devil,"[40] "doomed to undergo eternal punishment with the Devil."[41] The fact that they perish cannot be blamed on God, for it is his freedom: he is the potter.[42]

---

35. Ibid., p. 352.
36. Barth, *Church Dogmatics* II, 1, 28, p. 257.
37. Augustine, *The Enchiridion*, ch. 100.
38. Idem, *The City of God*, XXII, ch. 24.
39. Idem, *Homilies on the Gospel of John*, 48, 4.
40. Idem, *City of God* XXI, 24.
41. Ibid., XV, 1.
42. Ibid.

In Barth we observed that the line of thought was not completely coherent. In some way nothingness still came from the hand of God. In Augustine the system is not closed either. Over against the idea of the freedom of the will of God who governs all things as he pleases and makes all things good, in certain observations Augustine sees evil as opposed to God. Then he regards evil not as coming from God (and hence essentially good), but as *malitia,* malice, corruption, an independent evil source outside of God, welling up as a poisonous fountain in people.

What emerges then is that he who makes the superiority of the love of God primary cannot escape relating evil in some way to God, while he who posits the absolute freedom of God even to reject people cannot avoid breaking through the iron fixity of that notion. Only the lesser figures in the history of the church have presumed to maintain the extreme consequences of their thinking, and accordingly encountered a synod which condemned them.

In 849 that meant the loss of freedom for Gottschalk. He was locked up in a monastery at Hautvilliers till his death. In 1953 that meant a new church fellowship for Steenblok, a communion which turned his view into church dogma.

If we employ the image of the potter to say that God can do with people what he pleases, the question arises whether we must not then speak of arbitrariness. Is it not the case that in some unverifiable and incomprehensible way, a way one is fundamentally not even allowed to understand, God is just "messing around" in his world? Classic theology has always been afraid to attribute arbitrariness to God. But then are we not restricting God's freedom? God indeed owes an accounting to nothing and to no one. It is even impossible to evaluate his choices: by what standard could we measure them other than by his own being? When the image of the potter is used, the idea is not that God is arbitrary; the image serves to safeguard God's freedom. God cannot be bound to anything. One could say that he is bound to himself. But who but he himself will decide whether he is remaining faithful to his own being? God cannot be held responsible to any authority outside of what he himself is and will be. God cannot be measured by any image we have of him. God is God and therefore absolutely free. What he makes of that freedom is his own business. Who would presume to tell God how he has to make his decisions? "Where were you when I laid the foundation of the earth?" God asks Job (38:4). Who could possibly restrict God's freedom? What would be the criterion by which God's actions could be judged? Who could say, "What you are doing is not good"?

Still, it remains hard to acknowledge this in a concrete situation. Theoretically, one can construct such a model. One can even believingly confess that God is free and that what God does cannot be other than good; but amidst the events of history it remains incomprehensible. Now incomprehensibility belongs to the image of the potter. The clay does not understand what the potter is doing either. But it is not only incomprehensible; it is also impossible to handle or process emotionally and intellectually. That is the situation in which we humans find ourselves. We are not dead lumps of clay, but feeling, thinking people. The idea that because God is completely free to let a truck knock down and run over a child, one could in that case say that "this is for God to decide" is not something we can handle. To see a young father being destroyed by cancer is not something we can handle. When in Latin America people are murdered by those in power for no reason, and soldiers in Chile shoot at little children simply because they bang the lids of pans against each other, we cannot understand. Under these circumstances can a person still say, "That is for God to decide"?

This issue is even more pressing in the biblical stories. In the present, one might still say, "You may think that God is doing it, but that, of course, is nonsense. The way you think about suffering is completely wrong. The potter metaphor does not add up." But a person who considers the biblical stories as God's communication to us cannot escape having to admit that God sometimes does incomprehensible things in these stories. In many Bible stories it is explicitly stated that God willed the destruction of people. It was God's will that because Achan had stolen devoted things, his whole family should be murdered. God willed that, in order that his name should be established, a child should die in every family in Egypt. In every house a father and a mother were shattered over the loss of a child who died suddenly, not only in the palace of the hard-hearted Pharaoh, but also in the hovel of the poor woman who turned the mill (Exod. 11:5). And even the proud Pharaoh was no more than a means in God's hand. He had no choice. He was called by God to be proud and to be ruined as a result of his own hardheadedness. The fact that, according to Joshua, thousands of Canaanites—men, women, and children—were wiped out to furnish Israel room in the land God promised to them, even while others lived in it, is beyond our capacity to handle.

The book of Job combats the notion that a direct relationship exists between sin and suffering, or that God does everything for our good. But the course pointed out by the book is even harder to stomach. The book portrays the total absurdity of suffering. There the sufferings of a man are the result of a wager in heaven. Is not that arbitrariness? And the man who opens his mouth in protest can only be silent in the end. "I lay my hand on my mouth" (Job 40:4). For what is the point of a puny earthworm disputing with the mighty God who created the colosse of the animal world, who plays with untameable monsters as his own creatures, who in the beginning of creation formed the stars and called them by name? (Job 38–41). Who is man that he should argue with God? Is the way of "living with" suffering pointed out in the book of Job really a way out? Is it not the case here that one's last bit of support is undercut?

One could say, "True. That is what we find in the Old Testament. But then people did not yet have a clear image of who God is. They still regarded God as a God who willed these horrors, but later the religious consciousness of man developed and people saw that God cannot be that way." But what kind of criterion do we have for saying that in fact God is not like that? Is the revelation we have concerning God legitimate and that of the authors of Exodus, Joshua, and Job illegitimate? If in advance we write off everything in the Bible that does not fit our God image as ignorance of the author or something like it, the Bible loses its critical function with respect to our ideas and we will never get beyond the image we already had. Then we shall not find in Scripture any other God than the one we already had in our heads.

Now there is reason to say that in Christ we have the critical authority who places Old Testament pronouncements about God and his actions in another light. Is it not true that the New Testament speaks a different language than many writings of the Old Testament? That may be true in general, but we have to be careful not to play the New Testament off against the Old. Also, the New Testament speaks about God as potter and about man as clay. Moreover, the idea underlying this imagery is not only to be found in Paul; in John the problem of suffering is handled in a way that is not very different from that of the book of Job. I have in mind especially the familiar pericope about the man born blind (John 9:1-3). The disciples' question is whether his suffering is the result of the man's own sin or that of his parents. Jesus then says that the blindness did not arise from sin. But the argument Jesus advances for the man's suffering only makes the situation harder: he was born blind that the works of God would be made manifest. If the man had been blind as punishment upon sin, then one could still have discovered a certain rationality in his situation. But when God lets a child be blind from birth, lets him spend the years of his childhood and youth in darkness, lets him go through his adulthood as a beggar, only to show what he can do in healing him, can that be regarded as anything but arbitrariness? On the basis of God's freedom and omnipotence we would have to say, "God is free to do what he pleases. Good is what God

117

wills—even if the man is blind." We would then even have to take a position somewhere further back than the idea that God's goodness is actual, concretely filled goodness, for concretely filled goodness is a limitation of the freedom of God. If God wills to be really free without any restriction, then he is the absolutely omnipotent who can do as he pleases and owes no one any accounting.

Now why is it that we continue to have problems with the view that all things come from the hand of God and are therefore good? Why can we not put a period here, as would be proper in a chapter on the omnipotence of God? We cannot for two closely linked reasons: first, because we ourselves do not experience all things as good, and second, because the Bible has more things to say than, "All things are good."

If all things come from the hand of God, we also, including our thinking and our inner experience, come from his hand. God proceeded to create and created a human being who experiences suffering and is open to sin. Humans do not experience and treat the world as being good, something true not only of humans but also of animals with *their* pain and plants with *their* response to a lack of water and food. Because God acted as he did in the creation of this world, there is more than pure goodness afoot. Because God has not created us in such a way that we thankfully and joyfully accept pain and grief, the world is not pure goodness. That epithet would still be applicable if, masochistically, suffering gave us pure joy. Reality, however, is different. God's own actions, the decisions of his will, themselves give rise to the difficulties we have in calling the totally free omnipotence of God good.

This comes through even more clearly from within the biblical-theological point of view. In Scripture human deeds are viewed as coming forth from the will of God, but the same deeds are labeled as aberrant from God's ways (Isa. 63:17). It turns out that God's way and God's leading diverge. God's words and God's actions diverge. They themselves do not display the coherence of absolute omnipotence. God wills both one thing and another. God says one thing and something else happens. The words and deeds of God, his *debarim*, do not correspond. God's actions and words (and his words are actions also) themselves give rise to problems. Because he *does* things, there is dissonance. Problems do not arise from the general image of God's omnipotence, for then the world as emanation from God's being would consist of pure light. But the problems arise from the events of history, from contradictory experiences. Because the problems do not arise from "the eternal truths of reason" but from "the accidental truths of history," they cannot be resolved on the level of "the truths of reason." This means that *logically* there is no way out of the problems of omnipotence and evil. Arising as they do from the nonrecurrent, arbitrary factuality of history, from different wills, from the conflictual nature of the words and deeds of God, they can only be resolved from within the context of history; that is, not logically but chronologically. No logical response is possible to events that do not follow each other logically, that do not constitute a coherent whole of connected data. Events come in contradictory series.

Proceeding from the idea that all things come from the will of God we have to ask ourselves, "Just what does God actually want?" Does he, or does he not, will the sin of Israel? Does he, or does he not, want Pharaoh to let Israel go? Does he, or does he not, will the handicap of the blind man? The answers to these questions, questions which arise from concrete reality, do not lie in the absolute unity of logic. Just as the question arises from the words and deeds of history, so the answer can only come in the form of an event in history, in an act in which God speaks. God then must let us know what he wants. Accordingly, God's answer is not a logical conclusion: the Logos of God is an act, an "accidental historical truth," the sending of his Son, Jesus Christ.

We have come to the end of the chapter whose starting point is God's omnipotence. We have arrived at the absolute freedom of God, for whom *we* are the clay while for us *he* is the potter. We have also landed at a point where we realize "we cannot stay here." Here certain radically different things will have to be said. At the same time we have to note here that the experience of God as our potter represents a radically reverent posture of faith. It is one which hardly fits in our age, the age of man come of age. To many people the reaction of Job in the debate ("As God lives, who has taken away my right," 27:2) will be more congenial than his humble confession at the end ("Behold, I am of small account; what shall I answer thee? I lay my hand on my mouth," 40:4). For few people today will this also be an unbroken confession. It is mixed instead with uncertainty, inner doubts, and with prayer for change or acceptance. But none of the models discussed can be handled consistently unimpugned. That also applies to the models which are still to come. Perhaps the model discussed in this section calls forth the most problems in our time. Possibly many people will even turn from this God-image with loathing. It will not do, however, to dismiss this form of the experience of God's presence as inferior. It is a legitimate way of speaking about God, as much as the other models. In this form of the experience of God one hears a deep reverence for the Holy One whose Name is above every name. He is the Holy One who spoke to Job in the whirlwind (Job 38:1; 40:6). He is the Holy One who descended on Mt. Sinai with fire and lightning (Exod. 19), the Holy One before whom the seraphs around the throne cover their faces (Isa. 6). There is deep amazement when this Holy One deigns to look at me, a puny human being, and to grant his eternal salvation. He is the Holy One who created me and of whom I can and must say, "Though he should cast me into hell forever, I would still praise him."

When experiences of suffering invade our present existence, we may say to each other, as I often heard it said during my pastorate, "It is not people who are doing it to you." When it is people, your equals, who do it to you, you can vent your anger and in your confusion ask for an accounting. When it is people who do it to you, people who act on a level you should be able to understand, you are confronted with real mean-inglessness and the perversity of human possibilities which also illumi-nate your own possibilities. But in the actions of the Holy One our way is not hidden from him. The Holy One does what is right in his eyes, for who will ever comprehend him? When he acts we do not have to fight back and avenge ourselves; we may be silent before his greatness. This consciousness affords us comfort, and comfort never paralyzes: it is the source of the courage to continue, whatever be God's way with us. I am allowed to live because God has put me in this place and in this life. In the extreme this applies even if in his holy will this life is destined for judgment. It is better to be an object of menial use to be later discarded than a plaything of chance, or the manipulations and aggressions of people. Comfort is all the greater when it is confessed that this Holy One is the God who loves me in Jesus Christ. His way may be in hiddenness, in clouds and darkness, but, consoled, we sing: "If God, my God, is for me, who then is against me?" God may take me on strange roads, lead me through deep valleys, but he knows my way and leads me to the light. Then he may do with me what he wills. For my only source of assurance is that with all that I am and all that I experience I entrust myself to him.

III

GOD DOES NOT WILL EVIL

IN THIS CHAPTER OUR FUNDAMENTAL STARTING POINT IS THAT GOD IS totally good. He is love and grace, and he wills only the salvation and happiness of people. Accordingly, evil, suffering, and sin are not to be attributed to his will or work but come from another source. God, more than anyone else, opposes evil. In the models discussed in this chapter the omnipotence of God is problematic, just as in the previous chapter—in which omnipotence was our fundamental starting point—questions arose about God's goodness. In this chapter we will again discuss a variety of models, each of which resonates with Scripture in its own way. The point of view is totally different from that in the previous chapter. A person who has just finished reading it will have to reorient himself. For one person that will be a relief; another will have the impression that after dealing with the most profound questions related to God's omnipotence we are now wading in shallow waters. However, both points of view are equally necessary. Both concern the one God of Israel who in Jesus Christ is the God of the nations—the God who is the God of this world he has created but in which he is also present as liberator and judge so the power of sin and suffering shall be overcome by his goodness.

The first three models of chapter II could also have been given a place here. The chastising father is the good father. However, because the primary reference is suffering, and according to these models suffering comes from the hand of God, we have placed them in the previous chapter. They primarily proceed from the assumption of God's omnipotence, and though they may look for a way to make room also for the goodness of God it is secondary with regard to the confession of the role of God's almighty hand in suffering. Still, it is a good thing to consider that the models of sections 6-8 can also be described from within the viewpoint of God's goodness: God loves us; that is evident from the concern exhibited in the hand that strikes us. In order to avoid unnecessary repetition, however, we shall not develop this other view of the same images, all the more because the underlying ideas have already been dealt with in those sections. We shall now restrict ourselves to those models in which not only sin is against the will of God, but suffering too. Unattributable to his hand, suffering has its source elsewhere.

12. HUMANS DO EVIL

IF THERE IS A GOD, WHY THEN IS THERE SO MUCH MISERY IN THE WORLD? One answer to this question is, "You must not blame God for it but man." It is easy to point to God as the cause of suffering, but then we are ignoring our own responsibility. For when we survey the suffering of the world, that suffering can never be isolated from the actions of human beings. The largest part of the misery that comes to us in daily news reports on television has to do with what people do or fail to do. Reference to God can therefore easily become an excuse for not trying to arrive at change, and so for maintaining evil.

Familiar is the idea expressed in Lord's Day 10 of the Heidelberg Catechism, where all things are attributed to God. In this connection it is often forgotten that in the Catechism there is also a very different line of thought, one in which evil is charged to man. The question often raised in connection with Lord's Day 10—namely, whether God does not commit injustice—has already been posed and answered in another context by the Catechism itself. Lord's Day 4, question 9, reads: "But doesn't God do man an injustice by requiring in his law what man is unable to do?" The answer to it is this:

> No, God created man with the ability to keep the law.
> Man, however, tempted by the devil,
>   in reckless disobedience,
>   robbed himself and his descendants of these gifts.

Man, according to the Catechism, has deliberately taken a road in history which leads to misery. And no human being is able to free himself from the history begun by his ancestors. Every human being confirms over

122

and over that he wants to continue on this road. But it is not God's way; it never was and never will be. He is "terribly angry" about it (Answer 10).

"Man to man is a wolf," wrote Ovid. Human suffering is caused by humans; that is the passive effect of the aggressive human attitude described by Ovid. In simplest form this comes to expression in the conduct of one person to another. The school experience of some children is ruined because they are always being teased and humiliated by other children. One can often say that such a child "asks" for it. He grovels, so he is humiliated. But this precisely characterizes the human attitude: the moment someone is or acts weak, there will be "a tough guy" who wants to confirm it. The bleeding chicken gets pecked at. The weak person gets the blows. We can construct a theory about the frustrations that build up in tough guys who, in their powerless drive to affirm themselves, have to "act out," but this does not in the least alter the reality that these frustrations in human behavior apparently have to be expressed through aggression. Man to man is a wolf, and just as a dog is submissive to a bigger dog and in turn attacks the dog that is afraid of it, so human beings tend to admire the strong and bully the weak.

Humans suffer as a result of what others do to them. That is not only the case in the lives of children. Adults, too, inflict suffering on each other. They are more experienced, however, and can therefore do it in more refined ways. Of course some adults also straightforwardly beat up one another. That causes suffering, but usually not the worst kind. The worst kind is the drip which hollows out the stone; friendliness to one's face but falseness behind one's back; gossip which cuts down human esteem without the possibility of a defense; the scheming to advance one's position in a business; the contempt which comes out in diminutive words; the fact that people tell their own stories but have no ear for the story of another; the guilt feelings laid on the other and kept fresh; the claims made and impositions laid on a partner; the role into which the other is forced.

Adults have learned to swallow things, and generally know how to take the teasing, though the odd person never learns. Some feel every pinprick acutely and you can see it in their faces. Sometimes they become angry, but others see through the anger and perceive the impotence. But even the strong person who has learned to swallow a lot is hollowed out by the drip. For him too the moment may come when the tensions provoked by social interaction become too much. Then the pain may be the worse. There can be acutely painful situations in which people feel abandoned by their wife or husband, by their friends, colleagues, or superiors. Sometimes it is a matter of a person only feeling abandoned, sometimes a matter of really having been abandoned. Usually it is a mixture of both. In any case, this person was not received or approached in a way which was good for him or her. It is nonsense to fault God for this suffering. God does not will that people suffer, that they succumb to their problems. People are to blame for this. People have failed. They have wrecked this person. People have gossiped, baited, taken advantage. People have failed to listen to one another. God is on the side of the oppressed, not on the side of the oppressors. In his misery the oppressed knows he can call on God as his helper.

The psalms have great influence, especially those psalms in which persons cry out to God in their distress. Such psalms are read and sung from one generation to another. Generations of Israelites and Christians have been comforted by them. In situations in which they had no words, they found them in these songs. Psalms related to a very different situation than that of the reader can still serve as comfort. A sick person may be comforted by a song about someone being persecuted by his enemies. This shows a profound feeling of solidarity between believers living now and those who speak in this age-old volume.

An exposition of how various human afflictions are interwoven can be found in Hans Joachim Kraus. At bottom every enemy is a manifestation of the powers of chaos. Momentary suffering is a sign of "the waters and waves of the world of the dead." Kraus further points out that the individual psalms are not expressions of "private piety."[1] The songs have their place in the fellowship of the people of God. Fundamentally this situation still continues: the comfort of the psalms consists in the recognition of the fellowship of the devout across the ages before the face of the same God. It is not the incidental individual who sings, but the person who lives in the tradition of the covenant people.

It is striking to note how often in the Psalms the reference is to people who are in distress because they have been driven into a corner by others. Sometimes they are national enemies, gentiles who have come to ravage Israel (Pss. 74; 79; 80). But frequently it is personal enemies who beset the poet. It is precisely these individual psalms of lament which have had great influence. They are among the best-known songs of the psalter. Just think of Psalm 25, and especially Psalm 42. Pursued by the slander of enemies and involved in problems as a result of their scheming, the psalmists cry to God. False witnesses enter who attempt to bring about the fall of the oppressed, looking for an opening. In such a

---

1. Hans Joachim Kraus, *Psalms 1-59: A Commentary* (Minneapolis: Augsburg, 1988), p. 77. (See also excurses 4, "The Enemies," pp. 95-99; for the various genres and their "Sitz im Leben," see pp. 38-62. An extensive list of further literature can be found on pp. 99-111.)

situation, the poet of Psalm 27 says: "I believe that I shall see the goodness of the Lord in the land of the living!" (v. 13). If God were not there to help me in what people try to do to me, I could not continue. People trample on those in distress (Ps. 56:2). And where a person is in distress the number of people who trample on him increases steadily (Ps. 3:1, 2) and assume a proud position over against him (Ps. 56:1, 2), knowing their chance has come. But all the enemies disappear when we can say: "This I know, that God is for me" (Ps. 56:9).

When it comes to suffering which people inflict on each other, God is not the instigator, not the one who stands by with silent approval, but the challenger of evil. That is how we may relate to him in our misery. We may cry to him to rescue us, like the poets of these psalms. We may trust that he is near. When the Lord is near we need not be afraid. Then my adversaries may be many; they may drive me into a corner, but when all else collapses, the Lord is still my rock of refuge where I am safe from all intrigue (Ps. 71:3). Even if my pursuers have everything in their favor and get everyone to join them, then I am still not alone, for the Lord is with me. "With the Lord on my side, I do not fear. What can man do to me?" (Ps. 118:6). It is not workable, nor is it necessary, to cite all the texts in and outside of the Psalms where this attitude of faith comes to the fore. It is the believer's response to the promise of God that he is with us to deliver us when men arise against us, a promise which poets and prophets (Jer. 1:19) have heard and trusted.

People can suffer a great deal at the hands of others, but they can also suffer a great deal from what they do to themselves. We may suffer because of our fears. When we feel threatened by other people, it is a question whether others are really boxing us in, or we only think they are. When we are insecure, a well-intentioned word may be taken as a threat. Fear on account of something that is not there can make one's life unbearable, precisely because of the absence of a real threat. You cannot undertake to do anything against an evil you suspect or fear but cannot look in the face. The old rhyme which used to hang on the walls of doctors' waiting rooms can still be a daily reality to us.

> Most people suffer here
> from troubles which they fear
> but which may never come.
> So they have more to bear
> than God has meant for them.

Lives are made somber because they are always overshadowed by dark clouds of anxiety, clouds which gather into an *angst* which can no longer be handled. This suffering, however, arises from the suffering person himself. It is self-inflicted only. Not that the suffering is any less real or intense. People really do suffer from the suffering they fear, and often more than from the suffering that is obvious to all. In that respect, the old rhyme in the doctor's office is correct, including the last sentence—the burden he bears is greater than what God has laid on him. God has not given him this suffering. It is not God's will that we should lead our lives so somberly, in anxiety, shadowed by dark clouds. Jesus has shown us another way: to turn our heads, like flowers, to the light of the sun. "Consider the lilies of the field, how they grow; they neither toil nor spin. . . . Therefore do not be anxious, saying, 'What shall we eat?' or 'What shall we drink?' or 'What shall we wear?' For . . . your heavenly Father knows that you need them all" (Matt. 6:28, 31, 32). It is not the nearness of God which causes us to suffer and to be anxious; our anxiety does not come from him; rather he confers relaxation and relief. His presence makes us live without anxiety. We do not have to be afraid of everything that in the future may be lacking, of disasters that may come over us, for then too God is with us. Our greatest lack is a lack of trust in our heavenly Father who is present even when a sparrow falls from the roof (Matt. 10:29). By this I do not mean to say that it is always easy to trust. If there is one anxious person, it is I, fearing what is not there. But God is not to blame for that; I am. There is nothing we can do against imagined evil, we said. But we *can* do something against imagining it. We have to fight with ourselves, or somehow be comforted. We must look squarely at the fearful, self-destructive persons that we are, and take away their power. In that battle God is on our sides. He does not want oppression, including the oppression we inflict on ourselves. This is doubly true when it concerns the suffering we fear we shall receive at the hands of another person. By doing this we are not only doing an injustice to ourselves, but also to the other whom we distrust and reject. When Jacob fears Esau (Gen. 32:7), he not only does an injustice to himself but also to Esau. And he does not do justice to God who does not want him to be afraid and had in fact encouraged him at Mahanaim with an army of angels (Gen. 32:1ff.). When Abram and Isaac fear the king of Egypt (Gen. 12:10-20) and of Gerar (Gen. 20:1-18; 26:7-11), afraid these men will take away their wives, they are doing an injustice to those kings, to themselves, to their wives, and to God. They are rightly reproached by these heathen kings. Only God, who is opposed to this "way" of the patriarchs, can still save them from their predicaments.

We are now treading on the terrain of suffering resulting from our own sin. A great deal of suffering is our own fault, not only because of distrust or anxiety, but as a consequence of things we have done. We shall not repeat here what we have discussed in § 8. There the point was that God punishes us via the consequences of what we do. Here the point is that we are referring not to the punishing God, but to the responsible human. The drunkard is himself responsible for his misfortune. God did not will that he should get plastered and then step into his car. God did not will that he should endanger his own life and that of others. The problems are not attributable to God; they are attributable to humans. God wants to save people despite their guilt. God is the helping God. With one's guilt up front one can ask God for healing, for restoration of the relationships we have broken by our own wrongdoing. God clears away our troubles rather than gives them.

Psalm 38 is the song of someone who through his own fault is in deep trouble. "There is no health in my bones because of my sin" (v. 3). "My wounds grow foul and fester because of my foolishness" (v. 5). The song ends with the prayer: "Make haste to help me, O Lord, my salvation!" (v. 22). Also, in case of one's own fault one can call on the name of God as the God who saves, who also then does not want us to suffer. That is true even when we experience our suffering as proof of God's anger, as in Psalm 38 (vs. 2-4). Even then God is the God who saves us from suffering. On him one may hope and trust he will answer (v. 15).

In the case of suffering resulting from human sin, it is seldom only the guilty person who suffers. Usually an entire circle of people is affected, often even more so than the guilty person. The police record teaches us every day that the fault of one is the suffering of the other. There is the grief of friends and relatives. The relatives of the thief are counted in the category of the thieves. Esau suffers as a result of Jacob's wrongdoing and Jacob suffers the consequences of Laban's falsity. Uriah suffers under David, and emaciated Israelites suffer under Ahab. Here we are not dealing with the position of those affected; that has already been done. Now we are addressing the position of the guilty. Often the guilty person is blind to the suffering of others; at least he does not recognize it as his fault. God can punish him for the evil he has done. That may be an act of goodness toward the victim, though it is questionable whether it benefits him. Just how does it benefit the traffic victim that the driver who ran him down is now in jail? It may give him a sense of compensation, but at the same time it enlarges the tangle of suffering. Moreover, our topic here is not how God punishes. Our topic is responsible man and the saving God. The attitude of the guilty person vis-à-vis his victims, which corresponds to God's goodness, is not patiently to bear his punishment but to offer help. That is the only compensation which makes any sense. For Zacchaeus to restore the goods he has stolen—that is pleasing to God (Luke 19:8). This help may be coupled with the prayer that God will help the people who were hurt. When David had had the people numbered and they were ravaged by the plague, he prayed that God would remove the plague: "Lo, I have sinned, and I have done wickedly; but these sheep, what have they done?" (2 Sam. 24:17). Not that prayer can be a substitute for help. Such a prayer is only meaningful if it is accompanied by the deed. The deed is borne by people, which makes it an act of God's will.

Not every deed can be "made up." Compensation for damage suffered seldom offsets it. But the thing goes deeper. Even when the guilty person offers help to his victim, it in itself never makes up for the wrong done. Wrongdoing cannot be bought off, not even by exorbitant compensation. After all, a wrongful deed does not just damage another person's possessions or injure his health, but it affects his person. He himself has been violated. The guilty person who realizes that has just begun to experience the extent of his problems. As long as one can still do something and believe one can make some sort of reparation, one still has a positive sense of self in the face of the negativity of the wrong. But the guilt itself remains; it cannot be resolved by the guilty person. To be guilty makes a person helpless. The extension of help to the victim can be a sign that one recognizes his fault. It is even a necessary sign. Without it the recognition of the guilt incurred does not mean anything. It may equally well be a method to get rid of the guilt and to deny the essence of it.

Accordingly the guilty person remains stuck with an irreparable burden of guilt in a situation of complete dependence. The only way he can be freed is by forgiveness. When people are broken through their own fault, suffer on account of something that can never be undone or compensated for, God's way is the way of forgiveness. He is the one who does not desire this suffering which no human being can bear. He wills their deliverance; he wants to heal their hearts. Opposite the guilty stands the forgiving God.

Psalms of penitence search for this God. The poets who composed them and everyone who repeats them long for the grace which frees them from what has wrecked their life. God is a forgiving God. Poets and prophets knew him as such. He was their hope when they could do nothing to make satisfaction for the wrong they had done. For nothing can redress the evil committed. Guilt can only disappear in grace, in the gift of forgiveness. It is the gift which you as the guilty party receive, not the gift you give in compensation for your sin. In Christ God has confirmed this gift to humans. He *is* the divine gift of forgiveness, the presence of God who does not allow the person lost in sin to remain there. Often people have spoken of reconciliation as satisfaction. Correctly so. The New Testament refers to the suffering and death of Christ in that sense. Consider, for example, the sacrificial terminology of the letter to the Hebrews or of 1 Peter. Consider the role played in the New Testament by Isaiah 53 and the Lamb that takes away the sin of the world (John 1:29). But in that connection one must always remember that it is not the satisfaction the guilty person furnishes. It is the satisfaction given him as a gift of Christ. It is God who himself confirms his love to us as a gift of grace. God does not have to thank us for the sacrifice of Christ, but "thanks be to God for *his* inexpressible gift!" (2 Cor. 9:15).

Forgiveness is a gift of God. The gift of grace is the mode in which God deals with guilt. If that is his own mode of goodness, then it is also the mode in which he expects us to deal with each other. A person who suffers through someone else's fault can only liberate the perpetrator from the thrall of his guilt by means of the gift of forgiveness. The victim of the sin is the only one who can save the sinner. He is the only one who can make the impossible possible so that following irreparable guilt a healed life with an open future is again possible. The forgiveness of sin is the greatest gift people can give each other. By it individuals can extend to each other life toward the future. To withhold forgiveness is the worst thing one can do to a fellow human. It is to forbid him from having a future; it is uninterrupted murder. But unforgiveness also stands in the way of your own future. By it you also murder your own life. The sin of the other—the one you cannot forgive—remains a stone of stumbling in your own past, one over which you will stumble again and again. A moment ago we said, by your sin not only the other person's possessions or health have been injured, but he himself has been violated. He who cannot forgive himself exists in a violated condition.

To forgive is hard, even impossible. But harder than forgiving is the act of confessing your own sin and guilt. Both belong together. In confession and forgiveness two humans meet each other from whom the impossible is required. But this impossibility is realized as a gift from the forgiving God. The confession of sin before the face of God and his forgiveness does not compete with the confession of sin and forgiveness between people. On the contrary, they essentially belong together. One can never use confession before God and forgiveness by him as an excuse for not being reconciled with a brother or a sister. For forgiveness from the side of God expresses itself concretely in the gift of reconciliation between people. When from within the thrall of guilt people again find each other, that is the realization of the gift of the grace of God. If we view forgiveness in this light, we also realize that the gift of God's grace in Christ extends further than the walls of the church or the boundaries of Christianity. Christ is the Lord of the world—also and precisely in the reconciliation of human beings.

God wills neither the individual suffering, nor the individual guilt, of people. Now that which applies to the individual also applies collectively. Much suffering is not the fault of an individual, but of a group, a social class, a nation, an economic or political power block. We can ask God "why?" with reference to the hunger of the world. We can pray to him for protection from war and for relief for the oppressed. But we shall have to start by saying that hunger, war, and oppression are the consequence of human decisions. If there is poverty in the world we must not blame God. We must not even blame economic and social structures. For the structures are made and maintained by man. If in Columbia people are poor, then an overseas government which imposes import duties on roasted coffee in order to protect its own coffee roasters is also to blame. If the Columbians could roast their own coffee, they would have employment. If in South Africa blacks are treated as third-class entities, that is the fault of companies which continue to invest in that country and the fault of governments which do not consistently cut off all contact with it. Collective guilt is much harder to recognize and much easier to excuse than individual guilt. The situation in South Africa affords a clear example. If one country opts for total disinvestment and other countries do not follow suit, that action has little effect. Accordingly, it is easy to use the non-action of another as an excuse for one's own refusal to act, with the added motive that one wants these contacts in order to be able to exert pressure. But meanwhile nothing changes. Further, one can blame Western investors, but is not the South African government which instituted the system of apartheid primarily to blame? Every discussion of the guilt of others attracts attention away from those who are really guilty. But in a complex situation such as this, one can also draw the lines of guilt differently. Are not the South African blacks themselves at fault for allowing themselves to accept the role of slaves? If they were collectively to stop working, the economy of South Africa would soon grind to a halt. But they have accommodated themselves.

There is still another complication in the matter of collective guilt. It is the fact that a collective as such is not addressable. "The government," or "American society" does not make such a decision. Decisions are made by people who sit in cabinets, who run trade unions, who are directors of multinationals. Always it is Mr. X or Ms. Y who decides. The collective suggests that the decision of an individual does not have much weight. At least in our society collectives tend to operate in a context of ethical neutrality. It should be clear, however, that responsibility for a collective decision is not distributed over the members, but rests in all its weight on every member. Nor does the government stand by itself. A government speaks in the name of its people. We are all jointly responsible for the decisions the government makes. Every citizen of the United States is personally responsible for the policies pursued by its government with respect to South Africa. Accordingly, every American is also at fault for the continuation of apartheid. One cannot escape responsibility by saying that one votes for a party that favors disinvestment, though it is presently not in power. As long as that party has no responsibility to govern, one is talking into the wind. More important, however, is the fact that while one can vote for another party, demonstrate in the streets, and boycott South African products, one continues in the meantime to participate in the society as a whole. As long as one continues to take advantage of society with its provisions, its social structures, collective-wage agreements, its social security benefits, its monetary system, its streets and highways, its publicity channels, and even its court system, one remains co-responsible for that society and continues to be responsible for its sins. If one were to deny this, one would be saying the same as a multinational, which by its investments helped to maintain the system in South Africa, but which excuses itself by saying that the board members are all personally against apartheid. Dissuading a collective from the pursuit of a wrong policy can only be done from within by fully recognizing that one belongs to its structure, shares responsibility for it, and wants the company to change its policy. Protest is no compensation for shared guilt, only a recognition of it. If one speaks up and says "we are all guilty," that is the beginning of the change, the start of the liberation of all.

As individuals we human beings have a tendency to pass the buck. We tend to point out the mistakes of others. We note the splinter in the eye of another and miss the beam in our own. In the collective that is no different. Within a collective there is similarly a tendency to blame others for the wrong decisions of the community. We would not have done it that way. Looking outward, there is a tendency to attribute blame to another collective, to other parties, to other governments. But that can only serve to keep us from recognizing our own guilt. We can point an accusing finger in the direction of South Africa, but if we are honest we have to recognize that we are all jointly guilty. All together, we uphold the systems from which the kind of conditions that exist in South Africa, in Surinam, or in Chile arise. If people of a given nationality are known for their readiness to point an accusing finger, they may well ask themselves whether it is not to absolve themselves from much guilt.

Nations, governments, parties, and economic powers make decisions. They make choices opting for the course that seems best at the moment. Meanwhile, millions suffer as a result of oppression, poverty, and nationalistic preoccupation with prosperity. If we think or talk through these issues to the end, we end up feeling powerless. The structures to which we belong seem so inert, so impossible to move. As an individual you cannot change them. However, is that true? In the first place, as an individual you can do a great deal to relieve the distress of others, so that they become less dependent on the structures. A person who is no longer at the absolute bottom is less dependent on the system. Here too the drip hollows out the stone. Where increasing numbers of people have some breathing space, the colossus of tyranny has to totter. More essential, however, is what we said with respect to individual guilt: the extension of help can never be a compensation for guilt. Such help by itself, whether it be one or ten percent of our income, is cheap. Help is only really valuable if it is a sign of the acknowledgment of guilt.

Also, in the collective sphere what is primarily important is the acknowledgment of a common responsibility. Everyone who opens his mouth gives voice to this acknowledgment. A person who opens his mouth to acknowledge guilt for his community cannot place himself outside of that community. He cannot point an accusing finger. If he does point a finger, he can only point it to the suffering of countless people. That suffering cannot be compensated for with money, or made up with pretty words or slogans. There is not a single way to make it up. It is a burden of guilt you carry with you and from which you can only be delivered by forgiveness. Forgiveness is a matter of the community in which all are involved. Forgive *us* our debts. Poverty, oppression, hunger—none of these can be attributed to the will of God who has made some poor and who has made some rich, who has given masters and who has given servants. God wills neither the distinction between rich and poor, or that between master and servant. God wills peace, fellowship, and abundance for all. If there is poverty, it is because of what people have done and done against the will of God. We stand before him with the nameless misery of countless millions before our eyes. In our century television shows us how very guilty we are before God. When we look at the daily news, we are powerlessly watching our guilt before a merciful God as people who are merciless to each other. The enormity of our guilt is such that we cannot bear it, nor can we ever make up for it. But God forgives, forgives *us our* debts. The forgiveness of collective debts is an even greater manifestation of grace than the remission of individual debt. The place where our society belongs is the place where we as guilty people pray for forgiveness, in a way which shows that collective guilt and personal guilt are interwoven. The secret of the poets and prophets of Israel is this admission: *we* have sinned. In saying this they confess the guilt in which they are involved for all their people, the people alive at that moment and the people who have gone before.

Especially moving is Daniel's prayer (Daniel 9:4-19). "We have sinned and done wrong and acted wickedly and rebelled, turning aside from thy commandments and ordinances; we have not listened to thy servants the prophets, who spoke in thy name to our kings, our princes, and our fathers, and to all the people of the land. . . . To us, O Lord, belongs confusion of face, to our kings, to our princes, and to our fathers, because we have sinned against thee" (vv. 5, 6, 8). Considering our North American past there is much we can learn from that prayer. Perhaps we are more inclined to say with the Jews in Jesus' day: "If we had lived in the days of our fathers we would not have taken part with them in shedding the blood of the prophets" (Matt. 23:30). But such a denial of one's collective past only exposes one's own guilt. We belong to our ancestors, also in our sin and guilt. "Both we and our fathers have sinned" (Ps. 106:6). Both for them and for ourselves we can only ask forgiveness.

Now one can comment that perhaps this may apply to a believer, but that many North Americans would not dream of asking God for forgiveness as the only one who can break the bondage of guilt. Nor does it seem likely in a pluralist society that, say, the government will do it on behalf of the people. But it is precisely here that the importance of the role of the individual becomes apparent. Everyone who opens his mouth, we said earlier, gives voice on behalf of all to the sense of guilt. Everyone who opens his mouth to pray for forgiveness speaks on behalf of the entire community. Where a believer or a worshiping community confesses the sins of the nation as a whole, they speak as representatives of all. In Daniel's time they probably did not all pray his prayer either. It is the remnant in Israel, the faithful few. According to Jewish tradition, it is the last righteous person on whose prayer the world will be established. Both the humble prayer for forgiveness and the flaming protest on the street are ways in which a society gives expression to its sense of guilt. It is to be hoped that both groups of confessors do not despise each other, but view each other as speaking on behalf of and within the same community to which both belong. If one or the other is excluded, both the protest and the prayer lose their power.

Also, collectively it is true that the confession of a sin before God does not exclude, but includes, confession before one's neighbor. We need to confess our sins to the peoples of Africa, Asia, and America. This confession can be signaled in the extension of help to "make up" for the suffering we have caused. In the absence of a readiness to extend this help, the confession remains empty. But the attitude to which we are primarily called is an attitude of asking, asking for forgiveness which we can only receive as a gift. When the people of the North meet the people of the South, the former are not the ones with something to offer, but the ones who can only receive. A nation that perseveres in its sin and refuses to acknowledge its guilt remains fixed in the past. It is a nation without a future. It will always continue to look for structures which confirm the past, just so the past will not be laid open as one of guilt. When a people confesses its guilt, there arises openness to the future which it can enter when forgiveness has been received. But when another people refuses to forgive, that closes off the future of the first. Then you nail the guilty down in their past.

But you also nail yourself down in your own past. A nation that refuses to forgive the colonial overlord and exploiter is a nation without a future. It imprisons itself in its own injuries, and never becomes healed so that it can enter the future to its own benefit and that of others. If the extension of help is not an act of buying off a bad conscience, an attempt to polish one's own image, and if help is no longer received reluctantly—because, after all, "money does not smell"—but relief is extended as a token of the confession of past sins and it is accepted as a symbol of forgiveness—if all this takes place, the North will experience the miracle that it can give with joy, hesitantly perhaps, afraid to be rejected and uncertain whether the relief will ever be accepted, diffidently standing on the threshold of the South, the exploiter now entering as a beggar. Then the enslaved of the past will have the liberating experience that they can give the greatest gift—forgiveness—to the other nations; and these enslaved can be the road to the future for the erstwhile powerful.

As little as, collectively, the nations find it easy to take the road of confession of guilt, so little do the nations find it easy to take the road of forgiveness. It is left to individuals to raise their voices. It is the great ones of a nation who point out a way that is more excellent than that of industrialization and an increased gross national product—the way of forgiving love. But they are the nation's representatives, the remnant who speak for all. Those who raise their voices in forgiveness recognize those who raise their voices in confession. They meet each other; they constitute the reconciliation of the nations. They are the remnant, but also the new beginning who give shape to the miracle of the grace of a God who wants the nations to be reconciled, and who wants to open the future of mankind. God is the God who makes a highway from Assyria to Egypt so that together with Israel they may serve the Lord (Isa. 19:23-25). In the city of God the Israelites meet the people of Tyre and Philistia (Ps. 87:4). David and Goliath shake hands.

In the name of the God of Israel, the name of Jesus Christ, entire nations have been enslaved and exploited. Bible in hand, people have oppressed people. It is a denial of that God who even lets the accursed

Canaanite Tyrians share in his blessings (Ps. 87). It is a denial of Jesus Christ in whom the middle wall of partition (Eph. 2:14-16) was broken down and who is the Lord of all peoples (Phil. 2:11), in whom there is neither Jew nor Greek, slave or free, male or female (Gal. 3:28).

"Cursed be Canaan" (Gen. 9:25). In the beginning of Israel's life as a nation the Canaanites constituted Israel's biggest threat. According to a remarkable exegesis of Genesis 9, the reference there is to blacks who were cursed by Noah. This curse is said to be still in effect, an argument for viewing blacks as third-class "citizens." According to the text, it is not Ham who is cursed, however, but his son Canaan, the forefather of the Canaanite enemies of Israel. Even if one should trace blacks from Ham by way of Cush (Gen. 10), the curse does not apply to them; the biblical data concerning Cush are positive. Think of Ebedmelech who saved Jeremiah (Jer. 38:7-13) and of the first Christian from among the gentiles, the Ethiopian eunuch (Acts 8:26-39), even before the proselyte Cornelius (Acts 10). In any case it is wrong to use the table of the nations to oppress nations. What counts above all is that the accursed of Genesis 9:25 is blessed by the God of Israel, named after his city (Ps. 87:4).

What has been said above about relations between white and black, rich and poor, applies in all situations where collectivities clash. It applies to relations between social groups or classes (also when they are euphemistically called "social partners"). It applies to relations between East and West. It applies to relations between different church denominations. In the name of God wars have been waged and in his name people were burned at the stake. In the name of the preservation of a free Christian culture Hanoi was set on fire and the Vietnamese were attacked with napalm. In the name of the preservation of Christian civilization nuclear bombs and atomic rockets are being stockpiled. In the name of a classless society in which all people are equal citizens some are sent into psychiatric institutions. In the name of the liberation of the enslaved nuclear tests are being conducted. As though a Christian society can ever be based on the power of weapons and the conquest of enemies, instead of on faith in the unconquerable power of the love of Christ, who by his Spirit fills the lives of people. That is the power which hollows out all structures and systems from within. By that power Roman emperors fell. But after the fall of the emperors, the church exchanged the power of a victorious faith for the power of the sword and thereby denied its God. Nor can a classless society exist if it is founded on oppression. No equality is possible where one group of people has to fear weapon power of another group. Equality can only exist where people and groups of people confess their sins to each other and forgive each other, so they can leave old things behind and address themselves to the future. That is the road God wants people to take. If the earth is not a garden of peace and justice, it is not God who is to blame but people—people who refuse to give precedence to each other, to be beggars before God and each other. It is the fault of people who cling to the past; to their own past in order to cherish it and to put a good face on it, and to the past of others in order to continue to distrust them, who continue to deny them as people with possibilities of renewal, by a God who in Christ, the Lord of the world, made a new beginning with people.

If someone is in the hospital because his neighbor has pounded him on the head with a hammer, the blame clearly lies with a human being. That is true whether it is exclusively the fault of the neighbor, or also, and perhaps primarily, his own fault for endlessly provoking his neighbor so that at last in a blind rage he reached for the hammer. When blacks were dragged from Africa as less than beasts and then shipped to America on Dutch and English ships, it was the fault of humans that others underwent this suffering. If people in the interior of Bangladesh died of starvation while grain was rotting on the quays, then humans were to blame for their death. Much suffering is attributable to what people do or fail to do.

But is that true for all suffering? Can we blame people for the suffering caused by crop failures, famines, diseases, earthquakes? Natural disasters occur outside of human responsibility. What can a human being do about an earthquake or a volcanic eruption? What can he do about a flood or a crop failure resulting from drought? Who controls the forces of nature? Still, we must not be too quick to draw conclusions and to look for the causes of this suffering apart from man. If some of the money used for the arms race had been set aside for the reclamation of deserts, then people in Sahel countries would not have to suffer hunger. If people built bigger and better dikes, there would be fewer floods. We may attribute the great flood which occurred in Zeeland, the Netherlands, in 1953 to the chastising hand of God; but a Delta plan before that year would have prevented it. If people did not choose for economic reasons to make their homes in areas of great risk from floods and earthquakes, natural disasters would not claim so many victims. Lot still chooses to live in the Jordan valley on the plains of Sodom (Gen. 13:10ff.). Though it is dangerous, it is also fertile and rich. If all the money spent on sport were used to combat infectious diseases, would not malaria have gone the way of smallpox? If on the budgets of nations and alliances the items for space shuttles, F-15s, F-16s, and MiG fighter jets were transferred to cancer research, would not the cure of these diseases be much closer? People make choices. They make choices which may result in disaster and the suffering of millions. Some choices result in double suffering. The arms program, for example, stands in the way of the peaceful use of the means used, and at the same time holds the world in the bondage of fear.

God gives food to all flesh (Ps. 136:25). He opens his hand and satisfies the desire of every living thing (Ps. 145:16). God gave the earth as a garden to dwell in (Gen. 2). The earth is the Lord's and its fullness (Ps. 24:1), but he has given that fullness to man (Gen. 1:28ff.). Humans, however, have violated the earth and continue to violate it. By overuse, pollution, and mismanagement, the earth is exhausted. Although people see before their eyes what is happening, they continue these practices, so that environmental disaster is taking shape on a scale that defies the imagination. Nature is resilient; it can adapt itself endlessly. In the place where forests affected by acid rain used to be, and in the eroded soil of former tropical rain forests, new life systems will arise. Nature will survive the disaster. But whether fragile human beings will survive it—certainly in the numbers in which they now populate the world—is a question. World hunger is not attributable to the fact that God has created the world with inadequate resources. There could be enough, even abundance, for everyone. If there is hunger, the reason is that man is a poor manager of the earth. There is much suffering, ordinarily attributed to nature or to chance, which has to be attributed to man. Much suffering that people view as the striking hand of God is nothing other than the blows which people administer to themselves and to each other.

Still, there remains suffering which even in the most indirect way cannot be blamed on man. For the sake of clarity, let us take an odd example: if some time tonight a meteor came whooshing from space and struck the heart of New York, and hundreds of thousands of people, perhaps even millions died, then there is no human who could be accused of this disaster. Humans can prevent many bad situations or arm themselves against great misfortune, but certain events are totally beyond their control. However, before we say that, we must first be profoundly familiar with the human situations which are not or need not be beyond their control. And where suffering is bound up with human responsibility, there we are talking about human sin and human guilt.

Suffering is a universal experience. Throughout the world, to its most distant corner, there is suffering. There has been no time, no year, no day in history in which people did not suffer. The universality of suffering points to the universality of human guilt. Throughout the world, to its most distant corners, there is human guilt. There is no period, year, or day in history in which people did not sin. The Heidelberg Catechism rightly says that we daily increase our debt (Answer 13). From the universality of sin one could draw the conclusion that it is an inescapable fate, a feature that comes with human nature, which inevitably, over and over, assumes form in new deeds. This conviction might lead one to a habitual tendency to acquiesce in the situation of sin and guilt. One could then still speak of forgiveness, but figure that this forgiveness would have no effect on future action. That, however, would be a total denial of sin. Sin's primary character is that of an act, as Herman Wiersinga has correctly stated. He was not the first to say this, though few have accentuated this point as sharply as he. When we speak of sin, we are not talking about a universal fate, but about human acts proceeding from human responsibilities.

According to Wiersinga in the history of the church there has occurred a naturalization of sin, by which it was deprived of its active character and hence of its guilt. "Wisdom theology has often succumbed to the temptation to view sin as a tragic fate. Repeatedly the guilt-character of sin was eclipsed by its character as fate."[2] That, says Wiersinga, is in conflict with Scripture. "I think that the biblical tradition understands sin as act" (p. 76). "To sin" is a verb, both in the Old (p. 84) and in the New Testament (p. 92). Wiersinga does not deny that there are fatal aspects to the human situation (p. 80), but he refuses to call them sin. Sin consists in acquiescing in that situation (pp. 80-84), and not doing anything to enter into new relations with people. Doom-thinking arising from a mood of powerlessness is a sin against hope (pp. 160-167).

When people speak of the universality of sin they often refer to Genesis 3, the story of the Fall. But it is precisely the beginning of Genesis which shows with such clarity that sin is not inherent in creation. The creation is good. Sin arises from a human act. Man plucks the forbidden fruit and eats it. Man was responsible for the garden. Man knew transgressing the commandment would have consequences. Still he took and ate. That is the basic pattern of human sin. Man is responsible. He is graced with responsibility for the world in which he lives. He is responsible for the other human beings with whom he lives and with whom he has been placed in a society. Man knows that to ignore this responsibility has consequences which go far beyond his ability to survey. But he takes and eats. He oppresses and exploits. He overuses the land and pollutes it. By man sin came into the world, that occurring by way of one human deed, says Paul in Romans 5, with all the consequences in suffering that human sin brought with it, the final one being death. When Paul links sin in its collective character with the deed of

---

2. Herman Wiersinga, *Doem of daad: een boek over zonde* (Baarn, 1982), p. 79.

Adam, that is not to excuse the deeds of others. It is rather to set forth the guilt of all. "Therefore you have no excuse, O man, whoever you are" (Rom. 2:1). All are under the power of sin (Rom. 3:9). If Adam is man, the head of humankind, then every human has Adam's character. He poses his deed, he sins, he suffers the consequences, even when he wants to blame others. It is easy to blame others, to attribute to them the responsibility for the misfortune sin brings with it. It is easy to blame the conduct of our colonial ancestors for the world's poverty. But then again we deny the deed-character of sin. Then we would only be the victims of the sins of the past, and our children would only be the victims of the abuse of the soil by other people living now. But when the subject is sin, we are not primarily victims but first of all agents. If the world suffers it is because of *our* sins. I am personally not excluded. If we acquiesce in the situation that has arisen, we incur new guilt. If we view our situation as a consequence of the sin of the fathers, we are again seeing sin as fate, and the incentive to change that arises from the acknowledgment of guilt is lacking.

The prophets of Israel already opposed this attitude. Ezekiel reacts to a current proverb: "The fathers have eaten sour grapes, and the children's teeth are set on edge" (Ezek. 18:2). The prophet fundamentally rejects this proverb. Each person is directly responsible for his own situation. The Israelites reproach God, saying that though the fathers have sinned *they* must bear the consequences. Therefore they say, "The way of the Lord is not just." God's reply is clear: "O house of Israel, are my ways not just? Is it not your ways that are not just?" (18:29). They themselves must repent and act lawfully and righteously. They must be faithful and merciful before God and neighbor (18:5-9). And everyone will himself experience the consequences of his actions (18:20). For anyone to acquiesce in a situation of sin as doom is itself unjust. So also Deutero-Isaiah described it. When Israel abandoned hope, acquiescing in the situation of the exile, this prophet called on them to forsake their wicked ways and to return to the Lord, the God who regards the future as a way of unheard of new possibilities (Isa. 55:6-13).

It seems so obvious to say, "God does not will sin." But it seems the implications of that statement are not getting through to us: if we want to forsake the way of sin, we have God on our side. If from within the situation of our sin and that of our fathers we wish to enter upon a new future of right and justice, we have God on our side. His path leads to an earth which is on its way to being a garden of peace and justice. The king whom he calls is the king who delivers the needy and crushes the oppressor (Ps. 72:4). God leads the way in delivering the earth from the bondage of sin.

139

The prophets speak of a divine initiative toward a new covenant, a new people, a new world. Over and over it is God who takes the initiative. He is creatively at work to build the future. The subject of the new future of justice and peace is consistently that of the divine "I." One prophet after another, speaking in his name, says "I will make a new covenant with the house of Israel and the house of Judah" (Jer. 31:31). "For behold, I create new heavens and a new earth" (Isa. 65:17). For that reason Israel is called not to remember the former things, because God is doing a new thing (Isa. 43:18f.). Walking in his footsteps people shall be enabled to beat their swords into plowshares and their spears into pruning hooks (Isa. 2:4). For God will destroy the chariot and the war horse for the peace of the nations (Zech. 9:10). The authors of the New Testament epistles see the promise of the divine initiative fulfilled in Christ. In the resurrection of Christ God opened the new future. And us he has made alive together with him (Eph. 2:1). So we are called to the freedom of serving one another unencumbered by the powers of the past (Gal. 5:14; 6:1ff.).

When God leads the way to the new future, he does that in three ways. In the first place, he grants forgiveness. We have already seen that the guilt of the past pins us down in the past and keeps the door to the future closed. God atones for sin. Deutero-Isaiah, the prophet who as no other depicts God's possibilities for the future, begins by announcing pardon for the sin of the past (Isa. 40:1f.). Because guilt has been removed and broken hearts have been healed, courage and freedom to enter upon the future now arise. Part of the new covenant proclaimed by Jeremiah is that God will no more remember the sins of Israel (Jer. 31:34). When Paul speaks of the new life in which we shall live for the new righteousness, then what precedes this is that in the death of Christ our old life has died and we are saved by his grace (Rom. 6:1-14). The cross of reconciliation as the gift of God's inexpressible grace precedes the resurrection to a new life—and it is the only way to a resurrection. God gives to people space for a new life by liberating them from their past. Even the fratricidal Cain, the man who is in debt to his neighbor par excellence, receives a sign so that those who find him will not kill him (Gen. 4:15). Cain's fear of the consequences of his misdeed, a fear which made him dread to continue his life, is removed by God. That is the length to which the grace of God goes.

In the second place, God leads the way into the future by the renewal of people. People may arise to a new life. The Spirit of God transforms their hearts and hands for the cause of righteousness, so that they themselves begin to forge their swords and spears into instruments of peace. People are stuck in their past. Even when they know and will that which is good, they do not do it. They are stuck in the service of sin. That is the situation depicted in Romans 7. The entire discussion concerning whether this chapter speaks of Paul before or after his conversion is essentially of no importance. This chapter is about the human being, Christian or not, who is locked into structures which keep him locked in sin. These structures manifest themselves everywhere. They are the psychological structures because of which he keeps choosing sin. They are the accrued mental conditioning from which he keeps lapsing into his mistakes. They are the social structures by which his environment locks him into a fixed role. They are the economic structures in which you have to fight for your livelihood and are obliged to live in the mode of having, getting, and holding. They are the political structures in which you cannot escape the armed might used to establish the country's own structures. Enchained in every way in the structures of sin which bring with them misfortune and death, cause judgment and destruction, and finally ruin people, you cry out in desperation: "O wretched man that I am! Who will deliver me from this body of death?" (Rom. 7:24). But that is not the last word: "Thanks be to God through Jesus Christ, our Lord!" (v. 25). In Christ there is release from bondage, for his Spirit has set us free from the law of sin and death and led us into the freedom of life (Rom. 8:2). In Christ renewal is possible and real. Where the Spirit of Christ is, there in the place of sin grows love. In the place of estrangement an encounter occurs. Where exploitation thrived, tender loving care begins to burgeon. Where the Spirit of Christ teaches people, the spirit of their minds is renewed toward kindness and tenderheartedness (Eph. 4:23, 32). This renewal of our minds means acknowledging the will of God, "what is good and acceptable and perfect" (Rom. 12:2). From the vine God has planted spring the branches which bear fruit in mutual love (John 15:1-17).

In the third place, God leads the way to a future of righteousness by preventing an accumulation of sin. When God's hand is in history, it opposes sin. In Genesis 20 we read that God said to Abimelech: "It was I who kept you from sinning against me" (v. 6). God himself sees to it that a heathen king will not commit an act which would raise the walls of guilt between Israel and the nations even higher. Not so peaceful are the texts which say that God will destroy the wicked. Remember in section 8 we learned that God is a God who punishes. In the present context we may view God's judgment especially as a cleansing of the earth. When God arises to do battle, it is so that the wicked will not continue to commit injustice and violence and that justice and peace may flourish. Even the flood is designed to make room for a reborn earth overarched by the rainbow of God's faithfulness. If God rigorously

141

cleanses the earth, it is not because he himself wants to do it. He only does it because mankind had made the cleansing necessary. On account of the impenitence of people sin accumulates; as a result injustice grows and suffering increases, into a tidal wave of misfortune that can no longer be topped. It is a saving thing that God heads off the unrighteous. If God did not intervene, the earth would be consumed by its own violence. "If it had not been the Lord who was on our side, . . . then over us would have gone the raging waters" (Ps. 124:1, 5).

God leads the way into the future. That creates for us humans the possibility, in forgiveness and renewal, to travel the road to the future. God has taken away the paralysis of sin in order that we should forgive each other as individuals, groups, and nations, and remove the barriers which keep us from going into the future together. God sends the Spirit of Jesus Christ; he speaks the words of liberation; he calls us in admonition to a new life. But people offer so much resistance. Sometimes one picks up a few weak signals of renewal, but they are soon engulfed by the old voices, the old structures. People continue to make the wrong choices. Lot, Abraham's nephew, has not left the scene since the coming of the Messiah, nor are Jacob and Laban gone. Entire nations are still being led by windbags who blow themselves up into giants. The rich still join field to field and build their arched palaces—as though the Lord of the world were not the poor man who had no place to lay his head. People have not changed since the days of Amos. Amos fulminated against the rich. When a poor man has been forced to give his garments in pledge to another down-and-outer, he does not get it back until he has paid the last penny of his debt. The poor man has less money than the rich man, but the same mentality. Poverty by itself does not say anything about justice and love. The feet of the poor man do not automatically go the way of peace. Only he who is poor for righteousness' sake is truly poor. But who is poor because he sold all he had and distributed the proceeds to the poor? The God who dwells in heaven leads the way to a new world. God is enthroned in heaven and Jesus sits on his right hand. The Lord looks down from heaven to see if there are any that act wisely and do good (Ps. 14:2; 53:2). The psalmist then says he found none. "There is none that does good, no, not one" (Ps. 14:3; 53:3). Is the situation today any different? Who is the one righteous person? Let him or her stand up and report! But who, looking at the world's suffering and knowing what he himself helped to bring about, will call himself righteous? Everyone has gone astray. On account of one's personal and common guilt no one can squarely look another in the eye. We are all to blame for the fact that the curse remains intact. Every sin builds on a foundation of common guilt. Every sin adds to the measure of common suffering. Every sin makes its contribution to the death which has passed to all.

When we speak as we are doing about the collectiveness and universality of sin we enter upon terrain that in classical theology fell under the heading of original sin. In contemporary theology original sin is an embattled concept.

"Original sin" does not literally occur in Scripture. Psalm 51 and Romans 5 come closest to the subject. They are also the texts which usually serve as *loca probanda* for the doctrine of original sin. Romans 5, however, does not deal with the hereditariness of sin but with its universality. Materially the two concepts are closely related, but they are not identical. Psalm 51:5 reads: "Behold, I was brought forth in iniquity, and in sin did my mother conceive me." The intent of the text is not, anymore than Romans 5, to furnish a universal doctrine of original sin, but to put into words the totality of the sinfulness of the poet. His sin is not something incidental, but something interwoven with his whole being from its very first beginning.

Though original sin may not literally be in Scripture, the concept is inseparably connected with the corporate kind of thinking that emerges over and over in the Old and the New Testament. People are not monads but members of a body. It is one for all, as Paul asserts in Romans 5.

The great promoter of the idea of original sin in church history was Augustine. Although a variety of influences, Neoplatonic and Manichean, may have played a role, what was decisive for its development was the theme of Psalm 51: the sense of being a sinner right down to the center of one's being. A man does not just incidentally commit an occasional sin; it is structural, and only the liberating grace of God can liberate him and give him a new life with a new structure. In this structural evil all are involved; no one escapes it. It is congenital. Accordingly, the confession of original sin was not a general theory but a concrete confession of guilt. For various modern theories, see Wiersinga, pp. 63-68. He himself explicitly rejects the idea of original sin (p. 67).

It is a question whether it is correct to reject the idea of original sin. If we reject it, we are withdrawing from the collectivity of the human race and from there it is only a small step to washing our hands in the sovereign innocence of individuality. To give up the teaching of original sin is but one step removed from the assertion made in Germany after World War II relative to the concentration camps: "Wir haben es nicht gewusst" ("We did not know about it"). Only we must view original sin correctly. Not, in the first place, so as to be discouraged by it and say, "After all we are only sinners; we will never achieve anything anyway." The medieval view that baptism constitutes the washing away of original sin is not that unattractive. To enter into salvation in Christ creates new possibilities; the curse is broken wherever he appears. The attributed grace of Protestantism need

143

not exclude the infused grace of Roman Catholicism. They belong together as the one gift of forgiveness and renewal.

In addition we must not use original sin as a stale platitude with which to gloss over real sin. The situation here is no different from that of individual sin. In the latter case too, the general confession, "I am so sinful" can be a way to avoid looking at the concrete sins committed. No more than individual sin, original sin is then a general principle that does not have to be fleshed out. Original sin is sin and guilt which one generation takes over from another. Understood as such, it manifests itself in various ways.

a. Certain structures already exist and are in place. The one generation forms structures which have consequences for the next. The colonial structures our fathers have formed underlie the economic system in which we now live. Their sins of exploitation are continued in our sins of exploitation. However, we are not only the victims of these structures (and as victims no less responsible for those we inherited, since we confirm them) but also their producers. The structures we now form are the structures in which our children will have to live—at least if we leave them anything to survive with. The structures of Europe formed in the forties and the fifties entail that we, and presumably the generations that succeed us, will have to live in a divided world that is armed, not just to the teeth, but into space. The choice for coal or nuclear energy is decisive both for the environment of tomorrow (acid or radiation?), and for the economic power structures of the future. In the choice of energy the future still lies intellectually within reach. But the same continuation of our choices is operative in everything. The caricatures and theories of today are the realities of tomorrow. Our ideas create the world, and once in effect we cannot retrieve them. Today's formation of images concerning races and nationalities by generalizations, jokes, and caricatures creates the relations between the races and nationalities of the future.

b. The sins of the fathers too, by character and nurture, manifest themselves in the children. In the case of human choices it is hard to tell to what extent they are free, to what degree they are determined by nurture or the wider environment, and to what extent they arise as a result of genetic patterns. Presumably psychology will shift from one to another for the foreseeable future, with ethics at its heels. Undoubtedly, it is none of these factors by itself. In any case the choices are not made merely on the basis of pure individual freedom. Descent and environment certainly play a role. The character of a person is determined in part by what his parents were. It is the folk wisdom of the question, "Who is your father?" "From what nest does she come?" Positively or negatively, children bear the family stamp. Timothy follows the pattern of the

144

faith of his grandmother Lois and his mother Eunice (2 Tim. 1:5). The royal chronicles, in sketching the story of the kings of Judah, in each case report the name of the king's mother, a detail not mentioned about the kings of Israel. They are the sons of their fathers—enough said. But the kings of Judah are all descendants of David. One gets to know them by noting the line of their mother's descent. Who are you? Do you confirm the faith of your mothers or follow in the sins of your fathers? What you are, you are not only for yourself but also for your children.

c. We can also take original sin to mean that every child born is a new link in the chain of sin. No child is sinless. Sin is inherent in people, interwoven with their entire existence. No one is exempt from it. In the classic Reformed formulary for baptism the parents are asked to confess that their children "are conceived and born in sin." Some people have trouble with those words. How can one say of a newborn baby, which cannot yet make decisions, that it is already sinful? In the first place, it is a question whether one can say that a baby cannot sin. A baby that is only a few weeks old can already be thoroughly spoiled. The possibility of being spoiled implies the possibility of pursuing one's own interest. A baby knows very well how to get what he or she wants. In the process of the development of human attitude there really is no break between holy innocence and self-interest. The later life only confirms what was already present earlier. If there is a break, it is the break of conversion from egoism to the service of righteousness. However, this comment is not the most important. More essential is a second thought which implies that when as parents you say that your child is conceived and born in sin you acknowledge that this child is one in the chain of human generations, and does not stand outside the fellowship of others. There is no one who realizes perfect righteousness in life. Every human being has his or her flaws. Every human being fails. Every human being sins. By saying "Our child has been conceived and born in sin," we confess that "we believe that our child is not different from all those other children. We believe that our child also is sinful, carries sin within itself, and will sin. We really do not foster the illusion that our child will be perfect. And we do not want to reserve an exclusive place of honor for our child in the midst of all other children." Viewed in this way, the acknowledgment of original sin is a matter of realism and its confession a matter of solidarity. The denial of original sin, on the other hand, is itself a sin: the sin of not being in solidarity with all other sinners.

In classic dogmatic theology a distinction is made between original guilt and original pollution. Original pollution (*maculatio; peccatum inhaerens*) consists in the sinful nature every human being inherits. Original pollution means that every human being is a sinner, has sin within, and will also commit sin in life. These concretizations refer to original pollution: we need not entertain the illusion that a generation will arise that will all at once live sinlessly in righteousness. It is the sin one inherits from his parents and then proceeds to confirm and realize. Hence it is called *maculatio*, defilement, pollution. You are born a polluted person in a polluted world. By using the expression "conceived and born in sin" people have, historically, often posited a connection with sexuality. Not only was the pollution said to be transmitted but it was also said to be *caused* by the act of sexual intercourse and the conception which followed. In the nature of the case this notion is closely linked with a negative view of sexuality.

We already encounter this idea in Augustine.[3] Sin is rooted in concupiscence, which is the consequence of the primal sin of Adam. Concupiscence is not in the last place sexual desire. On account of this aspect of original sin, Wiersinga has turned against the whole concept. The notion that sin is inherited suggests to him that it is transmitted by a biological act.[4]

Also, if the linking of original sin with conception should be a denial of what original sin essentially is, we still cannot dispense with the concept, unless there is another which carries with it the same universality and carryover without these or other undesirable connotations. As long as we do not have such a word—I know of none and do not think it is necessary to come up with one—we shall have to maintain the word. A negative valuation of sexuality need not be incorporated in the concept of original sin any more than the transmission of a handicap needs to convey a negative valuation of sex. Negative associations with sexuality do not arise from thinking about original sin, but constitute another way of articulating the deep-rootedness of evil: sexuality is sin par excellence and every human being is actively or passively involved in it. No one escapes it. Because both lines of thought—the universality of concupiscence and original sin, as different versions of the fact that no one is free from sin—express the same viewpoint, the two are often, though not necessarily, interwoven. Augustine coupled the two; the ascetics regarded universal concupiscence as the real evil; I prefer the idea of original sin. The responsibility of every human in all his structural contexts can be better indicated with that concept than with the concept of innate primal desire. It is all too easy with this last concept to restrict evil to a narrow view of the seventh commandment, to the neglect of

3. Augustine, *De nuptiis et Concupiscienta,* I, 23, 25.
4. Wiersinga, *Doem of daad,* pp. 56, 64ff.

other sins. Besides, the main line of Scripture on sexuality is not negative. In Scripture there is some agitation against sexual evils (often having a religious coloring), but as a rule sex is not wrong. Again, one must not exaggerate the positive biblical valuation of sexuality because there are also indications of a positive valuation of abstinence.

Most familiar is the passage in 1 Cor. 7. Here Paul accepts marriage but prefers to remain unmarried, relating this not only to himself but to others, saying he wishes they could all remain single as he was (v. 8). One can attribute this to the "near-expectation" of the eschaton by Paul, but it is a question whether this motif has not been too easily employed to solve a variety of problems in the letters. In any case, Paul leaves room for different options and deems it desirable that everyone should live in accordance with the charisma each has received. Other texts in the New Testament do not stop there. In the synoptic gospels we are told that in the resurrection from the dead people do not marry (Matt. 22:30; Mark 12:25; Luke 20:35f.). In the world to come people will be asexual, like the angels. Accordingly, sexuality belongs to the perishable things of this world. This does not imply a rejection of it, but it does strongly relativize it. In later texts within the New Testament this tendency is confirmed. Revelation (14:4) writes concerning the 144 redeemed of the Lamb that they are *parthenoi* (virgins), seeing "they have not defiled themselves with women." Jude 23 speaks of hating "the garment spotted by the flesh." Of early Christian movements which viewed abstinence as truly Christian, such as the Encratites, Montanists, and many of the Gnostics, one cannot say therefore that they had no support in canonical literature at all.

Another argument for not coupling original sin to sexuality is that sexual intercourse is a single human act surrounded by a set of feelings peculiar to that act. By connecting concupiscence and original sin the idea could arise that original sin originates each time from this single act whereas in fact the incidental nature of that act militates against the principle of original sin. It is not the recurrent act which calls forth the sin; sin is an essential human datum from generation to generation which manifests itself in all human activity, including sexual. By referring to the sexual act as source, one invalidates the absolutely collective character of original sin; in that case the cause and effect of sinful human acts are reversed.

Besides original pollution, there is original guilt *(peccatum imputatum)*, even harder to place for twentieth-century man. Can the sin of one person be attributed to another as guilt? It would seem that Ezekiel 18 radically rejects this notion. "The soul that sins shall die" (v. 4)—period. Every person is responsible for himself. We already saw, however, that Ezekiel 18 is directed against an attitude of inertia. If, appealing to the sins of the fathers, one refuses to repent, one carries full responsibility for oneself. But there are also other lines of thought in Scripture, also in Ezekiel, which point precisely to the guilt of the fathers which the children bear. The iniquity of the fathers is visited upon the children, says the decalogue (Exod. 20:5). Not infrequently, the guilt of the fathers is confessed as one's own. There is a profound sense of common responsibility. One belongs to the group which is both extended in space and in time. One is co-responsible for what the group does. For what one person does all are responsible. The entire German nation is responsible for Hitler's actions. No one can excuse himself by saying: "Wir haben es nicht gewusst" ("We did not know about it"). And the truly great ones have been willing to acknowledge it and to suffer for it. They have been willing to bear the guilt of their people right into death, such as Dietrich Bonhoeffer. All Europeans are responsible for the Second World War; no one can back out of responsibility, not only because of what happened in Versailles in 1919 but also because of the dynamics of European culture which called forth the demonism of this regime and which, if we do not repent, will again call forth this demonism. There are signs aplenty.

Mankind is a collective entity no one can step outside of. We are a biological unity; we have the same chromosomes and a common gene pool. The person who refuses to feel responsible for the guilt of this collective of past and present places himself outside of this fellowship, whatever his reasons. He puts himself in the position of belonging to a select group which is not responsible for everything this collective contains within it. Discrimination is right around the corner. The confession of original guilt is the best remedy against every form of discrimination, self-elevation, or group formation. We are all in the same boat. No one can be excused. The acknowledgment not only of original pollution but also of original guilt is the real solidarity with all human beings past and present. That is the idea of the corporate personality which so often comes to the fore in Scripture: if one member suffers, all suffer. If one member is guilty, all are guilty. Whoever would deny this also has to deny the converse: if one member offers atonement, all share in it. If we reject this thinking in terms of collective unities, together with collective guilt and collective grace, we remove the core of at least the Pauline concept of atonement: one for all, by one man's obedience the many (intended inclusively, not exclusively) will be made righteous (Rom. 5:19).

Accordingly, humans share in responsibility for the suffering of the world; they are collectively guilty. No one can exclude himself. No one alive does not join in adding stones to the walls of guilt. No one can say that the common guilt is not his own. If all sin, that can never serve as an excuse for myself, as if that fact would diminish the deed-character

148

of my sin and the responsibility I bear. The collectivity is rather a multiplication of my own responsibility and an enlargement of the deed I committed to the massive dimensions of the billions who lived and are still living. My deed is the deed which confirms that all these deeds are opposition to God who created the world to be a garden; opposition to God who in Christ leads the way in renewal. Human deeds have made the world into a region of suffering, violence, and misery. Human deeds bring about nameless suffering. And every deed I commit—or, even stronger, my very presence in this world—confirms this state of affairs. If I did not believe in the unlimited possibilities of this merciful God, who is the gracious one because he is God and not man (Hos. 11:9), who has unlimited possibilities of forgiveness and renewal at his disposal, I would succumb under a burden of sin. At the same time I have to acknowledge that I cannot comprehend what that guilt is which mankind carries and which I carry as a human among humans. Man has posited deeds. Of mighty man the truth is as Faust said: "In the beginning was the deed." But the deeds of man, from the beginning to the present, have created a world of suffering which could only be saved by the one divine person who became man, who from the beginning was the Word.

In God's world man has accomplished something. Man has also created something. He has created sin and suffering. We may ask ourselves whether man was capable of that from within himself. Is man so creative that he can call something into being out of nothing? Is the human will so effective that it can call forth something that can be really threatening to the creative action of God? Nicolas of Cusa has said that man is a *deuteros theos*, a second God. But does man have this power apart from the power given him? Man is god; that is a thesis which can be argued. But he is and will always remain god in a secondary way. He is god because God has said, "You are gods" (Ps. 82:6). But God can just as easily deprive this secondary god of his divine status (Ps. 82:7). He is god with regard to his fellow man as Moses was to Aaron (Exod. 4:16), but before the holy God he has to remove the shoes from his feet (Exod. 3:5). Man may be almost divine, as the poet of Psalm 8 says, but he remains the fragile human being of whom the same poet says: "What is man that thou art mindful of him?" Would this creature be able to bring about something in the creation of the Holy One which the Holy One himself has not willed? Many New Testament data show rather that sin is a power to which man is subject and which surpasses him in power.

We have now arrived at the same point as before in section 9. Reference to the guilt of man is a foreground solution. We must continue our questioning. How can man possibly pose this deed? But as before

149

we can only proceed after a long pause in our thinking. We can only proceed if we ourselves thoroughly realize our own responsibility in the matter of evil. And if we then proceed, we can only proceed cautiously, afraid to go too fast, thus covering up the real evil we commit.

13. GOD'S PERMISSION

IF ONE ATTRIBUTES EVIL TO POWERS OUTSIDE OF GOD, BE IT DEMONIC POWERS or human responsibility, one safeguards the recognition of the goodness of God. Unaffected by evil proceeding from another source, God remains pure. But at the same time the omnipotence of God is subjected to great pressure. Now we can say that because in this chapter our fundamental starting point is the goodness of God, we have to ignore the omnipotence of God for the time being. But that is not how this starting point has functioned in the history of theology. Attempts were regularly made, when starting with God's goodness, to create as much space as possible for God's omnipotence, just as when people proceeded from his omnipotence they sought as much as possible to do justice to God's goodness. From this last endeavor emerge models like that of the chastising Father; all things come from God—that is primary—but he does what he does out of goodness. In the same way one can say God's goodness is primary, and at the same time try to find a model in which his omnipotence does not disappear. For then God appears on the scene as the powerless benevolence who has to stand by as powers or people, or the two together, destroy his work.

A classic solution to this dilemma has been found by speaking about the permission of God. God does not will evil; he himself does not act in it; it does not come from his hands, but he passively permits it. If he wanted, he could prevent evil, but for certain reasons perhaps known only to himself he doesn't. In support of this view a distinction is made between the *providentia* and the *praevisio* of God. *Providentia* means that in all things God provides—which accords with the usual doctrine of divine providence. God is the almighty and provides all things both good and evil. In addition there is *praevisio*, which means that God sees all things beforehand. God has the foreknowledge of it but does not himself provide it. It is foreknowledge *(praescientia)*. In his omniscience God sees beforehand that a murder will occur, but he himself is not the cause of it; he only refrains from preventing it. He passively permits it to happen. In the history of dogmatics this notion was picked up over and over to escape the dilemma between divine impotence and divine malevolence. But on the other hand there was intense opposition to the idea of permission.

Theologians who emphasize providence are as a rule declared opponents of the idea of permission. Calvin calls it "a foolish cavil,"[5] basing himself on Augustine's doctrine of providence. Heppe is more positive and discusses permission at length.[6] "Divine providence governs the bad as well as the good actions of men, the latter by an *actio efficax*, the former by a *permissio efficax.*"[7] In contemporary works of dogmatics one usually does not encounter permission as a theologoumenon. In its place one finds other concepts which express the same or comparable thoughts. Emil Brunner speaks of the self-limitation of God.[8] Berkhof speaks of the "defenselessness" of God.[9] We already referred to Barth's ideas about the relationship of God to nothingness. Those theologians who make the free will of man central do not need the idea of permission. They restrict God's relationship to evil to *prescientia* (foreknowledge). A classic example is the early theology of the Remonstrants.

In upholding the thesis of the permission of God one runs the risk that in order to leave both the goodness and the omnipotence of God unblemished one in fact abandons both. What kind of goodness is it that tolerates the occurrence of murder? What kind of omnipotence is it that can stand by passively? Far-reaching objections can be advanced against the idea of permission:

a. How can a good God make a creature that can sin? It may be that God did not cause every individual human act to come from his hand, but did confer the possibility of sinning given with humanity. This question is bound to arise every time; when basing oneself on the goodness of God, one seeks to safeguard his omnipotence.

b. Can God ever adopt a passive stance? Is God not always the actively present one? Does not his presence call forth that which he wills? Is not God's willing ever effective, as Barth has stated?[10] God cannot will passively. He is *actus purissimus*, the purest act, solely and purely act, as the classic formulation has it.

c. The most important objection is that passive permission does not relieve one of responsibility. In the doctrine of sin we are not only told

5. Calvin, *Institutes*, I.18.1, 2 (also see II.4.3).

6. Heppe, *Reformed Dogmatics*, 251ff.

7. Ibid., p. 274.

8. Emil Brunner, *The Christian Doctrine of God Dogmatics*, vol. 1 (London: Lutterworth Press, 1949), p. 251.

9. Berkhof, *Christian Faith*, 133-140.

10. Barth, *Church Dogmatics* III, 3, 50, p. 351.

of sin as an act but also of sin as omission.[11] If you were in a position to prevent evil but did not do it, you also would be guilty. If someone drowns in a canal while a trained swimmer stands by watching from the side, the latter is not free from blame. We can hardly praise him for his goodness. It is not for nothing that criminal law admits the possibility of guilt through gross negligence. This applies to negligence when evil strikes another. One might defend the thesis that it does not apply to evil committed by another. One cannot enter someone else's position of responsibility. But this objection is not well founded. If my son stands ready, stone in hand, to throw it through my neighbor's store window because he has a quarrel with the neighbor's boy, and I see it but do nothing—I only stand by watching—then I am right in expecting a damage claim instead of friendly words from my neighbor. Responsibility for what you were in a position to prevent goes far beyond that which concerns the actions of your children. If I could have prevented someone's deep misfortune at the hands of someone else, and I did not do it, I am responsible for the suffering of the unfortunate. If God permits the enslavement, murder, and ruin of people at the hands of other people, then God is co-responsible for these crimes, at least if he was able to prevent it. We may attempt to defend the holiness of God, his inviolability, but what is the point of this endeavor if by doing it we can no longer be honest and open with him? If we want to place God in a storm-free domain to safeguard him from all the questions humans ask and shield him from all responsibility for things for which we call human beings to account, then is he still the living God who wants to be there for man? Therefore, if it is true that there is permission on the side of God, we call him to account. And we understand Calvin's furor when he fulminates against the idea of permission because he cannot believe that a holy and sovereign God would degrade himself by passively anticipating or watching evil. God is not the God of "laissez faire, laissez passer" but the God who bears his responsibilities.

    d. One can also discover an argument against the notion of permission by checking out how the word "permission" is used in Scripture. According to one concordance,[12] in the Authorized Version (Statenbijbel) of the Netherlands the word "permit" occurs fifty-two times. The instances in which the reference is to permission by humans are not, of course, relevant here; but where the reference is to permission by God, one finds that each time it is stated that God did *not* permit something.

11. Heppe, *Reformed Dogmatics:* "sins of omission, by which that that the law enjoins is omitted; and of commission, by which that is committed which the law forbids" (p. 351).
12. Abraham Trommius, *Nederlandsche concordantie van de bijbel,* Den Haag.[10]

When Abimelech wants to take Sarah as his wife because he does not know she is married, one reads that God prevented him, for "I did not let you touch her" (Gen. 20:6). God rather prevents the evil that would have resulted from the sin of people. God frustrated Laban's evil intentions with respect to Jacob. "God did not permit him to harm me" (Gen. 31:7). God refuses to let Balaam curse Israel (Num. 22:12). He does not let his holy one see corruption (Ps. 16:10). Hence God is not the one to stand by passively when evil takes place, but is rather the one who blocks evil and sees to it that the evil plans of people are not carried out. On the basis of Exodus 32:10 one would rather get the impression of the opposite scenario: God is the active one and man the one who gives or denies permission. When God is angry with Israel he asks Moses, "Now therefore let me alone that my wrath may burn hot against them and I may consume them." Moses refuses, so it does not happen. Only if Moses permits it can God do evil against Israel. The issue of whether evil shall be permitted or not is one for people rather than for God. The faithful representative of Israel refuses permission. In this regard Moses is also the faithful representative of the God of Israel in that he does not permit the evil to come over his people, even when at that moment it is God's will to punish Israel. Talk of the magnitude of human power and hence of human possibility! In contrast to Moses there is Eli, the old priest from the beginning of the books of Samuel. He *is* the man of "laissez faire, laissez passer." He is that in relation to people: in everything his sons have the audacity to do, he fails to restrain them (1 Sam. 3:13). He is that also vis-à-vis God. When Samuel announces to him in God's name the judgment that will befall him and his family, he merely says, "It is the Lord; let him do what seems good to him" (1 Sam. 3:18). The consequences of Eli's permissiveness were as one would expect. True, in these pericopes God may be the angry one, a fact which may put pressure on his goodness (though not necessarily); in any case he is evidently not passively permissive. The permissive one is Eli.

We still have to take a closer look at a number of New Testament texts. In Hebrews 6:3 we are told that the author is about to change the subject "if God permits." Accordingly, the reference is to God's positive permission. It does not refer to permitting suffering or sin; in addition, permission here has the general significance of approval or consent against the background of the belief that ultimately God decides what will happen. It is a counterpart of James 4:15: "If the Lord wills, we shall live and do this or that." The reference is more to the positive will of God (if he also wills it, it will happen), than to a passive permission against his will. The second text is Matthew 19:8 (and its parallel, Mark 10:4), where the reference is to divorce. About that Jesus says, "Moses allowed you to divorce your wives," a reference to something definitely unwanted. One might say that "Moses" here means the commandment of God, for "Moses" is the Torah in which the commandment about divorce is found (Deut. 24:1). In view of the opposing desires of men God permits divorce. Jesus rejects divorce and motivates his rejection by saying that "from the beginning" it was not so, which shows that it is God's will that people shall not divorce and that the permission to divorce comes from Moses. The law is something additional which does not have the preexistent value of divine authority, compared to Jewish traditions about the preexistent Torah. Here Matthew is taking the same line of thought as Paul in Galatians 3:17: the law was added.

The last textual group which raises questions is Mark 5:13 with its parallels (Matt. 8:31; Luke 8:32). When Jesus cleanses a man possessed by demons, they ask Jesus for permission to enter a herd of swine. Jesus grants it. Since the early church (within which the gospels originated) acknowledged Jesus as the divine Lord we can say, Here is divine authority, proving itself as such precisely in the expulsion of demons which permit the occurrence of evil. The swine, which constitute the livelihood of the inhabitants of the region, drown. However, with this conclusion we are not properly appreciating the theological significance of the story. The demons ask for permission to enter the swine, unclean animals par excellence. They plunge into the *abyss,* a loaded word in association with demons. The abyss is the abode of the demonic (Rev. 11:7; 17:8; cf. Rev. 20:3; where Satan is thrown into the abyss from which his beast had ascended). The swine end up in the sea. In Mark 4:35-41 the sea is depicted as the waters of chaos which rise up in opposition to God and men. It is the primal chaos Jesus conquers by his word of power. Accordingly, in Mark 5 permission to enter the swine means that the demons are assigned to where they belong: they belong in unclean animals, and end up in the abyss, which leads to the sea. But the sea is the power of chaos which Christ has overcome, where the demons are destroyed, taking the swine, *their* swine, with them. Hence permission given the demons is not the decision to permit evil, but the cleaning up of evil. Even in giving permission the Lord, in the superior power of his saving act, is *actus purissimus.* The permission of Mark 5 is more a radicalization of the non-tolerance of evil than an acceptance of it. Evil is permitted to seek out evil in order that it may be totally destroyed.

All in all there seems to be plenty of reason to abandon the idea of the permission of God. Still, though I am not enthusiastic about the stereotypical way in which as a rule the idea is used, I want to argue for it. If we reject permission as nonsense, we are not doing justice to the attempts of people at least to say something in their dilemma. It is an attempt to exempt God from evil as well as to shield him from the charge of impotence. To be sure, we do not have to protect God; his identity is what it is; but the aim of theology is to look for formulations which do justice to God. We need to find words which allow us to speak about him correctly. Also, the word "permission" is one which has been found in order to avoid doing an injustice to God. For that reason we cannot dismiss it so easily. We shall have to dig more deeply—check to see if the counter arguments are strong enough for us definitely to write off this attempt, which, like all theological attempts at articulation, is debatable; check to see if perhaps there are new formulations which have the same intent as the old concept of permission, but are free from its disadvantages. Ultimately, as with every theological concept, the pros and cons have to be balanced.

We shall begin where we ended the attack on the idea of permission—with the biblical data. It seems marvelous to be able to say that when in Scripture the matter of the permission of evil by God comes up, the reference is precisely to his not permitting it. That is also in complete agreement with the line of thought we are pursuing in this chapter: God does not will evil. Still, upon closer examination, this view cannot be maintained. It "works" only if one uses a modern translation. The moment we turn to the original, as so often when we do this, the matter proves to be different. The verb "to permit" serves, in the Old Testament, to translate the Hebrew words *natan, nuach, natash*. In the first place these words have a much broader meaning than "permit," or a directly related word. *Natan,* for example, means first of all "to give." If we then look at how the words are used, we find that in the Old Testament God is often the subject of the "giving" of evil. When evil subsequently comes to pass, it seems very much as if the reference is to something active that God does in contrast with passively "permitting" it. In cases where *natan* results in something happening, the Authorized Version usually translates it with the word "cause" (e.g., "I will cause them to be removed," Jer. 15:4). But *natan* does not always have an active meaning. It can also mean "to let": I let them go. A clear example is Psalm 81:12. There the Authorized Version has, "So I gave them up unto their own hearts' lust" but the Hebrew only means: "I let them do what they wanted." Accordingly, if we examine the Hebrew text and note that words which can be translated by "permit" mean that God permits something that people or powers themselves insist on, we get quite another picture. God abandons Israel to Babylon (Isa. 47:6). Especially in Jeremiah and Ezekiel it is repeatedly stated that God leaves them to the sword (Jer. 15:9; 25:31; Ezek. 32:20), to the fire (Ezek. 15:4, 6), to famine (Jer. 18:21), and a variety of other disasters. God leaves people where they are. He leaves Israel to

155

its fate and lets the heathen have their way. "I will leave you in the hands of those whom you hate" (Ezek. 23:28); "I will leave them in the hands of their enemies" (Jer. 34:20).

In most instances God's activity and passivity coincide. His decision to let Israel's misfortune come is active: it is judgment. But the realization of it occurs at the hands of evil powers which threaten Israel continually. They simply did not have a chance, because God protected Israel. When God decides to suspend his protection, then his people fall a prey to the power play of the nations and the disasters of nature. In 1 Kings 13 we find the remarkable story of the prophet who acts against Jeroboam in Bethel. Because there he eats bread against the express command of God, he is killed by a lion. His fellow prophet then says: "the Lord has given him to the lion, which has torn him and slain him, according to the word which the Lord spoke to him" (v. 26). An extreme interpretation of this statement in one direction is: "The Lord let him be killed by the lion" (i.e., God no longer protected him and when the lion came he was finished). However, the idea of judgment and the remarkable fact that the lion and the donkey together stand beside the body, point in another direction. One could then opt for another extreme: "The Lord has given him to a lion which killed him" (i.e., God threw the disobedient man to the lions). But that interpretation too is resisted by the context, because the lion does not devour him, something which one would expect in the case of the disobedient being thrown "to the lions." Not as if, according to the author of Kings, the God of Israel could not be that way. That is evident enough from the story of the children who were devoured by bears because they jeered at Elisha (2 Kings 2:23-25). But in 1 Kings 13 the situation is more nuanced in the remarkable commingling of a judgment and allowing a serious misfortune to occur, the same remarkable commingling of activity and passivity we encounter in the lion. Whereas 1 Kings 13 leans in the direction of the active meaning of *natan*, in Psalm 81:12 it is the passive meaning which predominates. To surrender someone to his own thoughts means to cease to exert influence on him, to let someone go in the way of his own choice, to take your hands off him.

If one has problems with God's permission, one can as much as possible stress the active side of these texts. For the person who wishes to be an advocate of the omnipotence of God, that is no problem. But for someone for whom God's goodness is the core of his theological thinking it *is* a problem. If we want to flesh out 1 Kings 13 as actively as possible, then God indeed throws the unfaithful prophet to the lion. Thinking from the perspective of this chapter as we are, we benefit from the most passive interpretation possible: God withdrew his hands from the unfaithful prophet and the accident happened. The exegesis of this type of text is bound to be heavily influenced by our dogmatic bias relative to the omnipotence and goodness of God. Coming from the direction of his goodness we can discern in these texts that the authors sense a passive disposition in God; it is, to be sure, a consciously chosen, but nevertheless a passive, disposition. If a person rejects this, he ends up with an active God who is so hard as to be incompatible with the traditional ideas about his goodness. Whoever, conversely, would claim that to understand these texts we must base ourselves on the omnipotence of God restricts the meaning of the above-mentioned Hebrew words in an unacceptable way. In that case, particularly a text like Psalm 81:12 suffers distortion.

What emerges here is that the idea of permission can in fact boast a biblical basis. One can say that it is a somewhat one-sided solution, but that is just as true of the idea of omnicausal omnipotence (and all the other models we have discussed, for that matter). Permission is a legitimate attempt to express certain biblical nuances. From the above discussion it is also clear that the idea of permission arises especially from the notion of the goodness of God. A person who swears by divine omnipotence has no need to interpret verbs of which God is the subject in a passive direction, even when the actions denoted by the verbs are hard on people.

The objection that in the framework of permission God is only passively involved in the events of the world, a situation in which his active presence is said to be excluded, is already challenged by the above. In the above-mentioned texts activity and passivity are not mutually exclusive. The passivity of God is an active choice. Especially in the prophets the recurrent pattern is that God is angry with Israel and this anger is effectuated in withdrawal from his people. It is an active movement of God away from his people by which they are left to their fate. Hence, divine permission of evil is not an expression of pure passivity. In the history of Saul we are shown how far this activity can go. On the one hand we learn that a king is appointed for Israel. In the choice for a king they reject God. The words are almost bitter: "They have not rejected you, but they have rejected me" (1 Sam. 8:7). God then has Samuel depict to them the consequences of their choice: misery on a large scale. But if Israel persists, Israel gets its way, by God's permission. "And the Lord said to Samuel, 'Hearken to their voice, and make them a king' " (1 Sam. 8:22). Here the picture is especially that of passive permission: "Let them have their way; I am taking my hands off." The result is announced in the conclusion of Samuel's speech: "And in that day you will cry out because of your king, whom you have chosen for yourselves; but the Lord will not answer you in that day" (v. 18).

A later redactor of the Saul story combined this starting point with another view of the king: the king is God's elect, the man who will lead the people in his name. This view comes to expression in chapters 9 to 11. In this way the path is cleared for the story of David, the king who is the man after God's heart (1 Sam. 13:14), for whom the Lord will build a house forever (2 Sam. 7:11, 16). From the conjunction of the two stories in the present redaction of the books of Samuel came the pattern that God permits the choice of a king against his own wishes, but subsequently uses him on the road that leads to his salvation. What he passively permits he actively uses in a positive way. The shadow of God's "no" continues to hang over the history of Saul, but it becomes the shadow of the light of his "yes" over the history of David. The penumbra of the evening of judgment when God hides the light of his face proves unexpectedly, as a result of God's choice of the son of Jesse, to be the dawn of the messianic king's day and his kingdom of peace.

God's permission is an act of surrendering people to their chosen ways and to the powers that surround them on account of their sin. That is the main accent of the biblical data concerning "permission," even when God manages to give a sudden turn to that permission. But we must pursue this line of questioning, however, for we have not yet touched upon the core problem of permission. The fundamental question, after all, is "How, given the goodness of God, assuming he is Lord of the world, can man nevertheless do and suffer evil?" Each of the above texts refers to already existent evil to which God responds by permitting the occurrence of another evil. The disobedient prophet of Bethel already exists. The unfaithfulness of Israel precedes the Babylonian invasion. But how can the antecedent evil be explained? Ultimately, the issue in permission is that which concerns evil in its totality. Does that also fall under the heading of permission? In preceding sections we repeatedly discovered that the foreground solutions which had biblical roots were not isolated from the deeper questions, and that the final questions did not have to be answered differently than the foreground problems. That was the case with sin and original sin; that was the case with the suffering that comes from the hand of God. A certain foreground solution proved each time to be rooted in a deeper stratum. In view of the amount of biblical data and their degree of clarity it is better, however, to put it the other way around: a foreground solution concerning God and the world turns out each time to be capable of being thought through to the end without taking us to a terrain that lies outside the biblical framework. It even seems to me that the distinction between "foreground" and "fundamental" solutions lies completely outside the purview of most biblical authors. For in keeping with the way in which God is bound up with the world, he is totally—right down to the very last questions—bound up with the world and there is no other God than he.

If we do make use of the distinction between foreground and more fundamental questions, it is only in the interest of a clearer analysis, not because there would in the end be a difference in the way they are answered. We have to begin by making distinctions and by analyzing; the unity between the different conceptions will have to emerge from the investigation. In fact, in comparing the different models what comes out over and over is that foreground statements are statements about God's being. Explicit statements about his being kind are rare in Scripture; but foreground statements stand out against the background of the concrete history of redemption. At the same time they are a sign that the words about God's action in history are sustained by the consciousness of the being of the acting God. This means that if what we say in the foreground about God is true, it is true to the very last stratum of background. In the history of dogma this view has led, in A.D. 344, to the rejection of the opinion of Marcellus of Ancyra, who thought that the Trinity was only economic, not ontological. If God is triune in his relations with men then he is also triune in his being. If we now say that according to Scripture the aspect of permission plays a role in human reflection on God in his actions in history, and that the model of permission therefore has a legitimate place in it, then that model has a legitimate place in all our speaking about God. If permission is a legitimate term for speaking about God when it concerns his active response to human deeds, then permission also precedes human deeds, just as in everything God precedes human beings. God, it is true, reacts to human deeds and is influenced by them, but he is not shaped by them.

Now, to be sure, as to the idea that God's permission precedes sin as well as expresses his displeasure over the sin of humans by leaving them to their fate, God's permission is based on the general principle that one must not make a distinction between the action of God in history and his preexistent being. Still, it is desirable again to verify this principle in biblical-theological terms for every theologoumenon. Now, we have already remarked that explicit statements about God's being are rare in Scripture. This is understandable, because as a rule it is God's action in history, his reaction and appeal in the concrete human situation, which constitute the direct subject matter of the texts of the Bible. One might be led to dismiss all further questions as irrelevant, but this would threaten the continuity of God's action. His action is sustained by who he is, and he is who he was. Accordingly, in the midst of God's reactions to and approaches toward people, those texts light up which speak about God as preceding and encompassing all things. They are the final fixed points to which the changes of history are oriented, the distant beacons in the fullness of the flow of history—God's history with men.

When it comes to permission, there are also places in Scripture where it is not a reaction which people deserve on account of their unfaithfulness. The most striking example occurs in the framework story of the book of Job. Here is a man who is perfectly faithful, yet God permits him to suffer. God himself did not take the initiative; that came from Satan. But God did let Satan go his own way and so also the Sabeans; he permitted the wind to destroy the house sheltering his children, and he permitted the sickness which struck Job. There is a heavenly permission—preexistent and transcendent, if you will—antecedent to all earthly events. Also, the book of Job shows the commingling of the activity and passivity of God. Job is not afflicted by God himself; God permits Satan to do it. He is allowed to go as far as God permits. "Behold, all that he has is in your power; only upon himself do not put forth your hand" (1:12). "Behold, he is in your power; only spare his life" (2:6). God permits it up to a point and Satan does it: "So Satan went forth from the presence of the Lord, and afflicted Job with loathsome sores" (2:7). At the same time God is very closely involved in the entire process. He actively permits Satan to go ahead. He himself gives his consent, so that what Job says in his discourses is understandable: "God gives me up to the ungodly, and casts me into the hands of the wicked" (16:11). Also, the initial challenge came from God: "Have you considered my servant Job, that there is none like him on the earth, a blameless and upright man, who fears God and turns away from evil?" (1:8). Hence, in transcendent permission there is the same ambivalence that is present in withdrawal from an unfaithful people on account of their sins; here too there is no pure passivity, but permission based on a decision of the will.

In classic dogmatics people also tried as much as possible to repress the passive element in permission. Heppe states that this permission is efficacious.[13] God furnishes all the technical conditions necessary for the evil deeds of men: he provides the iron; he furnishes the human knowledge needed to forge it; he gives man the capacity to think and to choose; he even gives him the capacity to raise his hand to strike another. The only thing God does not actively create is the choice of a man to raise his sword and to kill his victim. On that point and on that point alone God is passive. Only there God remains uninvolved. God is not to blame (even though he took care of everything which made the murder possible) anymore than is the storekeeper who sold the knife with which its victim was killed. Of course, here too the analogy is flawed, and many

13. Heppe, *Reformed Dogmatics*, p. 274.

objections can be raised. If the storekeeper knew in advance what the murderer planned to do, was he right in furnishing him the weapon? Why, in the long chain of things and thoughts, is there suddenly this exception? Is that "for the sake of the cause" a matter of convenience? Indeed, it is only a solution for the situation in which one cannot possibly square the goodness of God with his omnicausal omnipotence, and God's omnipotence is for a moment "deactivated" in order to safeguard his goodness. Though the classic idea of permission, as Heppe for example developed it, is to be evaluated positively, in many ways it fails in practice. Still, that is no reason to reject the idea itself—witness the modern elaborations of classic nuances which in this context also continue to fascinate twentieth-century man as ways out.

The form in which God's permission can best be expressed today consists in saying that God gives space to man. God did not create man as an automaton—doing what God has programmed him to do—but as a being who can choose. Man was created in freedom to be a real partner for God. Man is called to love and obedience. If man has no other options but to carry out the will of God, one can hardly speak of "obedience" when he does in fact carry out God's will. After all, he could not do otherwise. Obedience occurs when one has a choice between ignoring a command and fulfilling it and then decides to go the way of fulfilling it. The other possibility is open but rejected. Obedience is manifest in free choice.

The relationship between obedience and freedom is extensively discussed by John A. T. Robinson in *The Human Face of God*, where he characterizes the essence of obedience in a christological context: "He was fallible—yet when the crunch came he did not fail."[14]

In process theology freedom is viewed as the possibility to increase one's *enjoyment*. God takes risks, but he has to in order to escape the emptiness of the void, the undifferentiated all. Simultaneously, freedom is openness toward the future and simultaneously the driving force of history by which both God and men arrive at a higher mode of being. "Increasing the freedom of the creatures was a risky business on God's part. But it was a necessary risk, if there was to be the chance for greatness."[15]

The case with love is no different from that of obedience: love is not one being forced to care about another, but consists in the free surrender

---

14. John Arthur Thomas Robinson, *The Human Face of God* (London: SCM, 1973[2]), p. 94. Robinson bases his views on Tillich; see, for example, *Systematic Theology*, vol. 1, pp. 201-6. Also cf. Berkhof, *Christian Faith*, pp. 184-86.

15. See Cobb and Griffin, *Process Theology*, p. 74. See also Cobb, *A Christian Natural Theology: Based on the Thought of Alfred North Whitehead* (London, 1966), pp. 92-98.

of one's life to the life of another. Another way, the way of unfaithfulness, is open, but one opts for the way of love. In God's choice of a partner who owed him obedience and was able to offer love, God made room for another being beside himself who could also choose the road away from him. When the human partner no longer has that option, he can hardly anymore be called a partner. Then he is no more than an extension of the omnipotent will of God who fills all things. If there really is something outside of God, if God has created something that does not exist within his own divine being but has an existence of its own; if there is something that does not remain locked up within the walls of the will of God, then God has created it as an "opposite." Only then is it really independent. Only then is it a partner. That applies to the whole creation. It applies especially to man. The creation of the world, and even more the calling of man to obedience, is the most clear-cut form of permission: God permits another alongside himself who can make another choice. That is not a passive permission. God has actively chosen for it. He himself has willed it. He has chosen to give a place to man where man has space. God made space for man from which he himself retreated. That is the impossible miracle of creation, a creation which is no emanation from the overflow of God's being (in which case creation would again still carry God's being within itself), but a real creation by which something comes into being that really can and may be other than God and exist alongside him.

The fact that God gives space to man is an act of love. God did not owe it to anyone; it was and is his own free choice. Accordingly, permission is not something negative, not an emergency solution, the kind of which the classic scholastic model all too clearly has the typical features; permission is love. It is the self-emptying love of God. God filled all things, but he relinquishes some of his power to make room for man and so to make room for mutual love. It is indeed mutual love. Only if man is a true partner, a being other than and over against God, can God love another, and only then does his love remain enclosed within his eternal being. By creating man, God creates room for the expression of his own love, just as by creating man God makes room for man's answering love to the God who created him. Now the more independent man is, the more space there is for the expression of human love and the more God's love can assume concrete form. Accordingly, one can say that in the space God makes for man in creation, he already expresses the love by which he in Christ saves the lost. These are not two different loves; it is one and the same love in which God moves outside of himself to enter a relationship to one who is not himself.[16]

16. Brunner, *The Christian Doctrine of Creation and Redemption, Dogmatics*, vol. 2

The less the other is the extension of the will of God, the sharper the profile of God's love. God creates room for his love by creating man and equipping him with freedom to choose between obedience and disobedience, between love and unfaithfulness. Man has used the choice to bring about disobedience and unfaithfulness. That, however, does not affect his independent position over against God. Rather, it only makes that independence explicit and manifest. Nor does human disobedience affect the space of God's love. That gets its deepest hue and form precisely by contrast with man's disobedience. God's love is most apparent in relation to the human being who is most estranged from him and who has completely squandered the space of the freedom God gave him. This human being has laid hands on everything that belonged to God; he wanted to be as the Creator. This human being was not destroyed by the superior power of God's being; instead God gave him space—all kinds of space, the space of all his power and being— and God positioned himself alongside of him, the partner not of the obedient, but of the disobedient man. God emptied himself to the degree that he relinquished all power. The most secularized human being is the human being most encompassed by the love of God. The godless human being is the human being beloved by God as the ultimate "opposite." In the godless person God's love comes to its clearest manifestation.

Especially in Lutheran theology the notion of the self-emptying, the kenosis, of God has played an important role. The term comes from Philippians 2:7 where we read that Christ "emptied himself, taking the form of a servant, being born in the likeness of men." Christ had divine power but emptied himself of it in order to become man. God expends all his glory on man. In that love, in the one man Jesus Christ, obedience and disobedience came together. Unfaithfulness was conquered by love which embraced the worst apostasy; and the end of the road away from God—death—and that death on the cross, is encompassed by the love of him who relinquished the very last degree of power by choosing for death. A dead man has no power left at all. He is delivered up to whatever people want to do with him. Jesus Christ, who is the revelation of the mighty God, delivered himself up past the point where any power reaches and every will stops—and so he was the God of human beings. He permitted them to do all they were minded to do. And they did with

---

(Philadelphia: Westminster Press, 1952): "The kenô which reaches its paradoxical climax in the Cross of Christ began with the Creation of the world" (p. 20). See also Brunner's "The Self-Movement of God," in *The Mediator: A Study of the Central Doctrine of the Christian Faith* (London: Lutterworth Press, 1934), pp. 285-302.

him whatever they pleased, just as they did with John the Baptist (Matt. 17:12). In that way God wants to be God, by completely making room for people, by relinquishing all his power, and by making room for all his love. If anything of God is all-encompassing, it is not his omnipotence. That he gave up. All-encompassing is his love, past the very last boundary.

Now does this mean that when the idea of the space God gives to human beings is consistently applied as the ultimate form of permission, the omnipotence of God vanishes and we have to drop the concept of omnipotence? Not at all. The power to relinquish omnipotence is greater than the power compulsively to cling to power. Compulsive retention of power ("a thing to be grasped," Phil. 2:6) has something anxious about it. It is then as if God cannot cope with the idea of relinquishing some of his power. The inability to tolerate responsibilities beside one's own is a sign of weakness rather than of strength. God is able to relinquish *all* his power and puts *all* responsibility into the hands of men. That is no admission of weakness but a sign of strength. When God relinquishes his omnipotence it is an exhibition of his absolute superiority. It is the superiority which is able to be defenseless because it is not an anxious self-preserving power which can be hurt or even broken. This power is not the power of violence but the power of defenseless love. It is, as Berkhof has pointed out, "defenseless superiority."[17] The love of God is so great and so all-encompassing that nothing falls outside of it. Wherever we roam or stay there is God. However, that is not the God who is the rearside of every event, but the God who defenselessly surrenders himself to men—to be despised, to be mocked, to be denied, to experience their disobedience—until they have killed him and it is clear that this God cannot be kept dead, because even as one who is dead he is alive. In the absolute defenselessness of death the superior power of his love asserts itself and he rises again unconquerable.

One can flesh out this defenseless superiority in an authoritarian way so that God makes infinite room for men because he knows that soon, in a moment of time, he can restore everything in accordance with his omnipotent will. God is then like a father who romps with his kids. They are allowed to do with him whatever they please. They may throw him to the ground, sit on him, tie him down, and gag him. He permits it all. For he knows that the moment he thinks it is time to stop he will just get up, break the threads with which they tied him up, and with one hand lay them all down on the floor. Similarly, God plays his game with

17. Berkhof, *Christian Faith*, pp. 133ff.

us, lets us enjoy our supposed power; but it does not really mean anything; our heavenly Father only lets us toy with him. If we think about it for a moment, we know too that this is reality—that all our human fuss is merely the shadow of a morning haze.

However, at the heart of this idea there is much more: God really wants to be defenseless. His divine defenselessness extends to the death of God, leaving people to live in complete godlessness. God is absolutely at the mercy of the other. Amidst all the power-hungry humans, God is present as the wholly other, not demanding but giving; as the God who continually subjects all systems and ambitions to criticism; and so, as the defenseless one, he lives eternally and can never be overcome by any competing power whatsoever.

In this way, by permission and in defenselessness, God is present and alive as one who continually subjects the world to criticism because the world proclaims power, not defenselessness. Though he gives man all his desired space, he is unavoidably in our midst. However, we can also flesh out the idea that God gives space to the world and to man in a less dramatic way. Then we do not say God is present in our midst as the defenseless one. Rather, we state that God actually withdraws from the scene. In the place where he created man he has given power to man. In the place where he called the universe into being the laws of physics are in force. In these places God no longer asserts himself or intervenes. That is the viewpoint of Deism: God is present at the beginning of the world, but beyond that he does not involve himself with it. God-talk only serves to express in words the possibility of our existence; beyond that, it says nothing about the present. The deistic viewpoint is to be taken deterministically: God is the clockmaker who started the whole thing, but for the rest it runs by itself. It is a mechanism; everything is determined in advance. But that is not what is at stake here, for in that fashion everything *is* regulated by God. The point is that, though God certainly furnishes the initial thrust, he allows everything beyond that to take its own course—in accordance with its nature. Every creature displays the measure of freedom that belongs to it. Man has a great measure of freedom which he can use at his pleasure. God does not direct him, but lets him choose his own way, for God has retreated from the world. For that reason one cannot observe God's presence in the world. All one observes are the regularities of nature and the free choices of man. That is how God has willed it. God created the earth to be independent. The end is totally open, be it a kingdom of peace and righteousness, or the destruction of the world. In all other views concerning permission and, even more, in all the other models we have discussed, the future, though open, is always one in which God is involved and becomes manifest. The "processing" of suffering and guilt is possible particularly with a view to the end. Even when suffering is due to human sin, the sin is before the face of that God who ultimately acquits or condemns people. In the above non-deterministic conception of the deistic standpoint, the end, from a theological point of view, is completely open. God is only present at the beginning, and for the rest it is up to us to sort things out.

According to Tillich man is destined for freedom. "Man's destiny is determined *by* the divine reactivity but *through* man's self-determination, that is, through his finite freedom."[18] Still, even in Tillich man has no absolute freedom. God remains the sustaining ground of his freedom in the polarity of freedom and determinateness (see *Systematics* vol. 1, pp. 201-6).

At first, the idea that God gave the world complete freedom may seem attractive. It also seems to agree with the contemporary experience of reality in which only the laws of nature and human choices play a role. One could even find biblical proof texts for it, e.g., Psalm 8, where all things have been subjected to man. But precisely the same psalm pictures man in his smallness vis-à-vis God. More essential, however, is that this idea—that God is merely at the beginning and not at the end—is diametrically opposed to the eschatological thinking of the greater part of Scripture. One could perhaps appeal to wisdom literature where judgment is rather that of folk wisdom than the final judgment of God. But wisdom literature too knows that the fear of the Lord is the beginning of wisdom (Prov. 1:7), and the least eschatological book of the entire Bible, Ecclesiastes, speaks of the spirit returning to God (Ecc. 12:7). Accordingly, if God is at the beginning, then the end is no different than the beginning. The prophetic books and the New Testament Scriptures are even more end-oriented in their theology. Here criticism of the world arises before the face of the God who judges and the hope of the world lies in the future of the Lord.

In process theology there is much more room for the future than in other conceptions which base human freedom in the space God creates for him. In its representatives God is not the sustaining ground of freedom, but the inviting call that comes from the future. Man is lured to richer possibilities but has the freedom to follow or to resist the call: "God is that factor in the universe which establishes what-is-not as relevant to what is, and lures the world toward new forms of realization."[19] In process theologians the risk God takes is greater than

---

18. Paul Tillich, *Systematic Theology,* vol. 2, p. 150.
19 . Cobb and Griffin, *Process Theology,* p. 43. A clear summary of this idea in process

in Tillich. Still, also in their work, God remains continually present as the unity of all that is and was, and the inviting call of higher realization in the future. God's invitation can be frustrated by the inertia and recalcitrance of man, but he continues to lure. One can even say that the pressure increases in proportion to the degree the world falls behind the possibilities extended. God does not really retreat. Momentarily he gives man space in which to choose, and immediately returns with his new invitation.

One can advance arguments, even in a biblical-theological sense, for virtually all models and emphases. However, that is very difficult in the case of Deism, certainly in its non-deterministic form, not only because it lacks an eschatology but also because in Deism God is no longer relevant for the present. Suppose it were true that God had only given the first thrust to the world and had then allowed it free play, with the possibilities and impossibilities of human freedom; then we would not now have to take him into account. Then we could not even take him into account, for he has let go of the world. All the words of the Torah, every prophetic exhortation, every promise and every criticism would then be completely meaningless. The message of the kingdom of God issued by Jesus Christ is then a matter of human choice, and the claim it represents is then no more than the inspiration of the human spirit, and everyone is at liberty to pose or counterpose an alternative.

Accordingly, we do not "fill" God's permission in the manner of Deism, but rather with the space which God continually gives his partner for love and obedience, or in the manner of God's "defenseless superiority." That is the positive side. At the beginning of this section we also saw the possibility of the negative side: that in wrath God lets people go their way. That however is not an act of retreat in the manner of Deism where God does not let himself be influenced by the world and the world is not influenced by him, but a retreat based on an intimate relationship. Only on the basis of a close relationship can one react by saying, "I am leaving you." It is not God's absence as uninterestedness but his absence as injured love. If in our time God seems to be the absent one, totally out of reach, we should ask whether we have not arrived in the situation of Psalm 81: "I gave them over . . . to follow their own counsels" (v. 12). Is it not possibly the case that after twenty centuries of Christianity, after long series of bloody wars of religion, after years of slave trade and colonialism, and two world wars, God is releasing us to follow our own counsels as people with whom he cannot do anything anyway? Is it not

theology can be found in G. D. J. Dingemans, "Schepping in eschatologisch perspectief," in *Kerk en theologie* 34 (1983), pp. 293-311.

possibly the case that God has given us up to the choice of those who have no vision, the choice of bread and games, governed by the laws of economics and by anxiety over how to spend one's leisure time, without relationships and without hope? God can withdraw himself until the level has been reached about which the prophet Hosea says: "Even if they call to him on high he will by no means lift them up" (Hos. 11:7; translated from the Dutch—Trans.). In the succeeding verses the same prophet shows why God's absence and the negative content of his permission can never be the definitive form of his relationship to Israel, any more than the cross was his definitive relationship to Jesus, but that in no way detracts from the reality of his absence vis-à-vis Israel and from the reality of the godforsakenness of Jesus.

If in our day we interpret the absence of God as his decision to permit people to follow the counsels of their own heart on account of their impenitence, sooner or later we can expect a horrible awakening. Withdrawal in wrath on the basis of love, encompassed by a love that is greater than the wrath, has the character of the lesson that we have to learn by bitter experience. Because people are pigheaded regarding their own history, the experience may have to be very bitter. If Verdun, Auschwitz, Dien Bien Phu, Hanoi, and Beirut are a foretaste, then what will we not have to go through before we learn to go the way of the righteousness and love of the God of Israel? If we interpret the absence of God as judgment, then we also have to ask whether that absence is not a favor. In the days of Amos people were looking for the day of the Lord. Surely God would at last set things right! He should no longer be silent, no longer permit the things that were happening. But the prophet was not enchanted because people were at last asking for God. His answer was, "Woe to you who desire the day of the Lord! Why would you have the day of the Lord? It is darkness and not light" (Amos 5:18). If God is about to set things right, should we not prefer his silent absence over his presence in judgment? The idea that God is leaving us to our own resources may be frightening. There is a sense of being left to the uncertainty of our own choices and to the play of great powers. It makes one uncertain because one does not know where to go in a freedom that is too great for a human being. But is not God's absence a favor? Are we not enjoying God's favor in order to muddle on with God's permission, even in the uncertainty of our decisions and false choices? God has retreated from the scene; come, let us continue to make our messes for as long as it is day, before the darkness comes in the day of the Lord.

We are now coming to the subject of God's patience. In 2 Peter we read: "The Lord is not slow about his promise as some count slowness, but is forbearing toward you, not wishing that any should perish, but that all should reach repentance" (3:9). Permission is also a form of patience. God is not washing his hands of us. He has not yet reached the end of his patience. He is still giving us a chance. It is "the day of grace," the hour of acceptance. It is the silence in which we are permitted to live—before the storm of his wrath. Accordingly, permission is the goodness of God in judgment. God's patience goes a long ways. He is merciful and gracious, *erek appayim:* it takes a long time before he begins "to blow." ("He is slow to anger.") For he knows what we are made of, mindful that we are dust (Ps. 103:8, 14). To this dust he gave space and allowed it to overrule him; he left it room in the wrath of his love and the love of his wrath.

14. EVIL AND THE EVIL ONE

IN THE FIRST SECTION OF THIS CHAPTER WE DISCUSSED SIN AS HUMAN ACT and suffering as human guilt. For evil we have first of all to go to ourselves. We can also, however, describe evil as a power. This power of evil effects sin as well as suffering in the world. Sin is not something consciously at our disposal, something a person chooses or rejects, but a mystery beyond man by which he is infected. Sin corrodes man, and its symptoms become visible in the sinful things people do. This powerful character comes to light primarily when people are driven to wrong actions against their will. In this connection it is not even of importance whether others label this action as wrong; the primary question is whether a person recognizes his own action as incorrect and still does it. The conscious choice of thinking and willing is one other than the road actually taken. You may consciously plan, at the next visit of the neighbors, not to indulge in gossip; but once they have arrived it starts automatically, against your real intention. It just happens. Over and over people do things other than they intend. Apparently there is a power stronger than they are. It is an insidious urge which takes a person captive and brings him where he does not want to go. It is like an intoxication which takes over the controls, a strange passion which inhibits and even suspends his willpower, his choices, his common sense. Following the disenchantment comes a sense of guilt. I have allowed myself to go where I did not want to be. I have not resisted. The failure is experienced as guilt, and at the same time we cannot handle the guilt; for in spite of all our good intentions we continue to fail. A situation of powerlessness results. We are victims of a power greater than ourselves. But though victims we are at the same time guilty, because we are not the people who by our most fundamental choices we want to be, and who in our heart of hearts we should be. The deeper our sense of being victims, the more guilty we are.

The discrepancy between will and action may embitter the lives of people, especially when they envisioned a high ideal. The real person proves over and over to be different from the ideal. A solution for this disturbed sense of happiness can be found in saying that you must accept yourself as you are. You have to live with your real self, not with your ideal self. Come home to your real self and do not let yourself be controlled by some authority you may or may not have projected. The moment you accept the fact that the action you did not will is not wrong, but an expression of your own being, the spell of that power will be broken. You are now no longer estranged from yourself in this action, but you are being precisely who you are. If, on the other hand, you follow your ideal image, you are following not yourself but an image. It is precisely in pursuing the ideal image that the estrangement occurs.

Now it is certainly true that this reversal of the process of estrangement may help. People can have strange fixed ideals which unnecessarily mess up their lives. Still, the issue itself is more complex. In the first place, what is "strange" and "unnecessary"? Is the ideal strange because, viewed statistically, it is exceptional? If we follow this line we deprive people of their right to uniqueness. The exceptional may be more valuable than the general. Uniqueness preserves tension and color in humanity. Another more basic objection—the notion that one must not live by an ideal image of oneself or of others but should and may live according to what one is—is the end of all ethics. Ethics is based on the existence of a critical standard for our actions. There is an image of how reality should be, in contrast to the image reality displays. Accordingly, if one calls the attempt to conform to the desired image "self-estrangement," no ethics is possible—unless one means by "ethics" the notion that one should in fact be liberated from ideal images. The truly good and the truly free human being no longer lets himself be estranged by what he ought to be. But this argument is circular, for the man governed by ideal images—that's the way he *is*. My ideal image is a part of my thinking. "Come to yourself" then means, "Come to yourself *with* your ideal images." I still again have to accept myself as an ethical being. Then we are back at the beginning. Accordingly, "come home to yourself" means either a reversal of ethics, or it means that we make no progress whatever. In this connection the demand to suppress one's ideal image is just as hard as the demand in classic ethics to pursue the ideal image. "Come to yourself" is *also* an externally imposed ideal image. In that ethic one becomes the prisoner of one's own feelings and drives and all criticism is taboo. Such a life can only exist in a totally splintered society in which people live and roam as monads who do not care about each other and whose only goal is the distant vision toward which they are traveling. Hence self-acceptance may be of relative help in relieving the pressure of one's ideal image when one threatens helplessly to succumb under a burden of guilt; but when self-acceptance is chosen as one's fundamental life posture, one ends up in an even more impossible situation. Accordingly, self-acceptance is to be taken therapeutically rather than ethically.

For as long as we humans are ethical beings, it is inevitable that we will experience the power of sin in opposition to the will to live good lives, even when we no longer use the word "sin," but euphemisms like "fail" and "fall short." The Christian manner of dealing with this power is not that we a priori call "good" the conduct that happens to be ours, but that recognizing our lives do not conform to the ethical norm, we know of forgiveness. Forgiveness is the only way in which people can be liberated from the vicious dialectics of choice and compulsion. In forgiveness sin remains sin. Humans are sinners; but in their sins they are beloved, not rejected. Forgiveness is the deepest form of love; it is the way of Christ. The sinner is not urged to regard sin as something else: sin continues to stand in all its starkness. It is even increased because all pseudo-piety is unmasked. John 8:1-11 is typical. The woman sinner brought to Jesus by scribes and Pharisees is not advised to accept and to continue her adultery. Jesus says, "Go, and do not sin again." At the same time, in the face of Jesus' criticism the piety of the accusers proved to be no more than a soap bubble. But the woman is accepted in her sin and forgiven so that she can begin a new life.

Precisely this latter point, however, is a problem. For the moment one wishes to begin a new life one discovers that sin is indeed a power which we do not control but which controls us. It is the sin which rules us so that we do what we do not want. Forgiveness, therefore, is not only forgiveness of the one act, but forgiveness of our subjection to evil. Forgiveness is extended not only to what we do but also to what we are. Only thus is forgiveness really liberating.

Sometimes people themselves experience the power of sin. That happens when they know that their will and their conduct diverge. But if sin is a power, it may also begin to influence our will and mind so that we no longer experience sin as sin. Sin as a power is then so interwoven with our whole self that we follow it uncritically and without a struggle. This brings us to the question of what sin is. In this discussion we described sin especially as the discrepancy between the ideal image and the reality of self. In that case a person without an ideal image, the person who lived totally in the present, could not be a sinner. Moreover, not all ideal images are alike. Consequently, it is impossible to employ our ideal images as the final criterion. In the Christian church the criterion for ethical conduct is not anyone's ideal image, but Jesus Christ. That does not mean we have to imitate Jesus casuistically. That is not even possible. We barely know anything about the life of Jesus of Nazareth. The "quest of the historical Jesus" has especially made clear that for us the life of Jesus is only known fragmentarily. We have no more than a number of separate "moments" which come to us in the theologically charged contexts provided by the evangelists. But even if we had a detailed biography of Jesus which showed how and why Jesus in certain situations acted as he did, that would not help us. For the situations of Jesus of Nazareth are not our situations. The casuistic imitation of another person is not a road we can travel even when that other person is Jesus.

Discipleship is not a matter of imitation, but of living in the grip of the spirit of another, in this case the Spirit of the Other. At stake is what comes to us from the essence of the other person. In the case of Jesus that is the essence of his divine mission in which he totally devotes himself to the Father's will and is totally "the man for others." This love is a love unto death, one that does not begin from a base in human wholeness, but from a base in divine glory (Phil. 2:6). Accordingly, the norm of the love commandment is no other than the norm of Jesus Christ: to love God above all and your neighbor as yourself. It is the criterion of the Spirit of Christ, which proceeds from him and animates people. Where people do not act in accordance with, or better, from within this Spirit, they are in sin. Precisely where this life in sin is not recognized as such, sin is most manifest in its character as a power. It is a small thing when people fight against a power they do not want, compared with the situation in which people are absorbed by a power which controls their entire existence—conduct, mind, and will—so that they are no longer conscious of this power. At that point people are really slaves of sin, robots directed by an invisible will which eliminates a person's real calling. This power is not manifest from within the person himself. He is taken up into it and cannot position himself outside of it to criticize it. This power becomes manifest only where the God of Israel manifests himself. It is revealed in the law of which Christ is the fulfilment. Christ makes people manifest as people delivered up to sin.

The New Testament, especially the Pauline literature, brings out this sin-dominated situation of man. Where the light of Jesus Christ begins to shine, there people are manifestly the will-less instruments of sin. They were dead in trespasses and sin (Eph. 2:1). Sin is often pictured as an almost personal power. It finds opportunity (Rom. 7:8), and rules (Rom. 5:21). It is as if there is an evil will outside of people which takes them captive and drags them where Christians do not wish to go but to which the heathen are helplessly delivered up (Rom. 1:21-24).

If sin is a power which controls people, the question arises as to what is the cause of their subjugation. An initial answer is that man has delivered himself up to it. Like Faust he has sold himself to evil. Man has opted for sin, and with the first sin all other sin broke loose. The door was opened through which sin, like an irresistible flood, overran the whole of human existence. That is true collectively, symbolized in the story of the Fall (Gen. 3). In the wake of one sin comes a flood of sin. One can also understand it individually. In the act of taking that first step on the road of sin one loses control, caught up in a process one can no longer escape. This may occur in a hidden and incomprehensible way; the process may also be observable, one sin evoking the other. The sinful act is followed by denial, the lie; one lie demands another until the tissue of lies is so thick it can no longer be sorted out and human relationships are profoundly disturbed. One deed produces a stream of sins and suffering.

Now the power of sin does not exist by itself. Sin is a manifestation of the power of evil. The entrance of sin into the world is accompanied by a great flood of evil—by suffering, misfortune, and fear. When the door was unlocked it opened to the realm of darkness, filled in every nook and cranny with evil. This evil presses forward, bringing people into the grip of sin, suffering, and death. In Romans 5 Paul says that by one man sin came into the world and death through sin. Both are different manifestations of the one dark power which conquers the world. Death bears the sign of the power of darkness, of nothingness, of evil. In light of this no distinction can be made between hell and Sheol, the realm of the dead. Death takes people into the realm of the dead. But the realm of the dead is also the domain of evil. It is the domain of the power which perverts the creation willed by God and ultimately takes it into the abyss. By the one human act of sin the monster was released, and no one gets it back into its pen. As an insidious poison sin and death pervade the world in which we live.

By the sin of man the world in which we live has become the domain of sin. Nothing is left of the freedom for which man was created. Once we lived in a state in which it was possible for us not to sin, *posse non peccare*, says Augustine. But that changed into a state in which it is impossible for us not to sin, *non posse non peccare*. This tradition, namely that sin as power extends to all humans, can be found throughout the whole of church history, from Paul, via Augustine and Anselm, to the reformers, and via the reformers to most Protestant confessions. Linked with the continuation of sin is the continuation of suffering and death. We live in a world in which the creature groans for redemption and longs to be set free from the bondage of decay, from the suffering of this present aeon to which man has brought himself and the whole of creation (Rom. 8:19-26).

The idea of the encompassing power of sin has been developed at length in the letter to the Romans. In later theology the first eight chapters of this letter continued to furnish fresh impulses toward dogmatic formulations. In this connection it is often forgotten that the letter to the Romans is a single whole in which the relationship between Israel and the church is a central theme. The moment this is lost sight of and one allows Romans to end at 8:31 there is a continual risk of reducing the corporate basis of the letter to a theory concerning the state of individuals. Consequently, instead of being the starting point of the message of all-embracing salvation, the teaching of original sin becomes an individual psychology of frustration.

Augustine resumed the line of Romans 5 and developed it. Before the Fall man was gifted with "prima gratia," by which if he wanted he could attain righteousness, *posse non peccare*.[20] After the Fall man was only able to sin. Adam's sin becomes *peccatum haereditarium*.[21] Parallel to the transition from possible sin to necessary sin *(non posse non peccare)* is a transition from possible mortality to necessary mortality, *non posse non mori*.[22] Death is sin's concomitant.

Anselm speaks of a *"necessitas peccandi."* However, more than Augustine he emphasized the conscious choice of man to commit sin. As a result of the corruption of his nature man lost the possibility of choosing the good.[23] The guilt of man, as guilt before God, is infinite and total. To one who would question it Anselm addresses his winged words: "You have not yet considered how great the weight of sin is."[24] Calvin, in his *Institutes,* follows closely in the footsteps of Augustine.[25] See also *The Heidelberg Catechism* (Answer 7). The Belgic Confession goes beyond Anselm by viewing sin not only as an act (be it an inescapable one), but by locating it in infants before birth (Art. XV).

If we view the entrance of the power of darkness as a consequence of the opening of the door by a human deed, then the cause of suffering continues to lie in man. Though by his deed he achieved an effect that far exceeded his own capacities, nevertheless at the beginning there was his own deed. The consequences of his act, however, infinitely transcend

---

20. Augustine, *De Correptione et Gratia,* 11, 31; 12, 33.
21. Augustine, *Retractiones,* I, 13, 5.
22. Augustine, *De Correptione,* 12, 33.
23. Anselm, *The harmony between God's foreknowledge, predestination, grace, and free choice,* 3, 7, and 8 (see also *The virgin conception and original sin*).
24. Anselm, *Cur Deus homo,* I, 21.
25. Calvin, *Institutes,* III, 1.

it. This idea leads us also to view evil, which goes beyond man, as something which precedes man. Evil is more comprehensive than human decision. Consequently, man does not dispose of evil. He is not able to restrain it. Human capacities are not adequate in the face of evil. If evil precedes man and exceeds human power, the decision over whether or not evil will rule cannot lie in human hands either. For then man would transcend evil after all. It is therefore natural that the thesis that man opened the door to evil was reversed, turning into the idea that evil itself entered the world and tempted man to sin. Only in that way does evil really precede man. In the effectuation of sin the space which evil had in the world became manifest, bringing with it suffering and death. In the story of Genesis 3 human disobedience was prompted by the speaking serpent.

Consistent with this line of thought is the view that sin does not exist in isolation, but is called forth by temptation. Man has the option of saying "yes" or "no" to it. Evil comes to man from without and man either does or does not consent to it. The Spirit of Christ brings people to resist evil, but outside of the fellowship with Christ man is "delivered up" to temptation.

If temptation is present behind every sin it is also present behind the primal sin. In that case too, evil came from without. In Barth's description of nothingness it is not only the power to which man by his own fault succumbed, but even more the sinister emptiness which threatens the world, presses toward and into it, as the shadows of the coming night penetrate the evening and darkens the daylight. To be sure, in Barth nothingness is not preexistent. It comes into being at the same time as creation; it is the reverse side of God's electing creation, the possibility God passed by when he chose the other possibility of the good creation. But in developing the idea of nothingness Barth attributes to it all the traits of a power domain which exists outside of man and precedes human sin. Because nothingness is present, man can and did, in fact, succumb to it. However, man does not create it; that power he does not possess. Nothingness derives from the divine "no," just as creation proceeds from the divine "yes." And just as man himself does not opt for the divine "yes" (but the initiative lies with God), so the initiative of reprobation also lies with God. It is his divine "no." So nothingness, though it does not precede creation, does precede human choice and is immediately effectuated in human choice. For the moment man chooses [evil] he no longer allows himself to be sustained by God's choice; his choice is no longer God's, but the choice of the possibility God has rejected. Accordingly, there is a subtle dialectic between the nothingness which precedes man and the evil that is contemporaneous with human choice, between power and guilt. But because the rejected possibility is not the counter-pole of the human act but of divine election, the notion of nothingness as a power which transcends man (who can only exist as a choosing being and hence as a being who chooses his own rejection) predominates.

Hence there is an evil power which precedes and transcends man, the power which has seized control of the world. It is a power God does not will but rejects. Accordingly, if man is victimized by the power of darkness, God is on his side. God is the God who liberates man from the power of sin. God in Christ makes people alive, people who were subject by their trespasses and sins to death (Eph. 2:1). When Paul speaks about the power of sin and the body of the death to which we are subjected, there is deliverance by Jesus Christ, our Lord (Rom. 7:25). The curse of sin and death is broken by incorporation in Christ (Rom. 6) and life by his Spirit (Rom. 8:1-30). Accordingly, God is not the one who parcels out suffering to people, who lets people die, who even makes people sin, but he is the God who liberates people from suffering, who wills their life and liberation from sin.

Jan Van der Werf, a pastor in Utrecht who was incurably ill at the time, wrote a number of articles for a local church paper under the title: "Writing from my sickbed." Writing from within his own situation Van der Werf discussed what faith in God meant in time of illness. The second article is entitled "Reply to Martin Hart," in which he responds to the author of *A Flight of Curlews,* who in his youth had learned in church that God apportions to people all things, both good and evil. He was the God who made his mother ill, who gave her the cancer which destroyed her body. Hart breaks with God and with the church which confesses this God. Van der Werf replies that Martin has a mistaken view of God. The God he pictures is not the God of Jesus Christ. When Martin Hart speaks of the God who laughs satanically and invents cancer of the throat for people, Van der Werf says "no." The God of the Bible is the God who, when he saw we were being completely ruined by the anti-powers, jumped in after us. He acted not to content us with the notion that "a sorrow shared is a sorrow halved," but because he himself wanted to do battle in Christ with these powers. In the wilderness of suffering one gets from God this message: "Remember, this God died at the hands of those anti-powers, but in his death he pulled them along with him into death, so that soon there would and will be victory. And it is God's fatherly hand which brings me this message and rouses me to hang in there."[26] The God whom we encounter in Jesus Christ is a

---

26. Jan Van der Werf, "Schrijvend vanaf het ziekbed," in *Hervormd Utrecht,* 1978, p. 243.

loving God who protects and saves people, not a God who allows people to be slaughtered or their lives ruined by a guilt he has himself imposed on them. He is the God of mercy who comforts us and is present in our midst as Comforter (John 14:16). Man is a fragile being, a puny creature caught up in an unequal struggle with the sinister powers of sickness and death, a helpless being doomed to lose in the struggle to remain free from sin. But this creature may know that God is on his side. Therefore he need not be afraid, but can take courage for the struggle. If he had to fight for his salvation alone, he would be doomed. But God goes with us and leads us and works for our salvation; indeed he fought for and won our salvation in Christ. Together with him our struggle is not senseless, even when the power of evil far exceeds our own and is as intangible as the air that slips through our fingers. For towering high above the gigantic powers of darkness is the overarching superiority of the love of our heavenly Father who raised Christ from the dead.

Up till now we have especially spoken about evil as an impersonal power. We have already remarked, however, that in the Bible evil power and its manifestations are sometimes referred to in personal terms. According to several texts, evil comes to us through personal powers. The best-known text, presumably, is Ephesians 6:11, 12: "Put on the whole armor of God, that you may be able to stand against the wiles of the devil. For we are not contending against flesh and blood, but against the principalities, against the powers, against the world rulers of this present darkness, against the spiritual hosts of wickedness in the heavenly places." It is not clear precisely what is meant by all these concepts. What is the difference between principalities, powers, world-rulers, and evil spirits? What *is* clear is that we have here a representation of supernatural beings which seek to influence life on earth. First-century Judaism had well-developed images of this kind of being. Some were positive, others negative. The positive ones are the angels of God, his servants and messengers. In some writings (e.g., 1 Enoch), there is an extensive angelology divided into ranks and classes. Over against the messengers of God are the evil powers. They too have influence in the world. People are protected by their angels (think of the story of Peter's release from prison in Acts 12:15); other spiritual beings attempt to ruin their lives. Nations, too, have their angels. Michael is the angel who fights for Israel. But the Persians have a supernatural ruler who stands in opposition to God's messenger. When a heavenly emissary finally comes with an answer to Daniel's prayer, he has to recognize he would have come sooner had he not been held back by the prince of the army of the Persians; only the angel Michael's intervention decided the battle in his favor (Dan. 10:13).

These supernatural beings are mentioned in very different books of the Old Testament. Sometimes they appear in the form of a human being. When Abraham receives three guests they turn out with increasing clarity to be angels, messengers from God. One of them even turns out to be the Lord himself (Gen. 18). People who turn out to be angels appear to Gideon (Judg. 6:11-24) and the parents of Samson (Judg. 13). The angel who encounters Balaam is evidently distinctive (Num. 22:22-35). First he is invisible to Balaam; subsequently, after his eyes have been opened, he immediately recognizes the angel. Angels who are visible only to people whose eyes have been opened also accompany Elisha and his servant (2 Kings 6:16ff.). Often these persons are good beings who come to bring a divine promise or message. They are revelations to people of the will of the God of Israel. They are really *melakim*, messengers. In other instances, however, they bring misfortune. The angel of death who moves through Egypt (Exod. 11 and 12) can be interpreted in both directions: he brings misfortune to the Egyptians, to be sure, but salvation to Israel. The situation is different with the angel mentioned in Genesis 3:24. This angel is pictured with a flaming sword in order to block the way to life symbolized by the tree of life. Still, this angel too is a messenger of God. Accordingly, he is no personification of the evil power who opposes God. If he threatens people, it is because God wants to threaten people.

When it comes to supernatural beings, the angels sent by God predominate in both Old and New Testament. Angels appear in the history of Jesus from the annunciations to Zechariah and Mary (Luke 1), to the resurrection. Angels appear to Peter (Acts 12) and Paul (Acts 27:23) as saviors and messengers.

There are also evil powers, however. Psalm 91 speaks of the terror of the night and the destruction that wastes at noonday (vv. 5 and 6). Especially in the late texts demonic beings appear with increasing frequency. In the time between the testaments this development continues. The New Testament has no extended demonology anymore than an extended angelology. But the powers which rise up against the power of Christ are very much present. On the one hand are the invisible powers which threaten people, powers to which Ephesians 6 refers. This representation of evil powers occurs especially in the epistles. Man on his own is no match for these powers. But in the power of Christ one can remain standing. His power as the power of love is greater than the power of demonic influences. "For I am sure that neither death, nor life, nor angels, nor principalities, nor things present, nor things to come, nor powers, nor height, nor depth, nor anything else in all creation, will be able to separate us from the love of God in Christ Jesus our Lord" (Rom. 8:38, 39). On the other hand, especially in the gospels and Acts we find the view that the demons take possession of people and even animals (Mark 5:13). They manifest themselves in the people they possess. Present here is not the invisible power which threatens all people unseen, but a demon who takes possession of an individual and controls his actions and faculties. The demon-possessed are deaf and dumb (Mark 9:25); they beat themselves; they are extremely strong (Mark 5:3-5); they rave, foaming at the mouth (Luke 9:39). But the gospels also agree that the power of Christ overcomes the demons. They fear him because they recognize him (Mark 1:24). In the Spirit of Christ the apostles also cast out demons (Acts 5:16). In the story concerning the sons of Sceva (Acts 19:13-16), Luke reports that only people who work by the Spirit of Christ have power over demons. People who do not work by that Spirit are beaten up by the demons, even though they use the formula of the name of Jesus and operate as a team of seven (the number of divine fullness). Following in the apostles' footsteps the church also practiced exorcism. In certain periods exorcism was even an official ministry. In modern times it has been relegated in most churches to a minor role or ceased to exist altogether. Exorcism has been driven out to sectarian groups or to individuals within the churches, people who in the West are certainly viewed with suspicion. To most people, including those in churches, exorcism seems more like quackery or messing with the sacred than an exercise of Christ-given authority.

From the third century the church had official exorcists who played a role especially in the preparation of candidates for baptism. In the Roman Catholic church this function is now reduced to a part of the priestly consecration, and exorcism still occurs only in stylized form in the classic ritual of baptism. By special mandate from the bishop the exorcism of possessed persons is also still permitted. Lutheran churches have abolished exorcism. With their horror of magic, churches of the Reformed type have never accepted it.

In Protestant circles exorcism again gained publicity through the work of Johann Christoph Blumhardt (1805-80) in Möttlingen and Bad Boll. Blumhardt practiced faith healing and was involved in exorcisms. Through this he acquired great fame. Striking in this connection is the emphasis on the name of Jesus, clear likewise in the book of Acts. Via his son, Christoph F. Blumhardt (1842-1919), he exerted influence on Barth. Blumhardt's first exorcism was described by his son.[27]

A third picture of evil powers occurs in apocalyptic literature. There they are soldiers in the army of the evil One. They are the angels

---

27. Christoph F. Blumhardt, *Die Krankheitsgeschichte der Gottliebin Dittus* (Basel, 1943[8]). See also Johann C. Blumhardt, *Die Heilung van Kranken durch Glaubensgebet* (Leipzig, 1922[8]).

of the devil, symbolically represented by a dragon. They conduct a supernatural battle with the angels of God who, under the leadership of Michael, defeat them (Rev. 12:7-9). And Paul speaks of a messenger of Satan.

In addition to representations of angels and demons, we find in Scripture still other, more mythically conceived images denoting the power of evil. Here and there in the Old Testament we encounter reminiscences of ancient creation myths of Babylonian or other origin. Isaiah 27 refers to Leviathan, represented as a serpent or sea monster. The Leviathan is, in the first place, the crocodile. In Job 40 and 41 it is an ordinary animal: though frightening to people, it is not as impressive as a hippopotamus or rhinoceros. But the crocodile became a symbol of a primeval monster, a dragon in the sea, comparable to primeval monsters like the Babylonian Tiamat. Thus Leviathan symbolizes anti-divine power. But this power is overcome by the God of Israel. In Psalm 104 the Leviathan has been subdued to the point where God made him in order to play with him (v. 26). The question whether the reference is to the crocodile or the mythical monster of primeval times fails to do justice to the imaging, associative thought of the oriental poet. Even if it be the crocodile, it is still the Leviathan. Every mention of the crocodile in a religious text immediately evokes the image of Leviathan even more than in ecclesiastical literature where every reference to a snake is associated with the devil.

A conception similar to that of Leviathan is that of the primeval monster Rahab we find in Psalm 89:10 and Isaiah 51:9. On the one hand Rahab stands for Egypt (Ps. 87:4). But in associative mystical thinking Egypt, the primeval monsters, and the crocodile are all combined. If in Egypt the crocodile is divine, that can only heighten the anti-divine character of the animal for Israel. But Rahab and Leviathan have been overcome by Israel's God. In Psalm 74:12-17 all the associations come together.

A related conception is that evil as anti-divine power is embodied in the sea itself. The waters lift themselves up against God and his city (Ps. 46:3ff.; Ps. 93:3ff.). What emerges here is the heightened consciousness of the desert nomad for whom the sea is fear-inspiring, a threatening boundary-reality which comes storming at the land in order to overrun it. For the Israelite the sea is taboo, certainly from the time of the Phoenician-Canaanite threat to Israelite religion in the period of the kings. The Phoenicians with their Baals may rule the sea; Israel wants no part of it. When it is reported that the ships of Jehoshaphat were wrecked at Ezion-geber (1 Kings 22:48), so that Israel fails as a seafaring nation, that event, in the narrative style of the early prophets, is not without a

180

pointer from the hand of God. The sea may roar, its waters may lift themselves up, but they cannot affect the throne of God (Ps. 93:2) any more than that of his anointed—God has chosen him as his firstborn (Ps. 89:10, 27, 29). The image of the sea as an anti-divine power recurs in the New Testament, in the story of the storm at sea (Mark 4:35-41). But also in this story Jesus faces the demonic and overrules it. Whether it be the evil of primeval chaos in the waters which lift themselves up, or the demon who holds a human being in bondage, both obey the voice of him who is the mighty one. In the end, in the city of the messianic kingdom, the sea will be no more (Rev. 21:1) or remain only as a sea of glass (Rev. 15:2), a sea which has lost its chaotic, threatening character. The chaotic power of evil which threatens human happiness has then been overcome by the power of Christ.

In the mythical mention of primeval monsters or the waters of primordial chaos the concrete issues of human life are elevated to the status of an encompassing power. The crocodile becomes Leviathan, the sea primordial chaos. In this mythical parlance the most primitive feelings of people are addressed, feelings associated with fears and chaos which transcend the prosaic realities of the moment. They do not represent fear of a specific visible reality, but an undefined dread which fills people, dread of the loss of the basis of their existence. They are comparable to the archetypes of Carl G. Jung. Perhaps the primordial monster of Western man is the spider rather than the crocodile. In any case, the name is not the most important. Images can change. There is, however, a difference between Leviathan and the archetypes. The archetypes belong to the structure of the human psyche. They are domiciled in man, a part of himself. Leviathan and Rahab, though they directly touch the same foundations of the psyche and represent primitive fear, are conceived as being outside of man. They are a power which threatens man, the world, the whole creation. Though there is kinship in psychological function, the primordial monsters as powers which threaten both the inner and outer worlds of man are more comprehensive. They create havoc with the bases of human existence, threatening to separate man from the foundations of life, his existence as creature. The sea and Leviathan are references to a power which challenges human existence, forbidding it to be.

But the Holy One sits enthroned above the waters, which are silenced at the command of his Anointed. God does not permit the powers to ruin the basis of our existence: he wants us to be. He has said "yes" to our lives, and he will not permit the ground to be washed away from beneath our feet, neither by the concrete threats of the moment nor by the encompassing threat of indeterminate evil which holds the world by the throat. The concrete threats of the moment are no more than manifestations of the primal threat. If the all-encompassing primal threat is subject to the power of the Lord, then what can its diverse manifestations do if he is near in the name of Jesus, the Lord?

Evil, among all the evil powers, is also described as an absolutely personal power: evil as such summed up in the person of the Evil One, total evil in one person. Evil is not merely the dynamic of a vague power; it has a name. A name makes someone into a person, something more than a function of the collective. The Evil One is a personal power: Satan.

The word "satan" literally means "accuser." The satan exposes the evil deeds men do. He searches out whether there is evil in a person. This examination may take the form of a challenge. People are incited by the satan to do evil. Only in that way will it become evident that the person is really righteous (compare the role of the satan in the book of Job). Consequently the accuser is also the tempter.[28] Beside the earthly there is also the heavenly accuser. Initially, as in Job, he was still pictured as a member of the heavenly court. Later, he is God's opponent who incites people to do evil. In the Old Testament this function of the satan comes most to the fore in 1 Chronicles 21:1: "Satan stood up against Israel, and incited David to number Israel." In the parallel story of the census in 2 Samuel 24 we are told that the Lord incited David. It is clear the author of 1 Chronicles cannot square this with his God-concept. Consequently he attributes the incitement to sin to Satan. Here we see the beginning of the later development in which Satan is God's adversary who opposes the well-being of the people of God. In the angelology and demonology of Jewish texts from around the beginning of the Christian calendar, Satan occupies an important place. The world of supra-mundane beings increasingly acquires a dualistic character: Satan and God, each with an army of servants, of bad and good angels, are each other's antagonists. God is the good power, the light; Satan the evil power, the darkness. Especially in the Qumran literature this view is developed at length.[29]

On account of the dualistic opposition between God as light and the prince of darkness, it is often assumed that the idea of Satan was taken over from Parseeism. That would correspond with the late period in which the concept was used in Israel. The dualistic imagery of God and his adversary is said to have originated only through contact with the peoples of the East during and after the Exile. This may partly be true, but it does not adequately explain the broad interest which the concept of Satan enjoys in Judaism. In the first place, there are older texts in which the idea of the divine adversary also occurs. Von Rad (op. cit.) already points out that, though the prologue of Job in its present form may perhaps be late, the story itself has to be placed in a much earlier period. Though in Genesis 3 the word "Satan" is not mentioned, the role of the serpent is no other

28. Kittel, *TDNT*, vol. 2, pp. 73-75.
29. Kittel, *TDNT*, vol. 7, pp. 154-56.

than that of Satan in the later texts. Also, the concepts of Leviathan, Rahab, and the demonic sea are rooted in very ancient motifs of supra-human antagonists of God. In the second place, the idea that the notion of Satan is both late and of Parseeistic origin is used to disqualify it. That which is late is said to be adopted and non-genuine for the religion of Israel and, accordingly, theologically inferior. The religious-historical research of the last centuries has shown that there is little that belongs specifically to the religion of Israel and is not found also and usually earlier among other nations, except the acts and perhaps the name of the God of Israel. Israel used concepts from other religions when they were useful, and rejected them again when they became dysfunctional for the articulation of the content of its faith. In that regard Israel did not act differently from the church, which also continually adopted and still adopts concepts from without when they may serve to communicate the faith in a particular time.

Accordingly, when Israel adopted the concept of Satan and in the post-exilic period again refurbished very ancient motifs of divine adversaries, there must have been reasons. At that moment they needed those concepts, whether new or very ancient, just as they proved useful in ancient times before they were settled in the land. In the intervening period they were apparently less distinctly in the foreground, though not altogether lacking (reminiscences occur, e.g., in 1 Kings 22:22, in the lying spirit in Ahab's prophets; in the masked criticism of seafaring in 1 Kings 22:48; in ruling over water by means of a prophet's mantle in 2 Kings 2:8, 14). The observation that the concept has possibly been adopted is of less interest than the question *why* it was adopted or reactivated. It could be that it has to do with the demise of the threat of idolatry. In the period before the exile the worship of JHWH was continually threatened by devotion to the gods of other nations, especially the Canaanite-Phoenician Baal, the Lord's antagonist. A religion is always under threat either from without on account of other religions, or from within on account of the infidelity of its confessors. A pure faith is always under challenge. Since religious experiences always have to be expressed in concepts, there also has to be a concept which puts in words the threat or challenge of the true religion. For the period of the kings, the obvious concept was that of the strange God. Israel had its own God who was being threatened by the alien Baal. After the exile Israel radically renounced the worship of alien gods. But the religious challenge remained. Another concept was needed: that of the satan or those of ancient mythical images were suited. This fits into the framework of the universalization of the JHWH faith. The Lord is not the private God of Israel over against other gods. He is the God of the entire world and the other gods are vanities (Isa. 44). Opposing the universal God is not the vain power of the god of a Canaanite tribe, but the power of universal evil.

Accordingly, the concept of "the satan," like that of the powers of chaos, is linked with the universalization of the faith. It is not necessary, therefore, to disqualify the idea; it is rather to be viewed as a forward step on the road of redemptive revelation leading toward all nations. Only universal salvation is under assault from a universal prince of darkness. Only a world in its totality, from the beginning the world of God, is threatened by the chaotic powers of primeval times. Only in a period in which faith is nationalized can one deal with threats to it by means of the concept of a foreign, non-national, god. The moment one realizes that the foreign god does not exist, and the faith is still threatened, one discovers that evil does not just come from others but that the arch-threat lies also at the root of one's own being. If the other nations are not excluded from the Lord, then Israel is not exempt from the attacks of his adversary. If the true God does not exclusively belong to Israel, the false god does not exclusively belong to the Gentiles. The religion of Israel could only manage without a concept of an all-embracing primal evil in the brief span of time when the great powers of the Middle East momentarily ceased to push the internationalization of culture, politics, and religion, and small nations like Israel were able to build their own national culture, politics, and religion. When that time was past, Israel either had to fall back on ancient myths or look for new concepts. The concept of Satan, the Evil One with a personal face, in the end proved to be the most fruitful.

The fact that Satan is a universal concept, which replaced the exclusive idea that Baal was the Lord's antagonist, is still noticeable in the name Beelzebul or Beelzebub which refers to Satan. Beelzebub comes from Baalzebub, one of the many manifestations of Baal. In 2 Kings 1 we read that the sick King Ahaziah sends mesengers to Baalzebub, god of Ekron, to inquire whether he will recover. The prophet Elijah then asks whether there is no God in Israel. Hence from the start Baalzebub was an alien god. Later the name is transferred to the universal adversary of God, Satan. In this connection it is not clear whether Beelzebub or Beelzebul is the original form of the name; but even if it is Beelzebul, the distortion undoubtedly arose under the influence of associations with the story from 2 Kings 1.

As a rule the idea of Satan functioned in Judaism and Christianity as the polar opposite of true faith. Hence Satan had a secondary function derived from faith in God. Only he who confessed God also acknowledged Satan as his adversary. Only on the odd occasion, in the liturgy of Satanists, does Satan function independently as a god. This religion can probably only exist as a derivative of faith in God, though internally it functions independently. Satan is the primary object of worship. Public Satan-worship is very widespread in Western Europe and North America today as branches of an earlier (and still existing?) clandestine devil worship. In devil worship, in which ancient Celtic influences and negative Christian concepts were combined, sinister practices—child sacrifices and sacrilege—took place, especially in areas with a strong Celtic substratum in the population.

From the last centuries B.C., and perhaps even earlier in Judaism and subsequently in Christianity, Satan is viewed as an anti-divine person. The name given this evil personal power is not always the same. Some terms have the character of a proper name, like Beelzebul; others are purely predicative epithets. Central are those words which refer to the incitement of evil. He is the deceiver (Rev. 12:9) or Belial (2 Cor. 6:15). The expression "sons of Belial" occurs rather frequently in the Old Testament. The reference is to people who are a law unto themselves, closed to righteousness, open to every evil. They are people who have sold themselves to evil. The origin of the word Belial is not clear,[30] but the content is not in doubt in the Old Testament: it concerns total devotion to evil. In the Pseudepigrapha and Apocrypha Belial can therefore become the term for Satan. In the New Testament this usage occurs (probably in adulterated form) in 2 Corinthians 6. As Belial, Satan is the power of evil, and people who have fellowship with him seal themselves off from fellowship with God and his righteousness. The epithet "the evil one," which occurs repeatedly in Matthew, is of the same nature. The Evil One attempts to seduce people into sin, as is evident from the antithetical parallelism of the sixth petition of the Lord's Prayer (Matt. 6:13). It is the Evil One who slips false Christians into the church, the weeds amidst the wheat (Matt. 13:38). This parable also shows the hidden operation of the power of the Evil One. Almost imperceptibly he proceeds to do his work. He is the father of lies (John 8:44), insuring that the Word of God cannot strike root in the life of people (Matt. 13:19). People who live outside of fellowship with God in Christ are in the power of Satan. Accordingly, he is also the ruler of this world (John 12:31) who opposes Christ and his church (John 16:33). In Christ the new aeon has dawned. Over against the God of that new world stands the god of this age (2 Cor. 4:4). He is "the enemy" (Matt. 13) of God, an expression frequently used in the Middle Ages for Satan,[31] and of the kingdom which comes in Christ.

Finally, he is the devil, chief of the demons, the real background of the alien gods (1 Cor. 10:20). He it is who drives people apart and causes estrangement between God and people. He is the slanderer and thus the source of all estrangement and division.

30. Kittel, *TDNT* vol. 1, p. 607.
31. Cf. the exclamation of the main character in *Mariken van Nieumegen:* "Ghi syt die viant vander hellen" ("You are the enemy from hell"), ed. G. P. M. Knuvelder ('s-Hertogenbosch: Malmberg, 1968[8]), p. 18.

In the Septuagint, *Diabolos* ruins relationships. He is the "adversary."[32] In the Greek outside the Septuagint, *diabolos* usually has the meaning of "slanderer," one who brings shame on people. But applied to Satan this act is not just one of slandering people in the sense of "speaking about," but also one of providing the occasion of slander: inciting people to evil so that they can be maligned. As a result, the meaning approximates that of "accuser," specifically the hypocritical accuser who has himself incited the sin. By the incitement to sin and the denigration of the sinner relationships are broken.

Under the *diabolos* as head are the *daimonia*. Demons have no existence of their own but are totally subject to the devil,[33] which is why they are messengers of Satan.

From the epithets cited it is clear that Satan primarily has to do with sin. He is the power of evil who causes people to sin. He is Christ's adversary; as the power of darkness he opposes the Holy Spirit. In Christ and his Spirit the kingdom of God has come; he puts an end to the dominion of the devil. But the devil does not yield the field without a struggle. The church is continually forced into battle (Eph. 6:11ff.), apocalyptically depicted by the struggle between Michael and the dragon with his angels (Rev. 12:7-9), just as Christ had to fight to resist the tempter (Matt. 4:1-11). In Christ God is present in the world. But at his heels is the devil, embodied in Judas. "One of you is a devil," says Jesus to his disciples (John 6:70). The Greek also permits the translation, "the devil," the devil par excellence, almost as a proper name. It is tempting to posit the incarnation of the devil over against the incarnation of the Son of God. But for that purpose this one text is insufficient. Besides, in the gospels Jesus and Judas are not on the same level. Judas is one of the twelve who follow Jesus and hence is to be viewed as a member of the church. But in that position he fully carries out the function of the adversary who betrays the Messiah. He is the son of perdition (John 17:12); and although in him the Scripture is fulfilled—in his delivering up of Jesus he serves the way of God who delivers up Jesus—the evangelists nevertheless depict him in all his negativity, one whose ending is not positive (Matt. 27:1ff.; Acts 1:18-20). He misses the atonement; he misses the risen Lord; he misses the dawning kingdom in the Spirit.

Judas is a sign of the demonic presence within the church of Christ. But we cannot apply a black-and-white scheme here: Peter himself is addressed as "Satan," at the ironic moment immediately after his confession that Jesus is the Christ (Matt. 16:23). The use of the Hebrew word

32. Kittel, *TDNT*, vol. 2, p. 71.
33. Ibid., pp. 1-20.

"satan" in the New Testament excludes the possibility that Jesus was using the term in the general sense of "tempter," as though he only wanted to say: "Do not tempt me not to go the way of the Father." The reference is very much to Satan in the full sense of the word—the Satan is as present in the mouth of Peter as he is in the person of Judas. Satan is also present in true believers and if it were possible he would—via the pseudo-Christs—also lead them astray (Matt. 24:24). The distinction between true and false Christs is as subtle as that between tares and wheat (Matt. 13:24-30). The lines between the kingdom of Christ and the kingdom of the ruler of the world run right through the church. The line between the old aeon and the new, between the old man and the new, runs right through the churches and Christians. In that field of tension lives the church; on this boundary it wages its battle of the Spirit against the flesh. It is not exempt from the goings-to-and-fro of the Evil One. It is the church which prays to be delivered from him (Matt. 6:13), for it knows he is prowling around as a roaring lion, seeking someone to devour (1 Pet. 5:8). This roaring lion cannot always be distinguished from the Lion of the tribe of Judah (Rev. 5:5), any more than Christians can be simply distinguished either as weeds or as wheat. Satan can make himself appear as an angel of light (2 Cor. 11:14). The true deceiver comes in the guise of righteousness; or, as in the old Dutch figure, he comes in stocking feet rather than in wooden shoes. The messengers of darkness present themselves as angels of light, the servants of Lucifer; it is no wonder that the people he uses and in whom he works are no monsters with pointed ears and goat's legs, black and repugnant, but in appearance like the pious who are filled with the Spirit of Christ, unrecognizably similar until the day of the harvest.

Within the present framework it is not meaningful for us to discuss all the representations of the devil or of devils, often depicted very plastically as teasing satyrs or tormenting spirits. Our concern is with the function of the devil as an anti-divine power, as the evil one who threatens—not infrequently in a subtle way—the kingdom of God which has come in Christ.

In the first chapter we noted that evil has two faces: that of sin and that of suffering. From the material discussed so far the devil clearly has to do especially with the first. He is the driving power behind sin. But what of suffering? Is that also a product of the influence of the Evil One? In the story of the numbering of the people as 1 Chronicles 21 tells it, though Satan is the source of sin, the suffering of Israel is God's punishment of sin. When the stringent monism of 2 Samuel 24:1 is ruptured, the author of Chronicles does not pass on to a stringent dualism in which all evil proceeds from Satan, and all that is good and gracious comes

187

from the hand of God. Suffering comes from the hand of God as judgment upon sin, and sin in turn comes from the temptation of Satan. This need not detract from the goodness of God: when God punishes his people, it is attributable to his righteous judgments. It appears to be an acceptable scheme, one in which God is exempt from evil. Still, it raises a big problem. If it is part of God's goodness that he righteously judges sin and hence punishes the sinner—but sin is at the same time caused by the devil—then God is dependent for his action on the devil. To put it in philosophical terms, the devil is the primary cause, and in the entire chain of sin, guilt, and punishment, God is a secondary cause. In this manner the devil forces God to punish people and hence to make them suffer. The real and ultimate cause of suffering is then still the devil and God is merely a phase, an instrument on the road initiated by the devil. However, this would constitute a great breach in God's freedom, as though he could be forced to impose punishment by the machinations of the devil. God just *has* to punish when Satan as the accuser presents the facts.

Other passages show, however, that such a necessary chain of deception-sin-judgment-suffering was not, in any case, universally recognized. That is clear from Zechariah 3. In a vision the prophet sees Joshua the high priest as representative of Israel. Satan accuses him of his filthy garments, which render him ritually unclean. The accusation is rejected, however, not because it is unfounded (there is need for a clean suit of clothes) but because God chooses Israel. God's gracious election takes precedence over Satan's accusation. God is free to choose and to break the chain of sin and punishment. Hence God's punishment and Satan's temptation are two separate matters not necessarily connected by logic. They may go together, but they need not. That is entirely up to God. His judgments cannot be explained, not even in terms of the temptations of Satan.

Now there are other Bible texts where Satan himself has a hand in suffering. Again we come upon the book of Job. Satan leaves the heavenly counsel chambers and takes his measures, measures because of which Job loses his stock and his children perish. In the second round Satan goes forth from the presence of the Lord and afflicts Job with sores. Here Satan is explicitly the cause behind the suffering of Job. It is not right, however, to conclude from this that suffering in general is therefore the work of the devil in the same way that he is the background of sin. In the book of Job suffering, to Satan's mind, is no more than a function of temptation. By causing Job to suffer Satan attempts to make him sin. But suffering is not necessary for this purpose. The temptation to sin can also arise from material abundance and power. In Matthew 4 the devil attempts to lead Jesus astray by promising him all the kingdoms of the world. He also appeals to his sense of honor: "If you are the Son of God command these stones to become loaves of bread." Hence suffering and temptation are not necessarily associated.

All biblical-theological constructions show that there is much more openness than uniformity to temptation, and so it is here. All we can say is that this tendency is also present, though the other is not excluded. There is no simple linkage between temptation and suffering. But we can say that the idea that Satan is the ultimate source both of sin and of suffering is not foreign to the biblical scriptures. In the book of Job it occurs incidentally. But structurally we encounter the idea in the New Testament, where Satan is the great antagonist of the kingdom of Christ. All that belongs to the old aeon belongs in his domain. Sin belongs to the old aeon, as does death. When we discussed the idea of sin as power we saw that with the entry of sin the whole domain of darkness came into the world. Sin brings forth death (James 1:15). A direct connection is made between the power of sin and death as the culminating point of the suffering of the world: a person is imprisoned in "this body of death" in "the suffering of this present time" (Rom. 7:24; 8:18, 23). These texts do not mention the judgment of God as a link between sin and death. Sin itself brings death with it. It is natural that, if one thinks in terms of the power-character of sin, the personified power of evil should also directly bring death in its wake. If Satan is the tempter, then death is born from the success of his activities. In the Gospel of John, where the contrast between this world and the coming one is especially prominent, the ruler of this world is also called the murderer from the beginning (8:44). The lie inherent in temptation brings death to people, just as Christ who is the Truth (John 14:6) has the words of eternal life (John 6:68). When the devil who led people astray is thrown into the lake of fire and brimstone (Rev. 20:10), death and Hades are thrown in after him (Rev. 20:14). They belong together. When he is gone their rule is definitely over. Death and Hades follow him into ruin, which at the same time implies the dawning of the new heaven and the new earth where there is neither sin, nor tears, nor death. When the devil and death have left, God dwells among men in eternal life (Rev. 21:1-4).

In a totally different way Satan is involved in the suffering of human beings when, in the context of divine punishment or purification, he torments people. Accordingly, here God is not the executor of the punishment of sin brought about by the temptation of the devil. Instead, the devil is the executor of the suffering God wishes to impart to people. Paul receives a messenger of Satan in order that the grace of God should be sufficient for him and he would not be too elated (2 Cor. 12:7-9). Paul

189

himself, in the name of Christ, delivers an impenitent sinner up to Satan in order that in the day of Christ he might be saved as one who was purified (1 Cor. 5:5). Also, according to 1 Timothy 1:20, people are delivered to Satan for the purification of their lives.

Hence Satan is primarily the one who tempts people into sin and stands in the way of the kingdom of God. Because in this he is the ruler of this world, death follows in his wake; because he is the prince of darkness he carries the whole world of darkness with him. In the third place he is in the service of God and the church of Christ for the purpose of purifying people.

In the course of centuries these three aspects have remained decisive for the figure of Satan. Though various images of him may be formed, from that of black satyrs to deceivers in priests' clothing, these images consistently embody the above-mentioned attributes of the devil. In some periods belief in the power of the devil was deeply rooted in broad layers of the population, as in the late Middle Ages, while in other times he is barely mentioned. Since the Enlightenment belief in the devil and demons seemed a thing of the past; it seemed merely a matter of time before the last remains of this "superstitious" kind of thinking would disappear. In recent times, however, a change seems to be in the air. Both among theologians and non-theologians are those who do not as a matter of course discount belief in the devil.

Parallel to the increased interest in all sorts of paranormal possibilities, belief in negative paranormal forces also is increasing. In some charismatic circles within the sphere of Christianity an existential understanding of demonic powers is evident. We already referred to the influence of Blumhardt. Barth attributes to the devil the same ontological value as to nothingness, which is a negative value but no less real for that.[34] Berkhof views the devil as a representation which points to a background reality and therefore ascribes to the devil only a secondary and derivative reality.[35] But since all religious speech employs referential language and therefore consists of images, the distinction between representation and reality does not hold water here. Brunner regards the idea of the devil as inseparably bound up with belief in Christ, although he sees clearly that the idea raises many questions.[36]

With this we have arrived at the issue which is probably the most important one of this entire section: that of the hermeneutics of the biblical data concerning Satan. Particularly in the New Testament evil is

---

34. Barth, *Church Dogmatics* III, 3, 50, pp. 302-49 (see also pp. 502-31).
35. Berkhof, *Christian Faith*, pp. 201-2.
36. Brunner, *Dogmatics*, vol. 2, pp. 134-35.

personified in the form of a real, existing figure. Satan is represented as a person. And demons are real entities, invisible to be sure, but their effects are observable. The question is now whether in the twentieth century we must picture Satan as a real person (an invisible one of course) and affirm the existence of demons, or whether it is permissible to think that the biblical images belong to a culture and a language which we cannot simply take over. Is not this mention of demons, devils, and primeval monsters a form of mythical speech, while in order to say the same thing we employ a conceptual apparatus consisting of abstract concepts or words which designate functions? Is the devil only present in an antiquated language or is he present among us as a personal power?

This question has been posed most radically by Rudolph Bultmann in his famous article, "New Testament and Mythology."[37] In his answer Bultmann is equally radical: "It is impossible to use electric light and the wireless and to avail ourselves of modern medical and surgical discoveries, and at the same time to believe in the New Testament world of spirits and miracles."[38]

There certainly is reason for proceeding to a "demythologizing" of the material handed down to us. A significant change occurs already if we substitute "evil" for "the Evil One." Modern people have no experience of the presence of the devil; they do have the experience that evil is a power stronger than themselves which goes beyond our human thinking and willing. Evil as an impersonal power is conceivable; the Evil One as a conscious will which is the power behind evil is not conceivable. The same is true of demons. We no longer call people possessed. We have other words for the condition. A person with "a dumb spirit," for example, is a person with a psychic block who cannot express himself. People who used to be called "possessed" have come to be known as sick persons whose illness sometimes had a diagnosable physiological cause. We now speak of schizophrenia, hysteria, epilepsy, and we know better than to approach the sick as being demon-possessed. What we have before us is not a demon, only something demonic in the sense that we stand powerless before an evil, before human suffering. "Demonic," then, is a word which expresses our inability to help, not a word that refers to a will existing outside of us and which can take possession of us.

One can extend the process of demythologizing and view, say, the

37. In Rudolf Bultmann, *The New Testament and Mythology and other Basic Writings,* Schubert M. Ogden, trans. and ed. (Philadelphia: Fortress Press, 1984).

38. Ibid., p. 5. See also "Zur Frage des Wunders" in *Glauben und Verstehen: gesammelte Aufsätze von Rudolf Bultmann,* vol. 1 (Tübingen: Mohr, 1954), pp. 214-28.

economic and political structures as powers which rule the world. Evil is not a supra-sensual devil, but the structures of a capitalistic or (in the eyes of others) a communist society. We can of course posit a mythological image of a devil behind the scenes, but that can only hinder us in the attempt to engage in the sober analysis of existing structures. If we call a given structure an instrument or perhaps even an incarnation of the devil, we lose the clarity of mind needed to lay the structure really open to criticism. A societal structure can thrive while being termed diabolical or devilish. For once this label has been applied the correction or modification of the structure is no longer possible; only its destruction makes sense. After all, the devil does not permit himself to be corrected. Since the destruction of a societal or political structure, certainly in the large economic and political power blocks, is well-nigh impossible (regardless now of its desirability), it can peacefully pursue its business despite the barking dogs. For dogs which bark about devils and demons in public do not have any political bite.

One can also call a given culture or society demonic because of a lack of clarity about the real centers of power. Where, for example, is real power located in Western society? In the hands of political leaders? In the mass media? In the multinationals? In protest groups? Because it is unclear who influences us (possibly through an unidentified advertising program) and exerts power over us, we are in a state of powerlessness. This may lead us to suspect that in operation there is an unverifiable and intangible exercise of power which no one—not even the above-mentioned "agencies"—can lay their fingers on. One can view this nameless power as a modern form of the devil, as the ruler of this aeon. In this naming of indefinable power factors we are, however, again involving ourselves in a mythological obscuration of reality. In this case, too, this process absolves us from the obligation to track down the channels of power and to discover its source, which does not consist in a mythological figure but in concrete people working through concrete structures. Demythologizing cannot stop halfway. It has to press forward to the sociological and human reality in which we live.

Hence we can take still another step and observe that reference to structures is also a form of mythological speech. Structures are abstractions from reality. They are abstractions from people who make the decisions and act. If we would fully unmask what people once called the devil, we could not stop at the "mask" of structure, but see within the structures the people who make them. They are the devil. The evangelists who said of Peter and Judas that they were "Satan" and "the devil" were more radical in their demythologizing than modern people who locate evil in the structures. If the devil is this concrete person, then he cannot again hide in the myth of structure. The devil is not a being outside of us to whom we are subject, but he exists within us.

Even of my own "self" I can still make an abstraction. Of my being, my character, my nature, my bent (possibly shaped by nurture and environment) I can make a myth which abstracts me from the concrete acts and decisions of the moment. My concrete choice of the moment— that is the core of what is at issue. Pivotal is the decision of the moment. If we are going to demythologize we should do it radically, as Bultmann correctly maintains. What is really essential occurs in the decision of the moment: whatever goes beyond that is mythical abstraction. At stake is what happens "here and now." If we make the wrong choice now, in this very moment in which we are living, we are the devil. But the moment we view this mythological figure apart from this decision as a power existing outside this moment we are excusing ourselves. With this conclusion we are back at the beginning of this chapter: the origin of evil lies in ourselves, our own wrong choices and our own wrong actions. If we proceed to demythologize the devil we come out at our own decisions.

When Bultmann proves unwilling to demythologize the concept of God, he is not really consistent. By speaking of being addressed by the grace of God, he again escapes to a world outside of non-recurring momentariness, and makes the choice of the moment dependent on a power outside of myself.[39]

At this point the question arises whether, after all, there is not more to be said in this connection. Is every reference to the devil indeed meaningless and can we manage without mythological language, with just our human responsibilities and choices. These responsibilities are certainly real, as we clearly saw in section 12. But we will remain on the surface if we do not probe more deeply and allow all the data we have meanwhile processed to disappear in the shrouds of myth. Mythological speech does not exist for nothing: it serves to articulate the unsayable in another way. Also, people in earlier ages had their secularized language as a vehicle. They also spoke about a sick person as a sick person. Not every sick person was "possessed." They knew all too well of human responsibilities. The apocalyptic seer of Revelation who speaks about the devil, dragons, and angels knew very well what political power and economic structures were. Just check him out on it. But there are matters too big to be covered in the language of secondary causes. For them the

---

39. For the idea that the notion of the devil serves as consolation, to deliver humans from unbearable responsibility, see Berkhof, *Christian Faith*, p. 203, where one also finds additional literature concerning "the happy doctrine of the devil."

allusive speech of mythological language is needed. Realities exist which exceed the reach of rational human thought. For that reason we now have to reverse the process of demythologizing.

It turns out that my personal choice in this moment of decision is not as free as I should wish. My choice is determined by who I am and by my history. The crossroads at which I now stand is determined by all the previous choices at earlier crossroads. I cannot just arbitrarily choose a road; I can only choose those roads available to me at this crossroad, where I have landed as a result of earlier choices. This means that as a result of my history my choice is extraordinarily limited. As a result of who I have become and where my place in society is I have only very limited choices. Not only am I determined by who and what I myself am; in my decision-making I am equally and probably even more determined by the entire structure in which I live. I am bound by a thousand ties to other people and to my responsibilities toward them. There is a power which is far above me. Moreover, the microstructures of my situation are interwoven with the macrostructures of world politics and the world economy. And every human being, no matter how highly placed, is conditioned by unknown centers of power which co-determine his choices.

This line of thought still remains within the framework of inextricable connections and forces we cannot control. Though they may be inextricable, they remain immanent and can teach us both how complex the world is and also, perhaps through bitter experience, that demythologizing right down to the level of personal decisions is a fiction. Unless we keep our eyes open to the reality of the world in which we live, demythologizing is a utopia. The situation is as eschatological as the new heaven and new earth, which can only come into being via a transvaluation of all values. Only in the eschaton will the devil cease to exist. As long as neither the process of demythologizing nor the realization of the kingdom of God on earth has occurred, the powerful myth of the structures or the myth of Satan will exist. The only difference is that in the eschatological vision of the coming kingdom of God the hidden power is the Evil One, and in the eschatological vision of demythologizing the hidden power is the evil of the intangible powers and structures of human society, human history, and the human spirit.

Also, in still another respect demythologizing is superficial. For it is based on the optimistic nineteenth-century premise that in principle the world can be made transparent and explained right down to the ultimate (scientific) causal connections. There is much we do not yet know, but that is not a fundamental limitation; it is merely a quantitative lack of knowledge. They are the holes in the Swiss cheese. Awareness has grown in recent times precisely in this: that next to a quantitatively unexplored area of rational knowledge is also an area that is qualitatively inaccessible. Knowledge of this area can only be obtained with instruments other than our physical senses; it only opens up to us if, by receiving the Spirit, we are made willing to stand inside the current of this power. We cannot tap this qualitative area with the logic and objectivizing methods of the natural sciences. It is shortsighted to think that the human senses could grasp the ultimate dimensions of existence. Human reason can grasp more than the human senses, but the human spirit can see more deeply and has a higher reach. And beyond the human spirit dimensions of life present themselves which no ear has heard, no eye has seen, and which have never arisen in the heart of man. Human contemplation includes more than that which presents itself to the five senses; human beings live with and think about more things than are visible to the eye.

It is a striking fact that precisely within the natural sciences a strong movement has arisen which fundamentally relativizes human knowledge as objectivizing knowledge. Absolute knowledge does not exist; the process by which humans come to know is interwoven with the whole of reality. Over against Albert Einstein, who regarded the fragmentariness of knowledge in modern physics as a provisional quantitative gap, stood the physicists of the Copenhagen school, men like Neils Bohr and Werner Heisenberg. The uncertainty-relationship became a symbol for the idea that one can only think in motion, in relation to that with which, and the person with whom, one works, and that one can never know absolutely. This idea has been developed at greater length in philosophy by Alfred North Whitehead, especially in his books *Adventures of Ideas, Modes of Thought,* and *Religion in the Making.* According to Whitehead, all of past world history with which human beings are bound up, right to the most remote corners of the universe in time and space, streams into them, as does the inviting call of the future to enrich the cosmos. In that web of relationships humans make their choices, which immediately become a part of the material with which new choices are made.

Parallel tendencies may be noted in philosophers who tend to work more with the material of the social sciences. Max Horkheimer, in *Die Sehnsucht nach dem ganz Anderen: Ein Interview mit Kommentar von Helmut Gumnior,* practices a critical dialectic which is also critical of the criticism of religious concepts from the past. Also, the myth of demythologizing must be demythologized. In his book *Negative Dialectics* Theodor W. Adorno writes along the same lines. "Objectified legality is the converse of a state of Dasein in which men could live without fear."[40]

40. Theodor W. Adorno, *Negative Dialectics* (New York: Seabury Press, 1973), pp. 88-89.

"We do not yet live in a fully automated society; our world is not yet totally administered."[41] This openness offers us the only possibility still to accomplish many things, be it all very provisionally.

This is not to say that these philosophers advocate belief in mythological representations. They rather push demythologizing to the very end. This is certainly true of Horkheimer and Adorno, who turn their backs on all ontology. Physicists are more inclined toward ontology, certainly Whitehead; but his religious notions also are not mythical in the real sense. What these philosophical ideas specify and have in common is criticism of the simple variety of demythologizing represented by Bultmann, which characterized "enlightened" Western culture in the middle of the twentieth century, especially in the sixties, and which still shows its footprints, even though it is evidently in retreat.

In the period behind us we have excluded metaphysics. We have trouble with real personal powers outside of our existence. But the person who has trouble with the reality of the devil had better remember that the same worm which gnaws at belief in the devil also gnaws at belief in the existence of a personal God. The difficulty we have in thinking about the devil is the trouble we have with metaphysics in general. All the arguments we can advance against a personal will called "the Evil One" apply with equal stringency to a personal will who is God. Concerning both of them, we can only be persuaded from without that they are not just impersonal powers but persons who speak to us. Otherwise we at best arrive at a highly neutral abstraction: "evil" or "the Supreme Being," never "Satan" or "the God of Israel." But if we limit ourselves to the abstraction of "the essence" of the world, evil presents a stronger case than love. The structure of the world is rather a structure of alienation, of "the struggle for life" and of "the survival of the fittest," than a structure of love and grace. He who abandons hope for the person speaks to our hearts from the other side, and abandons hope for the world, because anyone who keeps his five senses alert can only observe that the final structure of this world is that of evil. Accordingly, the expectation of an ideal state based on societal analysis is mythology of the negative kind: a conclusion from a non-existing reality. Hope exists only because this world has been judged and because in dimensions of life beyond us love is stronger than evil. The person who does not believe in a Will which transcends this world has to live without any foundation of hope. However, the person who believes in the person of God and does not dismiss God language as replaceable mythological speech can have no rational arguments for rejecting Satan as a person. If Satan were

41. Max Horkheimer, *Die Sehnsucht nach dem ganz Anderen: Ein Interview mit Kommentar von Helmut Gumnior* (Hamburg, 1970), p. 87.

no person, it would have to be evident from the structure of revelation itself. That point now requires further examination.

According to the Old Testament, the God of Israel is mightier than the primeval powers of chaos. He rules over the sea. Rahab and Leviathan are defeated by him. In the New Testament Jesus and others cast out demons in his name or by the power of his Spirit. When his disciples go out on a mission in his name, Jesus sees Satan "fall like lightning from heaven" (Luke 10:18). The ruler of this world opposes Christ but is judged (John 16:11), and Christ has overcome the world (John 16:33). Blumhardt's motto, "Jesus is Victor" applies to demons at all times.

If the victory of Christ has real significance, must we not conclude that since his coming—in any case since Easter and Ascension when he was exalted and received the name that is above every name (Phil. 2:9ff.)—the power of Satan has been broken? Up to the coming of Jesus he was the ruler of the world. Demons were free to manifest themselves by taking possession of people. But Jesus expelled the demons. Satan and death were defeated. In their final opposition to Jesus, the demons asserted themselves more boldly in the period of his coming than ever before. Just before their final defeat they seem—in their madness—to be winning (Mark 9:26). At the very moment at which Jesus begins his work Satan attacks him personally (Matt. 4:1-11). He seems to be victorious when the Messiah dies on the cross; but actually it is his defeat. Christ is victor. In the early church people pictured Christ making a triumphal march through hell, his prisoners tied to his victory chariot. It was proclaimed right in hell that Jesus is victor (1 Pet. 3:19; probably also Eph. 4:9). Jesus' victory is said to be the reason why there now no longer are possessed people, that demons no longer haunt our houses, and that we need no longer reckon with the devil as a personal power.

However, if we take careful note of the New Testament data, the matter proves—as usual—to be more complicated. True, the devil, demons, and death have been defeated, but at the same time they are still there. The victory is caught up in the eschatological tension between the "already" and the "not yet." The power of sin has also been broken. Christians are dead to sin, for they belong to the new aeon, but at the same time they are told not to let sin reign in their mortal bodies (Rom. 6:12). Christ is the victor over death, but the chapter which is most expressive of his resurrection and new life (1 Cor. 15) also states that death is the last enemy to be destroyed (v. 26). Also, after Easter the demons are stronger than seven men with their incantations (Acts 19:13-16). In the world in which the church is situated Satan goes about like a roaring lion, and continues to do that even after Jesus' descent into

197

hell and ascension to heaven. Revelation 20 not only mentions the binding of Satan, but also his release (v. 7). Accordingly, the victory of Christ is an eschatological datum. This means that, though we may live in the certainty that in him victory has been accomplished already now, we also have to live with the reality of waiting and of the struggles which continue until he comes—the "not yet."

There is no reason to assume that what was true for the church of the first century does not apply to the church of the twentieth century. The Third Reich was certainly not less demonic than the Roman Empire in the second half of the first century. If ever there was a demonstration of diabolical power, then certainly it occurred in the Germany of Hitler. Also, in the twentieth century people are dominated by unknown forces, forces which destroy their lives no less than first-century forces destroyed the lives of "the possessed," sometimes in blind madness, sometimes as an insidious poison emanating from angels of light, sometimes in blunt apathy. We may use other names; we may perhaps be better able to isolate or confine the victims; but we are not able to liberate them to a life of light and true freedom.

If we believe in the personal existence of the devil and demons in the New Testament era, we have no reason whatever to doubt their existence in our day. "There is also a real devil with his legions and a real hell," writes Barth.[42] They are as real as evil in the world is real. I am not pleading for an overheated belief in the devil, demons possibly lurking behind every tree or in every fellow human. But we do definitely have to reckon with Satan as a power who attacks the kingdom of God, and as a personal will who leads people astray. We do definitely have to take account of the demons which infest our lives, not only in the dark but also as angels of light in the middle of the day. We need not, like Luther, hurl inkpots at the devil, but it is very much in our interest not to ignore his existence. The only ones who benefit from such denial are the demonic powers themselves. It allows them to operate undisturbed— they do not then have to show their teeth. But meanwhile we are stuck with unnamed evil that haunts the world. As long as it is unnamed it remains elusive and intangible. When we begin to assign names to evil in accordance with its truly demonic character it may seem frightening. It is always frightening when an indeterminate power, even a natural force like electricity, is no longer ignored but given a name. But this act of naming and recognition is the means for learning how to relate to these powers. It may seem frightening to speak of demons and of the evil—to recognize that they exist. But it is not denial which liberates people—

---

42. Barth, *Church Dogmatics* III, 3, 50, p. 310.

then we remain stuck with a vague neutral force which nevertheless unconsciously corrodes the human soul. We must call the powers by their names, knowing they are powerful and that with our human weapons we are not able to combat them. Human weapons can only confirm their power. To attempt to combat demonic powers with nuclear weapons is only to grant these powers the victory in advance. Over against the names of the unnamed powers stands the power of the name of Jesus the Lord. Liberation from demons is not accomplished by denying their existence, but by conquering them through the power of Christ. His power is greater than the power of the devil. The devil goes about looking for victims, but the community of faith is in the hands of its Lord. The weapons against Satan are truth and justice, faith and salvation, the Word of God—all of these sustained by prayer (Eph. 6:14-18). The evil one is overcome in meditation, prayer, and action in truth and righteousness. In the church the sixth petition of the Lord's Prayer has increasingly become a dead formula. Extemporaneous prayer, though it knows formulations which correspond to prayer for daily bread and forgiveness, seldom includes formulations asking for defense against the Evil One. Recognition of the evil power can only open our eyes to the power of Christ, who is Lord not only over the human world but also over those powers which far exceed ours. He is Lord not only over those who are on earth, but also over those who are "in the heavens above and under the earth."

In this context I should wish to argue for fresh reflection on the role of exorcism in the church. New developments in the Roman Catholic Church could perhaps lead to the abolition of the last formal remnants of exorcism. It would be more desirable if the rite, like so many other rites in the Catholic Church, were to be infused with new life. In Protestant churches, and specifically in the churches of the Reformed tradition, only a few people involve themselves in exorcism. The result is that the action becomes esoteric, surrounded by an aura of unverifiable mystery. Protestant churches would do better if they jointly undertook to reflect on the place and meaning of exorcism. Then it would no longer be a private matter of a few individuals on the borderline of sectarianism, but a fully ecclesiastical matter for the church which prays, "Deliver us from the evil one." In our culture one cannot expect general acceptance of exorcism on short notice. It is a matter which requires the most delicate handling. But if caution should prevent us altogether from dealing with it, we would be doing an injustice to aspects of the Christian faith which can only be ignored on pain of estrangement on the one hand, and sectarianism on the other. The attendant risk is that soon the exorcists, having mushroomed overnight, would go to work at random, without being sustained and supervised by a church community. It would be a sign of wisdom, then, if the churches themselves would reflect upon the function of this very ancient rite in advance.

15. GNOSIS

THE NOTION OF SATAN IS PART OF A DUALISTIC WAY OF DEALING WITH THE problem of God and evil. God is good, and evil originates with a power opposed to him. Dualism is based on the premise that God is in no way the author of evil. He did not will it; he did not introduce it into the world; it has nothing to do with him; on the contrary, it is that which is absolutely opposed to God, that which God opposes. Accordingly, it is not something we have to accept from the hand of God, but something we too have to fight.

Within the framework of dualism, however, the concept of Satan is not the only possible position. There exists another position which consists in the thesis that evil is inherent in the world and came with it. The situation then is not that there is an evil metaphysical power which threatens the world as God's good creation from the outside—the earth itself is the anti-divine. Existence on earth in itself constitutes estrangement from God. This idea has been developed most in gnosis or Gnosticism. Gnosis, a wide current in religious and philosophical thought in the first centuries A.D., climaxed in the second century.

In recent literature a distinction is usually made between "gnosis" and "Gnosticism." The latter name is then reserved for the explicit formation of a school of thought and the more or less institutionalized religious movements in that period, while "gnosis" is the term used for a broader movement which had a strong impact upon the whole body of thought at the time.

Gnosis was part of the intellectual climate of that time and is not therefore bound to any specific religion. Jews, Christians, and pagans were all influenced by it and all had to adopt a stand in relation to it. It would take us too far afield to discuss the different gnostic systems here. As is to be expected with a movement which is successful in a given period of history, gnosis displays a wide range of schools and currents within which a broad spectrum of nuances are again possible. Here we shall restrict ourselves to the main theme not only as it was articulated in the established schools but also as it leavened the entire culture of the time. At the same time we shall have to be careful lest the subject become so general that it lacks definition.

Characteristic for gnosis is a scheme of opposites: light-darkness; spirit-matter; divine-earthly. This dualism expresses itself first of all in the realm of thought. In fact, this is where gnosis derives its name: gnosis means knowledge. Ordinary everyday knowledge is based on observation, experience, thought. It occupies itself with the material and psychic world. Over against it, however, stands another kind of knowing, and that is the true knowing, the knowing of the spirit. It is the intuitive contemplation of the true essence of things, specifically the true essence of the self. It is knowledge, not of what you are in everyday life—eating and drinking, working and sleeping, thinking and talking—but of what you are at the level of the fundamental self: a spirit who far transcends the earthly. It is a kind of knowing you cannot learn, but which comes over you like a shock. Nor, therefore, is there gradual growth toward it. It is a sudden change as a result of which you view yourself and the world in a different light and you experience that your spirit is a source of eternal light elevated far above earthly matter. Pivotal in this gnosis is the recognition of your true being, a positive experience of transparent light which you recognize as your own home and in which you find residence.

This light is a part of the divine, eternal light, a spark of the eternal fire. It is the spirit as a part of the eternal Spirit. When we arrive at gnosis we have to return, and do return, to the eternal source. This eternal source is God, the source of eternal light, the total unity in which there is no trace of the earthly or the material.

Belonging to this dualism in knowledge, therefore, there is also a dualism between God and world. God is the true light, the full, all-encompassing spiritual knowledge. Opposed to it stands the material and psychic world which opposes God. It is not spirit. This material world has been created by a demiurge who is an inferior God. In Christian gnosis he is usually presented as the God of the Old Testament. He created matter in order to catch sparks of the light in it. The spirit was imprisoned within the body. Accordingly, matter, the earthly and the physical, is negative. Furthermore, rational thought is of this world and therefore negative.

In some gnostic systems we find a tripartite division in which thought is superior to matter but inferior to spirit. As a result the Valentinians recognize three groups of people: *hulikoi*, people who live purely material lives; *psychikoi*, people who reflect on things and belong to the church; and *pneumatikoi*, the people who behold the true knowledge. Though the *psychikoi* are higher than the *hulikoi*, by comparison with the spirit the psyche is also negative.

The various gnostic schools have different answers to the question of how this negative material world came into being. According to some it was there from the beginning. They advocate a basic dualism between good and evil, between spirit and matter. Because the darkness was there the light wanted to conquer it. Within itself the spiritual source is silence (sige), the abyss (buthos); but spirit emanated light and so formed the spiritual world of the aeons, lower heavenly beings, among which was the Logos. However, some attached themselves to matter and waited for the call to return, for a ray of light to ignite the spark and to remind it of its true being, in order that, after leaving the earthly prison, it might be reunited with the Spirit. At the end of time matter perishes, and silence again prevails; only the Spirit remains.

Other schools speak of a transcendent fall. The eternal Spirit was surrounded by transcendent beings, like the Logos, the Sophia, the original human being. One of these beings fell by leaving the source and then created matter, or was incarcerated in matter as punishment, or fell in love with matter. In that way humans were created bearing within them sparks of the fallen Wisdom, Sophia. By the call of the Logos they must be reawakened.

In both systems the first enlightened One played an important role in this process. In him the true knowledge again came to light; in him the true being of man, his divine descent, again became manifest. It is natural that in Christian gnosis the person of Christ was this first enlightened One: the Light of the world. For the problem of the relation between God and evil, therefore, gnosis has a simple solution: evil is bound up with matter, earthly existence, the polar opposite of God. God has absolutely no dealings with matter.

Ethically this view may have very different outcomes: asceticism, libertinism, or something in the middle. But in all three the essence is contempt for the world. Asceticism means shunning the world as much as possible. Libertines trample on all earthly laws and give free rein to the body. It counts for less than nothing. In between is this attitude: do not wear yourself out shunning the world. Why should you? The world does not matter anyway. And do not pursue pleasure. Why should you? After all, it is not real anyway.

In gnosis suffering and sin have nothing to do with God. We do not even have to pose the question how suffering is possible in the world. For gnosis the physical-material world, together with our earthly conduct, is itself a continual evil. Of course evil occurs in such a world. Therefore, the guilt of the act is not the important thing but the foundational guilt of incarceration in matter. The spirit is above all that. The real essence of a person is not affected by evil. Only the Spirit affects the

202

spirit. Only one's material body or earthly psyche can be affected by suffering and sin, but that is not important. That does not affect the relation between spirit and Spirit, the relation which coinheres with God.

In the second century the church was embroiled in a hard struggle over gnosis, one that ended in a rejection of all gnostic systems. After that gnosis in its extreme form never again became a problem. But its fundamental pattern continued to make itself felt throughout the history of the church. In every period, sometimes in wide circles, sometimes in small groups, the contrasts have continued—between the spiritual which is higher and the material which is inferior, and between the truly heavenly which endures and earthly illusion which perishes. Much asceticism, though not all, is conditioned by the idea that the earthly is inferior—a necessary evil as long as one exists in this inferior world— and that the truth and meaning of one's existence lies in the spiritual. This trend of thought has continued right into our own times. Today too, people believe that the world in which we live is a world which will perish. Accordingly, the future of the believer is not on this earth as the kingdom of God, but in heaven. As a rule this entails contempt for corporeality and for pleasure in material things, and hope for the re- demption of the soul. The earth and its beauty are opposed to God, and fortunately will pass away.

> Away world! Away, treasures!
> You cannot grasp
> how rich I really am!   *Da Costa*

Because this world is opposed to God, it is expectedly full of injustice and suffering. And because we live in this world and in the flesh, our spirit is continually threatened. The flesh lusts against the spirit. A lust for mundane matters, for riches, for beauty, and especially sexual desires threaten the purity of life with God. As long as the Christian is in the world there is continual conflict.

Liberation from this evil world is expressed in two ways:

a. After death the spirit goes to God. To die is to be freed from the world. It is also to be freed from fleshly desires. Soon we shall leave everything behind us and our souls will ascend to God. We shall go to heaven and there with God we will be happy. As children of the light we do not always experience this. Of ourselves we are bound to the earth. We live in this world. We are held back by carnal ties. But the believer knows that this does not compare with the splendor of heaven, and in his best moments he can let it all go and look forward to heaven.

b. The issue is viewed from the perspective of the world as a whole, not individually. The whole earth is destined to pass away. Soon this world will be destroyed and believers will be taken up into heaven. Then this earth will be annihilated. Characteristic for this line of thought is the disposition completely to write off this world—a tendency that is not restricted to any denomination in particular. One can find it in Catholic monasteries, in elitist Protestant circles, in the revivalist movements of recent times. In the Netherlands this view and the matching lifestyle occur most explicitly in the circles of the ultra-Reformed.

However, contemporary types of asceticism differ substantially from primitive Christian Gnosticism. Gnosticism operates with the model of emanation. The spirit proceeds from God, a spark of the divine descended to the earth. It is a heavenly category, incarcerated on earth in matter, awaiting its release to return to the one source of light. In contemporary models the spirit is not an emanation from God. It is created by God, and the contrast is between the *created* spirit and *created* matter. Hence, the difference between ancient and contemporary models is the distinction between emanation and creation. But for gnostics and the ultra-Reformed the final destination is the same: the spirit is destined to return to God. It is immortal and goes forth to a destiny in the heavenly light. Matter and the body are destined to perish. Those in this earthly life who are not spiritually allied with the Spirit of the imperishable God but remain bound to the earth will not share in the eternal light. They will remain incarcerated in an infinite existence of darkness and pain. The spiritual person is oriented to his or her ultimate destination; accordingly, despite the difference between thinking in terms of emanation or creation, in both there is great resemblance in the fundamental pattern of the religious life. This is especially determined by contempt for the earthly—also and precisely when people know themselves bound hand-and-foot to the earthly. It is this bondage which shapes the struggle for a pure spirit oriented to God.

Another characteristic is the assumption of the spirit in the divine light. In the *eschata*, what is central is not the resurrection of the body but the immortal soul. Immortality points to something divine as opposed to the mortal body. Sometimes the resemblance is even greater; that occurs among the ultra-Reformed when the Fall acquires cosmic features. Then man as a collective being is first of all man in fellowship with God, but the Fall then binds him to earthly desires. This comes close to the gnostic notion that the soul has its origin in God as opposed to the inferior earthly matter from which the body was formed.

Of this Arnold Albert van Ruler says, "How do they speak of man's being a sinner? If I am not mistaken their entire mode of thinking and speaking about this matter is determined by the apostle's image that we are 'dead' in our sins and trespasses. . . . A sinner is a dead human being. . . . That is how the sinner is born." To which van Ruler responds by asking, "Does sin have the character of fate in common with death?"[43]

In a much weaker form the tradition that the heavenly is the real and the earthly the inferior has been dominant over long periods of the history of the church. The moderation of the gnostic model as a rule consisted in the fact that the earthly and physical were not viewed as the wrong and the heavenly and spiritual as the good; rather, the heavenly was viewed as the higher and the earthly as the lower. That which is inferior is also less important. One must primarily invest himself in the spiritual and only work for the earth when necessary. We find these ideas, for example, in the antithesis between God's kingdom and the earthly kingdom (*civitas Dei* and *civitas terrena*) in Augustine, in his contrasting the enjoyment of God (*frui*) and the use of the earth (*uti*). One finds the contrast in the two-kingdom doctrine of Lutheranism but also in the construction of opulent cathedrals as "the house of God and gate of heaven" (*domus dei ac porta coeli*) amidst the poverty of the Middle Ages.

It would be wrong to view all these and similar phenomena as direct expressions of Gnosticism. There is a distant kinship in the longing for a future in heaven transcending the reality of the earth which lies in evil, a future in which the spiritually enlightened already participate. The boundaries of gnosis are unclear and its ideas gradually, via asceticism and world avoidance, faded into criticism of earthly structures. To use gnosticism's own imagery, it is like a fire whose flames rose high into the air at a certain period and in a certain movement of history; at its moment of maximum intensity the whole world was lit up by its glow and light; some people more, some less, but no one remained unaffected and at no point could one draw a line at which gnosis ceased; the fire still glows through the centuries so that even now one cannot draw that line. One can also reverse this line of thought: in all religions there is a relative distinction between the divine and the human, the holy and the secular. It is symbolically expressed by such terms as "heavenly" and "earthly." There is also a distinction between good and evil, between light and darkness. When that distinction is radicalized to the limit, and all contrasts can be divided into two fixed groups, and there is no interwovenness which makes a division into two realms impossible, then one arrives in the world of Gnosticism.

43. Arnold Albert van Ruler, *Theologisch Werk*, vol. 3 (Nijkerk: Callenbach, 1971), p. 107ff. (see also pp. 82-183).

Question: what can still be called "gnostic" and what cannot? It agrees with the character of Gnosticism to give an ambiguous answer to the question. It is an atmosphere in which one lives; it is like the air one breathes; it is the elusive Spirit which touches one's own spirit. In the precise sense of the term, Gnosticism no longer exists, at least not in the official works of theology. As far as I know, no theologian will unre-servedly say that matter itself is evil. But the spirit of Gnosticism still haunts the church, perhaps less in the theology of the schools than in the churches, and in groups which often occupy themselves intensely with the faith.

Opposed to this trend, in the church a strong current flows which resists this scheme of high and low and the withdrawal of the believer from the world. Van Ruler was a great advocate of the acknowledgment of the earth as a positive God-willed matter. The title of one of his articles is, "How does one appraise matter?"[44] The answer to that question is positive. The earth, the material, and the physical have a positive theological value. What happens at Koningstraat 38 (van Ruler's residence) is as important as Golgotha, and the sports stadium must not be neglected in favor of the communion table. Van Ruler loved sharp formulations and antitheses. Sometimes they seem exaggerated. But as a result his positions became clear. One must not file away the sharp edges. At the moment it is especially van Ruler's pneumatology which is getting attention,[45] more than his appraisal of the earth. That is not, however, because his ideas on the latter are said to have been superseded; on the contrary, it is so generally accepted that the earth is important—including politics, economics, and sports—that van Ruler's articles on this point do not seem to say anything new. It no longer needs to be said that the earth must not be assessed negatively and that we are not *only* spiritual Christians full of longing for the heavenly light. In contemporary theology the predominant tradition is that which accentuates the positive value of the world, culture, and politics. The high/low schematism is not at all in vogue. The linear schematism of history, the line that runs toward the coming kingdom, is preferred. Heaven has been replaced by the new earth and the new earth became a world with another face. In this context it is frequently remarked that the hierarchical

44. Van Ruler, "Hoe waardeerst men de stof?" in *Theologisch Werk* vol. 5 (Nijkerk, 1972), pp. 9-18. In the same volume, cf. "De waardering van het aardse leven," pp. 19-31.
45. See, for example, J. J. Rebel, *Pastoraat in pneumatologisch perspectief. Een theologische verantwoording vanuit het denken van A. A. van Ruler* (Kampen, 1981); R. Bohren, *Dass Gott schön werde. Praktische Theologie als theologische Ästhetik* (München, 1975), § 69; F. O. van Gennep, "Recente ontwikkelingen in de praktische theologie," II in *In de Waagschaal* 11 (1982), pp. 569-78, esp. p. 576.

scheme was Greek and the linear view of history typically Jewish, or better Hebraic. I do not share that view. There are two different approaches which Jews and Greeks have in common. It is a question rather of the period in which Jews and Greeks lived.

It does not do to compare Jewish data from the ninth and tenth century B.C. with Greek data from the third. One must compare Jewish and Greek texts from the beginning of the last pre-Christian millennium with each other, and similarly those of the end of that millennium. Then there are indeed differences, but they are not as big and of another character. One must not compare the judges and David and Goliath with the philosophers of the Greek enlightenment or the Stoa, but rather with Homer, and Ecclesiastes with the Greek philosophers of his day. Otherwise, one draws the same false conclusions as when one compares Ecclesiastes with Homer, concluding that Greek thought consists in faith in men led by the gods, men who fight for earthly values, and that Jewish thought consists of scepticism with respect to life, and that for Jews the true home of the human spirit is with God. The culture of the Eastern basin of the Mediterranean was much more a unity at that time than is often supposed. One must not forget that the easiest connections were made over the water.

It is incorrect to dismiss the high/low scheme as Greek and to conclude that the Christian church, rooted as it is in the tradition of Israel, must reject this scheme. For that matter, even if it did come from the Greeks, one could still argue over that conclusion. Even if it originated with the Greeks and was foreign to Israel, the church is not forbidden to use it as a vehicle for the formulation of its faith in God. In the preceding section we already remarked that Israel as well as the church have both continually adopted concepts from without. If the church of the Greek fathers deemed Greek concepts the best vehicles for the articulation of the true Christian faith it would have been folly not to use them. Accordingly, the explanation why the high/low scheme was rejected on the basis of the Jewish-Greek antithesis is doubly wrong. The high/low scheme as well as the scheme of the line of history are both Jewish and Greek, and both are useful for the communication of salvation to the world.

When in the second century A.D. the flames of the fire of Gnosticism rose high in the air, they did not come out of a void. A long road led to that point, one on which the tendencies of gnosis became increasingly more visible. Especially in the first century gnosis began to manifest itself more and more. If the concepts of gnosis, be it in a non-extreme form, are useful and may be viewed as legitimate vehicles for the articulation of faith in Christ, it would be desirable to find at least initiatives in that direction in the New Testament. The authors of the New Testament, at least in part, lived in a world in which gnosis began to gain ground. Gnostic thought was not foreign to them. Some New Testament authors in fact took a stand against these ideas. If against this trend no positive use of these gnostic schemes was made at all, their legitimacy within the Christian church would be rendered very suspect.

In the greater part of the Old Testament one finds neither the idea that the human spirit is of divine origin and has a divine destiny while the flesh is inferior, nor a preference for a hierarchical scheme over that of the linear progression of history. But in Ecclesiastes 12:7 we find an initial suggestion in that direction: the spirit returns to God who gave it. By contrast with existence on earth there is an eternal home with God to which the spirit returns. One cannot interpret the spirit here as the human breath of life which God has created and which belongs to God. That is still the case in Genesis 2, where we read that God breathed into the nostrils of man the breath of life. Ecclesiastes 12, first of all, speaks explicitly about the eternal home to which man is going, and this points to a continued existence of the human spirit. Also, the framework of Ecclesiastes is very different from that of Genesis 2. In Genesis 2 the reference is to man who, called into being by God himself, is permitted to live on earth as in a garden planted by God. In Ecclesiastes earthly existence is trouble and sorrow. It is vanity, even the vanity of vanities. It is air, and our earthly endeavor is the pursuit of wind. The Hebrew word translated as "vanity" is *hebel*. It means "a gust of wind"; hence it is something empty, meaningless, an illusion, a nothing. That describes life on earth. It gives one no foothold whatever; it passes like a breath of air, until it is over. But the spirit departs from this vain existence to an eternal home. An eternal home or "a home for eternity" denotes a firmness conferred upon it by its nearness to God. David receives an eternal home; God will build him a house that is sure and established, a kingdom that will last forever (2 Sam. 7:16). A related text in Psalm 89 states, "I will establish his line for ever" and the parallel "and his throne as the days of the heavens" (v. 29). Accordingly, in Ecclesiastes the imperishability of the spirit, enduring as heaven itself, is contrasted with the transience of the earth. The dust of man—his body—returns to the earth and the spirit returns to God who gave it (12:7). As a result, everything one does in this earthly life is "vanity of vanities." Ecclesiastes 12, or for that matter the entire book of Ecclesiastes, remains a flinty stumbling block for every theology which claims that the hierarchic scheme is non-Jewish. Ecclesiastes knows no historical progression, only senseless repetition. The scheme is cyclical rather than linear. In addition, Ecclesiastes knows of the imperishable human spirit, coming from and returning to God, as opposed to the earthly vanity associated with matter. One can only escape this stumbling block by representing Ecclesiastes as "Greek thought." But that constitutes an a priori selection of Old Testament material on the basis of the theory that is to be proved.

In the final centuries before the beginning of the Christian era, a more dualistically tinted movement arose in Judaism, in which the soul is pictured as eternal, and at death it leaves behind a transient earth. A further development is the idea that the soul is pre-existent and comes from the realm of God, an idea which, in view of the word "return" (shuv), seems to be presupposed in Ecclesiastes.[46]

In the New Testament the high-low scheme is present much more often. This is most clear in the letter to the Hebrews. In this letter one finds the notion that for every earthly thing there is a heavenly counterpart. There is an earthly high priest and a heavenly high priest, an earthly tabernacle and a heavenly one, an earthly sabbath and a heavenly one. The earthly is perishable, the heavenly permanent. Christ is the heavenly high priest who by his entrance into the heavenly sanctuary has opened the way to the eternal sabbath for us. Some authors have seen in the letter to the Hebrews a pronounced gnostic scheme, that of a descending and ascending redeemer, in which the heavenly savior descended into fallen, material existence. The scheme of high and low, heavenly and earthly, and the description of the final destination of man as rest corresponds to Gnosticism. Such notions are so general, however, that others must be added for us to be able to accept kinship with gnosis. But a more precise analysis teaches us that the resemblance to gnosis is only very superficial. The contrast between high and low has a very different function here. In gnosis the heavenly is bound up with the human spirit and material earthly existence as such is evil. In Hebrews the whole man, spiritually and physically, is of the earth. No divine spark descended on earth and entered man. For the author of Hebrews, earth is not the prisonhouse of the higher spirit but the prefiguration of the heavenly. The two belong together. Though temporal, the earth is nevertheless a positive prefiguration of heaven. Accordingly, the course of earthly life is also essential. It is the road to eternal rest. Hebrews has a clear sense of history. The scheme of high and low is supplemented with that of the old and new, or that of before and now. A strong accent falls, to be sure, on the relativity and provisionality of earthly life. The church is the people of God on their way to an abiding city in the footprints of the forefathers (Heb. 11). So on the one hand Hebrews shows similarities with Gnosticism, especially by employing the scheme of the heavenly

46. Kittel, *TDNT*, vol. 6, pp. 368-89, esp. pp. 377-80.

and earthly, the perishable and imperishable, and the stress on provisionality. But these similarities can be explained in terms of the general movement of thought in the second half of the first century as it tended toward Gnosticism. On the other hand, both on account of the absence of the idea of the spirit as the divine spark and on account of its sense of the course of history, Hebrews can certainly not be called gnostic.

The idea that earthly events were adumbrations of heavenly reality—an idea which originated in platonic philosophy—gained great influence in the Eastern churches via the theology of John Damascene and especially of Pseudo-Dionysius Areopagita. There too the eschatological goal is rest as the final end of human history. In the liturgy the church celebrates the new life, the life that consists not in human political activity but in the rest of eternity, surrounded by the church of the ages which enters that rest. When the Christian church engages in earthly activity, when it makes changes in the tradition of centuries, it is not traveling on the way to heaven, but is removing itself further away from the eternal liturgy. There are features in areopagitic theology which are reminiscent of emanation, a theory in which the world is alienation from God. The division of an earthly and a heavenly liturgy, however, keeps the earth within reach of the divine goodness and blocks the idea that the earth as such is evil. The totally different understanding of the relationship between liturgy and human activity in the Eastern and the Western world is a continuing barrier in ecumenical dialogue.

The situation—if one wants to answer the question whether there could be gnostic influences in the New Testament—is more difficult in John's gospel than in the letter to the Hebrews. In John's gospel Jesus is the one sent by the Father. He comes from above and descends to the earth. He possessed a glory before the world was; he left it behind and prays that he may receive it again (John 17:5). He who believes in him is also "born from above," of "water and the Spirit" (3:35). They are the children of God who are not born of the will of the flesh (1:13). Because Jesus was the one sent from above, he does not belong in this world (17:14). For the ruler of this world is the devil (12:31). Belonging to his domain are the people who do not believe in Christ, who therefore are not born anew by the Spirit (3:18). The use of the word "world" *(kosmos)* may create the impression that the spatial scheme is decisive and that John therefore had a view similar to that of gnosis. The alternative, after all, was the use of the word "aeon," "this age," a word with a much more temporal aspect than *kosmos.* However, in contrast with other New Testament authors, the word "aeon" does not occur with this meaning in John. Preference for *kosmos* over "aeon" could perhaps indicate a preference for a spatial image and thus point in a gnostic direction. But if we draw this conclusion we forget that in gnosticism the word "aeon" was very important, not as "age," but as an intermediate heavenly being with a domain of its own. Accordingly, if John had wanted to use gnostic structures, the word "aeon" would have been an obvious choice. The absence of "aeon" points to opposition to Gnosticism rather than to a preference for their scheme. Also in another respect there is an essential difference. The Logos, the Word, was sent by the Father. He is a preexistent divine being, just as in Gnosticism, but when he descends, he comes not to a foreign domain but to his own (1:11). The world is not a counter agency hostile to God; all things were made by the divine Logos himself (1:1-3). The world is the realm in which the devil rules but also the world which God loves (3:16). The world as such is not evil; it is evil only in its perversion. The question concerning the ultimate source of evil is probably not of interest to the Gospel of John. Evil exists, Satan rules, and God saves by sending his Son. In any case evil is not automatically given with the existence of the world.

Another essential difference is that the spiritual man, rather than being a divine spark which must be liberated from its prisonhouse, must be born anew. The point is a new spiritual creation rather than a return to the source. Actually, in John the situation is no different than in Hebrews: there are echoes of gnostic patterns; the comparison between the two is not totally unfounded and theologians who stress the resemblance can find a good many arguments for their point of view. But at the essential points the two diverge. Moreover, the author of the Gospel of John appears to be writing in an environment much more heavily influenced by gnosis than that of Hebrews, which can still unfold its own ideas unhindered by the tensions which gnosis was to introduce into the church. The author could make carefree use of the tendencies which were in the air. John has to engage in explicit confrontation and faces the difficult challenge, on the one hand, of exploiting the language and thought of his environment and, on the other, of resisting the gnostic tendencies which he considered a barrier to faith in Christ. To a large degree he uses the language of his gnostically influenced environment and at important points gives to that language a radically anti-gnostic twist, for example, when he says that the Logos has become flesh (1:14). By doing this he paved the way for the great second-century opponent of gnosis: Irenaeus.

In the case of Paul and his corpus the situation is not essentially different. Paul uses the word "aeon," but primarily in its temporal meaning. This aeon is succeeded by the revelation of the sons of God, an event for which believers long (Rom. 8:18ff.). This world is indeed an ungodly world, but not because in essence and origin it was evil; it is evil on account of the sin of man (Rom. 5). The perverted world is bad, not the world which God made. The world is not vain as such, but it was subjected to futility by an active agent (Rom. 8:20). In Paul, as in John, there are echoes of gnosis, to be sure, but at critical moments it is rejected. Christ is the true wisdom, the *sophia* (1 Cor. 1:24); to confess him as Lord is to live by the Spirit (1 Cor. 12:3), not by an esoteric wisdom.

In other New Testament writings the situation is not fundamentally different. It would take us too long to deal with all this at length. It is indeed also interesting to note that, apart from James 3:5 (where *hule* means forest, not matter), the words "matter" *(hule)* and "material" *(hulikos)* do not occur in the New Testament at all. In Gnosticism the contrast between material and spiritual *(hulikos/pneumatikos*, with *psychikos*, animated, in between them at times) plays a large role. The writings of the New Testament in no way refer to this antithesis. Flesh *(sarx)*, not matter, is the polar opposite of the Spirit. In the New Testament "flesh" has an ethical meaning, not a cosmological one. The person who does not live with Christ in a new life is carnal. "Flesh" is not corporeality as such, but earthly existence as perverted by sin. The world as such is not evil—it is God's creation, which has been made evil by sin. This evil has profoundly corroded the world, so that the authors of the New Testament can no longer speak ingenuously about the "world," "flesh," and "man." There is no neutral nature. All that exists is a world corrupted by sin which resists the Spirit of Christ. This world is not cosmologically evil on account of its materiality and man is not evil on account of his corporeality, but it is ethically corrupted by the sin which man has chosen and which controls him where the Spirit of Christ is not in charge. For the Christian church this implies a call to be reserved in relating to the world. The world is not neutral nor even positive; it is the sinful world in which the deceiver is in control. It is subjected to evil, though it is not inherently evil.

Hence the New Testament is not gnostic. Links with gnosis exist because of the shared cultural situation and the climate of thought which were influenced by gnosis. Asceticism and reserve toward the world can be a legitimate Christian posture, but not because of the world's being earthly. In the first century the Christian church consciously rejected the gnostic position and explicitly confirmed its choice for the sake of Christ, a historical human person, in whom the Word became flesh. Even less does the Old Testament know the idea that the earth is inferior or evil. All we can point to is a tenuous line running toward dualistic Jewish views via the pessimistic wisdom teaching of Ecclesiastes. But in the New Testament the church consciously headed in a different direction.

For more literature, cf. Jacques Dupont, *Gnosis: La connaissance religieuse dans les Épîtres de Saint Paul*, and Bultmann's article in *TDNT*, vol. 1, under *ginōskō*. See also the articles under *Aiōn, gé, cosmeō,* and *pneuma* (see, besides the articles already mentioned, also vol. 6, pp. 389-455). For an interpretation of the letter to the Hebrews in light of gnosticism, see Ernst Käsemann, *The Wandering People of God: An Investigation of the Letter to the Hebrews.* Extensive criticism of this work occurs in Ronald Williamson, *Philo and the Epistle to the Hebrews;* another exegesis can also be found in C. K. Barrett's article, "The Eschatology of the Epistle of the Hebrews," in *The Background of the New Testament and its Eschatology,* W. D. Davies and D. Daube, eds., a volume in honor of C. H. Dodd. On pp. 363-93 the thesis is defended that for the author of Hebrews it is history which is determinative.

For the gnosis of the second century, see esp. Robert Haardt's *Gnosis: Character and Testimony.* A twentieth-century version of gnosis and a plea in favor of it can be found in Eugen Heinrich Schmitt, *Die Gnosis. Grundlagen der Weltanschauung einer edleren Kultur: Die Gnosis des Altertums,* vol. 1; *Die Gnosis des Mittelalters und der Neuzeit,* vol. 2 (new editions of both parts: Aalen, 1968).

Accordingly, in its radical form Gnosticism is diametrically opposed to the Christian faith as articulated by the authors of the New Testament. That is not to say that aspects of gnosis cannot be incorporated in Christian theology. We already said it is the extreme form in which ideas which also occur in wider circles are posited which make Gnosticism into Gnosticism. Within the spectrum of themes propagated by Gnosticism there can, within the church, be a variety of nuances; for example, in the evaluation of the earthly, of matter, and of history. However, when quantitative differences are elevated to the extreme, they become qualitative differences. Then it is no longer an issue of more or less but of all or nothing. Where the earth in its materiality is said to have nothing good; history and human action are emasculated and become a mere flight to heaven, ethics melts into esoteric knowledge, and faith is forgotten in favor of direct vision, a boundary has been crossed. To this the church of the first century said "no," and this extremism the church of the second century passionately resisted. Throughout the centuries the crossing of that boundary remained a temptation for the church because the absolute contrasts are always present in relative forms and the boundary between "much" and "all" is a subtle one.

Often the radicalization of gnosis also rendered suspect other forms of world avoidance. But this—in light of the New Testament data—has proven to be wrong. For that reason we have to spend a bit more time on the forms of world avoidance in the history of the church to which we referred at the beginning of this section. In the context of the rejection of Gnosticism, an impulse may easily arise also to reject all gnostically tinted or even all ascetic tendencies. We discover, however, that these tendencies as such are not to be rejected; in the New Testament it is only their radicalization which merits resistance. This means that, in the church, to work with concepts oriented to gnosis always involves risks, since every concept has the potential in certain circles for being radicalized. But does not Christian theology always function between a rock and a hard place? Is it not precisely where the last things which can be said are said that the fiercest tension and greatest joy arise? At this critical point world avoidance may and must be positively assessed.

We have seen that to most New Testament authors the world, though not inherently evil, has been perverted and become evil. In actual fact it lies in evil, a situation which calls for reserve toward it. We need not shun the earth because it is the earth. But we do have to exercise the greatest possible prudence in relating to the world. For in that world the evil one is in command. Everything people do is perverted as measured by the standard of God's original intention with the world. Accordingly, the Christian church adopts a critical attitude toward earthly greatness. Power on earth is all too easily power based on violence. What does it profit a person to be powerful on earth and to be outside the kingdom of God? What does it profit a person to be held in honor if it causes him to forget to render honor to the glorious one? What does it profit us to be rich if we are poor in love? What benefit is there in relationships perverted by injured souls? All that belongs to the world bears the marks of estrangement and temptation. The more we become engrossed in earthly greatness, the more prominent we are in the group to which we belong—whether that be in the higher echelons of government, on Wall Street, in a synod, or in the world of popular entertainment—the greater the danger that we become small in the kingdom of God. The more we grow in the grace of Christ, the bigger the chance that we do not count or are at most tolerated in earthly structures. As Christians we are called to abstain from sin, for we have died to sin. But sin has become "enfleshed." There is a covenant between sin and the world, between sin and our earthly existence. Our flesh is no longer neutral. It militates against the Spirit of Christ. Therefore, to fight against sin always implies dying to the world, that is, to the perverted world, the world in which in fact we live. There is no other. We must die to our flesh. That does not mean to our bodies. The issue runs deeper. We are dealing with the whole of our earthly life, including our spiritual achievements. Our spirit is not a divine spark; it too belongs to created, sin-sick existence on earth.

As we think from within this perspective, we arrive at a life of sobriety and ascesis. We live on earth; we cannot dispense with our daily bread and so we work. But life on earth becomes the road to the kingdom of God, where our real joy is. There we delight ourselves, free from the perversion of sin, and hence are really free at last. It is the distinction Augustine made when he spoke of using and enjoying. Enjoyment is present only in communion with God.

This posture is that of practical dualism. Cosmological dualism is based on the idea that the world as such is evil. Practical dualism acknowledges the goodness of the earth as God's creation. At the same time it sees that in practice this world has become a fallen world. Sin cannot be ignored. Corruption and brokenness are not to be ignored. Practical dualism therefore follows the line taught by John and Paul. Only where the Spirit of Christ is can existence be renewed. There man's existence is illumined. The light is not the divine spark of his spirit. That light is the grace and love of the crucified and risen Lord, extending to the whole of our life and determining our daily conduct. Creation is an area of light around the cross of Christ, says Noordmans.[47] This creation as renewed does not express itself as earthly glory, but in the glory of the crucified among the poor and despised. It is the glory of the foolishness of the cross which the world cannot deal with, a glory which irritates the legalistic "devotee of principle" and on which the power of the powerful comes to grief. It is the glory of anchorites and monks vow-bound to poverty. It is the glory of the sober people of the Reformed tradition with their black suits and subdued looks.

However, in all the different traditions and currents we observe the risks of the temptations of the world. Anchorites carried the passions of their hearts with them; monks ate the good things of the earth; the Reformed, whose sobriety turned into frugality, filled their houses with riches. But the corrosion of evil went even deeper. The flight out of the world itself became glorious. The moment the anchorite became a celebrated saint his renunciation of the world was over. Anchoritism became rubbish. As soon as monasteries and monastic orders gained power in the world, the silence of meditation and prayer passed into the organization of a power which can be more perverse than a dictatorship. When the Reformed became emancipated they raised their voices in the street; all at once they were right with a vengeance, in a manner peculiar to all the emancipated.

Then it is again the small and despised who are the sign in this world of the light of the cross shining in a world in which even people who have seen the light prefer the darkness of greatness to the light of renunciation. Then comes a foolish monk who preaches to the birds. Then comes the fool who abandons his career and, talking about salvation by grace alone, locks himself up in a remote castle. Then comes the

47. Oepke Noordmans, *Herschepping* (Zeist, 1934), p. 83.

quiet prayer of the pious who, in a world of people all of whom are right in their own eyes, sigh, "How long, O Lord?"

If the world is perverted by sin, that means not only guilt but also suffering. People who are led by the Spirit know of oppression by the pseudo-saintly, the pseudo-powerful, and the pseudo-wise. They then open the book of Psalms and recognize the songs of the persecuted. They do not raise their voices on the street but sing, either in their hearts or their assemblies:

> Thou knowest all my woes,
>   O treasure Thou my tears;
> Are they not in Thy book,
>   Where all my life appears? (Ps. 56:8 in verse)

They know of slander and mockery, like the ancient poets. But they also say:

> My foes shall backward turn
>   When I appeal to Thee,
> For this I surely know,
>   That God is still for me. (Ps. 56:9 in verse)

But practical dualism goes further. Not only are Christians the persecuted on earth. Earth itself is a place of suffering. Never again can it be seen apart from the brokenness of sin. For that reason the best of life is but toil and trouble (Ps. 90:10). The earth is a vale of tears. So Christians are not surprised when they suffer and are afflicted by sickness and death. It hurts them. Their hearts are tender. They suffer indescribably under the pain. They cannot do without the infrequent partners who share their journey. They shrink at the sight of the suffering of the world which is estranged from God. It was the anchorites, the monks, and the pietists who went into the world to help and console. They did not administer development programs, but they helped and spoke of the grace of God. And when compassion and consolation in the name of Christ became development work, they pulled out. For when the world becomes developed, the powerful become great and the rich become powerful.

Practical dualism entails the longing for heaven; happiness is not to be found here below. Believers understand the apostle Paul: "My desire is to depart and be with Christ, for that is far better" (Phil. 1:23). They remain wanderers on earth, seeking a better country (Heb. 11:13-16). Our home is above; on earth we are but strugglers, our existence one of suffering. Even our faith is embattled and weak. In many ways we all stumble. In rigorously Reformed circles people often refer to themselves in the third person. Then they talk about the person who is able to forsake the earth and totally focus on Christ, about the tender person who is led by the Spirit. But at the same time they know their earthly existence to be so interwoven with the perversion of sin, right down to their deepest selves, that they cannot imagine themselves to be that person. Also, this posture can become an alibi, a process in which the spiritual man becomes a fiction and carnal man a beast. Beside the asceticism, dualism always has within itself the corruption of libertinism. But it can also be awe before the miracle that God, taking the lost earthly creature, should by the Spirit of Christ make him into his child and let him share in the heavenly light. It is the same trembling awe which comes through in 2 Corinthians 12, where Paul also speaks about himself in the third person. Here he refers to the heavenly vision and finds it inconceivable that the person who has that ecstatic experience should be the same person who can glory only in weaknesses, the person who was buffeted by a messenger of Satan.

Practical dualism does not inquire into the cause of evil. To the question where evil comes from it may very well apply another model, that usually being that man is the guilty party. For God is good, the gracious one. He is our only hope of deliverance from this world of sin and suffering. Practical dualism is not so much interested in the past, in where lie the roots of this broken world; it is more interested in the reality of the present and even more in the hope of the future when God will deliver us from this vale of tears. The practical dualist does not primarily ask "Why?" but rather, "How long?"

At the same time, however, he trusts that the time still remaining is a time in the hands of God. God knows our sufferings and struggles, and will lead us on our journey even though it be a journey through depths which may be long and dark. In the deep vale of the world, with all its suffering, Christ says to us, "Be of good courage; I have overcome the world" (John 16:33). In him God not only knows our suffering and struggle, but also delivers us from the burdens of battle. When it comes to the relationship between God and evil, God is the God of compassion who delivers us from this world. The world is not saved; it perishes. But God saves his children. He saves them through death. When they have borne their cross to the very end, God the Father sees them from afar, embraces them, and brings them home to celebrate (Luke 15:20-24). At the feast God's children are the beloved, and he wipes away all their tears (Rev. 21:4). We need not ask God "Why?" We do not need in desperation to ask: "How can God permit this?" In our deepest distress we may raise

217

our heads, tears filling our eyes, to the God who is our hope, who loves us, who will help us through suffering and will some day give us eternal joy. That joy will be so great that all the suffering of the world will be as nothing by comparison (Rom. 8:18). Because that is the prospect before us, a prospect God himself has given us, we find the courage to persevere in the world.

In this connection there is one figure in church history about whom something must still be said: Marcion, a theologian of the second century. Marcion posed the thesis that the God of the Christian church is different from the God of creation. In that respect he agreed with Gnosticism. Marcion supposed that first there was a God who made the creation, the God of the Jews and of the Old Testament. But now, in Christ, a new God has come and the time of the Creator God is past. Accordingly, for Christians the Creator God is the wrong God. To acknowledge him is to deny that Christ is the real Lord. To maintain his position, Marcion gave up the entire Old Testament, the book of the Creator God. Marcion also left out of his canon large parts of the New Testament. He only kept, and that in a purified form, the Pauline letters and the gospel of Luke. Part of Marcionism is rigorous world avoidance: taking part in earthly pleasures is service to the Creator God, but we must participate in the new kingdom of Christ.

There is strong kinship between Marcion and gnosis, specifically in the position that the earth is evil. But there is also great difference. Gnosticism is based on a cosmological dualism, a hierarchical scheme, and the absence of historical progression. Marcion, on the other hand, proceeds from a historical dualism, a scheme of earlier and later, old and new. In any case, by adopting this scheme, Marcion showed he had a better understanding of the old aeon and divine sonship as Paul understood it. However, the separation of the God of creation from the God of Jesus Christ, the God of Israel from the God of grace, was non-Pauline and ultimately intolerable to the church. For that Christianity was too deeply rooted by Jesus in Israel, and in the tradition in which he had lived. But before the church arrived at this decision much water had flowed under the bridge, and the church was seriously divided. For a time the number of Marcion's supporters was larger than that of the later orthodoxy.

Especially Adolf von Harnack devoted much attention to Marcion's theology. In his monograph *Marcion: das Evangelium vom Fremden Gott,* he drew a number of parallels between Marcion and Luther. This relatively positive assessment was later criticized. A more recent view can be found in Edwin C. Blackman, *Marcion and His Influence.* Also of interest is the theology of Marcion's pupil Appeles who, while tracing both creation and grace back to one principle, at the same time tried, in imitation of Marcion, to maintain the tension between the two.[48]

Gnosticism proceeded from the idea that the divine spirit was the good and that as a result of emanation from the fountain of eternal light the spirit fell into evil. Consequently, it was imprisoned in matter which consisted of or arose from alienation from God. God is the absolute source of the good: the further a thing is from him, the less good it is. Evil consists of matter, but part of the explanation for this is the enormous distance between the fountainhead of light and the darkness of matter. This led to the idea that evil consists in the lack of the good. Evil is not an independent "something," but only the absence of the good, just as darkness does not exist independently, but is only a deficiency of light. Accordingly, evil is not a position, only a negation. Thus, also the problem of the existence of matter is solved. Matter is only the coarse situation which originates from a lack of the refined purity of the light of the spirit.

If we adopt the position that evil is merely the absence of the good, the problem of the origin of evil is solved. God is good, the source of pure light. Light radiates outward from him and the more the light shines, the more the darkness becomes manifest. The larger the circle filled with light, the longer the circumference where darkness is manifest, just as a larger island has a longer coastline than a smaller one. As the circle of light around the cross of God's good creation grows, the darkness of sin becomes more manifest.

The idea that evil is merely the negation of the good is not typically gnostic. In Gnosticism this idea only occurs in extreme form. But also within a model in which from the beginning the world is God's creation, it is possible to think that though the creation was good and though it was made by a good God, with its appearance—which is not the goodness of God himself—deficiency also makes its appearance. In relation to the glory of God creation is deficient. And on the boundary of the good creation there is nothingness.

Barth's doctrine of nothingness displays features of evil as negation. Nothingness is the possibility which God bypassed. It is the unreal reality which originated when God electingly created the world. In creation itself the sign of nothingness is the darkness of the night. Night is not nothingness itself; it belongs to the good creation of God. But it exists on the outer limits of nothingness.[49]

Harnack once said of Barth's theology that it resembled that of Marcion (which for Harnack meant a positive valuation rather than a disqualification). It cannot be denied that in fact the gnostically influenced theologian of the second century and the church father of the twentieth share certain characteristics. They have the christological concentration in common: only Christ is true and he judges all else around him. From this angle one could call Barth even more gnostic than Marcion, since in Marcion the world outside of Christ is created by another God. In Barth, on the other hand, all that is outside of Christ has succumbed to nothingness, the non-willed impossible possibility. As a result evil and hence also

---

48. Adolf von Harnack, *Marcion: Das Evangelium vom Fremden Gott* (Leipzig, 1921[8]), pp. 231ff.
49. Barth, *Church Dogmatics* III, 1, 41, pp. 117-33, esp. pp. 130ff.

sin lose their active assertive character. Election and reprobation are so concentrated in Christ that human responsibility tends to be crowded into a corner.[50]

Though in the basic structure there is commonality between Barth and Marcion, there is also a great difference between them. It is precisely the shading in the basic theological structures which determine the theological position. Extremely antithetical structures do not make for the most interesting theologies. Of importance are the fine nuances which in theology make the basic structure useful or non-useful. With respect to evil, the difference between gnosis and Barth is that in the former evil is the utter absence of God, while in Barth, in a strange and indirect way, it came from God. It exists in the remarkable mode of being which is peculiar to nothingness. But given the fact that it proceeded from the negative choice of God—rejection—it is no longer merely negation. It is incorporated in the way of election, the way of the saving God. In gnosis every form of existence outside of God is as such a form of straying from the light. In Barth existence outside of God is not apostasy, but the basis for reconciliation and hence the basis for the covenant. No gnostic will call a world fallen under nothingness, "the external basis of the covenant." Marcion would never describe the world of the Creator God as the good creation, the basis of God's covenant of love and faithfulness. In Barth creation calls forth rejection in its electing character. Consequently, rejection is no longer merely dismissal; it is also a position, serving the glory of Christ. Rejection is divine rejection: there is an act of God behind it. Accordingly, rejection and subsequently nothingness is not mere deficiency but an act, be it an act of not-willing, an act of God's left hand. Nothingness is not positive, nor is it merely negative.

With this position Barth aligns himself with classic Reformed theology. Also Heppe, in his classic compendium of Reformed scholastic theology, remarks that evil is neither something positive, nor something purely negative. It is a *privatio iustitiae*, a lack of righteousness but also an *actuosa privatio*, a robbery. It is an "active quality opposed to the good . . . the absolute opposite of righteousness."[51] Accordingly, the difference between Barth and the Reformed tradition is especially that, whereas the tradition sees the assertive aspect of evil as especially inherent in the human deed, Barth sees it rather in the divine act of bypassing the rejected possibility, hence as an act (be it negative) of God.

16. GOD IS DIFFERENT

THE SET OF PROBLEMS THIS BOOK IS CONCERNED WITH IS THE FIELD OF tension between the omnipotence and the goodness of God. God is the

---

50. For an elaboration of this, see my dissertation *De menselijke persoon van Christus* (Callenback, 1980), pp. 56-59.
51. Heppe, *Reformed Dogmatics*, p. 323.

almighty—nothing happens outside of him. Nothing is more powerful than he, for he is the highest power. He is also the highest goodness. There is no darkness in him. All categories—goodness, freedom, and love—are ultimately grounded in him; all that exists in the way of earthly and human possibilities owes its existence to divine possibilities. He is the highest goodness, the highest power, the highest freedom, the highest love. He is these things in an all-encompassing way: he is the all-good, omnipotence, absolute freedom, and love itself. Because God is the *One* who transcends all things, he even transcends his own attributes. Omnipotence, all-goodness, freedom, and love are all references to the being of God in the absoluteness of his oneness, the oneness of all that is. God is the highest being, true being in an absolute sense.

Conversely, this means that all being can only exist in dependence on this One Being. Such properties and categories as exist do so because of God's eternal being, even his own properties. This is all the more true of our relative properties. They only exist in absolute dependence on his absolute properties. Our goodness, our power, our freedom, our love are possible only because God is good, powerful, free, and loving. This is true not only of the properties mentioned, but of all the positive possibilities of human beings, say, wisdom, joy, faithfulness, and mercy.

Now it turns out that human categories such as love and freedom, power and goodness, are frequently contradictory. Power is misused and experienced by others as violence. Freedom is restricted by love of neighbor. In the case of people, given their relative possibilities, this may be irksome or sad, and may occasion inner psychological conflict, but it does not occasion logical conflict. After all, there are many people with many possibilities capable of realization. But there is only one God. Now how can God's oneness be preserved, and at the same time all his properties in their all-encompassing character be maintained? How can absolute love and absolute freedom be squared? Freedom for a person means to be completely determined by one's own choice. Love means to be completely determined by (the needs of) the other. Now one can solve this problem by saying that one's freedom is not restricted if one chooses freely to allow oneself to be completely determined by the other. But that is a pseudo-solution. The person who freely opts for love is indeed free. But to be loving that person has to choose for love. The freedom to choose for hate is excluded. Consequently, freedom is restricted and hence no longer absolute. Accordingly, there is a logical contradiction in the concept of the one all-encompassing God. Either God is the absolutely One (but then he cannot in an absolute way encompass all properties), or he encompasses all properties in an absolute way (but then he cannot be the absolutely One).

However, the idea that God is the absolutely One, the true being, is even more problematic. We stated above that God's properties are the extrapolation, to the absolute degree, of our positive properties. But humans also have negative properties such as hate, egoism, stupidity, slackness. If God were really the one all-encompassing being, he also has those properties in absolute form. Then he is absolute hate, total egoism, infinite stupidity, complete slackness. Not only can these properties not be squared with other properties of God; they also do not in any way fit the image of God that underlies the concept of God as absolute being. At stake in that concept is the ability, amidst the relativity and chaos of the world, to see in God the one fixed point, the one stable being. But if God is relativity and chaos to the infinite degree, the sense of the representation of God as absolute being is gone. For then also the conflicts of the world are imported into his being to the infinite degree. Then God can no longer be the absolutely One. If all things, love and hate, wisdom and stupidity, power and slackness, must belong to the being of God to the infinite degree, the result can only be that at the beginning of all being there is a spiritual "big bang" in which oneness only calls forth chaos.

Thus we note that basic to the conflict between the omnipotence and goodness of God in the pastoral situation of human beings there is a philosophical notion of God. Why does my suffering raise questions? It is on account of the all-encompassing character of the power of God. How can he permit this suffering? After all, he could have prevented it. Or conversely, in light of the absolute goodness of God, how can he give me this? Is he not my loving Father unreservedly committed to my happiness? Because we believe in the one God who is absolutely powerful and absolutely good, a God whose omnipotence and whose goodness must be accepted without qualification, we run into conflict over suffering. In his book *A Flight of Curlews*, Martin Hart voices his inability to comprehend a God who as a merciful Father not only gives me health but also sickness. That is to say, a philosophical paradigm is not just a theoretical plaything invented by a learned man in the quiet of his study but the ground on which people stand, and in which, in their daily lives with all the experiences they encounter, they find a basis for processing their existence.

The paradigm concept is derived from Thomas S. Kuhn, *The Structure of Scientific Revolutions.* "Paradigm" Kuhn understands as the basic view which underlies scientific research. No one can be totally unbiased, or completely objective, as he engages in research. Everyone has his tradition, educational background, and cultural horizon. Within that context he will interpret all data in a certain way and even observe some things while being blind to others. Some data simply fall outside of the world of his experience. When, as a result of cultural change there is openness toward new things, or when as a result of this openness new things come to light, a new paradigm comes into being. That is not a simple matter; it is a burdensome process, for not only does one have to deal with new, hitherto unknown facts, but all old experiences and interpretations also come to stand in a new light.

An example of a change in paradigms in the natural sciences is the Copernican revolution, in which the old view that the earth stood still and was the center of the universe was replaced by the concept of a revolving earth. Another example is the revolution occasioned by quantum mechanics, which replaced the mechanical-physical image of the preceding centuries.

Also, the revolution in biology—from an earlier concept of fixed created species to today's evolutionistic view—is such a change in paradigm. These examples already make clear that paradigm change occasions much tension. It is not merely a remote theory or hypothesis that is being replaced; in reality, one's whole manner of being in the world changes. Changes in natural science, accordingly, have to do with changes in one's understanding and experience of the world and of faith. In theology, such changes of paradigm explicitly bear this stamp. For that reason they are even harder to realize than paradigm changes in the natural sciences; or better, cultural changes shaped by the new paradigm are easier to assimilate in the natural sciences than in theology. In theology we still experience the greatest difficulty assimilating Copernicus—man is not the center of the universe.

In his theory of paradigms Kuhn reacts against Popper, who does not view science as being programmed by paradigms but believes that we can only develop very provisional theories. Not without reason his best-known work is entitled *Conjectures and Refutations*. One tries out theories until they no longer prove to be tenable and subsequently one ventures out on a new path. In my opinion both views are right. The truth is that Kuhn is dealing with the fundamental structures of scientific thought and Popper proceeds from the theories possible within a given paradigm. Kuhn says, "You cannot see everything and what you see you see in a certain way." Popper says, "Attempt to arrange what you see in your own way as meaningfully as possible." In fact, then, they are talking about different things. That is even true when they are talking about the same examples. Precisely theology can learn that what to one person is a paradigm which fundamentally shapes his views is to another no more than a provisional model. To one person an apocalyptic description of the new heaven and the new earth following the millennium can be the perspective in terms of which the entire world of present, past, and future is interpreted; to another it is no more than an interesting theory whose tenability is perhaps worth testing. To one person the idea that Paul radically rejects the Jewish law constitutes the basic structure of his theological thought; to another it is a questionable, antiquated hypothesis. In the one case Kuhn is right, in the other Popper. But the person for whom the paradigm of another is no more than a provisional or antiquated model should not think that he has no paradigm of his own. And to another person *that* paradigm may be no more than a replaceable model.

Where the experiences of people can no longer be "placed" in light of a philosophical paradigm they lose their bearings and lapse into despair; such people suffer intensely. As long as an experience of sickness or other adversity is still supported by the ground of their existence and can be fitted into it, that experience is acceptable. But as soon as the experience can no longer be placed, their lives are uprooted. This sense of being uprooted lasts until the experience is fitted in, or until the philosophical paradigm has been adjusted so that the experience can be placed, or until a completely new paradigm has been found in which the new experiences have a harmonious place. As a rule, in such a new paradigm the experiences which made it necessary have a key function. People fit most of their experiences into their view of reality without difficulty. Some experiences cost real effort and lead to a modification of their existence. They enrich their life view. But in some situations people arrive at a completely different fundamental life choice, not because they like it and want to try something new, but because they have to. The change of paradigm for the interpretation of reality is a matter which cuts so deep and produces such dislocations that no one goes out in search of them. But the experiences of life can be so radical that the old foundations no longer serve and a new basis for living has to be found. In theology such a change of paradigm constitutes a conversion. It need not be a conversion to the Christian faith. It may be only a turning away from that faith. It may be a turning from one non-Christian to another non-Christian paradigm. It may be a shift from one paradigm of being a Christian to another fundamental view of Christian belief. For (fortunately!) Christian theology is too rich for one paradigm to suffice. But in all cases the shift is experienced as a turning away from an earlier existence. One has become another person. One not only has learned new things; one has changed. One has not become an enriched person; one has at last begun to live, be it perhaps as a poor man or as a child, from the bottom up.

A change in paradigm does not only occur on the individual level, but also and predominantly on a collective one. Discoveries are made which can no longer be assimilated in the old system. During the decline of cultures there are individuals who articulate the changes of the world. They are the forerunners of the new spirit which is breaking in and which is verbalized by the great men and women of the new period. Once the change has taken a hold, return to the old is no longer possible. People can no longer be as they were before. The man of the Renaissance can never again practice scholarship, never again theologize, never again believe, enjoy, and love as did medieval man. The old has passed away, the earlier understanding of reality has died, for the new has come. In

224

the last centuries the great shifts in theology had to do especially with the experience of man as an independent being and with the rise of the sciences as a related phenomenon. Theology has had to search for a view of reality in which these realities have been factored in. That endeavor has only been partly successful. In this connection the coming of age of man has been assimilated more than the natural sciences, with which theology has never been able to reach a settlement. The preferred method of theology is to ignore them.

Our time has provided new experiences which cry out to be factored into our theological thinking. The experiences of Verdun and Auschwitz, the worldwide horrors of terrorism and oppression, all demand processing. It is the responsibility of theologians to give these experiences a place within a theological framework. If theology fails here, it can itself be written off. For if theology leaves untouched experiences which cannot be fitted into our thinking about reality related to God, it occasions the disordering and dislocation of human life, until a new framework has been found. If the theologians do not do it, others will, and people will correctly view theology as belonging to an age which is past once and for all. We can also put it another way: if the church can find no answer to the question of what Auschwitz means in relation to God in a theology in which this experience can be assigned a meaningful place, people rightly turn their backs on the church. It is clear that the collective experiences of this century cannot self-evidently be fitted into the old God concept. This is evident from the sense of dislocation which haunts Christians. Either changes have to be made in the old God concept or a total reversal must occur. The intensity of the estrangement makes one suspect the latter is needed. We have to go back to square one. It is the task of all concerned, of the entire church, to find the way. It is the task of theologians to take the lead. If no answer can be found to Auschwitz, while no answer has yet been found either to Galileo and Darwin or to Kant, the time of Christian theology, at least in Western Europe, is over. Suffering, the natural sciences, and the estrangement of the Enlightenment determine the face of the twentieth century. A theology which has no answers but at least gives expression to its perplexity can help twentieth-century man find a way. But if it never shows a way out and if others always come up with a new paradigm before theology does, it has made itself superfluous. And a theology which does not even struggle intensely to find a way to cope with suffering and the challenge of the natural sciences— thinking that the answers of earlier ages are adequate or that these problem areas can be skipped over as we approach the twenty-first century—either dies in tradition or loses its continuity with tradition, and veers off into a space above this world, the world of the history of humans.

Of great significance for the God concept in the twentieth century has been the theology of Barth, who posed this thesis: we must not base ourselves on a general God concept in which God is the absolute extrapolation of human possibilities, but on the concrete revelation of God in Jesus Christ. If we base ourselves on human possibilities we come out badly, for then we only encounter ourselves. If human power has to be the point of departure for divine power, one trembles to think of this God. Barth started his theological career exactly at the end of the first World War. With the shots of Verdun still in his ears, surrounded by the demolition of human might, he could not see God as a super-Kaiser. When God is linked up with human power and the human potentate uses God as confirmation for his naked power, that can only lead to catastrophe. Accordingly, Barth was among the first to see what national socialism meant. In the Barmen theses of 1934, he and others resolutely rejected the linking of Christian faith and human power. God is not an abstraction from our reality: he is Jesus Christ.

In Barth the rejection of the linking of the idea of God with the super-Kaiser or the super-Führer has to do with the influence of C. Blumhardt. Blumhardt regarded human "flesh," expressing itself in human egoism, as the principal source of opposition to the coming kingdom of God. Flesh only seeks its own interests and serves only itself. Faith in Christ is diametrically opposed to that. It seeks only Christ and his grace, Christ who in serving made people free. Christian faith does not consist in a search for power and for a demand for one's rights: it is forgiveness and grace. Barth rejects every attempt to ground faith in human possibilities. One can find God neither in human power nor in the human psyche. In them man only finds himself. And if man proceeds to extrapolate from himself in order to find God, he will merely find his own self-elevation, his own violence, and his own egotism raised to an infinite degree. This God image is an idealistic abstraction from his own reality.

How then can we find the true God? We do not find him; he presents himself; he posits himself in his revelation, in Jesus Christ. Jesus Christ alone is the true God, and nothing or no one else. If we want to know who God is we must look to him. If we want to speak of divine properties or attributes, we must refer to the deeds of Jesus Christ. Accordingly, our faith must not be directed toward that which we human beings accomplish, toward what we experience in life or feel in our psyches, but solely toward Jesus Christ. Therefore the only revelation of God can be found in the Word via the Scriptures which testify of him. God is not an abstraction from our our ideas, but concretely present in the Word who is Jesus Christ.

A fundamental disagreement developed between Barth and Gogarten over the concepts "concrete" and "abstract" (on this see Peter Lange, *Konkrete Theologie? Karl Barth und Friedrich Gogarten "Zwischen der Zeiten" (1922-1933); eine theologie geschichtlich-systematische Untersuchung im Blick auf die Praxis theologischen Verhaltens.* Barth is of the opinion that what is abstract we derive from our human reality. It is only our idea of God, not God himself. The God who is present in history in Jesus Christ, however, is concrete. For Gogarten the concrete is first of all the earthly reality in which we live, the political, social, and psychological structure of the human world. If God is not associated with that and recognizable there, then any nice things we say about Jesus Christ as the true revelation of God will be unsubstantial. To talk about a God who is not visible in our human existence now is an abstract matter. A God who is only the uttered Word is an abstract God.

The impasse arising from these two positions is fundamental for the theology of the last centuries. Either God is merely the projection into infinity of ourselves and hence no God, or God is "the wholly Other" and not accessible to human knowledge. In the first case, the deity of God comes off badly; in the second, the human knowledge of him does. As a rule, the solution is found in the position that faith is a private choice. God is not cognizable; one has to believe in him, a process in which faith becomes a private decision of man. God's existence can no longer be inferred from the world: he is absolutely transcendent, and can only be believed. But by this process one arrives at an inner contradiction which can only mean the end of every form of the knowledge of God: if only a personal choice is decisive for belief in God because God is "the wholly Other," then personal choice is also powerless to posit God. For also that choice and that belief is something from this world (*diesseitig*). It is a psychological event. What remains is only the Word uttered over our heads. But also that Word, the moment it is uttered or even thought, is *diesseitig*, an earthly phenomenon. That is even, or especially, true of Jesus Christ. In our human world he is a human phenomenon. Basing ourselves on the absolute transcendence of God we end up in absolute scepticism. In that connection faith cannot help either. Nor can the dilemma be solved dialectically, for if one tries to solve the problem of the unbridgeable distance between God and man dialectically, in the melting down of concepts, one ends up with a confusion of God and man which erases all boundaries. All distances are bridged in dialectic. There is no solution in thought; a solution only occurs in the history of the divine-human encounter, when the Transcendent deigns to reveal himself to man and hence is no longer the Transcendent One. Revelation is either the end of transcendence or it is no revelation.

"No one has ever seen God; the only Son, who is in the bosom of the Father, he has made him known," writes John the evangelist (1:18).

227

That means the end of every natural theology. We only know God in the Son who is our God. Accordingly, for our ideas about God and suffering we have to resort to Jesus and not to abstract ideas about omnipotence and goodness. Jesus loved his own to the end. He was faithful unto death. He is the gracious One, who bargains for the unopposed withdrawal of his disciples (John 18:8) and himself travels the road of imprisonment which leads to death on the cross. God is not a distant God existing in a supramundane world of abstract ideas, but he is one of us. The Word has become flesh. God became man, and chose to dwell among us. He entered our humanity to bring true humanity to light before the face of God. Humanity does not consist in power based on violence but in the power of love. Humanity is not the egoism of the flesh; it is self-sacrificial faithfulness to one's fellow human being. In Jesus Christ natural theology is turned on its head: man does not determine what is divinity by projecting his will to power and egoism on God, but God determines what true humanity is. He does this by revealing himself in the man who came not to be served but to serve.

The question is, how does God, who reveals himself in Jesus Christ, relate to evil? For an answer to this question we must not proceed from abstract theories but from Jesus Christ himself. Primary in the revelatory action of Jesus Christ is the Incarnation. In that event his entire further course is encapsuled. The Incarnation means that he descended from heavenly glory and became a man bearing all the burdens of man. He who was in the form of God emptied himself and was born in the likeness of man (Phil. 2:7). He who was the Lord became a servant. This means a condemnation of the evil of sin. Sin is not to be attributed to the will of God, but is opposition to him. For sin is the power of the flesh. Sin is our egoism and preoccupation with personal power. When God reveals himself he exposes sin. God is different, totally different, from sinful man. God does not lust for power. God is not selfish, but is driven by a desire to serve. God has in mind the advantage of the other. If Jesus Christ is the revelation of God and the only source of knowledge concerning him, then it can in no way be said that sin comes from the hand of God. For it was precisely the coming of Christ which brought this to light: sin is opposition to God. It is only when in Jesus Christ God shows us who he is and what his will is that it becomes evident that we humans are different from him and do not live according to his will.

Hence God exposes sin as something that runs counter to him, his will, and his being. He breaks sin by opposing it to the end and conquering it. But he does not do this by annihilating sinners with lightning and thunder, so removing ungodly humanity from his holy presence. For then his rule would be based on violence after all, and the egotism of his

228

honor would be greater than his serving love. The holiness of God is the holiness of one who is different from us. He breaks the power of sin by being with sinners in the flesh, by himself—in his Son—bearing the judgment upon sin. He himself takes up the cross of his own accursedness. All the human power in the world cannot invalidate this love. Where people lay siege to heaven to be equal with God they can only confirm the love of him who lets himself be besieged. When to confirm their own power people cried "Crucify him!" and nailed the Son of God to the cross, they only succeeded in confirming his divine holiness, the holiness of him who, when he was reviled did not revile in return, and who when he suffered did not threaten (1 Pet. 2:23). And at the same time they confirmed their own ungodliness, the fact that man with his violence is wholly other than God. In the face of Jesus Christ man in his human striving for greatness can only confirm both his own lostness and the superiority of the love of God.

Accordingly, God reveals to us that he does not will the power and violence of the flesh. The way of power, the way of the Kaiser or of the Führer, is not his. God breaks this power by delivering himself up to humans. In the face of that love the bluster of tyrants and the scraping of egoists comes to nothing. They can bluster and scrape till they collapse. And right to the moment when they collapse they have only succeeded in confirming the justice of God. In the process God's invincible holy love is manifested, a love which the sin of sinners can never void but only confirm. Consequently sinners, though blustering and scraping, are not outside his kingdom but are encompassed by the love of him who prayed: "Father, forgive them; for they know not what they do" (Luke 23:34). They knew even less what they were doing than superficial reflection on this text would lead us to suspect. Their ignorance did not just consist in the fact that they were blinded by hatred. Their ignorance was much deeper, consisting in the fact that they did not know that in their raging they were serving the God of love. It is the ignorance of Caiaphas who, speaking on a level far above what he knew, announced, "It is expedient for you that one man should die for the people, and that the whole nation should not perish" (John 11:50). To this the evangelist adds, "He did not say this of his own accord, but being high priest that year he prophesied that Jesus should die for the nation, and not for the nation only, but to gather into one the children of God who are scattered abroad" (vv. 51-52). These godless tyrants prove to be priests in the kingdom of God. That surpasses the comprehension of any human. It is the miracle of the strange God for whom the reprobate is the elect and the elect the reprobate. The elect Jesus, God's own chosen one, dies as a reprobate on the cross. The reprobate wicked prove to be chosen to confirm the love of God in their capacity as priests and prophets.

Barth developed this idea extensively. Cain, Esau, Saul, and Judas are all reprobates. But the reprobate are never a separate category of people apart from the elect. The reprobate are elect and the elect reprobate. The elect Judas was reprobate but simultaneously chosen to confirm the self-surrendering love of Christ. The reprobate Saul was the chosen man to bring to reprobate Gentiles the name of the reprobate Messiah of the elect people of Israel. Where God appears in concrete form in Jesus Christ our human divisions and categories in no way add up anymore. Everything breaks apart on the rock of the one God who can only elect himself by rejecting himself and who elects himself by allowing himself to be rejected.

Accordingly, God exposes the evil nature of sin and breaks it at the same time. Sin does not proceed from his divine will, yet it is serviceable to the revelation of the glory of his love, as is the evil of suffering. The predominant classic Reformed idea was that all things came from the hand of God. This view is not based on the knowledge of Jesus Christ, however, but on the idea that God is the cause of all things. It is based on our idea of God, not on God as he really is. There is suffering in the world; but God is not above it as the dispenser of it. He came to be among us in our suffering, which Christ took upon himself. The Messiah as divine being is not the Lord in glory and light; he is the suffering servant of the Lord in shame and darkness. The deepest suffering is suffering in solitude, but God himself broke through it. For in our solitary suffering there is present the one forsaken by God who had earlier been abandoned by all humans. But this forsaken one is the true God, who came that we could never again be forsaken by God. For however deeply forsaken we may be, precisely in the deepest state of forsakenness and darkness the Crucified One is near to us. And where he is, God is. And when all humans have abandoned us we are in the presence of the one true human. True humanity consists in being with the suffering, forsaken one in his forsakenness. That is not something we learn from theories about human rights and human dignity; that is something we only learn from God who encounters us in Christ. In the true humanity of God in Christ Jesus the power of suffering is broken by the nearness of love.

In the story of Jesus it is evident that suffering is not conferred by God; on the contrary he goes out to be with the suffering. This is not only manifest on the cross, but throughout his earthly life. He was prepared to stoop down toward a lost world in order to save it. He seeks out the lost and becomes an advocate for the despised. God chose not the strong of the world, but the weak and the despised. He liberated publicans from their greed, touched lepers, and caused cripples to walk. He fought with and drove out demons and calmed the waves of the storm. When people cried out in distress, he was their helper. Here is God in all his concreteness. He is not the Kaiser-God; he is the God of compassion. He is not the super-God who is approached most nearly by the superman, but the God of Jesus Christ. He is not approached by misfits, underdogs, invalids, the unemployed, the weak, and defectors from the doctrine of race and soil; no, he is near to them in his divine saving compassion.

Suffering also has to do with death. Suffering is not only the social experience of being solitary and abandoned. It is also physical suffering, the decay and total degradation of human beings. In death everything is over. Barth speaks about death in various ways. On the one hand, death is part of being human. Barth would probably not say, "Dying after all is natural," for the word "natural" is too heavily loaded in his theology. Whether a thing is good or bad does not depend on nature but on God's dealings with man, dealings which include death. For human time is limited time. As creature, man does not have eternity within himself: he has the time allotted to him by God. Man is in time, and hence bounded. It is only in creaturely delimitation that time comes into being. Time, too, is created, given conjointly with the delimitation of the creature. Finite humans meet their boundary in death, given by God to man as creature. In principle the same is true of suffering in the form of a physical defect by which human existence is robbed of its lustre. When people are afflicted by a handicap or by illness, is that defect real? Or does it owe its existence to our having before our eyes an ideal image of being human derived from the Renaissance or from Athens rather than from Jesus Christ and from Golgotha?

Genuine humanity does not consist in the ideal average of physical and spiritual forms. In Athens, the person who does not meet that standard will always suffer on account of his defect. But at Golgotha we see not the ideal man but the despised man. There we have before us not the strong military commander, the muscular athlete, or the fearless hero, but the feeble silent man who in Gethsemane was so scared that his sweat became blood, the man who could not even carry his own cross, who, as he hung from it, asked "Why?" as though he did not want to accept the consequences of his own words and actions. But this man is the true human. He is the sign of human dignity, the dignity of the undignified. In his presence no one need suffer on account of his defect, for the defective human is the human being of God. "Who is blind but my servant, or deaf as my messenger whom I send? Who is blind as my dedicated one, or blind as the servant of the Lord?" cried Isaiah (42:19). He is the man who does not open his mouth (Isa. 53:7), who will not cry or lift up his voice or make it heard in the street (Isa. 42:2). True humanness is humanness that is not great and balanced in all things. For that reason suffering is not an inhuman but an arch-human matter, as arch-human as is Jesus, the suffering but truly human being. Therefore suffering is not evil; it belongs to the humanness of humans made by God. He who opposes this human being and seeks his glory in human fantasy and dignity is a human being in a state of degradation. He is the human being who wants to reach an ideal that will never be reached, because it is an abstraction from the reality of man in his God-given existence. Man is no more the man of our ideals than God is the God of our ideals. God and man are both to be found in Jesus Christ.

However, Barth can also speak very differently about death. Death is also alienation, a sign of absolute forsakenness. Then we are talking about death as judgment, as the impossible possibility of not being there for God anymore. Then death is linked with the power of darkness, with nothingness, the possibility God bypassed. Death, then, is being where God does not want us to be, where he, the living one, can also never be. Jesus Christ, however, robbed death of this power. For he who enters death in death meets him who was obedient unto death. In the realm of the dead he descended into hell. Jesus Christ bore the divine judgment, enduring rejection and forsakenness. In our own judgment, in the midst of death, we are together with Christ who, in death, is the living God. Consequently, death has lost its judging character of absolute alienation. In death we are together with the other who is the Other.

It is impossible here to mention all the places where Barth speaks about the relation of God to man in his lostness. In fact his entire theology is suffused with this theme. In every section of his *Church Dogmatics* the above-mentioned ideas can be found.[52]

Barth's position has proven to be of great importance for the pastorate. A classic example is the work of Eduard Thurneysen, *A Theology of Pastoral Care*. A modern version of Barthian views in pastoral theology (where there is a specific address to the question of the relationship of God to evil) can be found in Manfred Josuttis, *Praxis des Evangeliums zwischen Politik und Religion: Grundprobleme der praktischen Theologie*. In the meantime Barth's position has also caused the

---

52. Of special importance are the volumes I, 2; II, 1; III, 2 (esp. 45, 2, "The Basic Form of Humanity") and IV, 1 (ch. 14: "Jesus Christ, the Lord as Servant"). See also his little book *The Humanity of God*.

About our existence within time, see C.D. III, 7, pp. 67-69 and esp. III, 2, 47 ("Allotted Time"). See further III, 3, 49. About death as judgment, see esp. III, 3, 50, pp. 310-12: "That nothingness has the form of evil and death as well as sin shows us that it is . . . the comprehensive negation of the creature and its nature" (p. 310).

necessary problems in practical theology. For a discussion of these problems and for further literature see the articles by F. O. Van Gennep.[53]

At a later point we shall take up the far-reaching assimilation of Barth's position by Moltmann, especially in *The Crucified God*.

Barth has been of great importance for church and theology. It is a liberating thing not to have to speak of an omnipotent all-encompassing Supreme Being whose mighty hand holds within itself all the contrasts and suffering of the world, and instead to be allowed to speak of God's concrete presence in Jesus Christ. In that context God proves to be different than we could ever have conceived in our ideas about God and the world. In the pastorate these views have proven invaluable for people who could no longer stomach belief in divine government as it was confessed in Lord's Day 10 of the Heidelberg Catechism. It was the liberation whose echoes we pick up in the article by Van der Werf mentioned earlier: "A grim protest like that of Martin Hart against Lord's Day 10 is appropriate. The little vocable 'God' should not evoke the idea of an omnipotent supreme being who shuffles the cards and hands to one person or another the jack of spades; it should make one think of the Father of Jesus Christ who fought with death and won. As loftily as Lord's Day 1 of the Heidelberg Catechism can speak about Christ as our only comfort, so icily cold is the wind which blows out upon us from Lord's Day 10 and in which we can no longer sense anything of what is really happening in the name of this God." Not the icy wind of Lord's Day 10 is our God, however, but his concrete presence in the love of Christ.

When we refer to the relationship of God to suffering we should base ourselves on the concrete God. In that connection we should also proceed from the concrete situation. We can construct elaborate themes about the cause of evil. How did it originate in this world? How can it exist in a world that is God's? Why does God permit it? We can also say that all these questions and theories are in fact not very relevant. We have to deal with the concrete fact that sin, suffering, and death are realities. All that goes beyond that fact plunges us immediately into speculation. Accordingly, we must proceed from the givenness of the world with its sin and suffering. It is a world which far exceeds the reach of our human competence, a world of which we have learned that it only heads further toward destruction to the degree that human power, competence, and control increase. If that was not clear to us after Verdun, it should have

53. Frederick O. Van Gennep, "Recente ontwikkelingen in de practische theologie," in *In de Waagschaal* 11 (1982), I, pp. 538-47; II, pp. 569-78.

become totally clear to us after the death camp of Auschwitz, after Hiroshima, after the horrors of Indochina. If the highest human achievement consists in an insane arms race in which we count our rockets as though they were scores in a soccer match, we need not have any illusions about human greatness. But in the light of Jesus Christ our situation is finally illuminated as a totally human one. In that situation, however, God wants to be concretely present because he is a different God.

Moltmann worked out this idea even further than Barth did. Christian theology is the theology of hope. This hope is grounded in the resurrection of Christ. But the resurrection is that of the Crucified One, because he proves to have been God by rising from the dead. The church has always been afraid of Theopaschitism. God must remain free of all affects. Over against this position Moltmann states that because of the fear of attributing to God such affects as pain and sorrow the church has never taken seriously the confession that Jesus is God. The Crucified One is God. God is not devoid of affects, not an unmoved being; he has a heart. In this regard Moltmann goes much further than the earlier kenotic views in which it was said that God emptied himself of his glory. In that context the real essence of God remains his omnipotence, and his self-emptying is only an act of compassion. To Moltmann, however, suffering, smallness, and weakness belong to God's essence. Only through alienation and fear can God be really God. Only by dying on the cross is he the living God. If God truly reveals himself in Jesus Christ, we are shortchanging his revelation if we deny that suffering is part of his essence. Then we continue to entertain the idea of a God with the face of a Roman emperor. But the face of God is the face of the Crucified One. The hands of God are pierced hands. The heart of God is a pierced heart. Every other notion of God is the product of our own fantasy, not of the concrete God of Golgotha. In that case we are not dealing with the real God, but with an idol made in our own human image and likeness.

Moltmann's ideas about God's relationship to suffering are most developed in his book *The Crucified God*. Basically the same ideas occur already in his article "Gottesoffenbarung und Wahrheitsfrage" in *Parrhesia*, a volume published on the occasion of Barth's eightieth birthday. For a good understanding of Moltmann it is well to read his entire series about the doctrine of God (besides *The Crucified God; Theology of Hope: on the ground and the implications of a Christian eschatology; The Church in the Power of the Spirit: a contribution to messianic ecclesiology; The Trinity and the Kingdom: the doctrine of God*).

Moltmann is of the opinion that his ideas are most closely approximated by Luther. For the rest of the Christian tradition Moltmann has less appreciation, though, to him, Luther was not consistent enough. Besides being indebted to theologians like Barth, Luther, and Pannenberg, Moltmann derived many of his ideas from the philosophers of the Frankfurter school (Adorno; Horkheimer) and from Ernst Block.

God is the suffering God. According to Moltmann he is also the rejected one. He suffers as an outcast. He suffers outside the city at the place of judgment, "outside the camp," as the letter to the Hebrews puts it (13:11-13). He suffers outside the established order of a society where rank and station, position and dignity determine a person's worth. But in the underside of society master and servant are equal. Among outcasts there is no longer any distinction between high and low, but all are equally low. A pariah falls outside the caste system. But where all rank has ceased to play a role, there is God. He is among the outcasts, the downtrodden, the crucified, and the tormented. He subjects ordered society with its neat classes and functions to racial criticism. The society of the bourgeoisie is not the society of God, for God is among the classless. He does not *dwell* among them, for the classless have no homes. They have been evicted from them. They have no place to lay their heads any more than the Son of man does. Nowhere are they safe; the shouting soldiers carrying swords and sticks break into the quiet of the garden. The truly powerless do not even have the possibility of protest: they have been beaten to a pulp. They have been struck, but do not strike back. They do not have the strength, for they are the weak. They are persecuted but they cannot flee, for no one puts up with them. Nowhere do they amount to anything. Nowhere is there for them a fatherland. Nowhere are they at home in a world of power, of structures, of privileged party members, of the rich in money or inheritance. The world conspires against them; proper citizens and the venerable pious head the parade in protest against the pariahs who despise God and his law.

In the midst of these rejects is the reject Jesus Christ. In the midst of these wandering Hebrews is the Son of Abraham. In the midst of the ungodly is the crucified God. In the midst of those who want nothing to do with God or his law is he who has fulfilled God's commandment to love one's neighbor. He is the Samaritan who is spat in the face because he blasphemes the God of Israel. But the Samaritan is the good Samaritan. His crown is made of thorns, and the anointing oil of his kingship is his own blood. His ornaments are his stripes and his medals are wounds struck, each of them unanswered. The shouting at the feast of his coronation is the cry for a cross. That is the concrete God of the world.

But beyond contempt, beyond the rejection in which the classless and the classified divide the world, beyond all that there is suffering. The classless are themselves a class, all equal in their exclusion but different from the others. If God were only the God of the outcasts, he would not be the God of all. Something could certainly be said for the notion that God is only the God of the lost. "God chose what is low and despised in the world, even things that are not, to bring to nothing things that are," writes Paul (1 Cor. 1:28). In the gospels too we encounter such thoughts: the first shall be last and the last first (Matt. 20:16). In the parable Lazarus the beggar ends up in the bosom of Abraham, and the rich man in torment (Luke 16:23). But the confession that Jesus is God goes beyond that. Jesus is not only the outcast but the *suffering* outcast. What person is there who does not suffer? The rich man in his villa suffers just as well as the poor man in his hut. The ruler in his palace suffers just as well as the slave on the plantation. But not all suffer to the same degree. God is the suffering God, as God close to the suffering, and closer to those who suffer more. That too can be argued. The prominent have their reward already on earth, Jesus said in the Sermon on the Mount (Matt. 6:2, 5, 16). In Jesus' company the poor man, who was brought in from the gutter, sits in the place of the rich (Luke 14:15-24).

But beyond the experience of being an outcast, and beyond suffering, there is death. In death every distinction drops away. In death there is no rank and class. One person does not die more than another. Dead is dead—there is no distinction. The way to it may be different; the end is the same. The living may surround the dead with more or less splendor. To the dead it does not make any difference anymore. Death comes equally to the poor and the rich, the classless and the highly classified, to the pious and the ungodly, to the dictator and the political prisoner. Death extends its reach to all. No one escapes it. All are doomed to die. But in the midst of the doomed is the Crucified One. He was killed. God did not exempt himself from death. Even in death God is the concrete God. He is not the immortal but the dying God, one with those who are doomed to die. In Jesus the song of the pious Israelite became a reality: "If I make my bed in Sheol, thou art there!" (Ps. 139:8).

When Christians of the early church started to confess that Jesus is God they revolutionized religious thought. They consistently held to the divinity of Jesus. He is not just adopted as son; he is the eternal Son. God is *really* present in him, in this concrete earthly form. Both the rejection of adoptionism and the rejection of docetism served to secure the thesis that the earthly Jesus, together with his concrete history ending in suffering and death, is the true God.

The motives of the early church do not always coincide precisely with Moltmann's emphases. In the earliest period the idea that the crucified is the revelation of God did play an important role, particularly in the Pauline literature. Consider 1 Corinthians 1:23: "we preach Christ crucified, a stumbling block to Jews and folly to Gentiles." Later, in Athanasius and Cyril of Alexandria, for example, especially the theme of eternal life played a role. Only God has life within himself. Consequently, life can only be received through fellowship with him. Accordingly, the flesh of Christ received in the Lord's Supper has to be truly divine. The accent shifts therefore from the cross to the Incarnation. In the relationship between Barth and Moltmann we see the line reversed. In Barth the Incarnation is central—God is really present in Christ. His pivotal text is John 1:14: "The Word became flesh." In Moltmann the cross is central. God is the suffering one who is with those who are doomed to die, with the outcasts. For him the core text is Mark 15:34: "My God, my God, why have You forsaken me?" "God forsaken by God"—that is the focal point of the trinitarian event in which suffering humanity is taken up in Christ.

Many of the ideas sketched here can be found in the theology of Luther, who also made the person of Christ central. "Jesus Christ and no other God." In Jesus God emptied himself of himself. On the cross God was really forsaken by God, "God forsaken by God." To this last line Luther added, "Who can grasp it?" Who can comprehend the forsakenness of God on the cross of the one true God Jesus Christ? Is that not in conflict with every representation that could be made of God? Does it not conflict with all human logic? Luther, who loved opposites, would be the first to concede this point. He was convinced God can only be known in contradiction. God is not present in our human ideas, nor in our logic. God's power is not manifest in a superior attitude and pride, nor his glory in self-display and fanfare. God is present in this world *sub contraria specie,* literally "in the opposite of what you see." His power is present as weakness, his glory as shame, his light as darkness, his wrath as a cross.

For the theme of the hidden God who reveals himself in the concealment of the cross, see Reinhold Weier's recent book, *Das Thema vom verborgenen Gott von Nikolaus von Kues zu Martin Luther.* In it even more literature can be found. In Luther the hidden God is not another God who is unknowable and may turn out to be different from the *deus revelatus* in Christ, but the same God as Christ. He is concealed from the natural man who wants to infer God from the world. The only true God manifests himself in the hidden manner of the cross; accordingly, he can only be known by faith and cannot be deduced in accordance with the rules of human logic.

The question with which people struggle is this: "How is it possible that this broken world is a world in which God is present?" Luther answers by saying that this is precisely what is needed for God's revelation in the world. Every presence of God is *sub contraria specie*. For the world is the opposite of God. God is eternal, the world temporal. Accordingly, when the eternal God reveals himself in this temporal world he does it in an antithetical manner. In other respects too the world is antithetical to God. God is just, the world unjust. God is holy, the world ungodly. Accordingly, every self-disclosure of God is the opposite of what the world considers divine. Hence, this world is not a revelation of God in the sense that we can read the essence of God directly from nature or history. The world only hints at the presence of God; it is only a sign, a question, and a reference to what is invisible. For in his being God is the eternal and transcendent one. So, to be sure, the general omnipotence of God is vaguely evident from nature, but in Christ the true nature of divine omnipotence is manifest. But precisely in him the revelation of God is most present *sub contraria specie:* God on a cross; God who makes his presence manifest in the crucified and accursed one; God who reveals himself in the injustice of the world, in the weakness of man, in the ungodliness of popular fury, in the impermanence of death. That is the greatest possible antithesis. That cannot be understood from within the human mind. That can only be understood from within the Spirit of God, for whom the foolishness of the cross becomes wisdom.

In the cross of Christ all the darkness comes together. All the sorrows of the world come together in him. All the "whys" of man are absorbed into the cry, "My God, my God, why have You forsaken me?" On the cross the wrath of God floods in upon the world. At the same time there is the pointer to God as he really is: one who saves this condemned world and reveals himself to the world as only he can, by entering into its total lostness. All the "whys" of the world cry out for this merciful God, and on the cross those realities come together. Present in the darkness and suffering of the world is the cry to the antithetical God, and in the darkness and the suffering of Christ this antithetical God is present. The God who dwells in a high and holy place is with whoever is of a contrite and humble spirit (Isa. 57:15). That reality was fulfilled to the utmost in the cross of Christ. There the high and holy God bowed down to the lostness of the world. He clearly wants to dwell with the accursed.

At the same time, by this very fact a judgment is pronounced over all who attempt to elevate themselves above this lostness in pseudo-power and pseudo-piety. If Jesus is God, God's revelation to the ungodly, then God reveals himself in the suffering one, in accursedness, in the cross. Thus every cross in this world points to the one cross of the crucified God. Where must we look for God in this world? Nowhere but in the cross, in suffering, in death. Suffering and divine presence are not opposites; they belong together. They are only opposites to those who have not gotten to know by faith the gracious foolishness of God in the cross of Christ.

Moltmann is of the opinion that in his discourse about the suffering God he is turning his back on an age-old prevailing tradition in the church. The church always opted for the God of power. That impression can be supported with evidence from history. The idea that God the eternal can suffer was the occasion around A.D. 200 for the rise of a term of abuse, "patripassianist" or "father-sufferer." Peter Volla, a preacher in the fifth century, by too closely linking Christ's suffering with the essence of God, caused a riot in Constantinople. There are numerous examples like this in the history of the church. Over and over people who spoke about a God of the powerless and a suffering God were condemned as heretics.

The question therefore is whether the position of all those who say that God is concretely present in Jesus the crucified Lord, and who do not believe in our idea of the "impassible" God, in fact constitutes a break with tradition. Does it especially conflict with the roots of that tradition in the Old and New Testament, and with Jesus Christ in the entire context of Israel and the early church? If so, the idea of the suffering God would be a turning away from the Christian faith, for then this faith would not be related to its own beginning, Jesus Christ. The christological concentration found in this position may already prompt us to suspect the reverse, though in itself this is no guarantee of authentic Christianity. After all, was not Jesus himself the first to point away from himself to the Father? Accordingly, in the doctrine of God would not concentration on Jesus be downright unfaithfulness to the Son who only wished to obey the Father who is greater than he (John 14:28)?

Another indication that the idea of the suffering God is not alien to the Christian tradition can be found in the fact that, despite all the ideas about a powerful God, there have consistently been people who spoke about God as one who can only be known in the crucified Christ.

Already around A.D. 200, the modalists taught that Jesus is a mode of divine presence. He was God in the mode of suffering. He was God himself, the true God; but he was that in a certain mode. At that time the Roman bishop Zephyrinus stated, "I know one God, Jesus Christ, and apart from him no other who was born and who suffered." Their opponents derisively called them "patripassians." For if Jesus constitutes the divine presence to that degree—including his birth and suffering—then God himself, the Father of all the ages, suffered. Though at the beginning of the third century the modalists were condemned, the focus on the essential unity of Christ with the Father reappears in the Alexandrinian Christology of the fourth and fifth century. In the sixth century this culminated in the formula of the Scythian monks adopted by the emperor Justinian and so, as the custom was in those days, by the church—namely, "that one member of the holy Trinity suffered in the flesh." This idea closely approximates that of Patripassianism, at least so far as the suffering of God is concerned. In their doctrine of the Trinity, following in the footsteps of the Greek fathers in the fourth century, they made a much sharper distinction among the triune persons. Already Cyril of Alexandria had moved toward this position in accentuating the union of Christ—who was truly God—with human nature. However, in the fourth century and later, people continued to reject the notion that God could suffer. They solved the problem by saying that God the Son suffered in the flesh. What suffered then is the flesh, for God himself cannot suffer. Thus arose the contrast between the phrases "in his divinity" and "in his human nature," which we also find back in Lord's Day 10 of the Heidelberg Catechism.

Moltmann places the idea of the suffering God in a strong trinitarian framework. It is the Son who suffers. But at the same time he states that in the suffering of the Son the Father also suffers. Besides, Moltmann is nowhere near using the schematism "in his divinity—in his human nature." Jesus is one. He is the one who, being God, brings true humanity to light. Essential to Moltmann's thinking is precisely that as sufferer Jesus is truly God, for suffering belongs to the essence of the Trinity, in which the Son must die to the Father. But the moment the Son dies to the Father, the Father dies to the Son. In Barth, where the trinitarian framework is much less strong, the idea that Jesus is the only God is even more pronounced. But because he relates this primarily to the Incarnation and not to the crucifixion, resemblance to Patripassianism is much less striking, although the connection was noted at an early stage from within the circle of the orthodox-Reformed.[54]

Luther's resistance to patripassian formulations was even less firm than it was in the time of the later ecumenical councils. In that regard he followed the wandering monks of the Middle Ages. Luther replaced the Aristotelian-scholastic idea of God with an emotional God concept. Luther's God is not without affects, and above all, God can only be found in Christ. Zephyrinus's formula cited above would not be out of place in the theology of Luther: "I know no other God than Jesus Christ and apart from him no other who was born and who suffered." If throughout

---

54. See Y. Feenstra, "Theopaschieten" in *Christelijke Encyclopedie* (Kampen, 1961²), pp. 357-58.

the history of the church there is such a stubborn tradition of a suffering God, the idea can hardly be alien to the Christian faith.

The central question, however, is how the Old and the New Testament as the writings which are at the source of the Christian tradition of which Jesus Christ is the center, themselves speak about God. Is he devoid of affects or is he the suffering one? A glance at the prophets can already teach us that the idea of a God devoid of affects originates in the Stoa (which accordingly honored the ideal of *apatheia* as the highest form of humanness), rather than in the Hebrew prophets. The God of Israel is an emotional God. He is moved to compassion over his people. He suffers when they are unfaithful. "How can I give you up, O Ephraim! How can I hand you over, O Israel! . . . My heart recoils within me, my compassion grows warm and tender" (Hos. 11:8). That God is far from being devoid of affects. He is the God torn by compassion and by anger. Whichever of the prophets one turns to, over and over we encounter an emotional, wrathful, furious, merciful, and empathetic God.

The God of the New Testament is not a different God. He cannot be another God, for the early church lived out of the Old Testament. It was their holy Scripture. The God of Israel of whom the prophets spoke was their God because he was the God of their Lord. And Christ was their Lord because he was no other than the Lord of Israel, precisely because in him they recognized Israel's Lord, in an even more involved and intense way than ever before. In their experience he had demonstrated his mercy promised to the fathers (Luke 1:72f.). In Jesus Christ the early church recognized the emotive God of Israel. He is the suffering one because he came on our behalf. The most direct evidence for this comes to us in those pronouncements in the New Testament where Christ is accorded divine honor and majesty, and where in the same context there is reference to his suffering. Philippians 2:6-11 knows Christ as the one who was in the form of God in preexistent glory, but the same Christ is the slave who was obedient to death on the cross. Colossians 1 speaks of him as the one by whom all things were created and in whom the divine fullness dwells; but in the same breath it says he made peace by the blood of the cross. In Revelation we encounter the Son of man depicted in divine metaphors as flaming fire and burnished bronze (1:15); and at the same time as the Lamb, standing as though it had been slain, who discloses the divine secret of world history (15:5, 6). In the different traditions of the New Testament, therefore, it appears that the glorified is the preexistent one who is also the suffering one. In this Paul goes furthest in this direction, although as is evident for the examples cited, this datum is by no means restricted to the Pauline literature. Within the scope of this book it is not necessary to deal with all the passages on this theme. As soon as one discovers that Jesus Christ is divine, even the presence of the God of Israel, and that the Lord of the Christian church is no other than the Lord of the Septuagint, one continually encounters texts in which the Lord is the suffering one and God the crucified.

We do wish to mention one more text, 1 Corinthians 2:8: "None of the rulers of this age understood this; for if they had, they would not have crucified the Lord of glory." "The Lord of glory" is a parallel formulation to "the God of glory" (Acts 7:2) and "the Father of glory" (Eph. 1:17). The expression fits in a context in which the glory of the God of Israel is attributed to Christ. Expressions and phrases from the Old Testament which refer to the glory of God are used in the New Testament for Christ. To people used to the Septuagint, the combination of "Lord" and "glory" must have prompted immediate associations with God dwelling in unapproachable light who nevertheless communicates to humans. The glory is the glory of the Lord, the *kabod adonay*. The Lord of glory is the Lord of the divine glory. The formulation makes us think of a theophany. But the theophany of the Lord is the crucifixion. The divine glory is the glory which becomes visible at the cross.

Now one could interpret 1 Corinthians 2:8 in such a way that the crucifixion and the glory of the Lord were only indirectly related. Thus one could say that the Lord of glory relates to the glorified Christ, who is now worshiped as Lord by the church. He who is now the Lord of glory was at one time crucified, but when he was crucified he was of course not yet the Lord of glory. After all, he received the name above every name only on the basis of the crucifixion (Phil. 2:9-11). However, the context of 1 Corinthians 2 points in another direction. The reference there is to the preaching of divine wisdom. Apparently the Corinthians look for that wisdom in earthly fame *(kauchma)* and glory *(doxa)*. The glory of the Lord has to become visible in power and in spirit. Over against that Paul posits that the wisdom of God is the foolishness of the cross. In the proclamation of the wisdom of God (2:7) the point is not signs or the wisdom of men (1:22), but the cross of Christ. *There* God's wisdom is manifest; *there* the divine mystery is revealed. The most divine thing in the world is not the signs of the Jews, nor the wisdom of the Greeks, but the cross of Christ. Therefore "what is weak in the world," "things that are not," were chosen by God. The line that runs through 1 Corinthians 1 and 2 is not very different from that of Moltmann's *The Crucified God.*

So the line of the gospels is really no different from that of Paul. In the center of the synoptic gospels is the transfiguration on the mount as a theophany. But this theophany is the beginning, not of power and glory, but of the passion history. The theophany ends in the cross, just as John indicates that the lifting up of the Son of man is the crucifixion (John 3:15).[55]

Next to the emphasis which identifies the divine with the crucified, however, we also find sections in the gospels where Jesus bears much more resemblance to suffering man. If in fact in those sections we should have to speak of the suffering God, it is not in any case explicit and we can only suspect it via the confessing church in which the gospel functioned. They confessed Jesus as the glorified, and in that light they transmitted the stories about his suffering orally and in writing. An important pericope of this type is Matthew 26:36-46. In that narrative Jesus comes across as a suffering, fearful human. Here we are not dealing with heavy theological statements which because of their extreme concentration and dialectical wordiness are hard to digest. Here we have a human story into which every human who knows what it is to suffer and to struggle before the face of God can enter existentially and immediately. Jesus here suffers as one of us; he suffers right down to the roots of his being. Here we see no evidence at all of preexistent divinity nor of post-existent glorification. Present here is only the suffering human who will soon be on his way to a cross because the cup will not pass from him any more than it passed from all those millions whose suffering ended in death. However, this pericope is also incorporated in the framework of the synoptic gospels with their prologues about divine intervention and the dawning kingdom of God, which have at their centers the theophany and the confession that Jesus is the Christ, the Son of the living God, and which have at their conclusions the appearances of the risen Lord. The story of Gethsemane functions in that framework. Also, this pericope was used by the church in its assemblies, where the confession was "Christ is Lord!" It was of that Lord that they told the story of his suffering and fear.

The fact that stories like that of Gethsemane functioned in the church of the first century is evident from the letter to the Hebrews, where both lines are interwoven, that of the divine redeemer who suffers, and that of the human Jesus who in his fears is one of us. Hebrews is both heavily theological and deeply human. No other letter gives a

---

55. For an extensive discussion of the texts about exaltedness, preexistence, and suffering, I must refer to my dissertation *Preëxistentie en postexistentie van Christus*, in *Schrift* 82, pp. 181-86, and especially in Pannenberg, *Grundzüge der Christologie*, Gütersloh, 1974[4]), pp.345-49. About the Kurios title and the application of Old Testament sayings about God, cf. my *De menselijke persoon van Christus*, pp. 194-99. On *doxa*, cf. *TDNT*, vol. 2, pp. 247-55: "It is to be noted, . . . that NT usage itself takes a decisive step by using in relation to Christ a word which was used in relation to God" (p. 248).

more vivid picture of the fact that Jesus' deep humanity and therefore the deeply human character of the suffering of the church was at the same time heavily theological for the early church. Hebrews says explicitly what Matthew and Mark say implicitly. Hebrews 4 and 5 speak of the suffering high priest. He was in great fear "with loud cries and tears" (5:7). In that he was one of us. This means he can understand us in our fear, or in our struggle against the temptation to stop believing (4:15). Pressure on the Christian church can be so intense that one gives up being a Christian, as those addressed in Hebrews were being threatened. But when that pressure is intense we may know of Christ who was tempted in all things as we are. He can understand us; he can sympathize with our weaknesses because he suffered along with us. But this suffering one, who suffers along with others to the very depths of his being, is the Son (5:8). And the Son bears the very stamp of the nature of God, who endures forever and is superior to the angels (1:3ff.). When everything proves impermanent he remains the same, for he is God and king (1:8-12). Therefore if we speak of God, a wide stream of New Testament tradition says that God manifested himself in Jesus Christ the crucified, the suffering and praying human. God has come to stand beside us. He is not exalted in the light above without any understanding of us puny earthworms, but he is here below in the darkness, crawling over the earth like a worm, less than a man, kicked around and trampled on in the most dehumanized way possible. God is among the downtrodden of the world, among the unworthy, the non-persons, the foolish, and the despised. God suffers as they suffer. In that way Jesus is the fulfillment of the God of Israel who was afflicted in all of Israel's affliction (Isa. 63:9).

If God is the suffering one, then the signs of his presence on earth are not to be found in power, beauty, and achievement. The signs of his presence are the oppressed. It is the suffering needy human who points to the true God. The tears on the human face of the other are more the signs of God's nearness than the spires of a Gothic cathedral. God is more present in one broken human than in a massive church service where a thousand people sing "God himself is in our midst."

If God is concretely present in this world, he is present in the concrete existence of people (i.e., in the existence that cries out for the other who wants to be near us, and not in the sublime spheres where we sing ourselves away from the world and its suffering). To whom have we been a neighbor? That is where the will of God was done. And where it was done to the least of his brothers it was done to him (Matt. 25:40). In the one cup of cold water we gave, the one prisoner we visited, the one tear we wiped away—there we met God. In a poignant way this idea was developed by the Jewish thinker Emmanuel Levinas in his book *Het menselijk gelaat*[56]: God is present in the human face of the other. All ideas and theories about God tend to distance us from the concrete reality in which God meets us. God is not the general; he is the particular, present in the concrete and special situation of this one face that looks at us.

We are back here at the most ancient traditions of Israel, which say that the Lord's elect is the suffering one. His servant is the broken servant, his son the beaten one, his beloved the despised. It is the tradition of deutero-Isaiah which the early Christian church recognized in Jesus their Lord. It is the tradition again articulated in *The Last of the Just* by A. Schwarz-Bart.[57] This tradition enabled Jews to see the divine presence in the face of the dying brother in the death camp. In the gates of hell the God of Israel was present.

"Here we come to one of the deepest truths of Holy Scripture with which also the rabbis, who viewed suffering and martyrdom as the distinguishing marks of God's elect and beloved, were familiar," writes Aart van Roon on Ephesians 1:6 and 7,[58] where he poses a connection between the Old Testament, the rabbis, Pauline theology, and the Polish Hasidim in the concentration camps.

The concrete God whom the Christian church confesses is not the omnipotent eternal Supreme Being, but the crucified Christ—the God who shares in the suffering of his church. But he is more than that. He is also the co-militant God. When enemies threaten his people God fights with and for them. He is also the victorious God who conquers the enemies. The church says that not on the basis of a construct of an omnipotent Supreme Being, but on the basis of God's deeds. Just as concrete as the suffering and the battle is the victory. If it is a source of consolation in suffering that God suffered along with the sufferer, it is because the sufferer was glorified: God's deity was demonstrated in power. Moltmann treated the first line at length in *The Crucified God*. In his *Theology of Hope* he drew the other line, that of victory. The order is the same as that of the New Testament church; in terms of the confession of Christ as the glorified Lord the tradition of the suffering Lord follows. He is the risen one, but he is that as one who was crucified. The resurrection of Christ confirms that he is the Son of God (Rom. 1:4). For God fights against the powers, the enemies, even the last enemy.

56. Emmanuel Levinas, *Het menselijk gelaat. Essays van Emmanuel Levinas*, ed. and trans. by O. de Nobel and A. Peperzak (Bilthoven: Ambo, 1975³).
57. A. Schwarz-Bart, *The Last of the Just* (Bantam Books, 1961).
58. Aart van Roon, *De Brief van Paulus aan de Epheziers: De prediking van het Nieuwe Testament* (Nijkerk: Callenbach, 1976), p. 23.

Even more than Moltmann, Pannenberg in his Christology stresses the resurrection. In the resurrection the goodness of God is manifest: God does not abandon the person who puts his trust in him. God does not abandon the world to the powers of chaos. By God's raising Christ from the dead history is put in a new light, the light of God's apocalyptic victory over the powers.[59] Pannenberg's view is linked with the fact that he sees the future as judgment over history: the new events determine the meaning of the earlier. Thus in the resurrection of Jesus God's action determines the meaning of Jesus' life and death.[60]

The battle of God along, with, and for his people, like the idea that God is an emotive God, goes back to Old Testament times. It is even a fundamental given in the tradition of Israel's confession. God liberates his people, something demonstrated in the history of the night of nights, when with a strong hand and outstretched arm God delivered them from Egypt. Because God is the God who himself fights for his people, this night is greater than all other nights, as the Jewish Passover liturgy remembers to this day. When Pharaoh oppressed Israel and there was no escape, the Lord regarded their misery and delivered them. A people with small children and large flocks of sheep and goats escaped from the chariots and horses of Pharaoh. For the power of the Holy One is greater than the power of the tyrant. Israel bases its confession not on the all-embracing character of the ground of being, but on the liberating deeds of God. The oppressed are his people, but they are the oppressed whom he intends to liberate.

Israel most impressively voices the saving actions of God in song. Immediately after the story of the deliverance from the power of Pharaoh one encounters the song of Israel and Moses on the shores of the Red Sea. "The Lord is my strength and my song, and he has become my salvation. . . . Who is like thee, O Lord, among the gods? Who is like thee, majestic in holiness, terrible in glorious deeds, doing wonders?" (Exod. 15:2, 11). In the ancient song of Deborah (Judg. 5), the elements are moved ("the earth trembled, and the heavens dropped, yea, the clouds dropped water," v. 4) for the deliverance of Israel. The same ancient motifs resound in Psalm 18 and 68. "In my distress I called upon the Lord; to my God I cried for help. From his temple he heard my voice, and my cry to him reached his ears. Then the earth reeled and rocked; the foundations also of the mountains trembled and quaked, because he was angry. . . . He delivered me from my strong enemy" (Ps. 18:6, 7, 17).

59. Pannenberg, *Jesus, God, and Man* (Philadelphia: Westminster Press, 1968), pp. 66-73; 133-41. See also his *Glaube und Wirklichkeit: Kleine Beiträge zum christlichen Denken* (München: Kaiser, 1975), pp. 81-93.

60. Idem., *Grundfragen systematischer Theologie*, vol. 2 (Gottingen, 1980), pp. 66-79.

God himself fights for his people. Personal deliverance and the salvation of the people are interwoven in their songs. Every Israelite is king and every psalm becomes a psalm of David. "With the Lord on my side," says Psalm 118, "I do not fear" (v. 6). "They surrounded me like bees, they blazed (Hebrew, "were extinguished") like a fire of thorns" (v. 12). Where the God of Israel appears, there the enemies are quickly consumed, though for a moment their flames shoot high.

In other stories it is rather that God is in battle together with his people. He gives the victory, but he does it through human stratagem or battle. When he again strengthened Israel after the curse upon Achan, he gave them victory over Ai by prospering their ruse (Josh. 8). That is also Gideon's experience, who with 300 men defeats tens of thousands of Midianites (Judg. 7). Trusting the Lord, David defeats Goliath (1 Sam. 17). "In the name of the Lord I cut them off," sings the author of Psalm 118:10.

Consequently, the call also for deliverance continually resounds from these same psalms. "My God, my God, why hast thou forsaken me?" (Ps. 22:1). Under threat from his enemies the poet lifts up his soul to God (Ps. 25:1). For the only deliverance is in God's hand. If I had not believed I would see the goodness of the Lord in the land of the living—then my adversaries would have defeated me (cf. Ps. 27:11, 13). The two types of psalm belong together. They are interwoven. For that matter distress and deliverance often occur in the same psalm. The chosen one is the afflicted, but the afflicted also finds God on his side, even though the enemies number in the thousands (Ps. 3:6).

The New Testament saw Jesus as the fulfilment of the messianic king. He is the oppressed but as such he is the chosen one; or rather, conversely, because he is the chosen one he is the sufferer. There is no other chosen one, nor can there be. That has been demonstrated in the history of God's actions with his people. But the oppressed has God on his side even though the whole world, Israel and the Gentiles, are against him. He utters the words of Psalm 22: "My God, my God, why hast thou forsaken me?" (Mark 15:34), but his journey ends in the meal with the people of God (Ps. 22:22-31; Luke 24:30-35). He is the victor. The last song the oppressed Messiah sang was Psalm 118 (Mark 14:26). And God made the song come true: the stone rejected by the builders did become the head of the corner (Ps. 118:22; Acts 4:11). Therefore he is seated at God's right hand (Ps. 110:1; Acts 2:34) and appointed Lord over all things. All things are subject to him and have been laid before his feet. He opposes all his enemies and will overcome them until the last enemy, death, has been overcome (1 Cor. 15:25-27). Faith does not focus on the question where evil comes from. The believer does not look for a highest being as the final point of fixation for the ideas of the human spirit. Faith focuses on Jesus Christ, the Lord, the victor over oppression. The believer knows himself found by him who knows the oppressed. Coming out of the great tribulation, believers may celebrate the wedding of the Lamb that was slain (Rev. 19:6-10). For they belong together for good, gathered from the suffering of the cross and united for the kingdom of God. Gathered from the blood of the world they, the people of God, are united for life at the great Passover feast. At midnight, the night of nights becomes the night of the feast (Matt. 25:6). "And once it has been said that Jesus Christ conquers, then comes the moment that something can be said about God's government," writes Van der Werf on his sickbed. God's government does not mean that on the back of every event there is a placard reading "Made by God"; it means that he combats the powers of sin and suffering and overcomes them. That gives us the courage to persevere. Faith means faith in the God who is near to us in time of distress, as the one who suffers with us in our suffering, and in whose life we see the victory depicted before our eyes. "In thee they trusted, and were not disappointed" sang the ancient poet (Ps. 22:5). The church knows of the one person who in his oppression trusted, and perished with the oppressed. Thus he was the elect of God for the life that arises from the great oppression. Therefore we do not die as those who have no hope (1 Thess. 4:13).

The concrete God confessed by the Christian church is the risen Christ who combats the powers of evil and who has regarded our death and defeat. God is present where people are in combat against evil. Suffering requires that we take up the gauntlet, says Wiersinga. Suffering accepted as a challenge gains meaning. "It becomes meaningful and fruitful. It prepares a person for changing action." God is present where Christians do not go about with delusions of grandeur, but in meekness make themselves available to others, where by being present they break through the mute massivity of suffering by being a voice in the midst of silence, a possibility for relationship and deliverance.

When Wiersinga speaks about the challenge in suffering, following Sölle's *Suffering*, he has in mind something other than the challenge of which Cobb speaks. In Cobb it is a God-willed challenge intended to give more profile to the world. Suffering is chosen by God. To Wiersinga suffering is not willed; in itself it is an absurdity. But in this absurdity we are challenged in the imitation of Christ not to submit to chaos but to make the cross fruitful for others. Even senseless suffering is "limited in its meaninglessness by the attraction of a fellowship which takes up the challenge of suffering, incorporates it in its prayers of intercession, and goes to work on prevention and strategy."[61]

61. Wiersinga, *Verzoening met het lijden?* (Baarn, 1975[2]), pp. 111, 112.

Where that mind is present which was also in Christ Jesus who humbled himself and took on the being of a slave, giving himself in death for the other, *there* God is present (Phil. 2:5-8). God is present in the human face of the other. God is also present in the hands which dry the tears from the face of the other. He is not in the hand that strikes so that the tears come, not in the hand of the mighty any more than in the haughty glance of the proud man. Only where the hurt eyes meet and the human compassion that offers itself to the point of death, there the God of Israel is present.

If we base ourselves on the concrete revelation of God in Jesus Christ, instead of on a God image in which he is the source of all that is, we arrive at a very different understanding of the relationship of God to evil. There is another possibility, however, that of thinking of God as being at the end. God is not at the beginning of all things, as *causa prima*, but in the future. He is the goal toward which all things are striving. The most exposed representative of this type of theology is Pierre Teilhard de Chardin. According to him, in the case of God we must think of the definitive destination of the world. God did not make the earth as a finished product, something that can only exist as a showpiece for the greater glory of God. In that scenario a person indeed runs into the problem of how God could let that showpiece go bad. According to Teilhard we must see the formation of the earth as a beginning rather than as a terminus. The earth is the raw material that must be shaped for its ultimate end. Once it has reached this point, the "Omega-point," the earth is as God intends it to be. The whole history of conflict, of the struggle for life, of the evolutionary process, belongs on the road leading to that omega-point. Death, fear, and suffering belong to it as well. Only when the end has been reached will we be what God wants us to be, and know God in his essence, for then we shall correspond to his essence.

Christ came; in him the decisive breakthrough occurred. He is the firstfruits of the new creation. He is the revolution which gave the world a future with God. He is the first who will be followed by all of humanity. Accordingly, Christ ushers in the dawn of the new reality in which suffering and sin will be a thing of the past. But the process continues to the day when the whole earth will be full of the reality of Christ, and Omega is totally real; the struggle for life and the survival of the fittest go on.

Similar ideas have been developed by Karl Rahner, who advocates a transcendental Christology: man needs God but cannot find him. In Christ the fulfilment of the reality for which man is searching takes shape. He is the human being in whom God is near, in whom transcendentality meets transcendence.

One might say that Teilhard de Chardin and Rahner reintroduced, in a new dress, the old scheme of nature-supernature. No doubt this scheme plays a role, but why should not people, in a time that requires new reflection, work creatively with the possibilities available to them in their own tradition? It is rather to their credit that they are now saying new things from within the tradition they have assimilated.

The truth, however, is that the idea sketched above is not dependent on the scheme of nature-supernature. Evidently, people who are rooted in an entirely different tradition, like Pannenberg and Cobb, have developed similar ideas. For them history is an open process that only gains its meaning from the future. According to Pannenberg, the present is not only conditioned by the past; it is shaped especially by the future. The future will teach us what the past meant. The definitive fulfillment of history will not occur until the eschaton comes and history has ended. Only then can the deity of God finally manifest itself from what history has become as his history. As Christians, surrounded by the ambivalences and misfortunes which belong to history, we live facing an open future. At the same time, we are not living in a vacuum, because in the resurrection of Christ God has already given proof of his deity. Christ is the evidence that the future of the world will be God's.

In the writings of Cobb the future is still more open. God is the voice who invites us from within the future toward the realization of new and richer possibilities. Just what the future will be is an open question, although the goal is maximum enjoyment. To reach that goal we must assume the risks of history handed us by God. Whether these risks will produce enjoyment or frustration will appear later. Meanwhile, the luminous example of Christ, who assumed all risks and received the utmost in joy, offers the hope that we will not continue to struggle along in frustrated banality but will experience the heights of glory.

Accordingly, in all four of the theologians we have mentioned God is the future rather than the source. In all four Jesus is, in some way, the prolepsis of the eschaton. In all four the struggle which the world wages in failure and suffering belongs to the essence of history leading to the eschatological fulfillment of the man of God in God, and the God of humans in humans. Hence, suffering is taken up in the process, while in Christ we may trust that the process moves toward the new humanity which is liberated from the struggle for life, from frustrated transcendence, from the ambivalence of history, from the meaningless banality of undifferentiated existence.

The above conceptions tend to be optimistic. Teilhard de Chardin in particular has been accused of not paying enough attention to the real powers of darkness by viewing sin merely as a barrier in the process of evolution. After assimilating the criticism, Teilhard was less optimistic than he was in his foundational work *Le phénomène humain.* One must remember that the philosophical-theological works of Teilhard were not published until after his death.

Also, in Rahner we witness a development in which an optimistic evolutionistic transcendentalism is replaced by a more christologically-oriented theology in which Christ is the fulfillment of vainly questioning man.[62]

Within the present framework it would take us too far afield to analyze these views at length. Nor is that necessary for our purpose, since the problems we have already discussed would simply reemerge from another viewpoint. Broadly speaking, one can go three ways with the above conceptions.

1. One can circumvent the problem of goodness and omnipotence by saying that God is not outside of history but in it. History is not determined by a divinely set goal which has to be reached, but it is really and totally open. Only the future determines the meaningful content of history. In that case, however, the course of history is completely arbitrary. Who can tell where we will end up? Who says that Omega is not annihilation and that the final conclusion of history will not have to be completely meaningless? That, however, is a direction in which none of the above theologians wants to go. Every one of them already sees in Christ the breakthrough of fulfillment. For that very reason his place is so important because in him arbitrariness, meaninglessness, frustration, and discouragement are fundamentally overcome.

2. Accordingly, there is a Will which has set the goal and watches history on its way to the goal. There is planning and control, and a Lord of history. That raises the question why he, who is the Lord of history, should lead it to its goal by such a difficult path. One could say, simply because God has so willed it. With this material, via this searching human and this ambivalent way, he has wanted to do his work and reach his goal. The question is, if then that has to be accomplished by way of so much failure, with so much suffering of man and animal, with

62. Compare, for example, the articles, "The Eternal Significance of the Humanity of Jesus for our Relationship with God" in *Theological Investigations,* vol. 3 (Baltimore: Helicon Press), pp. 35-46, and "Christology Within an Evolutionary View of the World," in *Theol. Invest.* vol. 5, pp. 157-92, with his later works *A New Christology,* Karl Rahner & Wilhelm Thüsing (Seabury Press, 1980), and *Foundations of Christian Faith* (Seabury Press, 1978).

For the views of Pannenberg, aside from the article "Eschatologie und Sinnerfahrung," see also "Der Gott der Geschichte" in *Grundfragen systematischer Theologie* vol. 2, pp. 112-28, where among other things he discusses the views of Cobb. For the rest, in Pannenberg Christology is a much more central datum than in Cobb. In the latter one gets the impression that it is rather an appendix than the center.

millions of dead and billions of sufferers, then how significant is the sublime goal of that divine human being? If we then say, "That lies within the freedom and the will of the Overseer," we are back in the same place as when we said, "We are the clay and You are the potter." The complex of problems this model evokes, therefore, is one that is already familiar to us. Whether one views history from the end or from the beginning, the free will of God remains determinative for how he acts.

3. The above scenario restricts the freedom of history since it is bound to a prescribed goal. One could also conceive the final goal as not having been determined in advance but as given in Christ. From the fact that in Jesus Christ the eschaton is preestablished the future may correctly be viewed in light of him. Undoubtedly, this possibility is most likely in the thoughts of the theologians mentioned, certainly of the first three. But if the facticity of the event of Jesus Christ is determinative for the deity of God, then we are back at the line sketched at the beginning of this section. Jesus Christ is the reality of the new man, and therewith also the revelation of God's will and being. The difference with Barth is that according to him this Christ comes entirely from the other side, and, regarding the theologians cited here, he answers to a way which history goes and to questions which man asks. However, when we remember that according to Barth creation is "the external ground of the covenant," the question is whether the difference is that big. In both cases the creation is dependent on Christ, is directed toward him as goal, and without him remains meaningless frustration. In this scene, all sorts of things should happen, but they do not. Also, in the work of the theologians discussed here Christ does not necessarily or automatically arise from humanity, not even in Teilhard de Chardin. The fact that he is the new man is "an accidental truth of history," a gift that is extended to us; in Barth, conversely, the world already exists for the sake of the event of the coming of Christ—in creation the covenant is already an a priori.

IV

GOD AND HISTORY

17. WHICH MODEL DO WE CHOOSE?

IN THE PREVIOUS CHAPTERS WE DISCUSSED A NUMBER OF MODELS BY MEANS of which one can try to define what God's relationship is to evil. We placed these models more or less side by side. As a result, one section could contradict the other. We have deliberately chosen for this inconsistency. It mirrors the situation of the church. Within the Christian community people make assertions about God, including his relation to guilt and suffering. But the assertions of Christians vary. Often they even contradict each other. In the preceding sections we have tried to do justice to the different ways in which people deal with the problem of evil in relation to God. Undoubtedly, more such models could be found. Also, within the models described here a wide assortment of variations can be advanced. It is not possible to discuss them all at length. From the preceding it is sufficiently clear, however, that people can relate authentically to this complex of problems in very different ways.

But the task of theology does not end there. It rather just begins at that point. If we simply let all models stand in loose juxtaposition, everyone could say what he wanted. In that case no criticism would be possible and there would be no need to influence one another. Every person would then have to think as he pleased. Theology, however, attempts critically to review the assertions Christians make. They are tested in light of the real actions of God. For Christians do not make their assertions at random; they are of the opinion that in making them they are doing justice to God; they believe they are correctly saying that God is as they say.

Someone rejecting the idea that evil comes from the hand of God does so because he is convinced that evil cannot come from God; God is not like that. Hence, some say God is someone who confers illness on people; others say God makes no one ill. Both take this position because they think they are stating truth about God. Next comes the question, "Who is correct?" Having presented different models, we must now ask the question, "Which model is the correct one? For example, *are* we the clay and *is* God the potter? Or is evil purely a matter of human choice in which God is not involved?

Now we can begin by saying that the question cannot be posed in that way. In our discussion of the models it became evident that every way of processing reflects authentic experience. The discussion also showed that every model has biblical-theological roots, with perhaps the exception a narrow understanding of Gnosticism. If the Christian community recognizes that Scripture as the tradition in which Jesus stands is the decisive criterion for Christian theology (even if it is not the only criterion; there is also, for example, contemporary world events and the human psyche), the presence of biblical roots in the different models means that they can all legitimately make claims to being true. It should be clear that the Bible is much richer in views and much more variegated in ways of defining the problems which engage us than can be worked out in one book. For every model one can find texts which confirm what the speaker is saying. For one person that may seem easier than for another, but it is often merely a question of the spectacles one is wearing. Also, the different authors of the Bible have different points of view. Hence the question is not, "Which model is correct?" but "How are the different models related?"

Some models can very well be brought into a rationally unified picture. One can, for example, very well connect the idea that man is the cause of evil with the notion that God is the chastising Father. If God punishes evil, that presupposes that man is the evildoer. Accordingly, in practice there is usually a combination of several models in which one thing is more heavily emphasized than another. Models rarely occur in pure form and so do not simply exclude each other. However, that is not true for all models. There are positions which can in no way be logically squared with each other. If one person asserts that all things, including sickness and war, come from the hand of God, and another asserts that God never "confers" illness and that there is no place in his being anywhere for war, then no rational connection between these two viewpoints can be found without doing violence to both. "Less" and "more" can still be combined logically; "yes" and "no" cannot.

If no unity can be established between models, one can solve the problem most simply by opting for one of the two and ignoring the other. That is often what happens in the church. People swear by the providence of God and forget the suffering and fighting God. Or people swear by human responsibility and forget the omnipotence of God for whom all the nations are no more than a drop in a bucket and dust on the scales. A person who then represents other views is a heretic or one who still does not understood anything of theology.

One can also be less consistent and simply live with a variety of models. One moment one says one thing, the next something else. In any case that practice does more justice to reality. But in theology one cannot be content not to think through this juxtaposition of contradictory views. One has to ask how these models relate to each other.

Thinking the above material through may lead to the decision to let the two stand side by side. Then one opts not for a logical but for a dialectical relationship between the models. At first blush that is a very meaningful method. God is so great that we cannot capture him in a model. He will not let himself be imprisoned in a human line of thought. He will not let himself be locked into the opinion of one biblical author. He does not even let himself be imprisoned in the whole Bible. Just as Solomon acknowledged, "Behold, heaven and the highest heaven cannot contain thee; how much less this house which I have built!" (1 Kings 8:27); so we have to say, "Behold, heaven, even the highest heaven, cannot contain thee; how much less this book which humans have written." The temple and the Bible may be products of a divine mandate and a divine gift inspired by the Holy Spirit who spoke through the prophets, but they cannot contain God. Again, we have to acknowledge, "Behold, heaven, even the highest heaven, cannot contain thee, how much less this theological model I have constructed." Every model is too small and needs to be supplemented with another to convey in words the fullness of God's relations with the world. Even all models together are less than the greatness of the Holy One. If we say one thing, we also immediately have to say the other. If we say that man in rebellion causes evil, we immediately have to add that God sovereignly has the power of disposal over people. If we say that God is the potter and we are the clay, we immediately have to add that he is the one who suffers with us and is present in the face of our suffering fellow human beings. We will never be able logically to put into words the essence of God; always we will have to say one thing as well as another.

No single model can contain the fullness of God. Nor can the thinking of a single person contain it. Consequently, believers need each other in order to arrive together at a fuller way of speaking about the fullness of God. The members of the one body complement each other. Not only is there a dialectic of formulations; there is a dialetic of people. That which one person says immediately has to be supplemented with what another person says. In dialectic there is an attempt to do justice to the awesome distance between God and man. God is the wholly Other, the incomprehensible One who is nevertheless near to us. However, if in every instance in which we say one thing about God we also have to say the other; if it would be the art of theology to find dialectical formulations which express these antitheses in one sentence, we will in fact not say anything anymore. If in every instance in which an assertion is made about God the other has to be included, the assertion becomes empty. If every assertion is valid, then in fact no assertion is any longer valid. Then the concept "God" will die the death of a thousand qualifications. Then theology becomes impossible. Even the act of confession, at least if it aims to say something about God, will become impossible.

We saw that theology subjects the faith assertions of people to criticism. But that implies a restriction of the possibilities of faith assertions. Not every assertion is valid. If theological assertions are intended to be assertions of truth, they have to be falsifiable. Otherwise everyone can say what he pleases without any controls. That is the end of theology; that is also the end of the church's confessional statements. For a confession is an attempt, often over against other confessions or views, to say what the content of the faith is. Sometimes a dialectic is necessary in theology. One cannot comprehend everything. That is true not just of theology but of all scientific disciplines. If physics has to live with Heisenberg's uncertainty principle because physical objects do not allow themselves to be absolutely objectified, how much more true is it then that theology has to live with uncertainty and contradiction, a situation in which we cannot even find a formula in which to lay down uncertainty relationships. God, after all, is much less objectifiable than an electron. Dialectic has a critical function. When a person makes an assertion, the dialectical method immediately responds by saying that the assertion really does not cover the whole subject. Hence dialectic is an antidote to petrifaction and exposes all isms. But when dialectic is absolutized it turns into its own opposite. Then it itself becomes an ism. And then dialectical theology has nothing left to say. Absolute criticism is absolutely devoid of criticism because within it there is not a single point of verification by which to corroborate the criticism. The sister of dialectics is the negative theology which represents the view that one cannot make any positive assertion about God. One can only say what God is not. If negative theology means that one can only posit a broad framework for theology, a framework within which positive assertions are only relatively true, there is much to be said for it. But if negative theology is conceived absolutely, one lands in the void of skepticism.

We cannot let all models stand next to each other and say that everyone is right. Even if one desired it in dialectical fashion because God is too great and too comprehensive, the same dialectics will have to say that at the same time God is near and has given himself into the hands of humans so that we can think about him and make meaningful assertions about him. Hence again the question comes back, "What is the nature of the relationship in which the different models stand?" We saw that in part a logical relationship can help but ultimately does not satisfy us—without concluding now that therefore logic is taboo in theology. Logic is necessary and useful, but only insofar as it helps. We also saw that a dialectical relationship can help but is not absolutely satisfactory either. What is true of logic is true of dialectic.

Another alternative is to picture a spatial relationship between the different models. That would mean that *here* God is different than *there*. Here he is the chastising Father and there the potter. But this idea does not profit us very much. In the first place, for many people it is difficult to accept that for one person God would be one way and for another another way. That smells too much like arbitrariness. Of course, reality is normative, not the measure of acceptability. But suppose it was the case that God is different "here" than "there"; then either it is up to him to decide what he will be in each place (but that is no different from the view that we are the clay and he is the potter: God is free to discriminate), or the decision is not his (but then it is totally arbitrary how God is experienced, with an arbitrariness that is not even divine). In that case we are no further than absolute dialectics: God can be all sorts of things, it is all true, but nothing is universally valid. Further, this does not solve the problem which arises when two people commenting on the same event speak in different ways about God's involvement in the event. Then the question "who is right here?" remains. A spatial connection, therefore, is more a theoretical possibility than a real solution. It is more a speculation than theology. In any case it fails to do justice to the call: "Hear, O Israel: the Lord our God is one Lord" (Deut. 6:4). Like Israel, Christian theology is so deeply pervaded by this awareness—the awareness that for all peoples and nations God is the same; that even the separation between Israel and the nations has been overcome by him—that from here on we can eliminate this idea from further consideration.

The problem with the scenario in which the different models were placed in a dialectical framework was that no decisions could be made. There is no critical standard by which concepts can be limited. The result is that theology as a critical science and the church's confession as proclamation for the world are hollowed out. Accordingly, we must search for a criterion by which theological assertions can be measured— in our case, by which the ordering of models can be tested. Ultimately, of course, that critical authority is God himself. But saying that gets us into a circular argument: only God is normative for who God is. Our concern is a criterion by which God can be known.

That criterion is the acts of God. God's deeds tell us who God is. Solely from his actions and reactions do we know anything about him. Every assertion in which someone says, "God is . . . ," whether, "God is good" or "God is mighty," can be tested by the deeds of God. From those deeds it will have to be apparent that he is good or mighty. The acts of God have been recorded for us in the tradition of Israel and the early church. God liberated Israel out of Egypt. God led Israel into captivity and brought it home again. God sent Jesus Christ, in whom we may be his children. The Christian church is not called Christian for nothing: the witnesses who surrounded him are the beginning of the tradition of which he is the normative source. Through him the tradition of Israel, God's acts before Jesus, has come to stand in a new light as the way which culminates in him. God's deeds in the history of Israel and of Jesus Christ make it possible for us to make assertions about the nature of God's relationship to people.

This line of thought seems to lead us back to the final section of the previous chapter; God is the concrete God of history—hence God is Jesus Christ. This can indeed be a starting point, but we have to make some marginal comments:

1. In the revelation through Jesus Christ God did not perform one act but many. God's action occurs in time and is not always the same. The liberation out of Egypt is one event and the event of Bethlehem another. Even though Exodus 12 comes to stand in a new light as a result of Luke 2, that does not mean that Exodus 12 is merely a weaker version of Luke 2. God's acts in Egypt and with Israel are acts which are mirrored in a unique process of events.

2. The above becomes even clearer when we recall that God's action is reflected in a historical process in the world. The idea that there is not only a *creatio activa* (the creative action or speech of God) but also a *creatio passiva* (that which proceeds from his hands) is true of every divine action. On the passive side God's activity is effectuated in an earthly event which accordingly has a reality and value of its own. The event of the entry into Canaan is a fact with a reality and value of its own that cannot be absorbed by some other event, even if that event be the crucifixion or resurrection of Christ.

3. When God's acts take place, they are observed, recognized, and acknowledged by humans. Also, the human observation is part of the revelation, as is the human acknowledgment that in this event God is present in the way they say he is. Therefore the events are not objective facts as reflections of God's action; in order to become revelation they are bound up with a happening in humans in whom or in the presence of whom the event is realized. In other words, the event of the formation of human conviction constitutes a part of the divine revelatory action. Hence the different testimonies of humans, for all their variety, all have the significance of authentic divine revelation, and justice must be done to their variegated discourse. The human words are of no less importance than the Word and act of God. That which happens at Paul's and Luke's writing table, as reflex of what is at work in the person called Paul or Luke, is as much an event which mirrors God's action as what happened on Golgotha.

4. Accordingly, a sequence of events reflects the varied action of God. In this connection we must not, however, limit ourselves to the actions of God (and hence to the events) written up by the Bible authors. God's action continues. Now, too, God is the living, acting God. If God has not withdrawn from this world (and therefore has not become irrelevant to our thought and action), then current world events also have to do with God's action. Just how he has to do with them is precisely the focus of this study. Contemporary events stand in relation to God. Every new event calls for new reflection about what we have said of God. For that reason too theology is never finished: even if we were able once and for all to put in order all the acts of God's past revelation (which is never the case both because the human spirit is smaller than the reality it seeks to grasp *and* because people continue to think and to raise questions), then new events would have to be similarly processed. Otherwise God would not be doing anything new. We shall have to relate all contemporary events to the events of the past. Christian theology is not a repristination of the past, nor is it a summary of what the biblical authors say; rather it is the search for the mutual relationship between the important events of today and the normative events of the past. In this connection neither of these may be allowed to crowd out the other, on pain of the loss of the living God who has something to tell us. Between past and present stands the confessional activity of the church—shaped by a long tradition— which is subject both to the critique of God's deeds in the past and to the critique of contemporary events.

5. If we say that Jesus is the revelation of God, we are using the word "God" to indicate the significance of Jesus. The word "God" is no empty concept—it produces a certain picture in people's minds, one they had before Jesus Christ appeared on the scene. When they began to

write about Jesus Christ they found the word "God" an adequate expression for him. The word was charged with notions of power, rule, and the meaning and source of the world. Because the early church judged that Jesus had power, exercised rule, was the meaning of the world and the source of its existence, they called him "God." Hence "God" is predicate; and in the sentence "Jesus is God," subject and predicate cannot simply be interchanged. One could say, "Jesus is the only real God," as he is the only real Lord. But by doing that one has not made the concept "God" empty any more than the concept "Lord." It is precisely because of the meaning people assign to the word "God" that Jesus is so called. Hence there is a relationship between the idea "God" and Jesus Christ. What that relationship is, how the relationship has to be defined between the idea of "absolute omnipotence" and "absolute being" on the one hand, and Jesus Christ on the other, will have to be made clear. Judging by the New Testament and the entire Christian tradition, that cannot in any case be a purely negative relationship. The eternal Supreme Being (God with the face of a Roman emperor) and Jesus Christ have to do with each other in some fashion.

6. Taken together, the above two remarks again give rise to still another nuance. The fact that Jesus answers to the idea which people have of God is not merely a matter of language. For human ideas also are part of the earthly reality which comes forth from the hands of God. They are part of the *creatio passiva*. In other words, they are also a happening. The church's witness will just as much have to relate to the happening that someone thinks God is "the eternal independent Supreme Being," as to the fact that the world is chock-full of weapons and the fact that millions have been killed in the name of Christ.

There are, accordingly, a great many events which are related to God but whose interpretation in terms of the nature of God's presence can be extraordinarily difficult. Also, those events of which the biblical witnesses explicitly speak as God's actions are manifold and multiform. There are many deeds of God which cause people to speak (which as such is a new act of God). These deeds cannot all be reduced to one. They may be connected; they may place each other in a certain light; but each nevertheless has its own independence. All these acts of God have led to authentic ways of confessing his relationship to the world. They have also led to different authentic ways of speaking about his relationship to suffering and to guilt. What we know about that relationship we only know from those acts. On the basis of those acts, as events occurring around or in people, we arrive at very different models. Hence the relationship between the models has to do with the relationship between the deeds of God or—in terms of the passive side—with the relationship between the experiences of the event that points to him. The relationship of the one deed of God to the other is the only relationship we can discover between the different models because the sole standard of verification (or better, the only possibility of falsification) for our position lies in the revelatory action of God.

When it comes to a relationship between events as the passive side of a relationship among the deeds of God we end up with a chronological relationship. That, after all, is the way we order events which are not logically or dialectically connected. A chronological ordering of the models is the only way in which a theology which bases itself on the deeds of God as criterion for its assertions can achieve results. That does not mean that the one model must always come after the other and flows from it. In that case chronology would again turn into logic. History has its permutations; it is not a straight line to a well-defined goal. But it is a forward-moving line.

When we base ourselves on God's deeds, we base ourselves on the *history* of God's deeds and on the history of God. God is a God with a history he makes with people, one in which he himself moves from one deed to the next. For God is the living God. He is, as the classic dogmatics have it, *actus purissimus*, the very purest deed. Because his deeds are not reducible to one, his relationship to the world cannot be stated in just one way either. Each deed has its own character. Each deed is mirrored in the experience of people who confess God. Each time people are pressed to speak about God in a different way. It all depends on which of his deeds one focuses, on the yawning earth beneath the tents of Korah (Num. 16:31ff.) or on the joy in Abraham's tent when Isaac was born (Gen. 21:1-7); on Pharaoh's hardened heart (Exod. 4:21), or on Paul who was permitted to see the light from heaven (Acts 9:1-6). But if the deeds of God are not completely arbitrary, so that we would not be able to say one sensible word about them, we shall have to settle for a relationship between all those deeds that is historical, reflecting a history which God makes with people.

18. God Is Changeable

AS WE ALREADY HAVE SEEN, IN THE MIDDLE OF THE SECOND CENTURY Marcion asserted that the God of Jesus Christ is a different God from that of the Old Testament. The God of the Old Testament was a capricious God, wrathful and hard in his exercise of justice. The God of Jesus Christ was a God of pure love, compassion, and grace. The two were impossible to harmonize. The image of God which comes to us from the Old Testament is the image of a very different God from the God of whom Paul speaks, particularly in the letter to the Galatians, which most affected Marcion.

The church repudiated Marcion, consciously opting for the identity of the Father of Jesus Christ with the God of Israel. The church was not cut off from its roots in Israel. Nor was the church detached from its roots in the earthly society, which is the product of the Creator-God. For the Marcionite thesis that in Christ the Creator-God was replaced by the strange God of love was rejected. There is but one God: the God of Paul is no other than the God of Moses. Marcion was wrong, said the church.

With Paul's letters in one's hand, one can only say that Marcion was wrong. At the same time, however, the church forgot to ask itself whether perhaps in some respect Marcion was right. And that was undoubtedly the case. For God is not another God, but he *is* different. The church so strongly insisted on the oneness of God that in the divine image change was no longer possible. Among all the attributes of God "mutability" was taboo. For most of the history of dogma the church persisted in taking that position. God is an eternal, immutable being, without an "earlier" or "later," without a "then" and "now," without a "now" and "then." The world changes; everything is subject to change, but God never changes. One who starts to tinker with this fundamental idea of theology alters the basis of the certainty of the world. He removes the linchpin on which the world hangs.

Still, it is precisely in subjecting to criticism the thesis that God is absolutely unchangeable that one gains access to a meaningful way of dealing with evil, suffering, and guilt. As we saw, the problems with respect to the relationship between God and evil arose from the contradiction between these premises: "God is omnipotent" and "God is good." However, that contradiction applies only if we place the two premises in timeless juxtaposition. But the moment the time factor is introduced, the problem takes on a very different aspect. For then God can change in his being. Then he is not another today from who he was yesterday, but he *is* different. That does not mean we would have to conclude that God was first, say, omnipotent and is now good. That would be playing one divine attribute off against another, a process which can only lead to a de-divinization of God, a dissolving of his being into a number of separate attributes. Opposed to this is the classic dogmatic rule that the attributes of God mirror his being in its totality.[1]

Like all other attributes, "omnipotence" and "goodness" belong

1. Berkhof, *Christian Faith*, pp. 112ff.

essentially to the way in which God relates to the world. In thinking about change in God we are thinking about change in the attributes. If each of the attributes is a mirror of God's entire being, then every change of God will entail a change in attributes. Then "omnipotence" will not always mean the same thing. Today's goodness will be different from that of yesterday. If one drops the third premise, that of the immutability of God, one can no longer speak in such an absolute sense about "*the* omnipotence" or about "*the* goodness" of God, but only about the omnipotence as it was at a given moment or the goodness as it was manifested at a certain time. In other words, one can only read the omnipotence and goodness of God from the revelations of God's omnipotence and goodness in history. How did God's omnipotence prove itself and how was his goodness manifest? In that connection we must not look for an external norm by which we measure God's deeds to see if the deed of the moment was omnipotent, or measure God's action of the moment by an idea of absolute goodness and then decide whether or not God was good. There is no other norm for omnipotence or for goodness than the norm God himself sets. What goodness is at a specific moment is determined by the action of God at that moment. And if today God acts differently than yesterday, goodness today is different from what it was yesterday. God is the criterion for good and evil, for power and powerlessness. There is no authority above him to which he could be subject.

Only the deeds of God afford access to his being. Consequently, the history of God's action is the only norm for the determination of good and evil. When God commands Saul to destroy the Amalekites to the last man, woman, and child (1 Sam. 15:3), and the prophet with his own hands hews in pieces the survivor (1 Sam. 15:33), then at that moment that is good. It is the divine will, even a divine mandate. If today we are troubled that an entire people was killed and say, "but that cannot possibly be good," that cannot be said on the basis of an external norm to which the divine command was subject, as though an abstract idea of goodness floated over the heads of the Amalekites and Israelites and above the God who issued the command. To whom or to what would the God of Israel be subject? If today we do not endorse the extermination of a people, not even, rather, certainly not, on religious grounds, then that is because of a new action of God in Jesus Christ, by whom the nations were incorporated into fellowship with Israel, and because God was pleased to reveal himself on the cross and not with the sword. From within a new moment in history the norm for goodness became different. In the eleventh century B.C. it was good to exterminate the heathen; in the first century A.D. it is not good. If about the eleventh century we now say "that was not good," then that is true only proleptically with a view to Christ. Only in retrospect does the goodness of Samuel prove to be other than the goodness of the divinely sent Son of God. Accordingly, the norm for the goodness of God alters with the history of God's action, or to state this on the passive side, with the history of his revelation.

Now one could object that, to be sure, this is true of the knowledge people have of God at a given moment, but not of God himself. In the eleventh century Samuel did not know better than that God wanted the Amalekites exterminated, any more than the authors of Exodus and Deuteronomy knew better (Exod. 17:14; Deut. 25:19); but of course God himself could never have intended it. We must distinguish between three phases: (a.) the being of God; (b.) the revelation of God; (c.) the command given to Samuel. As we make a distinction between the last two one can ask whether or not the instructions Samuel gave Saul were in fact based on revelation, or, in this case, on instructions from God. Was the prophetic mandate a divine mandate? Now that is appropriate to ask not only for the prophet Samuel, but for all prophets. It applies as well to evangelists and apostles. Is their word in fact a reflection of the Word of God? It would constitute an absolute break with the entire tradition of Israel and of the church if the prophetic word of the Old Testament would no longer be in effect as the human verbalization of the Word of God. It would also be a break with Jesus Christ who, in the fulfillment of the prophetic word, saw himself as the one sent by God. To divorce the word of the prophets from revelation would mean the end of Christian theology. When the prophet says, "Thus says the Lord . . . ," that then is the word of the Lord. It would not be the word of the Lord only if it had not been substantiated. The word of prophets has to be confirmed in history (Deut. 18:22). The words of the prophets were confirmed in history, in judgment, in deliverance and salvation; they were confirmed above all in Jesus Christ. In him the prophets were proven true. Denial of the prophets is denial of Jesus Christ, who knew himself rooted in and borne up by the way of God and Israel.

There is not only the distinction between the word of the prophets and the Word of God, however; there is also the distinction between the will of God as the reflection of his being and the will of God as revelation. When God gives instructions through Samuel to exterminate the Amalekites, is it essential for God to give those instructions? If we should answer that question in the negative we should know what we are doing. In the first place, in that case God is playing a game with the life of a people. If, to save the ethical character of the being of God, we isolate the prophetic revelation of God from the heart of God, so that his speech only applies in relation to people but not to his deepest being, then there is a heavy price to pay. For if anything is unethical, it is that, while in your heart you know the salvation of people to be the highest good, you issue instructions to exterminate them.

There is still another argument against the separation of revelation and being: if God's being remains hidden behind his revelation, then we do not really know God through his revelation. But then it is no longer revelation from *God*. Then they are merely fantasies to conceal his real being. In that case God remains a mystery to us. A third motive is that we have no knowledge of God other than what comes to us via his revelation. If there is no such thing as prophetic speech substantiated by the acts of God, if these acts did not occur as reflected in prophetic speech, we know nothing of God. About a being behind the revelation of God, should that exist, we cannot say a word. However, the idea that such a hidden being exists militates against the idea that God really encounters people. God lays his heart bare. Jesus says, "All that I have heard from my Father I have made known to you" (John 15:15). But the prophets already spoke about the deepest inner self of God, his heart, his "bowels," which are directed toward Israel.

Hence the goodness of God is the constant decision of God as manifest in his action. It is the goodness of his history. There is no other goodness than the goodness which is God in his address to people here and today. The same is true of his power, his love, his entire being. There is no other being of God than the God who encounters us here and today. This idea raises the question concerning God's oneness. If God's being as mirrored in his attributes constantly changes in his separate deeds, can we still speak of one God? Does not God then consist of a large number of different and detached moments without any underlying essential unity? By postulating the changeability of God, are we not sacrificing his oneness? That is by no means my intention. Nor is it actually the case. For the oneness of God does not lie in an abstract concept of absolute unity in which there can be no variation. Such a unity would a priori exclude action and revelation. Absolute unity is a unity without life, for action and revelation require multiplicity. Action is different from non-action. The moment God acts he is different than when he does not act. Even if from all eternity he had intended the action, then the moment he speaks in order to effectuate the action, a change occurs. In that moment there is a difference between earlier and later. God created time. But when God created time for people, he also created time for himself. For time is the link beween earlier and later. It is the factor which unites the "before" and "after." The moment God does something more than remain by himself in the infinite circle of his own being and proceeds to act and to will, the moment he begins to create,

265

that moment time enters eternity (and not the reverse!). As soon as God begins to act something changes; there is an earlier and a later, not only in the world but also in the heaven of God. The situation with respect to revelation is no different; it is revelation to another, a second.

Action and revelation therefore by definition presuppose multiplicity. Even just one act already produces it. As the actions increase, so does the pluriformity. Each time God reveals himself anew, his revelation is multiplied. Each time something new comes to light. For unless it is something new, it is not revelation (i.e., an act of making known), but only a repetition of what is already familiar. And with every new datum people pick up about God, their relationship to God changes, even if they reject the thing revealed. And when a relationship changes, both partners in the relationship change.

The unity of God therefore does not lie in a concept of absolute simplicity. The unity of God lies in the unity of his deeds. It is a unity in pluriformity. God has an abundance of pluriform deeds and words: of deeds which speak of him, of words which are acts of revelation. God's mode of self-disclosure is that of *dabar,* word and deed in one. In the abundance of all these *debarim* there is not only constant change, but also a constant. The constant is that God proves to be the same God. Changeability and unchangeability are therefore most closely bound up with each other; continuity and discontinuity are most closely tied in with each other. There is a discontinuity of the differing deeds, but in the discontinuous series there is a continuity by which they are connected. In all the acts of God there proves to be consistency. He fulfils the promises. What he promised to Abraham, Isaac, and Jacob he gave to Israel in the days of Joshua. Despite Solomon's unfaithfulness the throne of Judah is preserved for the house of David. God proves to be consistent in what he says and does, consistent from one deed to the other. That consistency extends over hundreds of years; it is a unity of action which bridges the centuries. As far back as human consciousness can go, God proves to be consistent in his relationship to the world. Even in the event of the flood when things went to the brink, God held fast to what he began: to people living in a covenant relationship with him. God did not make a final break. From *olam,* from the very earliest beginning, there proved to be a constant in God's speech and action.

The consistency of God's deeds is most prominent in Deutero-Isaiah. When Israel thinks that with the exile all is lost and that God has changed by turning away from Israel, the prophet says that God does not just let himself be changed, neither by the unfaithfulness of Israel (40:1ff.), nor by the power of alien peoples (45:1ff.) and gods (44:6ff.). "I, the Lord, the first, and with the last; I am He" (41:4).

"You are my witnesses," says the Lord, "and my servant whom I have chosen, that you may know and believe me and understand that I am He. Before me no god was formed, nor shall there be any after me." (Isa. 43:10). God proves his faithfulness to Israel and no one can stop him. Characteristic is the phrase *ani hu* (41:4; 43:10, 13; 46:4; 48:12): I am he; I am the same. Psalm 102:25-27 says the same thing in confessional form: "Of old thou didst lay the foundation of the earth, and the heavens are the work of thy hands. They will perish, but thou dost endure; they will all wear out like a garment. Thou changest them like raiment, and they pass away; but thou art the same, and thy years have no end." In all the changes of the world God is the reliable one. The believing Israelite trusts that God is faithful to his promises, consistent in his deeds. It is the public acknowledgment of the Name "I am who I am" (Exod. 3:14), the God of Abraham, Isaac, and Jacob. When all things give way, the faithfulness of God does not. "For the mountains may depart and the hills be removed, but my steadfast love shall not depart from you, and my covenant of peace shall not be removed, says the Lord, who has compassion on you" (Isa. 54:10). We are not, therefore, talking about an absolute concept of divine immutability. We are talking about the certainty that God is faithful to his promises and about the conviction that he is able to fulfil them. But it is the same God who does new things and turns away from his anger. It is precisely Deutero-Isaiah who shows us that the stability of God's covenant, of him who is the first and the last and who does not go back on his word (Isa. 45:23), is bound up with his compassion for his people. The repeated "Comfort, comfort" with which Deutero-Isaiah begins (40:1) in Hebrew has the same root *(nacham)* as the word for God's repentance *(piel:* to comfort; *niphal:* to have second thoughts, to repent). A similar link occurs in the song of Moses in Deuteronomy 32: God's repentance (v. 36; again the *niphal)* and the certainty that he remains the same (v. 39) complement each other. God's faithfulness is the root of God's turning to grace, and God's repentance is the realization of his faithfulness.

God's deity stands or falls with the consistency of his deeds. The moment there is a definitive break the world will no longer be subject to the same God. If there is no longer any common component in God's revelatory action in relation to earlier generations and in the history of the present, then the history of the present can no longer be the history of the one God. Then we are living in a history that is no longer subject to the God of the fathers. We may be biologically connected with our ancestors, but we are no longer connected to the faithfulness of God who bridges the generations. Faithfulness is the biblical word for the consistency of the actions and words of God. The unity of God is not an abstraction; it is the unity of his faithfulness in which he does not forsake the work his hands have begun. With that faithfulness the deity of God stands or falls. As soon as God is no longer faithful to himself, he is finished with his past, with the work of his hands. Then this world, the result of his earlier actions, is lost for him. The moment God is no longer faithful, he is no longer the God of this world and no longer relevant for the world. Of the greatest importance, therefore, is the recognition of the faithfulness of God. Of the greatest importance is the discovery of consistency in the deeds of God. The greatest crises in the faith of Israel arose the moment they could no longer discover the component of constancy in God's relationship to Israel. Through the centuries it had been Israel's experience that God confirmed his word to Abraham. Sometimes they had moved to the brink of an abyss, but over and over the fathers had been rescued. The constant in God's works proved to be the choice he had made for Israel. Then came the moment, in the exile, that the line of continuity seemed to be broken. Then the cry arose: "O God, now where is Your faithfulness, Your honor? Now we have become like those over whom You have never ruled, who are not called by Your name" (cf. Isa. 63:19). Only new deeds of faithfulness can confirm the deity of God and demonstrate that he is more than the gods of Hamath, Arpad, and Sepharvaim (Isa. 36:19) which were no gods (Isa. 37:19).

When we have difficulty—in the history of the world or in our own lives—rediscovering something of the consistency which points to the action of the God who called us into being and made a covenant with us, then faith in this God again comes under pressure. Then we cry for the deeds of God which confirm his history with people.

There is, therefore, unity in God's action, but it is not a massive unity. It is the constant of his faithfulness, but that constant is caught up in constant change. The consistency of God's work is continually under fire to the point where Israel says, "Now where is your faithfulness?" Sometimes and in certain deeds that constant can hardly be discerned anymore; trust in the God of Israel trembles at the sight of the fathomless abyss of godforsakenness—until God again confirms his faithfulness.

Berkhof has spoken of believers' experiences with God as a cumulative process in history.[2] Now it is certainly not the case that the experiences, however cumulative and numerous, postulate God. To interpret the experiences as an action of God it is necessary that at the same time there is a minimal sense that God is the driving force behind the event. But human experiences in history do have the power to "falsify" God or to confirm faith in him. Every new deed of faithfulness signifies support for an already existing faith. If on one day of the history of the world an event would take place in which there was not a single thread of connection with all of God's promises and deeds, the deity of God would be broken. Then he would no longer be the God of this world.

2. Berkhof, *Christian Faith,* pp. 65-67.

Accordingly, Israel's doctrine of God and that of the church is based on the deeds of God. Its conclusion is that God is immutable in his faithfulness and at the same time continually changeable in his revelation. As a rule the tendency in theology has been to emphasize the immutability of God. The world is certainly changeable enough. It is a relief, amidst all the changes and uncertainties of the world, to be able to postulate the certainty of the unchanging faithfulness of God. As a result, the changes in God faded into the background. Thus God became a peg by which the changing world was hung on the wall of eternity, rather than a living person who warmly responds to the world and turns his face toward it. As long as his immutability was understood and experienced as the faithfulness in which a personal God did not abandon us, that view led to questioning the moment that faithfulness was no longer recognizable in the world. That questioning then led to a crisis of faith. But as soon as immutability became a principle, that could only have the effect of denying to God all emotionality. God became the eternally immutable, unmoved Mover, devoid of all affect. And that God is different from the God who encounters us in the Old and the New Testament, an emotional God full of moods and changes.

Of that too Marcion had become clearly aware. But here, too, he drew the wrong conclusion. Marcion could not accept the God of the Old Testament because he was an emotional, even a vehement God. Only the God of pure and simple goodness could be God. Marcion drew the conclusion that the God of the Old Testament could therefore no longer be God, a conclusion the church did not follow. But at the same time the church did nothing to honor Marcion's discovery that the God of the Old Testament was a vehement God. For that matter, Marcion had already discovered that this was true not only of the Old Testament but also of the New. To keep his own new God pure, far from the righteousness of the law which militated against the grace of faith, far from wrath and judgment, Marcion also had to delete large parts of the New Testament.

The God of the Old and New Testaments is an emotional, vehement, changing God, who pursues one course today and another tomorrow, who even changes his mind from one moment to the next. God is a God who one moment strikes out at the world so that mountains tremble and humanity shudders, so that the dead fall by the thousands, and who the next moment takes crushed humanity to his heart and comforts them the way a mother comforts a child (Isa. 66:13). The God who spoke through the prophets is no eternal immutable Supreme Being, but a God with a heart, always in motion. Throughout his entire history with Israel God is the living God.

The extent to which this is true may be seen from a couple of examples. Hosea 11 proclaims judgment over Israel. In emotional terms the prophet sketches God's relatedness to Israel. "When Israel was a child, I loved him. . . . it was I who taught Ephraim to walk, I took them up in my arms" (vv. 1, 3). A bit further the image of the working ox is used: "I led them with cords of compassion, with the bands of love, and I became to them as one who eases the yoke on their jaws, and I bent down to them and fed them" (v. 4). In every line we hear the voice of a God with an affectionate, loving heart. But at the same time Israel is charged with not paying any attention to this love. "The more I called them, the more they went from me" (v. 2). "They did not know that I healed them" (v. 3). Therefore Israel's measure is now full. God's affectionate tenderness now yields to vehement anger, for an outburst of temper that knows no limits. "Assyria shall be their king, because they have refused to return to me" (v. 5). "The sword shall rage against their cities, consume the bars of their gates, and devour them in their fortresses" (v. 6). Return is no longer possible. "And though they cry to him above he will by no means raise them up" (v. 7 [in the author's version]). Tender love has turned into boundless aversion. With that verse 7 ends.

Then for a moment it was quiet—the prophet was silent; the Holy One said nothing. For a moment it was silent in heaven. But the heart of the Holy One was not still. His heart churned within him (v. 8). Then follows the unexpected change: "How can I give you up, O Ephraim! How can I hand you over, O Israel! How can I make you like Admah! How can I treat you like Zeboiim!" The irrevocable divine decision of verses 5-7 has been revoked. God cannot carry out his plan, not because external powers would prevent him but because his own heart will not let him. And the irrevocable decision of divine wrath becomes the starting point of divine compassion. Israel refused to repent (v. 5). Therefore God turns around (v. 8). When it comes to immutability in Hosea 11, it exists on the side of man rather than God. Human beings are unchanging in their sinfulness. They never turn around. But God is different. He is the Holy One: utterly different from humans (v. 9), far above all human smallness. Therefore he is not unchangeable, but changes from the heart. "For I am God and not man" (v. 9). God is not miserably consistent like people; he does change from time to time. He will roar like a lion and is followed by people who come after him like trembling birds (v. 10f.), who understand what Jeremiah said: "For the Lord will not cast off for ever, but, though he cause grief, he will have compassion according to the abundance of his steadfast love; for he does not willingly afflict or grieve the sons of men" (Lam. 3:31-33).

Hosea 11, a vehement prophetic word, is a vehement oracle from a vehement God, but it does not stand alone in Scripture. Vehement prophetic words occur everywhere, from Moses to Malachi. Vehement words of God also resound from Matthew to Revelation. Sometimes the flames of the fire die down or smolder in a soft red glow. But unexpectedly they may erupt again like a volcano, causing the mountains to tremble and breaking the trees of the forest, while in his temple everyone cries "Glory!" *(kabod)* at the sight of the glory *(kabod)* of it all (Ps. 29).

The interaction between the unity of God's promises and deeds on the one hand, and the constant change in his deeds (as the mirror of a change in will and mood) on the other comes out in the use of the word "repent." On the one hand it is said, "God is not man, that he should lie, or a son of man, that he should repent. Has he said, and will he not do it? Or has he spoken, and will he not fulfil it?" (Num. 23:19). Israel gets to hear this confirmed by the pagan seer Balaam. Though the nations try to prevent the fulfillment of God's promises to Abraham in the life of Israel, though they hire a famous prophet and sacrifice numerous animals on the altar, God does not allow himself to be swayed. A promise is a promise. God remains unchangeable, irrevocably faithful to his election. Psalm 110 says that God will not change his mind about his election of the priestly king (v. 4). Conversely, even his wrath shows his steadfast purpose: "Compassion is hid from my eyes" (Hos. 13:14). "I will not spare, I will not repent" (Ezek. 24:14). Hence, both in grace and in wrath the Lord may be unrelenting.

The relationship between the two becomes clear in Zechariah 8: "For thus says the Lord of hosts: 'As I purposed to do evil to you, when your fathers provoked me to wrath, and I did not relent, says the Lord of hosts, so again have I purposed in these days to do good to Jerusalem and to the house of Judah; fear not' " (vv. 14, 15). God is not sorry about the choices he has made, whether they be to judge or to save. The unrelenting character of God is one side of the issue—expressed forcefully in 1 Samuel 15:29: "And also the Glory of Israel will not lie or repent; for he is not a man, that he should repent." His choices are irrevocable. But the same chapter which so forcefully proclaims this twice declares that God repented: "I repent that I have made Saul king" (1 Sam. 15:11). "And the Lord repented that he had made Saul king over Israel" (1 Sam. 15:35). Accordingly, there is in God both repentance and the denial of repentance. How are we to interpret this?

There are various possibilities.

a. In 1 Samuel 15:29 God says that he will never repent of his rejection of Saul; in verses 11 and 35 the reference is to a positive choice. Therefore the rejection of Saul is definite; the election is not. Apart from the far-reaching consequences this exegesis could have—consequences

271

which cannot be substantiated—it is not acceptable in view of the parallel in Numbers 23:19 where non-repentance has a positive meaning. We are apparently dealing with a customary formula.

b. Repentance and non-repentance relate to different situations. One moment God does not repent; the next he does. But this idea makes meaningless the statement that God will not repent: if after a little while he will repent, then the promise that he will not repent has no value whatsoever.

c. We can accept both dialectically. In any case, by doing that we are doing more justice to both. But we are then still stuck with the problem of every dialectic: that consistent implementation makes both poles meaningless. A non-consistent implementation requires further interpretation.

d. Apparently we must rather read the texts in such a way that non-repentance relates to a basic attitude of a structural kind, one within which all sorts of different choices can take place. God does not regret the promise made to Abraham, but in the realization of it he can, within the concrete circumstances of the day, make repeated changes in his actions. In this connection it must be noted that non-repentance apparently need not always be "forever"; it may be "for a long period." According to Zechariah 8:14 both judgment and salvation are successively "unrelenting."

More remarkable, however, is the fact that the texts which refer to God's repentance are far more numerous than those in which his repentance is denied. Over and over God proves to be sorry over something he has started. The first text about this in Scripture is also one of the most poignant: "And the Lord was sorry that he had made man on the earth" (Gen. 6:6). God regrets ever having started with man. He would have preferred that there never had been human beings. It is more often the case, however, that God wants to carry out his wrath and then changes his mind. The Lord repented of having said that Israel's fields will be eaten bare by locusts (Amos 7:3). The Lord is sorry that the angel of destruction is going around in the land of Israel to slay people with the pestilence after the census (2 Sam. 24:16; 1 Chron. 21:15). The Lord is sorry to see his people in distress (Ps. 106:45). Accordingly, the prophets repeatedly say that God will change his mind, that he will not execute his judgment, when Israel or other people repent (Jer. 18:8, 10; 26:3, 13, 19; Joel 2:13; cf. also Deut. 32:36). There is also prayer that God may reconsider and suspend the judgment he has already announced or is even in the process of carrying out (Ps. 90:13). The prophet Jonah is so convinced that God will reconsider and refrain from carrying out judgment that he loses all interest in announcing it. When as a prophet,

272

speaking in the name of God, you proclaim to people that God will judge them, the only result is that he makes you look like a fool, for he is sure not to do it (Jon. 4:2). In the end Jonah proved right: "God repented of the evil which he had said he would do to them and he did not do it" (3:10). However, there comes a moment when God's repentance over his plans to come in judgment is exhausted. In the name of the Lord, Jeremiah proclaims, "I am weary of relenting" (Jer. 15:6). Ezekiel too knows of the end of God's patience: "I will not spare, I will not repent" (Ezek. 24:14).

What this comes down to is that there is constant change in God's plans, feelings, and actions. It is often said of these data that they are only reported "as a manner of speaking," not actually real changes in God. It is anthropomorphic discourse—as if there were ever any other way of speaking about God than the anthropomorphic! *Everything* we say about God is said in human words. Those words either are, or are not, meaningful. Since words are not used without purpose, the people who in human words and earthly images say something about God intend to say something that does justice to reality. In the sentences cited above, the word "repentance" was used by translators who deemed it the most adequate rendering of the Hebrew word *nacham*. According to the authors of those texts that Hebrew word best conveyed who God was at that moment. In heaven there is perhaps a better word, but if that word is not intelligible to people it will be of no benefit to them. Then it does not constitute revelation and does not tell us anything about God. If God is to reveal himself, he must do so in human words which reproduce his intent and action as well as possible. One of those words is "repentance." It refers to a change in God's attitude toward people. There is perhaps another word like "regret" or "changing one's mind." But that does not alter the isssue: God changes his mind. Words like "repentance" and "change" are needed to report how the God of Israel acts and who he is.

The study of other concepts, such as "change" or "remain," yields a result similar to the study of "repentance." Malachi 3:6 is the only text I could find which states explicitly that God does not change (*sanah;* cf. Ps. 77:11 where the same conclusion is present by implication). On the other hand, Job 30:21 explicitly states that God does change (*hapak*). Where the English has "change" or "turn," one finds an entire spectrum of words in Hebrew. One certainly finds no doctrine of divine immutability in the Old Testament.

The God of Israel is a God full of movement: his judgment constantly shifts; new things are constantly being said in his name, and he repeatedly gives unexpected twists to history. One time he permits the world to be swept away in a flood so that the old is destroyed in judgment. Another time he says that all sins and judgments are past; the former things are not remembered because he will do new things on earth (Isa. 43:18ff.). One time he causes Israel to sin (2 Sam. 24:1); at another he is a forgiving and gracious God (Ps. 103:7-12). Marcion was right in saying that the God of the Old Testament was not devoid of affects, but vehement and changeable. He was right in saying that often God is other than the gracious one on the cross.

In Scripture events are viewed as effects of divine decisions. He takes the wagon of the world where he pleases. The reins do not slip from his hands, but that wagon does sometimes make a sharp turn. The God whose hand created all things and calls the stars by name (Isa. 40:12-26) is the same God who says "do not remember the former things," because he has a new plan. It is Deutero-Isaiah who, while he is so clear on the fixity and firmness of God's action, is also clear about the changes in God's action. One moment he gives Israel up to plunder, pouring out his wrath upon the people (42:24f.); the next moment he starts anew: "But now thus says the Lord . . . I have redeemed you" (43:1). Through the centuries the world sometimes takes a strange direction. The course of people's lives is often no less unclear. Not infrequently that course is so capricious that one cannot imagine anyone could say of it, "As the finger of God has written." But if we have difficulty believing that, is that because we have in mind the God of Israel, or because we are thinking of the God of Marcion, of Plato, or of Aristotle? To this day God conducts the course of the world where he wants to. No more today than twenty-five hundred years ago do the reins slip from his grasp. But today that course is unpredictable, as it was then. But if it is not God's course, then God is not God anymore. Then he is finished as God.

Sometimes the idea has been expressed that there is continuing divine revelation. In Israel God revealed himself in part—which, in view of the relationship between God's revelation and being, means that God himself is caught up in a process of development in the history of revelation. After the revelation in Christ God turns out to be adding new things to the knowledge the church has of him. The Spirit leads the church in the truth and causes it to share in ever bigger secrets. Now undoubtedly there is progression in the knowledge of God, just as there is progression in the action of God. But that is certainly no linear progression, a direct route to a pre-planned destination. The graphic of history is not one of linear ascent and still less the ascending branch of a parabola. It is a fitful line to which no formula can be applied. The way of God with the world is not something one can put in a computer. It is a strange zigzag course, one that excites hope and brings despair, a road of tears and blood, and at the same time one of laughter and life. History is labyrinthine; numerous alleys go nowhere, even alleys that started as avenues; sometimes alleys broaden into highways on which history whizzes forward at great speed. That is not something new; nor is that a reason to question whether this history had to do with God; it is only a reason to remind ourselves of the history of Israel, of prophets who interpreted this history as the reflection of the hand of God. It is a reason to remind ourselves of the devout who, in the psalms, confessed that their lives were led by the hand of God. It was the hand of that God who at every moment thought of something new and who changed in his judgments at every moment. But it was also the hand of that God who on the basis of all those changing deeds displayed arch-consistent faithfulness in which he bound himself to what he promised Abraham.

The idea that God is a changeable God who constantly changes in his judgments and conducts a fitful course in history may seem terrifying. It *is* a hair-raising thought—but what else do we want in a terrifying world in which we have to live? Suffering and guilt are terrifying realities. How real and how terrifying they are comes home to us every day on television. One can experience it every day in one's own surroundings. The world trembles on the brink of the abyss of irrevocable suffering as a result of irreparable guilt. It is terrifying to be in the world and to be a human being in the 1990s with the nuclear umbrella still above our heads. It is absurd to call nuclear weapons an umbrella as though they offered protection, instead of a menacing gathering of heavy thunderclouds already far above the horizon of our lives. If this umbrella ever stops anything, it is the water of a flood which can put out the conflagration of the world, the stream of grace that removes this guilt. It was terrifying to be in the world in 1348, with Black Death hovering over and haunting villages and cities, with horribly mutilated victims lying all around, and the possibility of losing in death all that was precious. To be human in history is to be human in a history of suffering, to participate in a history of guilt. If God is a God of humans, a God who has to do with this history, then God is a terrifying God. If God did not have to do with a history of suffering and guilt, then what would he have to do with? Is he then still the God of the world in which we are living?

Suffering and guilt are the fearsome mysterious and incomprehensible realities of our existence. But are not joy and reconciliation equally incomprehensible? Who comprehends the secret of reconciliation? Who will uncover the ultimate source of joy in the hearts of people? The entire history of God with men is a *mysterium tremendum ac fascinosum*. Life itself is an incomprehensible mystery. To be human on earth, to be human on earth and involved in a history with God, to be a human on *this* earth in a history with *this* God—who will ever decode the riddles?

In our uncertainty we may, amidst the chaos of world history, attempt to find a point, a pivotal point, that does not move. Amidst endless movement we may postulate an unmoved one. But the postulated Unmoved One is not the God of Israel. It is not the God who acts and reveals himself to humans. A God who is truly God can only reveal himself in human history, in the mobility of the chaos of history. One who looks for an unmoved God will only find a human postulate. To nail God down on one specific datum may seem reassuring, affording a person a foothold in the universe. It would provide order amidst chaos. But one who seeks the real God of the world will find no other than the Living One who performs acts. He is the variable God of life; but in that variability he is the God of unchanging fidelity to the history of the life he created.

19. JESUS CHRIST—GOD'S CHOICE

GOD IS A GOD WHO MOST DYNAMICALLY MAKES HIS WAY THROUGH HISTORY. Over and over he makes unexpected decisions. Over and over, in the conduct of his rule, there are unexpected shifts. What he has built he breaks down; what he has planted he plucks up (Jer. 45:4). He can never be figured out in advance. One moment he calls a king as the man after his own heart; then later he makes the same king sin in order to be able to punish Israel. And when his punishment is in process of being realized, he has second thoughts and is gracious to his people. God is not bound. In absolute freedom he goes the way he chooses, restrained, walled in by nothing. No one tells him what to do. No one can ask him, "What are you doing?" Autonomously, having only himself as law, he makes and leaves his footprints in the history of the world. Human rules do not ensnare him. He is the God who kills 185,000 Assyrians to secure the applause of a handful of Jews (2 Kings 19:35). He is the God who makes the brutal general Jehu king (2 Kings 9:1-6). The expression, "the zeal of a Jehu" refers to a commitment to the cause of God so rigorous that the God of Israel can no longer be recognized in it. Jehu has Jezebel's servants throw the aged queen out of a second-story window, and he brutally rides over her with his entire cavalry (2 Kings 9:30-37). He convoked a great feast in honor of Baal for no other purpose than to kill off the worshipers of Baal (2 Kings 10:18-36). It was not even a fair and

276

honest contest, as was Elijah's on Mt. Carmel (1 Kings 18). Jehu is a brute: his guiding principle is "the end justifies the means." "The zeal of a Jehu"—the phrase has a negative sound. But it is the negative judgment of a much later generation than that of the books of Kings. We may think, "Certainly it could never be God's intent that a king should restore the worship of Israel's God in such a horrible way," but of this view there is not a trace in First and Second Kings. The fact that Jezebel was crushed and then eaten by dogs is a judgment of God: so God decided, as Elijah predicted (1 Kings 21:23), and so it happens. Even Jehu had more respect for her than the author of 2 Kings deemed necessary. His idea is still to have her buried as a king's daughter (2 Kings 9:34), but the judgment of God has already taken care of the matter in a more efficient way: the dogs did their divinely willed duty (vv. 35-37). Accordingly, the verdict over Jehu's harsh and—in our eyes—false conduct is not, "You have done your best, Jehu, but that is not really what I had in mind," but the divine verdict on Jehu is this: "And the Lord said to Jehu, 'Because you have done well in carrying out what is right in my eyes, and have done to the house of Ahab according to all that was in my heart, your sons of the fourth generation shall sit on the throne of Israel' " (2 Kings 10:30). The criticism of Jehu was not that he was too rigorous, but that he had not gone far enough (v. 31).

The history of Jehu is only an example among others that show that the way of God does not answer to our norms of good and evil and that the manner in which God chooses and judges does not exactly square with our choices and judgments. God is a rough God, grim, and in our eyes even cruel. God does not have the refinement of a middle-class European or American. God at times weeps. He does not display the proud self-control of a solid authority figure—he can be inwardly miserable over his chosen Israel. Of course he chose a partner who was no good, who never was any good. By marrying a whore, the prophet Hosea gives the whole thing away in a symbol of God's union with Israel (Hos. 1–3). Is it any wonder that the marriage does not go well and that if there is to be a future for the two of them Hosea has to put up with all sorts of humiliations? Is not the covenant between God and Israel doomed to fail from the beginning? Can the covenant ever exist in any way other than by God putting up with an endless series of humiliations? And he does put up with them, even though from time to time he threatens and raises an angry fist.

God is not one you can figure out. Majestically he goes his own way. You can also say, He goes his own way with complete and fitful autonomy. Who will ever fathom divine government? Majestically he goes his way, and we humans can only exhaust ourselves trying to understand. The very ancient poet Agur—of whom we know nothing else—already said it (Prov. 30:1-4): "Why?" and "How can that be?" It is better not to ask; you cannot understand God in any case. Neither his actions nor his decisions are intelligible. The more one views the whole world as a theater of God, the less one understands him. The more one wants to let all of Scripture speak for itself—and not just those words we have first measured by a norm of what God could or could not actually have said—the more unclear the Bible becomes. The more we believe that the whole Word is revelation, the less we know who God is. We could perhaps restrict revelation to certain events in the world. We could restrict it to certain texts in Scripture. But then what is the criterion for our selection? Is that something other than the choice we already made in advance as to how we can imagine God to act and to be? But then we do not need revelation. Then there is no critical objective standard over against us of the real God with his real actions. And for that matter, what would we do with the rest which does not mirror God's action or speech in his name? The fascination and difficulty in Christian theology is that we have to do with a much more variable conduct of God and a much broader revelation than fits our construals. We cannot get a hold of God. We cannot lock him in our systems, not even in a system of mercy and grace. Always and again, God is different.

When we thus accentuate the variability of God's action, a question arises concerning the certainty God gives us. Is not God so changeable that a person never knows what he is up against; that everything a person counts on will be changed tomorrow? In other words, is a variable God one you can trust?

In this connection another question suggests itself: What is the difference, if any, between God and the accidental course of events? Behind the view described above is the idea that all things have to do with God. The process of world events is a mirror of divine action. Good and evil both come forth from his will. The two can never even be called good or evil in themselves, but only as related to another action of God in which the good of the one moment comes to stand in a bad light as a result of a new event. In this way, are we not robbed of a critical standard by which not only world events are measured but also human action? For human action too is a component in history and a reflection of the way of God. If on that way all moments are detached, what is the criterion by which my actions are judged, except that in a later stage I will think differently about them? And also this later stage is again followed by a new choice.

The search therefore is for a fixed point in history, a fixed point in the action and speech of God by which the rest can be measured. In the absence of that point, there is no thread of continuity in history; no ethics is possible—*God* is not possible. In the preceding section we started to answer this question by pointing to the consistency of God's deeds. Unity is not found in an absolute concept of simplicity, nor in an arbitrary choice of our own, but in the constant which exists amidst all the changes. We described this constant as the faithfulness of God. God does not act with absolute arbitrariness. He does repent, reverse himself, but the reversal is never total. In the final analysis what is not in any case alterable is the fact *that* God has acted. His deeds continue to exist, be it merely in his memory. After God has acted, he is in any case forever the God who has acted. Facts are hard, harder than bricks, van Ruler once remarked. A brick can wear out but a fact in history can never be undone. A person can forget it, but that does not mean that it has never been. With the very first deed of God he is irrevocably an *acting* God. But this is not the end: God is also forever a choosing God. Once God has made the decision to perform an act which has effect (and which act of God does not?), then he chooses. Even if later he plucks up what he has planted, he remains the choosing God, for he then opts for the alternative possibility. The moment God is more than a point of eternity turned in upon itself, creating room for something other than himself, he is definitely and for good a choosing God. Our existence as people presupposes a choice on God's part. Even if he should never choose us again and reject us once and for all, he is still a choosing God. For then he is the God who chose to be without people.

These, however, are merely some formal remarks about the immutability of God. He is unvaryingly an acting, choosing God. But there is more to be said about both adjectives, and it has to do with God's remnant. For, as we said earlier, God never reverses himself completely. His choice is never a turn 180 degrees from an earlier choice. In his new choice he always takes along with him something of the old, not only as a memory but as material for the realization of the new. That is not something one can deduce from a preconceived God concept; it is evident from the practice of his action. A striking example is the flood story. God is sorry he has made man and decides to destroy him. But he does not destroy all of mankind down to the last man. There is a remnant. It is only one family, but it is a remnant. And the remnant becomes a new beginning. A new humanity is in the offing, one that lives on the same earth under the same vault of heaven. Only in heaven something has changed. A "never again" has been sounded. A final decision has been made there. God decided never again to allow the waters to cover the earth (Gen. 9:11). Never again will God give up the earth to the primal powers of chaos, but he will maintain the orders. "While the earth remains, seedtime and harvest, cold and heat, summer and winter, day

279

and night, shall not cease" (Gen. 8:22). Accordingly, God again chooses for the world. The promises of Genesis 8 and 9 do not just stand by themselves. After God's choice for creation a new choice follows, one in which God's repentance of Genesis 6 has been incorporated. God has tried another choice; he has seriously thought of destroying humanity. He has been in the process of making that choice stick. But he did not carry it out to the end. He allowed a remnant to remain in order to build on it. After that experience God said "never again." The alternative, the road to ruin, was open. But God rejected it. That choice does not stand by itself; it is a choice made through a crisis. Through a crisis of "human-lessness," God again opted for people. That choice became "fireproof," a purified decision which can stand up to the flood of chaos.

Earlier we cited Agur: God is unfathomable. Who can know him? But the same Agur concludes: "Every word of God proves true; he is a shield to those who take refuge in him" (Prov. 30:5). The words of God are trustworthy because they have gone through a process of being refined by crisis. If the word of God to Noah is a purified word, it is true, and it cannot be viewed apart from the entire preceding history. Against the background of God's repentance over ever having made man, and of the waters of the flood, this choice of God gains its definitive power. God cannot go back on it. For his choice he is bound to the world, as is evident from the renewed earth after the flood. He remains true to the creation he began. In medieval terminology one can say, The *potentia absoluta* is limited by the *potentia ordinata*. In the beginning God was absolutely free. He could go in any direction. Before the flood God still had the freedom to give the earth up to the powers of chaos. However, in the Noahitic covenant God bound himself to his choice for the world. He does not ever again reopen and reconsider the issue of creating an ordered world, the issue of creating an inhabitable earth for man. God is bound by his own decision, not because it has been laid on him from without but because he so chooses. His choice bears the stamp of eternity, but also this time, the time of grace, it penetrates eternity.

This interplay between heaven and earth, between time and eternity, has been splendidly developed by Johannes Cocceius in his doctrine of the two covenants found in *Summa doctrinae de foedere et testamento Dei*. The covenant of works with Adam had been broken. The first dismantlement of it occurred in time in the Fall; the second occurred in eternity in the founding of the covenant of grace, the *pactum salutis*, between the Father and the Son. Following the earthly event comes the decision in the eternal counsel of God. In this interplay between earthly crises and heavenly counsels which carry eternal import, the formation as well as the realization of the covenant of grace takes place.

280

God's eternity is shaped in the crucible of his works in time. After reversing himself God confirms his choice for good *(ad ôlam)*. The destruction of the world by re-exposure to the powers of chaos was never again opened up to discussion; perhaps it was among humans, but never between God and humans and therefore also never between God and God in the eternal counsel. Decisions have been made which shape God's very being, not from without but by his own choice. God permanently ruled out consideration of the choice to destroy the world by letting it revert to chaos. He opted for the line of grace.

In history God continued the line of grace, not only by not going back on his choice for creation and against chaos, but also by confirming his grace in increasingly narrow circles. When after the flood people again turned into titans, perhaps not by wanting to be as God (Gen. 3:5), but certainly by wanting their own access to heaven (Gen. 11:4), judgment again follows: humankind is broken up into many nations. But amidst the nations, in Babylonia, there is the remnant of the one, Abraham, in whom all the nations will be blessed (Gen. 12:3). The choice of that one can never be viewed in isolation from the choice for the nations. In the call of Abraham God confirms his grace to all.

Each time things go to the brink of judgment and skirt the abyss of total ruin, there is also the narrow escape in which God's word is more and more purified. With increasing clarity he proves to be—again in the words of Agur—"a shield to those who take refuge in him" (Prov. 30:5). With increasing clarity he proves to be who he is, also in the history of Israel. Before the face of Pharaoh and on the shores of the Red Sea, right to the bottom of the sea of Rahab—chaos itself—-he proved to be the saving God who gave people a humanly habitable world. He proves to be who he is through the crises of the wilderness—past the golden calf and the disappointment of Kadesh-Barnea (Num. 14). In gripping language the poets of songs like Psalm 78 and Psalm 106 have articulated the line of God's faithfulness: amid continual unfaithfulness and crises God continually confirms his choice for Israel. When David became king the word of God was purified by many crises, even by the crisis of Saul's kingship. It is the line of the history of Israel as we have it in the redaction of the "historical" books of the Old Testament. It is not just history; it is the history of God's action which confirms his faithfulness, not in a self-evident superficial fashion but from crisis to crisis, moving to and past the brink of ruin, but ever saving, because God does not want to abandon his people. He always again repents of his wrath—until Israel enters the same crisis as humankind did in the flood. It was the greatest crisis in the religious faith of the righteous, because it was not the crisis of the strange gods, the Baals imported from without, but the crisis of

Israel's very existence in captivity and exile. Then the road led clean to the brink of the abyss. But again there was the remnant. In the crisis of ruin God proved unable to utter his definitive "no" to his people. The choice of Israel proves to be the choice of God's own heart, the choice of his deepest being. God's being is qualified by the election of Israel. That is evident not from the theoretical considerations, but from the consistency of God's action in relation to Israel over the centuries. The idea of the remnant does not derogate but underscores the firmness of God's words and deeds. The remnant indicates that the words and deeds of God have been purified and have passed through crisis. They are "a brand plucked from the fire" (Zech. 3:2), a precious possession for which God is prepared to burn his hands. And to the degree that the remnant of Israel knows itself to be the sign of God's faithfulness it also knows itself to be the remnant of the nations, the sign that God saves the world. After the crisis of the exile comes a new covenant for Israel (Jer. 31:31-34), a new action of God (Isa. 43:9-21), not only for Israel but for all nations (Isa. 49:6).

Accordingly, God increasingly turned toward grace and salvation, not with harmonious gradualism, but in the manner of the unpredictable God of the world, in a hopeless zigzag line. But in the confusion of events there are turning points, switches are turned, enabling the history of God's action to continue. In the tumultuous course of history there is Noah, Abraham, Moses, David, and Deutero-Isaiah. God can take many directions, continually charge, strike out and comfort, sometimes be incomprehensible, but over and over it is clear that he sticks to the decisions which confirm his faithfulness.

There is progressive momentum in history, on the way to the definitive turning point where the last decisive choice is made. That choice was made in Jesus Christ. Jesus of Nazareth identified himself with the lost. He accepted whores and publicans into his company and ate with them as a sign of religious fellowship. He proclaimed in the forgiveness of sins the dawning of a kingdom. For him fellowship with the most wretched sinners was not just a posture; it was the way he knew himself called by Israel's God. This was the choice of the God of Israel, the choice for the dregs of society, for the Samaritans, for sluts, for racketeers and extortionists, for the brutal criminals on the cross. God had made a choice for Israel, for the faithful remnant of his people—a choice for grace. According to Jesus, that choice had to be carried out so radically that the ungodly members of the nation would be first in the kingdom of God; and the faith of a Roman soldier (one of those dirty Romans of the occupation forces!) exceeded that of the devout Jew (Luke 7:9). He heard the voice of the Gentile woman who, though a "dog," was the first to be allowed to eat the living bread of the Messiah of God (Matt. 15:21-28). For Jesus was convinced that God had constantly gone that route—with the Gentile woman of Zarephath and with the hostile general Naaman (Luke 4:25-27). Jesus makes the claim that this is how God is, that this is God's definitive choice, the form of God's kingdom. He maintained this position until they nailed him to the cross, until he had to say "My God, my God, why hast thou forsaken me?" (Matt. 27:46), right into the greatest crisis in which for him the deity of God was at stake, in which God was absent and the man who confessed this God and lived by this confession was himself forsaken.

In Jesus things go wrong with man. He had opted for the way of the God of sinners; he had lived the way of that God and this road ended in death on the accursed cross. The way of the law in condemnation and judgment seemed confirmed. "Cursed is he who hangs on a tree" (Gal. 3:13). God punishes the ungodly one who made the wrong choice, who made claims he could not substantiate. God is the severe God who not only forsook Jesus but by that token also rejected publicans and sinners, sluts and traitors. God was not the God who opts for the sick beggar at the gate but for the rich man in his palace. God forsook the man who healed lepers and thus thrusts those lepers away from his own heart. God forsook the man who called the dead to life, and by that token God thrust the dying away from his nearness. There is hope for no one, for death has everyone in its power; and in the dying Jesus, who opted for the life of people, God forsook all who have to look death in the face. The tradition of faithfulness here falls in the ultimate, the very worst crisis, the crisis of the rejection of the definitively lost, the crisis of death. In the case of Israel God can be faithfully patient a long time, but if in the end they prove to be sluts and traitors he abandons them. The tradition of Israel only confirms that with which the tradition began: Jacob, the deceiver (Gen. 25:26; Hos. 12:3). He whose ancestor is a deceiver, who out of self-interest even deceived his own father, had better have no illusions. He who knows almost two thousand years of Israel's history had better have no illusions when at the cross of Golgotha the traitors and deceivers are rejected. The history of the Jews began with the patriarch Judah, who had children by a whore who proved to be his own daughter-in-law (Gen. 38). One who surveys almost two thousand years of Jewish history only sees a nation which conducts itself like a slut, like Oholah and Oholibah (Ezek. 23:4). He who knows Judah had better have no illusions when the whores on the cross are rejected. On the cross of Golgotha Naaman, the widow of Zarephath, the Syro-Phoenician woman, and the Roman officer, are all sent packing. Gentiles must not have any illusions about God, any more than may the sons of Israel and Judah.

At the cross of Jesus, it is either all or nothing: a world is saved or a world is lost. Either God is the God of sinners or God loses his deity. Those are the alternatives with which Jesus confronted God and which Jesus maintained to the end. And Jesus died. The human who carried all humans in his heart died. Therefore all have died. The history of mankind often skirted the abyss; in the death of Jesus the abyss opened. "Descended into hell," says the Apostles' Creed. Jesus went to hell carrying the world with him. The history of God's faithfulness often skirted the abyss. Sometimes there seemed to be an absolute break in his actions and his deity was threatened. But there was always the remnant with which God confirmed his faithfulness. There was no other beside him. But in the death of Jesus, the one person who confirmed his name, the line of grace was broken. The deity of God went under. The way of creation, of Noah, Abraham, and David, the way of the prophets, ran dead.

On the cross of Golgotha the hope of the world died. Then in heaven and on earth it was still. Especially in heaven it was quiet, even more than when Hosea stilled himself for a moment after his preaching of judgment. The stillness also lasted longer—to the third day. Three days is the time of preparation, the time needed for a good decision. The third day was the first day of the week, the day God said, "Let there be light." God saw the light and it was good. On this first day of the week God saw the darkness of the caverns of hell. And the darkness was not good. God could not opt for the darkness; choosing darkness would have meant rejecting himself. God chose the light, again. He chose Jesus as the light of the world. God raised him from the dead on the third day. The authors of the synoptic gospels had a very fine sense of what happened. The resurrection of Christ was the fulfillment of Hosea's prophecy: "After two days he will revive us; on the third day he will raise us up, that we may live before him" (Hos. 6:2). When God raises up Jesus, he confirms his goodness. He maintains the feelings that were already present in Hosea: "How can I give you up, O Ephraim! How can I hand you over, O Israel! . . . My heart recoils within me . . ." (11:8). God confirmed that he cannot let Israel go. He confirms that he cannot let the world go. Again he creates the light. He confirms that he cannot let Jesus go.

This time he did not skirt the abyss; this time the crisis, the most profound one, went through the abyss. Through death, the death of the cross, the death of the accursed, the death of him to whom God had said "no"; the death of him who was identified with Jacob and Judah, with harlots and publicans, with the occupying forces and traitors, with the Gentiles and the ungodly. After careful consideration, having passed through the most abysmal crisis, God said "yes" to the accursed. This human is his man. God confirms his claims. God confirms that he is the God of Gentiles, whether they are from Phoenicia, the land of Baal, Roman or Syrian. God confirms that he is the God of the Samaritans, of the woman who went through five husbands and was cohabiting with a man (John 4:18). He confirms that he is the God who wills the healing of the sick, the forgiveness of sin, the conquest of the demons. He is the God who wills that the lame shall walk, the lepers be cleansed, the dead rise. For he confirms that he is the God of Jesus.

God confirms the way already announced by the prophets: the true servant of the Lord is the light of the nations in whom God unfolds his new initiative. He bore our sorrows and assumed our diseases. He was counted among the transgressors (Isa. 53:4, 12). At Easter it was confirmed once and for all that God is the God of absolute grace who saves where no salvation is any longer possible. He saves even him whom he had rejected. Again, he repented after all. When God raises Jesus from the dead he proves to be the God with a heart, the God who can change his mind. Precisely in that regard he is faithful to the limit to the choice he made. For God loved Jesus. He did not let his Holy One see corruption. He could not forget him even in hell, nor forsake him (Acts 2:27). God could not detach himself from Jesus, not because he was forced, but due to the movement of his own heart. In his own being he could not tolerate the separation.

This last point requires further comment. It is not merely the case that Jesus went his way alone, made certain choices of his own, ran dead into the wall of Jewish and Gentile hatred, and that God then decided to save him from death. That is also true, but over and above that the idea we find particularly in the Gospel of John is that God himself sent Jesus. God willed that Jesus should go the way of the cross. God himself chose to bring his deity to light in this manner. Therefore for John the cross itself is the exaltation of Jesus. God himself had sent his Son to make public everything he knew of the Father. The ultimate revelation of God, there where his very being was exalted, is where Jesus, like the serpent in the wilderness (John 3:14), was lifted up on the cross. By his cross Jesus saves the accursed and those doomed to die. But that salvation is the choice for which God had sent him, "for God so loved the world that he gave his only Son that whoever believes in him should not perish but have eternal life" (John 3:16). The apocryphal letter of Barnabas extends the metaphor: those bitten by the serpent, who is the devil, as in Paradise, are saved by Christ, as Moses at God's command already indicated (Barn. 12:5ff.). God himself chose consciously to be the God of the cross, the God of love, who seeks out the lost because they are his own (John 1:11) whom he will not abandon.

God's decision was not a smooth one; it was made in conflict. Also, John's gospel requires the Easter story. And a later redactor found it necessary, apparently, to add another appearance story (John 21). Good Friday was God-willed. He opted for the way of grace in order to be the God of the crucified even before the cross was raised; but it took three days of decision before Easter came. Likewise, the Son opted for the cross, but it still cost him the thrice-repeated prayer in blood, sweat, and tears: "Father, all things are possible to thee; remove this cup from me" (Mark 14:32-42). It is the heavy conflict in which God is forsaken by God, in which God loses himself and chooses for the one way: the salvation of the ungodly. God chose to be *this* God—once and for all. For a human nothing can be worse than to die the death of the accursed, who in the name of God and man has opted for the very least. When God identifies himself with Jesus, he identifies himself with the crucified. In the resurrection of Jesus God himself becomes the crucified God. He confirms that he himself suffered the wounds and received the blows. He confirms that the death of Jesus was his own. What people did to Jesus they did to God. They crucified him. They killed him. But he let them. He let himself be crucified; he let himself be killed. In the glorification of Christ God made it clear he wanted to be this God, because he identified himself with the crucified.

There was a time when for God the choice was completely open. He could do what he wanted. In that way he was God. But he tied himself to his own way; he wanted to tie himself down. No one laid it on him. No one forced him to send his Son in the person of Jesus the crucified. But he wanted to. No one forced him to raise Jesus from the dead. But God wanted to—he did not want to leave him in death. God bound himself to the strange way of Jesus. Now he is the God who forgives sinners, heals the sick, and puts demons in their place. He is the God of Gentiles and Samaritans. He is the God of whores and publicans. He is the God of the crucified and of the dead. In God's past deeds this sometimes dawned but it was never as clear, all-encompassing, and finally definitive as in Jesus. One recognizes the God of Noah here, but in a much more intense fashion.

Marcion's idea that this God was another God is not totally far-fetched. God does appear to be very different in Christ. Still, it is not the case. In his eternal oneness God in the beginning could embrace everything: he could go the way he wanted. Good was what God was and wanted. In that God acted and made choices. Over and over he chose to be who he was and wanted to be. He chose eternal fidelity to mankind. He chose to be the God of the remnant of Israel. He chose for Jesus Christ. Increasingly, God articulated and defined who he was. And in every choice he rejected another alternative—until he definitively expressed himself in Christ, the Word, the Logos. In Jesus all other possibilities for the deity of God were rejected. Only in this way he could be and did choose to be God from that time on.

If Jesus is the definitive revelation of God, he is also the norm for the goodness of God. Consequently, all earlier choices come to stand in a new light. Earlier we remarked that good is what the will of God is—there is no criterion outside of God by which his deeds can be measured. But in Jesus Christ a criterion has been introduced within God himself. God is now "normed" by the choice of Jesus. In light of this criterion something can now be said in retrospect about the Gentiles. In the days of Saul it was good to exterminate the Amalekites. In the days of Joshua a command could be issued to exterminate all the heathen who inhabited the land of Israel. But in Jesus God opts for the heathen. From Israel to the nations there is now an open door. Therefore, there can never again be a choice like that of the days of Saul and Joshua. Yesterday's command God now himself rejects. Accordingly, the greatest consistency—God's fidelity to the world extended to the utmost in Jesus Christ—is at the same time the greatest change, in which all other choices which have been made now fall under the divine "no."

We have pointed out that God's revelation and being cannot be separated. If the old way which God took with Israel has become a closed road in Christ, something essential has changed within God himself. God has changed. God has ruled out for himself the option of exterminating the heathen. God has ruled out for himself the possibility of letting the lost be lost. God has ruled out for himself the possibility of letting the sick be sick. God has ruled out for himself the possibility of making a deal with demons. For God has chosen for Jesus.

The fact that the cross of Jesus, confirmed in the resurrection, is decisive for God's being can also be defined differently, by saying that the work of Christ has "eternal value." The value of Christ's cross is important not only for people as a sign of self-sacrifice given to the world; the cross actually reconciles them with God. A new relationship between God and human beings is initiated. When God enters a new relationship, something changes within himself as well. "Eternal value" means it touches the eternal One. There is no other eternity than that of God. The work of Christ is not just valid for the moment; it is valid once and for all. For it was divinely confirmed in the resurrection from the dead. It was even undertaken as a divine initiative. *God* was in Christ reconciling the world to himself (2 Cor. 5:19). It is his final decisive choice.

If Jesus Christ is the decisive change not just for the world but also for God, then God has circumscribed his own being in him. God has bound himself to Jesus. That also means a rejection of everything in heaven which does not accord with this choice. "To be in heaven," "to accord with God's choice" are phrases referring to divine nearness, to divine decisions, even to divinity, to the being of God, as the center from which all decisions flow. An Old Testament image for this is heavenly "counsel." We find it, for example, in Job 1 and 2, Zechariah 3, and in Genesis 1:26 and 6:1. There the heavenly consultation transpires of "the sons of God." We would probably describe these "sons of God" rather as God's attributes or decisions. In later Judaism the idea of heavenly beings is much more developed, serving to put into words the connections between heaven and earth without directly speaking about the being of God. Angels and preexistent persons and matters serve as a buffer between God and mankind. In this way divine revelation is secured without degrading the Holy One. In the Old Testament God is as a rule pictured more freely. He is the Holy One, to be sure, but One who is near to Israel, even dwelling with them. There heavenly counsel serves rather to indicate the possibility of variation in the divine decision-making process. Earthly history is not mapped out according to a certain fixed program: there is consultation in heaven about it. Eternal counsel is real and very much related to events in time.

In the council of the sons of God is a spirit which offers to go forth as a lying spirit among the prophets of Ahab to see to it that the king will die at Ramoth (1 Kings 22:19-23). Among the angels is one who goes around bringing pestilence and death in Israel (2 Sam. 24:15-17). Sometimes the divine council is narrowed down to the one who does the work of God, the angel of the Lord. In 2 Kings the angel of the Lord slays the Assyrians by going about as the angel of death (2 Kings 19:35). Sometimes the terminology within a single context passes from the angel of the Lord to God himself, as for example in Genesis 16. In verse 7 it is the angel of the Lord who encounters Hagar; according to verse 13 it is the Lord himself. Accordingly, the going about of the angel of the Lord in 2 Kings 19 indicates on the one hand that God himself kills the Assyrians, just as he did the firstborn in Egypt (Exod. 12:29), while at the same time implying a certain divine distance. God is more than the angel; the angel is not the fullness of his being. When God says in Exodus 33 that his angel will escort the people, Moses is not satisfied: God himself, with his fullness, his divine face, must go with them (Exod. 33:1-6; 14-17). Hence the angel of the Lord represents the divine presence, but is not the fullness of God. This is even truer for the other angels, for the sons of God, for the preexistent beings who inhabit heaven. They represent something of God and are at the same time far from being the fullness

288

of God. They are commissioned by God, who is behind them. But there is a "but" in the picture. It is true in the case of the angel of the Lord in Exodus 33; it also applies to the lying spirit in 1 Kings 22. God indeed sends them, but in part he holds himself in reserve, which is what Moses cannot bear. Angels represent an aspect of God but not God in his fullness. We can say that, too, is what God is like. God is the angel who saves Israel. God is also the angel of death in the Assyrian camp. God is also the lying spirit in the prophets of Ahab. But he is also the voice of truth in the mouth of Micaiah (1 Kings 22:28). God has many possibilities, for he has many sons.

Among them is (the) Satan. He is one of the many. That is how Job 1 and also Zechariah 3 speak of him. He is the heavenly accuser. It is his assignment to bring to light the negative side of people. He can even provoke them to that end by sending them all sorts of trouble. Accordingly, he is the tempter. But he is not a monster from hell; he is one of the sons of God in heaven. Hence, there is initially no discrepancy between 2 Samuel 24:1 and 1 Chronicles 21:1. When 2 Samuel says that the Lord incited David, he does that, according to 1 Chronicles, in the manner of Satan who incited David, just as God, when afterwards he punished Israel, does that by way of the angel of destruction. By gradual steps a difference develops between God and Satan. Increasingly, Satan becomes the adversary of God in heaven. We can also say God increasingly makes choices different from the judgment of Satan. God is increasingly less the God who wants to place the evil of men under judgment. In Zechariah we see the first signs of this new image. Satan is put in his place when he accuses Israel—represented by the high priest Joshua clothed in filthy garments—of its sins. God has chosen Israel. Election transcends the sin off which Satan lives. Satan is accorded increasingly less space in heaven.

In the New Testament this image is continued. The relationship between God and evil is depicted in graphic language. In Luke 10:18 Jesus says, "I saw Satan fall like lightning from heaven." Where the kingdom of God comes in Jesus Christ, neither the demons nor Beelzebub their chief have a chance. In apocalyptic language the author of Revelation depicts war in heaven between the angels of Michael, the angel of Israel's election, and the angels of the dragon called the ancient serpent, the devil, or Satan. Satan is thrown out of heaven (Rev. 12:7-11). After ravaging the earth (12:12), he is locked up in the pit of the abyss (20:1-3). Heaven no longer has any room for Satan. It is graphic apocalyptic language to indicate that in the presence of God there is no longer any room for the indictment of people, for provocation and temptation. Jesus Christ, the Lamb of God, is the definitive confirmation of Zechariah

3: God has chosen Israel, and through Israel all the nations, and there is no longer any room in heaven for Satan. His function is obsolete. Consequently, after Jesus Christ, one no longer hears language like that of 1 Chronicles 21:1. Satan can no longer incite people to sin, an act which ends in punishment from God. Even much less fitting is the language of 2 Samuel 24:1, that indicates the Lord incited David. One can only speak as James does, "Let no one say when he is tempted, 'I am tempted by God'; for God cannot be tempted with evil and he himself tempts no one" (1:13).

God repudiates Satan, the tempter and accuser. God no longer allows him a place in heaven. God repudiates the indictment of Israel, incitement to sin, and punishment. After definitively repudiating this way in Jesus, God made all these things evil. For the first time in Jesus Christ punishment, temptation, and indictment have come to stand decidedly in a negative light. Then what earlier had still been an open possibility for God became forever evil. God repudiated the heavenly accuser and thereby made him evil, the devil.

The Old Testament still refers to the sons of God. In Jesus Christ there can only be reference to the one Son of God, Jesus Christ, for whom God has chosen totally. In him the whole fullness of deity dwells bodily (Col. 2:9). He is *the* aspect of God's being which knows God's true being. He is the final Word of God, the decisive Word of God. He is the Logos in whom God fully expresses himself. Every other possibility becomes a diabolical possibility, one rejected by God. Every way of the world other than the way of Jesus Christ becomes a satanic way, one God can never want again. For he threw Satan out of heaven, choosing for Israel and the nations; he did this in final consistency with respect to his choice for creation. Jesus is the Son, the only begotten Son. He is the true God and eternal life (1 John 5:20). Angels of death and destruction no longer fit in his presence.

At this point we can also say a bit more about the relationship between the models discussed in preceding chapters. If we start with the idea that we are the clay and that God is the potter, we can now say that though in an absolute sense this has been true, now it can never be stated in that unqualified way again. God *had* complete liberty to fashion the world and human beings as he pleased. He could relate to them as he chose. But since the coming of Jesus Christ that is no longer possible. God can now only relate to people in the manner of grace. God can no longer act arbitrarily; he can only still act in accordance with the choice he made in Jesus Christ. Romans 9 cannot be read apart from Romans 10 (the proclamation of the gospel of righteousness by faith) and apart from Romans 11 (God has not rejected his people but will have mercy on all). That does not mean God's freedom is limited. That would be the case only if it had been an external power which forced God to make this choice. But God himself in freedom chose this way. He was "forced" to it only by the love of his own heart. From within the deepest part of his being God proved to be love and wanted to be no other than love.

When we speak of God's providence we can only speak of it the way the Heidelberg Catechism does, via the fatherhood of God in Jesus Christ. God does not apportion things arbitrarily; if he is the background of our total existence, his providential rule is always directed toward the salvation of sinners—their well-being, healing, and life. Ever since the cross of Golgotha, providence, far from being general, can only act and speak in the Spirit of Jesus Christ.

At one time God could be the punitive judge. He could destroy the world by a flood. He could exterminate the Amorites when the measure of their iniquity had become full (Gen. 15:16), and consume Sodom when there could no longer be found in it ten righteous people (Gen. 18:32; 19:24ff.). But at Easter he transferred judgment to Jesus Christ, to the human being who represents God's authority (Acts 17:31). Christ Jesus is the judge of the world seated at the right hand of God. Judgment over sin is in the hands of him who has borne sin. When someone suffers and views his or her suffering as punishment upon sin, we can only point to Jesus Christ who decides over punishment. He, however, is the one who forgives sins and heals the sick (Mark 2:1-12). He it is who does not respond to sin with fire from heaven (Luke 9:52-56), who does not condemn, even where all are under judgment (John 8:11).

When we view suffering as the chastisement of the Father, we can never again view it apart from the God who himself bore our sins, and by his own stripes gave us healing. The iniquity of us all was laid on him (Isa. 53:6).

When we view the evil in the world as human guilt, we cannot ever do that again without thinking of him who has atoned for it. Humankind does not exist in isolation from God with an unbearable responsibility of its own; God took responsibility upon himself in a person with a human face.

When we view Satan as a hostile demonic power who opposes God, we must remember in the first place that this power does not exist in isolation from God. He has never been more than the dog God kept on a chain. He never had power apart from the power he received from God. We must remember in the second place that God has said a definitive "no" to this power. He has been judged—thrown out of heaven. He has been repudiated by God and will no longer exist in a creation willed by God. As definitively as God in Jesus Christ said "yes"

291

to the world, so definitively has he said "no" to the inciter of sin, the revelation of sin, to the demonic powers of suffering, sin, and death.

When we speak of God's permission, we have to say he permits no other things than those which serve the realization of his kingdom in Christ Jesus.

God is the omnipotent. But he has decided to apply that omnipotence to the fulfillment of the way of Christ, because it is his own. Omnipotence no longer means that God can do all things in general, but that he brings about what he wills. The omnipotence of God is bound to the love of Christ, just as the goodness of God is no longer the absolutely open goodness but goodness defined by the cross of Christ. Now, is our remaining model only the position that God is different? Indeed, it is the only option left. But it can never be viewed apart from the other. If in Christ God is the electing God, that can never be viewed apart from the God who in the beginning had all possibilities at his disposal. Only because God is the potter and we are the clay election in Christ is what it is: a free divine choice. If we only say, God is Jesus Christ and Jesus Christ is God, we fail to do justice to the entire history which God has gone through, the history he carries with him in the depths of his being. God has a history behind him in which he continually distanced himself from his own rights, from all the possibilities he had, until only one was left, the alternative of Christ. God has a history behind him in which he confirmed to the end the first choice he made: the choice for creation, which is the choice for man.

To say simply "God is Jesus Christ" and to leave it at that is too little for the Christian faith. "God is the all-encompassing source" is also too little. The Christian confession is that the almighty God, creator of heaven and earth, has expressed himself in Jesus Christ as the God who wants to be the God of grace. To return to the old distinction: the *potentia ordinata* only acquires its true profile if it is viewed as the realization of the *potentia absoluta* and the *potentia absoluta* is never to be viewed apart from the content it acquired in the *absoluta ordinata*. We can never speak about God without speaking of both. We do this not dialectically, side by side, but chronologically, one after the other. Only thus do we do justice to the fact that God is the living God with a history. Only thus do we do justice to God who makes decisions, forever *(ad ôlam)*, eternal, and divine decisions. Something indeed happens in that history—not a war between God and an anti-god, but the way God wills in his faithfulness to humans, a process in which he loses himself and finds himself in the only Son, Jesus Christ. The human world is not the world of an ever-recurrent cycle; nor is it the back-and-forth movement of dialectics. It is the history of the acting God who is able to make radical decisions, able

292

to do radically new things, but who at the same time is radically faithful to the work of his hands.

In this connection we have to deal with the creation-mediatorship of Jesus Christ. Christ is God's definitive decision. That means God never again wants to, or is able to, view the world apart from Christ. God's relationship to the world in Christ is his true relationship to the world. All that is was created to stand in this relationship to God. The whole world is illumined by the light of grace. Nothing is created by God that is not linked with Jesus Christ, created by him who is the true God. By him all things were created. All things are of him; everything to which God directs his attention in the world proceeds from the Crucified. For God has ruled out every other mode of addressing the world.

However, the New Testament goes further, especially the letters to the Ephesians and Colossians. Ephesians (1:9) speaks of the mystery that has been made known. We could interpret this by saying, for example, that God knew in advance all that would be given in Christ, but only now has made it known. God kept it to himself for a time. In the preceding section we rejected this idea, because the history of salvation up to Christ would then be a mere game involving the suffering, guilt, and death of millions of people. The fact is that the mystery of which Ephesians speaks is deeper. It refers to that which in his deepest being God has always been and willed, but which in the course of history was fulfilled and assumed form in Christ. Ephesians 1 points to the consistency of God's action, a consistency which goes back to before the foundation of the world (1:4) but only definitively becomes a reality in the Beloved (1:6), in the Son of his love in whom we have redemption (Col. 1:13ff.) through his blood (Eph. 1:7). The way which culminated in Christ already began to appear in Israel's remnant; it was prefigured when even in Rehoboam God did not reject the house of David (1 Kings 11:13; 12:17). It was already announced when Abraham was called to be a blessing to all nations (Gen. 12:3), a promise fulfilled in Christ (Eph. 2:14-22). The dawning of the day of Christ goes back even much further. Already in God's faithfulness to creation as expressed in the covenant with Noah and in the promise inherent in the curse pronounced upon the first humans, the apostles saw the way of God which culminated in the Son. Ephesians and Colossians see that way as going back even further—when one looks at the creation of the world, in which God chose for humanity, one already sees Jesus Christ and no other—in fact, in God's first consideration of the world he already thought as has now . been proven to be the case in Jesus Christ. For election in Christ—by way of continual confirmation—is nothing other than the definitive confirmation of God's decision to make human beings. In God's first word,

"Let there be light" (Gen. 1:3), there already was an utterance of the Light of the world as God's Word.

Only now do people see who God has been from all eternity. Only now does it become clear who the Creator of the world is: Jesus Christ. Not only did it become known to humans; it also became known in God. He took the lead; he sent his Son; he chose long before we knew of it, making the choice he had carried within himself from all eternity. But it was a real choice. God was under no causal necessity to arrive at Jesus Christ. Right to the day of Easter he could have taken another way. God's decision to raise the Son is a real decision. It is accompanied by the rejection of all other ways. All other possibilities, the chaos of the flood, his wrath against heathens and judgment over Israel, are now past, concluded. That is not a matter of causal necessity for God; it is the reality of his history in which the consistency of his choices, starting with the very first, took form as his faithfulness. If from all eternity God had already willed this, and already was in essence, the reason is that God is faithful to himself and hence to the world. Implied in the confirmation of the deity of God is the confirmation of humans. At Golgotha and at Easter there are two: the electing God and the chosen man Jesus Christ. But in the election of Jesus Christ God elects to be God in the manner of Jesus. In Jesus Christ God elects himself. Accordingly, the chosen one Jesus Christ is the true God and none other. There are two here: God and Christ, the electing one and the elect. But in the elect the electing God chose himself, to be as the elect is. Accordingly, the two are one and the same. At the same time one can never speak of the elect in whom God chooses himself apart from him who chose from all the possibilities his freedom offered. About the Father and the Son we have to speak as two, but not as two separate Gods existing side by side, but rather as one succeeding the other: the electing Father who chooses himself in the elect Son. At the same time we can never speak about the Son alone. In all eternity he remains the elect of the Father. The choice and history of God are always carried along in the deity of God. Thus in all eternity God remains the Father and the Son—even when the Father has delivered all things, right up to the last part of his being, to the Son.

About the creation-mediatorship of Christ see Berkhof, where references to further literature are found.[3] A recent study on the subject, with special attention to views held within the Reformed churches, is that of Chul Won Suh, *The Creation-Mediatorship of Jesus Christ: A Study in the Relation of the Incarnation and the Creation* (Amsterdam, 1982).

3. Berkhof, *Christian Faith*, pp. 166-73, 292.

20. THE SPIRIT HAS TIME

20. THE SPIRIT HAS TIME

AMID ALL THE CHANGES IN GOD'S COUNSEL WITH RESPECT TO THE WORLD there is one clear constant: God's fidelity to the human being he created. Sometimes in history things skirted the abyss, but even then God proved himself faithful. Finally, his faithfulness to the world was demonstrated once and for all in Jesus Christ. In the cross and resurrection of Christ God proved himself to be the God of grace who seeks the life of people, not their death. He is the God who forgives sin, who heals the sick, who saves the oppressed, and seeks out the lost. In Jesus Christ God made this last decisive choice. Not "with the flick of his wrist," but through a crisis of godforsakenness God designated Jesus Christ as the elect in whom God chooses himself in his creative action. Until Christ there was openness, and God could choose any direction in his relations with the world. Over and over he went his variable ways, ways of wrath, ways of grace, ways of hope, and ways of bitterness. But in Christ God's one way, the way of grace, was shown. In Christ only one direction achieved validity—the direction of eternal life, of peace with God and of love.

If it is true that in Christ God made a definitive choice, if in him God wills to be no other God than the God who saves sinners, heals their diseases, and gives people eternal life, the question arises why after Christ there is still so much sin, why diseases continue, and why people die of misery. After the day of Christ's resurrection sin was not a thing of the past. People continue to cheat, hate, murder, and steal. People humiliate people. People refuse to bear the responsibilities which they must bear in light of the definitive choice of God. Neither sin nor suffering is a thing of the past since the first Christian Easter morning. People are still being held in chains. People are still being murdered. People continue to be sick. Death still prevails. Children still die.

Sin and suffering are not over after the resurrection of Jesus. On the contrary, as a result of Christ's death and resurrection sin and suffering have just become known in their deepest nature. Now that God in Christ has made his definitive choice, and accordingly in him the will of God has become totally known, it has become fully clear that every other way is a way away from God. In Christ it has become clear that the way of exterminating people cannot ever again be the way of God. From this point on every form of genocide is under a divine "no" to which it was not subject before. Since Christ it has become clear that God has defini-tively chosen for the lost and every rejection of people is subject to divine prohibition. In Christ God has chosen to heal the sick and every sickness has therefore become an evil which, far from coming from his hand, is

295

something he combats. Whereas before Easter death could still be viewed as the conclusion of a life that was full of days, after Easter death is the enemy that has to be annihilated.

Where God definitively chooses grace, there evil increases. The more stringent God's choice, the more evil that which falls outside that choice. When in Christ God chose, to the ultimate degree, for life and the reconciliation of people, then all that threatens the wholeness of human beings, all that violates the peace of their existence, became an anti-divine force which God has definitively rejected. Still, the peace of human beings is not only threatened, in innumerable ways it is being violated, while Christ is seated as Lord. His place is at God's right hand, the right hand which is mighty and performs deeds of liberation. "For God has put all things in subjection under his feet" (1 Cor. 15:27). But if all things are in subjection to him who is love, peace, life, and light, why then do hatred, brokenness, death, and darkness prevail? Certainly the story of the definitive choices of God is wonderful, but in the reality of life, which is our own life, does it in any way tally? Is not the answer clearly "no"?

In preceding sections we worked through a good many data, but there are more. We shall also have to work through the data about sin and suffering *after* Christ. If we are unable to give our twentieth-century experiences of suffering and sin a place in our theology, then that theology is abstract: christologically it may sound fine, but it will not say a thing about our own situation. Then the message of Christ will remain a light in the skies without touching the earth. But on the battlefield the wounded still die, whether the sun breaks through or the clouds gather. A light in the skies does not help at all if the situation on earth does not change. Therefore, the answer to the question how we must deal theologically, as Christian theologians, with the evil of the twentieth century after Christ is decisive for our theology.

In earlier expositions we stated that the history of God's dealing with the world is decisive for what we say about God. We must base ourselves on the factuality of events as the reflection of God's deeds. Only then do we keep our discourse about God concrete. The same is true here. We must base ourselves on the fact that the world bears a heavy load of evil. It would seem evident that after the resurrection of Christ there has been in the world no definitive breakthrough of the kingdom of God. It would seem evident that though life and peace are real for him, they are not real for all human beings. The New Testament also knows this complex of problems. The eschaton did not arrive immediately. The church at Thessalonica was troubled over the fact that death still reigned. Paul answered them that the eschaton does not come immediately but only at the moment when people no longer count on it (1 Thess. 4:13–

5:3). And Peter writes that God needs time for the eschaton, not wishing that any should perish but that all should come to repentance (2 Pet. 3:9). The longer the time between the resurrection of Christ and the situation in the church is prolonged, the need to reflect on the question why the eschaton is delayed and history continues becomes more urgent. Luke particularly addressed this question. His answer is this: between the resurrection and the eschaton is the time of mission. The choice of God in Jesus Christ must be made known to the world. The message of God's choice must reach the ends of the earth. People all over the world must be told what the decisive way of God is. On the Areopagus of Athens (Acts 17:22ff.), as in Jerusalem (Acts 23), in the provincial towns of Asia Minor (Acts 13:13–14:18), and in Rome (Acts 28:31), the message that Jesus is Lord and judge of the world must be sounded. The disciples become apostles, sent-out ones. The resurrection of Christ is gospel—good news that must be passed on.

According to Luke, the proclamation of the gospel of Jesus Christ is not a human but a divine initiative. It is not even a human work, but a divine one in which human beings are involved. It is the work of the Spirit. The book of the Acts of the Apostles, accordingly, begins with the act of waiting for the Holy Spirit and his outpouring. He is the driving force of mission. Therefore the time between the resurrection and the eschaton is also the time of the Holy Spirit. The Spirit is the divine presence, appearing in fire and wind, the signs of theophany (Ps. 18:10, 12). When the Spirit appears, Peter begins to speak. He proclaims Christ as the decisive turn in God's action. Those who rejected Christ were wrong. Full of the Holy Spirit, Stephen preached the salvation of Christ (Acts 7:55); disobedience to the gospel is resistance to the Spirit (Acts 7:51). The Holy Spirit prompted the missionary journey of Barnabas and Paul (Acts 13:2). He is the sender of the sent ones to proclaim the word of Christ which is now the Word of God (Acts 13:4). The Spirit indicates the route Paul must travel on his journeys (Acts 16:6ff.). The book of Acts is the book of the Spirit; the history of the church is the history of the Spirit.

What the Spirit does is to make known in the world, by way of human agents and human history, the decision that has been made in Christ. That takes time. God does not just work in a point of time, effecting his choice once and for all, but he works also in a process. It is only in that process that the once-and-for-all is realized. Only in the proclamation and the hearing of the message is God's choice for the world made known to the world and only thus does the choice of God become known, anew not only to himself but to the world. And if God's choice is a definitive choice *for* people, it also has to be his choice for *people*, not only concealed within the divine counsel but revealed to the world. The revelation of the salvation of Christ is as much a divine work as the decision of God realized in the resurrection. Both are aspects of God's choice once and for all to be the God of human beings. The history of the preaching of the gospel is no less divine than the history of the cross and the resurrection. The choice of God to be God in the manner of Christ includes the choice to be God in the manner of the Spirit. The choice of God in Christ is the decisive choice to continue in his dealings with and for human beings, accepting them as human to the ultimate point. The choice of God in the Spirit is to let humans as humans participate in this decision. For if humans do not participate in it, it is not a decision for humans. If God chooses for humans, he chooses for human history. Then God enters into the history of humans. They become his temple, a dwelling place of God in the Spirit (Eph. 2:22).

Now the activity of the Spirit does not only apply to proclamation. Salvation must not only be heard; it must also be realized. If it does not become real to people, then it is not a choice *for* people. In Acts, accordingly, proclamation and realization go hand in hand. If God in Christ has chosen to be the God who heals the sick, then that is realized through the Spirit. He animates the apostles so that in the name of Jesus they do signs. Luke at some length tells the story of the cripple at the gate called Beautiful. It is the story of a sign of the messianic kingdom foreshadowed in the preaching of the prophets and now confirmed in Christ (Acts 3). We briefly learn more of other healings, even through articles of clothing and the shadow of the apostles (Acts 5:12-16; 19:12). Victory over death is confirmed in the raising of Dorcas (Acts 9:36-42) and of Eutychus (Acts 20:9-12). The snake, symbol of demons, is rendered harmless where the Spirit of Christ is operative (Acts 28:3-6). Where the Spirit works, relationships among people also change. They no longer live to grab and to possess, but have all things in common; "and no one said that any of the things which he possessed was his own" (Acts 4:32-37). The Spirit distributes gifts to people, gifts of healing, prophecy, and faith (1 Cor. 12:4-11). But the gifts which the Spirit distributes are the gifts which Christ has given to people (Eph. 4:7-13).

Accordingly, it is by the Spirit that the new existence in Christ, the new life according to the will of God which came to light in Christ, is realized in the world. All men must be apprised of the salvation of God. They must be informed; they must know it. They must be taught to live on the level of the kingdom of righteousness and love. People must still go through the entire process to attain to what Christ already is, to participate in righteousness and love. The driving force of that process is the Holy Spirit. God himself took the initiative to enable people to participate in the salvation of Christ. God himself accompanies them on the way to the eschaton. God himself realizes the decision he made in Christ, applying it to the world. Consequently, God himself is involved in the process in which people are involved. There is the divine decision of Easter; there is also the divine history of the Spirit, which is the history of humans. In that history God realizes his choice for people and at the same time his own deity: his definitive faithfulness gains form in the peace of the world he created. Consequently, the way of the Spirit is as decisive for the deity of God as the cross and the resurrection. If God does not realize in the lives of people that he has once and for all chosen to be faithful to them, then either the choice becomes inauthentic or God lacks the capacity to realize what he chose, thus failing to realize his deepest being. In both cases the deity of God is broken. In the first case God is not consistent and his oneness is lost; in the second case there is a power greater than he. Accordingly, God is not only the source of all things, absolute freedom, and unbounded possibility; God is not only the choice he made in Jesus Christ to be definitively the God of human beings; but God is also the God who, in the process of history, realizes his decision as the Holy Spirit. That is the fundamental structure of the dogma of the Trinity. It is one and the same God, but without keeping in view all three we fail to do justice to the living God whom the church confesses and knows in Christ. As unbounded possibility he is the Father, *fons divinitatis*, the source from which all things flow. He is also the Son, the decisive choice, without whom God can and will not be God. He is also the Spirit, the driving force of the realization of God's choice without whom the deity of God in Jesus Christ cannot be. God is possibility, choice, and realization.

The understanding of the Spirit as the divine driving force in the realization of the divine choice is not a new datum which came at Pentecost. The Spirit is already the presence of God from the beginning. When there is a beginning, it is by the agency of the Holy Spirit. When God decides to create the world, it is his divine power which realizes this choice. His Spirit goes forth, moves over the waters, and creates life (Gen. 1:2; 2:7), just as the Spirit goes forth to create life all the time (Ps. 104:30). The Spirit of God is the animating power which makes life possible, conducts the history of the world, causes the prophets to speak, and inspires kings. When God made his first choice and decided to realize it in the creation of the world, he opted for time, for process, for life, not only that of the world but also for his own life as the source which nurtures all of life. Every one of God's choices, in its realization, is a choice to be God in the manner of the Holy Spirit, as the God who is the life power to bring forth a creation, to bring forth life. The moment God makes choices he is the trinitarian God, Father, Son, and Spirit: possibility, choice, and realization. One could even say that the Spirit is God to the ultimate degree: God who is life itself, pure act. Consequently, one can say as well that the deity of God depends on the Spirit, just as the Spirit depends on the Father.

In the preceding section we stated that God's definitive choice in Christ was already foreshadowed in God's first choice for mankind. The outpouring of the Spirit upon all flesh already dawned in the breath of God in Adam. In God's first choice for the world the creation-mediatorship of Christ already lit up. The Spirit's moving over the waters already adumbrated the Spirit who fills the world, awaiting the eschaton with eager longing (Rom. 8:19). The entire way of the Spirit is the way which issues in life in Christ. Even the way God chooses on his way to the decisive choice in Christ is the way of the Spirit. It is the divine act which heralds the birth of the Son. Conceived by the Holy Spirit, as the realization of a divine choice, Jesus Christ was born. At the same time, the Spirit was sent by the Father and the Son, in the shift God made when he decided to send the Spirit by whom his Son was conceived.

In classic dogmatics this interaction between Father, Son, and Spirit was expressed in the formula *opera ad extra sunt indivisa*. God's entire being cooperates in everything God does in relation to the world. In everything in which we relate to God, there is the possibility of the Father, the choice of the Son, and the effectuation of the Spirit. That is true of the creation, the incarnation, even the resurrection and the Pentecost event. The Son is raised by the Father in the power of the Spirit, but he himself also actively rises from the dead. The Spirit was sent by the Father and the Son, but he himself is active in sending forth the apostles.

Accordingly, the Spirit is God in the act of realizing the history of God's dealings with the world in the direction of Christ, toward the decisive choice in which God sought to be faithful to humans to the very end. We can also say God is faithful to his first act, to his own beginning. God is faithful to the process he began when he called the earth and earthly time into being by the breath of the Spirit. Therefore the Spirit of the beginning is the Spirit of Christ.

However, we have also seen that the way of God to Christ was not an established road. It is a way which can only be read in retrospect in the light of Christ, not guaranteed in advance. It is a way on which God went past many dead ends. It is a way on which wrath and ruin occurred. It was a way on which entire nations perished. It was a twisted way, swinging back and forth between possibilities which became impossibilities. Also, the rejected choices are ways realized by the Spirit. The waters of the flood were as much a divine piece of work as the breath of

Adam. The Spirit is not only the Spirit who inspires a king for his task (1 Sam. 16:13); it is equally a spirit from God who makes a king insane, totally unfit to rule his people (1 Sam. 16:14-23). The Spirit is the Spirit of truth (John 16:13), but earlier a spirit was sent out from God who was a lying spirit in the mouth of Ahab's prophets (1 Kings 22:21ff.). When God sends forth his Spirit man and animal are created, but when the Spirit of God blows over a field the grass withers and all flesh proves to be grass (Ps. 103:15ff.).

The way of the Spirit, as realization and revelation of the way of God's actions from creation to Christ, is not a straight line. The Spirit goes where he wills incalculably, just as the God of Israel proves to be incalculable. But this incalculable zigzag line culminates in Bethlehem and the Easter event. By way of the incalculable zigzag line of history God by the Spirit arrives at the revelation of his deity in Christ. The Spirit as divine Spirit goes by strange paths to reach his goal. Evidently that has not changed. For when the purpose of the Spirit of God is to realize God's choice for life—for forgiveness, for healing, for the salvation of the lost—his way through two thousand years of church history proves to be as strange as his way through four thousand years of the history of Israel.

We can also say it differently: the Spirit who proclaims to us the gospel of Christ at the same time has to bring us to the level of Christ. We are not parachuted behind the christological eschaton; we must, via our own spirit, be led by the Spirit to the eschaton that is contained in Christ. It is still facing us. In the manner of Christ it is already fully present, but in the manner of the Spirit it still has to be effected. In other words, in the manner of his choice (in the Son), God's definitive faithfulness to the world and to himself is already manifest, but in the manner of his power (in the Spirit), God's faithfulness still has to be confirmed. Consequently, the world on its way to the future lives in an open situation. Searching and shifting his course, the Spirit goes his way with Christians, as he went his way searching and shifting directions toward Christ. The goal of this way is not a matter of indifference: it can only be the kingdom of peace in Jesus Christ. On that decision God neither can nor will ever go back. But the way to that goal is indeed open. As always, the Spirit goes his way searching. One time the Spirit attempts one way, then another. On the one hand one can say that the way of the Spirit has become easier after Christ. He has been sent by the Son, poured out to proclaim and to realize the now familiar choice of God. The purpose is known. In the depths of his being God can heave a sigh of relief. For he decided once and for all to be gracious in Christ. He need no longer hesitate between life and death, between the fire of judgment and the warmth of love. God did heave a sigh of relief, and from Pentecost on his breath blows in the world bringing illumination. On the other hand, the way of the Spirit after Christ is more difficult. The Spirit who blows where he wills knows but one possibility. Wherever the Spirit blows, whether he storms or whispers, he cannot ever take people in any direction other than that of salvation in Christ, for God will never have any purpose other than to save people.

When after Pentecost the Spirit realizes God's salvation in the lives of people, it occurs in the way of process, in earthly history. For from the creation of the world the way of human beings is the way of process. Were God to choose another way he would not be choosing for humans. But this process is simultaneously the process God conducts by the Spirit. Consequently, the Spirit has at his disposal the fullness of God's possibilities. For the realization of salvation all the possibilities which moved history toward Christ are used again. In Christ God reached the end of the way, but as regards people he has to start completely from the beginning. By way of a striking hand and a thousand deaths, by way of lions and the stake, God by the Spirit conducts human history for the realization of salvation to bring people to the level of Christ. They must still follow his way in imitation of him. One may object that this does not agree with the love of God in Christ, that one cannot speak of the Spirit in these terms. But that is the reality of our situation. It is the reality not of people who lived in 1000 B.C., but of those living in A.D. 2000. If the Spirit of God works in the world and God is *actus purissimus,* then today too God acts through blood and tears. The people who follow Christ go the way he went before them. And the people who follow after Christ [in imitation of him] go the way he modeled most of all. The remarkable way of God with the world has not changed since Easter. But in *God* something has changed: he chose for our salvation once and for all. In preaching too something has changed: there is hope. Jesus went before us, via suffering; even via godforsakenness and death he won glory. That is the guarantee we have: God not only proves he can handle this way, but he also knows what he is doing. Since Easter he knows and since Pentecost we learn that this strange way through dark valleys ends in glory. The zigzag signs of the Spirit belong to the pattern which leads to the beauty of the kingdom of God. Precisely for that reason the way has not changed. If the way of Jesus to glory as led by the Spirit was the way of suffering and destruction, then the way of suffering and ruin is the best guarantee for the glorification of the world. Precisely therein the Spirit proves to be not a strange spirit, but the Spirit of Christ.

Now one could suspect that in the course of history there is growth toward the kingdom of God. We might expect that there is an increase of peace, grace, and life. We would expect to see signs of the kingdom. Sometimes people also point them out. Is not the social system in which we live a fruit of the Christian tradition? Is not the medical knowledge by which so much distress is alleviated a product of an attitude toward illness by which it is "de-demonized"? Is not the technical knowledge which makes our prosperity possible the result of a worldview which regards the world as created and not as sacral space? There is Christian culture. There is a Christian architecture which produced the beauty of the Gothic. There is a Christian literature in the tradition of which Thomas à Kempis wrote his *Imitation of Christ*. There is a Christian art of painting beneath the golden light of Rembrandt. There is a Christian philosophy exhibiting the depths of Pascal. There is a Christian music which attained the heights of Haydn's *Creation* and Handel's *Messiah*. There is a Christian ethic, supremely illustrated by the self-sacrifice of Albert Schweitzer. There is a Christian faith which produced the dedication and self-surrender of Bonhoeffer. One theologian stresses one aspect, and another a different one. One views the Christianization of the nations as a sign, another regards social justice as a product, and a third cannot conceive of a heaven in which no Mozart is played.

The signs of the kingdom exist. Renewal and hope dawn. A church has stood the test of the ages, and there is a deep-rooted Christian culture. These are signs. The moment we mention them we realize, however, how ambivalent they are. Do they not fit better in the optimistic context of the fifties and the sixties or even in the world image of earlier centuries than in the darkness which prevails in this decade? Is our social system really a product of the Christian tradition, or contrariwise, did the Christian church hold back the liberation of the disenfranchised? Is the ornate beauty of Gothic architecture not the reverse side of the blood, sweat, and tears of the poor of Europe? Did not music and philosophy transport people to heavenly regions while the earth perished in misery? Did not the light of Rembrandt distract the eye from the dark suffering of the world? Can Schweitzer's sacrifice compensate for the sale of blacks into slavery? Slave traders outnumbered self-sacrificing missionaries. Does Bonhoeffer's dedication offset the despair, and even more, the betrayal, of thousands? Has anything really changed since Pentecost? Must we not, if we are really honest, answer with a resolute "no"? Of course there are positive features, but did they not exist in earlier centuries also? Abraham personally provided food and water for his female slave when against his will but under divine guidance she had to go into the wilderness (Gen. 21:14). Amaziah, against the custom of his day (and ours!), allowed the sons of the murderers of his father to live (2 Kings 14:6). Socrates manfully drank the hemlock because he believed in the

303

truth. Is the beauty of the Acropolis less than that of Notre Dame Cathedral? Is Plato less profound than Pascal? Is the social legislation of Leviticus really worse than that of Washington? Ecclesiastes was correct: there is no progression in history. All is vanity, a striving after wind. No matter how passionately we long for the goal we have set, it never comes any closer. Our striving was already there in ancient times.

Must we not take one more step and instead of speaking of an increase in well-being speak of an increase of evil? As a result of the expansion of technical possibilities humans are now able to kill thousands at a time. The judgments which befell people in earlier ages are small by comparison with the havoc wreaked by humans in our century. The depths of turpitude of the Third Reich are deeper than any in history up to that time. The dead in Cambodia and Vietnam are numbered not in thousands but in millions. Human mismanagement affects the most distant parts of the earth. The technical arms of tyrants reach farther than ever before. And for the first time in history the doom of total destruction hangs above our heads. Not only is the individual exploited, but entire nations, even continents, are held in bondage.

Can we really speak of a divine presence in this world through the Spirit? Is the world really being saved? The deity of God depends on it, as well as the future of the world. If the Spirit does not realize God's choice in Christ, it is the end of the triune God. Either he is really God for the world or he is no longer God. If the realization of salvation is a divine *work* and not merely a creaturely unfolding of a given divine certainty, openness remains. God still has to be involved. That is to say, God still has to substantiate it. He has not yet substantiated it to the end. He has decided for it to the end. For Jesus Christ he has substantiated it; for the world he still has to fulfil it. Consequently, for God too the outcome is still open. The work of the Spirit is not a programmed computer disk that merely has to be played. It is an activity in which God is really present. Consequently, the future is not closed and sealed. Action carries with it the risk of failure. Something that is not programmed in advance can still go another way.

For that reason, the awareness that things may go worse for the world rather than better evokes enormous tensions theologically. If we entertain a positive view of the developments of world history, it is easy to say, "As the finger of God writes." Then we are able to see the signs of the coming kingdom of God. But if there is no ground whatsoever for optimism, then doubts arise as to the reality and worth of redemption in Christ Jesus. Then the question concerning the deity of God again surfaces. Looking for signs of righteousness is like looking for gold dust. The signs are certainly not more numerous than they used to be. The

304

existing signs are ambivalent. By contrast, the world is full of injustice, violence, and fear. Where is God in this world? Where is the Spirit as the breath-giving and breath-taking power of God? If the Spirit is not working, the deity of God is obsolete. If the Spirit does not change the face of the earth into the kingdom of peace and life, then the choice of God in Jesus Christ has not been substantiated. Then all "glad tidings" have been proven false. Either the world is being saved, totally saved, or God is no longer God. Christian theology cannot settle for less. If in these years the world is tottering on the brink of total ruin, Christian theology cannot but be under assault to the very limit. That assault is coming from without. It is warranted, because the Christian faith has made strong assertions. But are they being substantiated? It seems less so than ever. But the Christian faith is especially under assault from within. Not a single theologian, nor any Christ-confessor making statements about the coming kingdom of God, can escape the fact that the kingdom of God seems further and further away from us. No theologian can escape the fact that the deity of God is at stake and threatened in the world of the present decade, not only because people do not want to believe in him but especially because the realization of God's own choices fails to occur and does not even exhibit unambiguous signs on our horizon.

Then what arguments remain for continued faith in God? In the first place, there is the history of God's dealings. There is proven faithfulness. In the past God demonstrably "hung in there" with the world, saving it from total ruin. God was demonstrably faithful to his promises and realized his decisions. The earth reemerged from the flood. An infertile Sarah received a son. Israel was liberated from bondage in Egypt. Later, they returned from captivity. God raised from the dead the man who bore in his heart all human beings in expiation of sin. God did not abandon him to corruption, but lifted him to glory. We can extend the line: two thousand years of failure as a church have not yet brought the church to extinction, any more than four thousand years of the failure of Abraham's descendants have brought Israel to extinction. If the church—this church—the church of the exploiters, the pedantic, the guilty, and the rotters still exists, it gives one courage for the deity of the Spirit. Anyone who can work with such a bunch just has to be God. As the church has existed over two thousand years, so Israel has already existed for four thousand years. They exist purely by the grace of God; else they would have ceased to exist long ago. They survived the pogroms and their own wars. One who endures a relationship with the Israel of today just has to be God. Looking back on God's dealings as far as we can—*meolam*—we can only conclude that in fact he has been faithful. He even stuck with a world that did not ask for him. He stuck with slave traders and dictators. One who can keep such a world alive and going just has to be God. It is only a question whether he will stick with a world that works so hard at its own ruination as humans have done for, say, the last fifty years. Has not the point come where God has to give up on the world, call it quits, and thus give up on his own deity?

But is there not also a possibility of reversing this argument? If God can bear to be in relationship with this church, if God can stand this Israel, if God can endure this world, can he still be God? If the deity of God consists in his maintenance of the church, Israel, and the world while they continue to make a mess of things, then what does that deity mean? If God sticks with dictators, exploiters, slave traders, and manufacturers of atomic bombs, then must not every reasonable person prefer humanity to God and say of him, "I want no part of it"? We are here very existentially skirting the abyss. The faithfulness of God is good, but if in that faithfulness God's choice for love, peace, righteousness, and life is not being confirmed, it turns into its opposite.

Therefore the argument for continued faith in God requires an addition. The history of the faithfulness of God has never been a straight line. Salvation always came through brokenness. God always proved his deity on the brink of total disaster. Only one family survived the flood. Israel was saved from infanticide and slavery through the waters of the Red Sea. David became king after working himself into a hopeless fix among the Philistines (1 Sam. 29). God even proved his deity through utter ruination when his faithfulness was broken in the godforsakenness of Jesus on the cross, by raising him from the dead. If we see how God's faithfulness always becomes manifest as unexpected faithfulness, then there is every reason for hope in a world that does not ask for God. If we are now living at a time with these questions: "Where is he who brought up out of the sea the shepherds of his flock? Where is he who put in the midst of them his holy Spirit, who caused his glorious arm to go at the right hand of Moses, who divided the waters before them to make for himself an everlasting name, who led them through the depths? . . . Where are thy zeal and thy might? The yearning of thy heart and thy compassion are withheld from me" (Isa. 63:11, 12, 15); if from within the church the cry is sounded, "O that thou wouldst rend the heavens" (Isa. 64:1), and even this cry is no longer heard so that people no longer ask for God (though they cannot do without him), then there is hope that the moment has come in which God says, "Here am I" (Isa. 65:1). If the Lord of the church and of the world reached glory through godforsakenness, can we expect anything else for the church and the world? Evidently it is God's practice to let things go to the brink before the light breaks through. Consequently, it is not so much the positive signs with their ambivalence which give us hope, but the fact that we can recognize the way which the Spirit of God characteristically goes in the world as the way the Son went in the world. The Spirit is no stranger to the Son; he does what the Son has given him to do; he realizes the way of the Son in the midst of the world. If the Spirit is the Spirit of Christ, we cannot but expect that the servant will not be greater than his master (John 15:20), not only in oppression but in godforsakenness. Only through this darkness is there salvation for the church and the world. Also, the way of the Christian is the way of dying and rising. By faith we died and were buried with Christ. He is the certainty of faith in forgiveness and life. At the same time, we continually die to ourselves that Christ may be formed in us. In our dying we take off the old to lay hold of the heavenly glory (2 Cor. 4:7–5:10). That applies to the individual; it also applies to the world. The ruination of the world is the beginning of glory (2 Pet. 3:10-13).

A third reason for continued faith in God is fundamentally the real reason: God continues to address us. He has touched our hearts and will not let us go. Even though all the evidence is against him, even though he conducts himself in a way that would make one lose all hope, still we continue to believe in him. For he is our God. The Spirit works faith in the hearts of people in the hidden strata of godforsakenness.

We may ask ourselves why the way to the kingdom of God is not a straight line. In the first place we can only say that God has proven to act in this fashion. The history of God's acts is the surest basis for making assertions about God's dealings with the world. It has been observed, and through the centuries it has been confirmed over and over, that this is how God acts, which is why we have every reason to expect that God will act that way again. In the second place the way to the kingdom of God is not a straight line, because the way of Christ was not a straight line, but one exhibiting the deep break of the cross and the descent into hell. The way of Christ was not a crescendo, but the state of humiliation and exaltation. If Jesus is the decisive choice in which God opts for mankind, can God then ever opt for people in any way other than the way of Jesus—via the cross and forsakenness to joy, via judgment to glory? Perhaps we have to add a third argument: If in the final analysis God opts for grace, for the salvation of the ungodly, if God determines his deity to be the choice for the absolutely lost, can his choice ever be manifest in any other way than through forsakenness? Does not grace become absolute only where no single thread is left on which it can hang? Is not salvation divine and absolute only where people are absolutely lost? Thus, is not the abyss of ruin through which the world is passing, through which God the Holy

307

Spirit is leading the world, the foundation on which the deity of God in Christ is based? It is an extremely risky foundation. If the Spirit should leave the world in its lostness, that then is the end of the world and the end of God. But to say less than that is not good enough. Only by assuming this lostness can God be the saving God, the absolute Savior, which he is not because he had to but because he willed to be.

Up to this point we approached the question why after Easter there is still suffering and sin from the position that we have to be brought to the level of Christ. The Spirit has to bring us to where he already is, and it makes sense that to that end we have to go the way he went, with the essential difference being that he already traveled it, whereas we can only follow him. The Spirit effects the realization of God's choice in Christ in the world, and it is not strange that the way of realization confirms the way of that choice, with the understanding that our salvation is already contained in Christ. For him, however, the outcome was still completely open.

Yet we have to ask ourselves whether we can also answer the question in a totally different way. We have described the resurrection of Jesus as the ultimate consequence of the faithfulness of God. To the utmost limit God continues to uphold the work of his hand which he began. He saves lost mankind, which he began with and will not abandon. When he created them, God opted for human beings and in the end he opts for human beings in Jesus' resurrection from the dead. Accordingly, God is faithful to his choice. We have also stated, however, that God not only makes choices but also brings them to be. He is not only the Son but also the Spirit. When God decided to create man, he also proceeded to make man. There is a *creatio passiva;* something came forth from God's hands. God is present in the world through the Spirit, as the power which makes alive and puts in motion. When the Spirit works, something happens. God starts something and a process begins. Ultimately this process culminated in Jesus Christ. The history of the Spirit's action as reflection of the history of God's choice leads to Jesus Christ, and the outcome of this history is the consistent way of God which leads to the salvation of the world. But this is not the only process with which the Spirit began. God has turned toward the world in many ways. The lying spirit directed Ahab's prophets, and Pharaoh's heart was hardened. The Amorites and Amalekites were exterminated. There was the cruelty of Jehu. Thunder and hail came upon the Canaanites, and the split earth under the tents of Korah. All was the work of God's hands. And it was realized as the work of the Spirit. Not only the history of Israel, but also the history of the nations realized a divine initiative. And there processes were set in motion.

308

If God is faithful to himself in Jesus Christ, he is faithful not only to the way which leads to Jesus, but also to the Spirit, to all those processes initiated in a world of trial and error. Then he is faithful to the struggle for life and the survival of the fittest. Then he is faithful to the outpouring of his wrath and the sin of people. For so the Spirit worked, with all the possibilities the freedom of God afforded him. If the Spirit has to be faithful to the work of his hands, then he is also faithful to the failures he rejected. In other words, though God himself can make his choice for love and grace, he has to deal not only with his own heart but also with the reality he engendered by the Spirit. By the Spirit God posited something. That something is there, with its own existence. It is a unique reality engendered by God. Real faithfulness on God's part is not that he opts for grace and ignores all the processes of disfavor, as though the power of the Spirit could be denied. Accordingly, pneumato-logically the faithfulness of God means that he has to go on with everything he has set in motion. He has to go on with the hard realities of the world. He has to go on with the reality of sin; he has to go on with death, he has to go on with illness; he has to go on with suffering. If God does not go on with these, with what realities does he go on in this world?

This idea comes to a head in the aspect of human responsibility. God has created man as a willing, choosing being. Man is not just a wrinkle in the thought of God, but a reality engendered by the breath of the Spirit of God. If God is faithful to humans, he cannot ignore these beings in what they are. Faithfulness to humans means faithfulness to humans as they are and not to abstractions of them. God's faithfulness to humans is faithfulness to humans who make choices, wrong choices; who decide, and make wrong decisions; who sin, hope, and despair; who experience joy and sorrow. If on Easter morning God had glorified all humans with Christ in imperishable glory, making this decision over their heads without their even knowing of it, would that have been faithfulness to humans, to the creatures God himself called into being? If human beings are being saved, they must be saved as human beings, as thinking, willing beings created by the breath of the Spirit. The salvation of humans occurs, not apart from humans but with their involvement, or else it is not the salvation of humans.

The nearly impossible task of the Spirit is both to do justice to the fullness of his power which has effectuated itself in a great variety of ways and to God's choice in Jesus Christ who represents the choice for grace and life. Hence there is the irrevocable progression of the history of the world which cannot be broken off without negating God's choice for faithfulness to the world, and there is the absolutely critical authority of the cross and resurrection of Christ in which all other ways are placed under judgment. Only divine possibility has the capacity to realize both, but it is a possibility in which human beings are involved, the possibility of the Spirit. For that matter not only humans are involved; the whole creation renders service. The Spirit calls into play everything he began, but in Christ the great shift occurred: everything is now directed toward the one choice of God. God can never go back on Christ; everything he began in the world will now have to "fulfil" this pivotal and terminal point of history. The Spirit proceeds from the Father *(e patre)* but he proceeds from the Father through the Son *(per filium):* the work of the Spirit endowed with all the possibilities of God runs via the decision of Golgotha. The Western church has even added that the Spirit proceeds from the Father and the Son *(e patre filioque):* the work of the Spirit can never again be viewed apart from God's decisive choice, and this choice constitutes a part of the driving force of the history of the world.

The term *e patre filioque* has primarily to do with the intratrinitarian procession of the Spirit, the so-called *spiratio,* and not with the outpouring at Pentecost, the so-called *missio.* But the structures which apply to the one also apply to the other. We do not know anything of the intratrinitarian relationships of God except via his working in history. Discourse about intratrinitarian relationships, like discourse about the ontological Trinity, is an attempt to point out that God really discloses himself in his revelation and that behind it there is not a higher divine being that is concealed from us.

The Spirit was sent to apprize people of the salvation of God in Christ. But he accomplishes this mission via the normal human processes which exist: via the words of the apostles and the millions who take over and transmit these words. Paul has to undertake his arduous missionary journeys to make the gospel known to human beings, making use of human language, a process in which he is served by a knowledge of the Scriptures he has gradually acquired. Mission is not accomplished by a stroke of lightning from heaven. That is not how the Spirit works. The Spirit works with the human beings with whom he began, and thus God is faithful to the manner of the Spirit. When humans are being renewed in order to be raised to the level of Christ, that does not occur by way of a surprise attack gone over their heads; it is based on the joy of hearing the gospel and shaped by concretely formulated parenesis. The parenetic sections of the letters are not a necessary evil which actually detract from the gospel of love and grace but are the confirmation and reinforcement of that gospel: human beings are saved as human beings with their conscious, formulated choices. Christians are not passive toy figures wound up by the Spirit, but conscious, willing people called into being by the Spirit as *human* beings and now called to be brought to the level of God's choice.

God's purpose, however, is not only the salvation of the individual, not even the salvation of humanity, but the salvation of the world. All that the Spirit began is now directed to Christ and everything is called into play for that purpose. The competition of the struggle for life becomes the driving force or motive for people to proclaim the gospel. A minister working for an income remains a minister; a minister in the ministry for the sake of prestige remains a minister. The fear of punishment and the fear of becoming a social outcast serve the sanctification of life. One may consider this beneath the standard of Christ, because it certainly is. Christ is at the level of pure, freely chosen love and total sacrifice for the cause of salvation. But it is not beneath the standard of the Holy Spirit. For the Holy Spirit is faithful to what he began. He does not simply cast aside human psychological and social structures but makes them serviceable to the coming kingdom. When people are moved to come to the mind of Christ, that is work accomplished through the utilization of human words and feelings. When Philemon is summoned to welcome home as a brother the runaway slave Onesimus, it occurs in a context of respect for existing social structures and by means of the psychological skills of that sly old fox named Paul. That is the manner in which the Spirit works. It is not beneath the standard of the Spirit to call into play on the road of the kingdom all that humans carry with them in the way of possibilities and even nasty tricks. It is not even beneath his standard to use suffering and death to that end.

Regarding the models discussed in previous chapters, this means that, not having been rejected in Christian theology, they are all functional in the way of the Spirit. If God began to react to the world as an angry judge and people have begun to live by that experience, that reality is not terminated all at once. God is also faithful to the relationship he *had* with people. The wrath is not simply past, but it is now serviceable to the way toward the kingdom of grace. The law impels people toward Christ. God's hand continues to strike out at people, but it is now serviceable to the mature freedom of the love of his children. People remain responsible for their deeds and the suffering of numerous people is the fault of humans, but human responsibility, and even human failure, are ways toward salvation.

How this all goes, and will precisely go, nobody knows. Even the Spirit does not know. For the way which the Spirit goes is a process of real action and not the running of a computer disk. The Spirit uses everything. He is the Spirit who proceeds from the Father, from the boundless source of the possibilities of the God who is free. The Spirit first tries one way, then another. The Spirit pursues his strange zigzag line through history. He goes his way searching, breaking down what he had built and plucking out what he had planted. But what he broke down is rebuilt and what he plucked up is not thrown on the garbage dump of history. For history has no garbage dump: it is the history of the Spirit of God. Unless, of course, all of history is a garbage dump and God's way with the world has failed. But the resurrection of Christ is the hope-filled guarantee for life in the light of righteousness. The future lies open. The Spirit goes his way searching, directing himself to a goal that is now familiar.

It is an awesome thought that all things in the world have been called into play for the coming kingdom of God. All things work together for good, says Paul (Rom. 8:28), for those who love God. Individually it is already hard to assimilate the fact that the Spirit takes one's entire life history, rooted as it is in the long tradition of hundreds of generations of ancestors, and brings it to the goal of peace. But one cannot be satisfied with less. When he saves human beings he saves them with their whole tradition, their mental structure, their social connections. The entire individual is incorporated. The idea that all things come into play in the coming of the kingdom of God becomes even more difficult when we pass from the individual believer to the church as a body of believers. The Spirit leads the church with its entire tradition, its history of violence, its bourgeois outlook. "It has seemed good to the Holy Spirit and to us" wrote the ancient synods. That is true for the conciliatory apostles' convent at Jerusalem (Acts 15:28), but also for the Robbers' Synod of Ephesus (449) where the clubs of crude monks, not the spiritual vitality of the devout, determined the outcome. But here too we cannot be satisfied with less: the church is saved with its entire tradition or it is not saved.

The idea of the incorporation of the old in the way of the kingdom of Christ becomes completely unfathomable when we think of the world. All things must work together for good, not only the discovery of penicillin but also the development of the atomic bomb; not only the liberation of 1945 but also the preceding years. But either God goes on with this world, the world where such things take place, or God does not go on with this world. Now that in Jesus Christ God has once and for all decided to go on with the world, he has opted for the first. We may regret that. But it is the world's only hope. If we view the salvation of the world as the extreme consequence of the faithfulness of God, then this way which runs via blood, sweat, and tears, via human and in-human processes, is the only way.

God realizes his choices in the manner of the Spirit. It is his power by which things are brought forth. This is how time was created. In order to attain something with the processes and givens of creation, time is needed. If the Spirit continues to work with the creation, the Spirit needs time to arrive at the consummation of things. To do this well takes time. That already is the conclusion of 2 Peter when the question arises why the kingdom does not seem to be coming at all. "Since the fathers fell asleep, all things have continued as they were from the beginning of creation" (2 Peter 3:4). Golgotha and Easter also have not seemingly made a dent in its coming. The Spirit has left matters as they are. But that is not because of God's slothfulness, as though he did not follow through with things, but because of his thoroughness: ". . . not wishing that any should perish, but that all should reach repentance" (v. 9). Without this radical thoroughness salvation remains a job half done.

Accordingly, the Spirit needs time. Second Peter already comments that we must not pay particular regard to a millennium or two. The Spirit is the Spirit of God: he has all the time in the world. God does not fret over expending a millennium or two: he is patient—"long of breath." It is the long breath of the Spirit who groans along with the whole creation until the arrival of the eschaton (Rom. 8:22-26). The Spirit has at his disposal the rest of God, who can go his own serene way searching and groping, without hurrying, in the assuredness of his faithfulness. He is not in a hurry. We have all of eternity still ahead of us.

Now I can imagine two fundamental objections to the above: first, that this is a radical, speculative construction, and, second, that God is being pictured too humanly as a searching God. Both in summary are saying that we lack reverence in our encounter with God, that we are violating the mystery of his name, and we would do better to stick to his revelation in Jesus Christ. With the last I am in hearty agreement. We do best to stick to God's revelation in Christ. But then we must have the courage to stress all three of these nouns.

It is God's revelation in *Christ*. In him the definitive decision with respect to the doctrine of God is made. But it is God's *revelation* in Christ. God really enters the world. Human beings are really being touched. Michelangelo, in depicting the creation of man, shows God's finger a hairbreadth away from touching man. A tiny space remains. But in the hairbreadth space of a hand's touch man is an infinite space from clutching the life buoy. In Christ God really touches man. By the Spirit of Christ people are incorporated into the divine mystery. The Spirit is an awesome reality—God within us, penetrating the deepest part of our existence, the whole of our reality, soul and body. It is also *God's* revelation in Christ, revelation in the fullness of unrestricted possibility in absolute freedom, in which he himself goes his own independent way.

When God reveals himself in human history, he can only do that in human contexts, in events and worlds intelligible to human beings. Otherwise revelation is not revelation. But if God can indeed reveal himself this way, then also in these contexts, events, and words God is cognizable. They really do say something about God. Accordingly, God is as he reveals himself, and this is how God has revealed himself: "And the Word became flesh" (John 1:14). The divine being displays the structures of human contexts, earthly events, and human words. But in coming in the flesh he came to his own. The Word of John 1, the Word which was in the beginning (v. 1) and in Jesus Christ became flesh (v. 14) is the same Word that created the world. Man is the image of God. Man bears structural resemblance to God, not only in his faith, but in his existence. For a human being is more than his faith. At most one can say that his faith encompasses the whole of existence.

To speak in human terms, therefore, is not to display a lack of respect; it is to do justice to the confession that God is our God and that in Christ and by the Holy Spirit he did not remain a stranger to us. It is also to do justice to the manner in which Israel has taught us to speak about God. He is the living, continually acting God. He is the highly exalted one with the human face, who cannot be represented by an abstract image, but who is concretely present in the earthly and human history of Israel. He has the initiative; he is the one who acts (man is the image of God; the converse is not true), but in his initiative and deeds he is really present. Human history bears his image.

As to the first question, every theologian embarks on a road of speculation. Even every believer must, who works at a formulated confession of his own ventures on that road. In Christ there is divine action. There are the deeds of his saving revelation. But the moment we begin to speak of them we look for a framework in which to organize these deeds. And when we speak of Jesus we also look for a model in which we attempt to sort out and arrange the facts of revelation. That is even true of the most simple confession (e.g., "Jesus is Lord"). To the extent that we attempt to put into words more of God's salvation, to that extent we require a more complex model. Theology has to deal with a plethora of scriptural data divided over numerous authors and two testaments. It also has to deal with a world history of many centuries and an unassimilable mountain of material from the world in which it operates, the world to which the revelation is addressed and which is the object of the salvation of God. For that reason we search for a model in which we can represent this chaotic mixture in an orderly arrangement. In that manner the labyrinth becomes accessible. Every model is an attempt. No theology is perfect. We are always looking for a better model. Always new events and data are added to world history which cast a fresh light on the exegesis of the Old and the New Testament. Now one can do different things. One can lift one point from the mass of materials and arrange everything in terms of this one point of entry. As a rule, the choice of this center is not arbitrary. It is in fact a central datum that in Christian theology the central point of entry is the person of Christ. But the manner in which one makes him central (as representative, as substitute, as initiator, or whatever) also belongs to the choice one makes. Around this one central datum one can then group all the other data. Some are close to the center; others belong to the periphery of Christian theology. However, one must deal not only with Christ but also with the contemporary world, the world of politics, the world of the natural sciences. In that connection one must deal with the ideas of the human mind in which human language plays a role. In preceding sections an attempt was made to create a model that does justice to different aspects. There is not one vantage point, but several. An attempt was made to do justice to the absolute freedom of God and his unbounded possibilities; he does what he wills. That is a given on which biblical theology and the religious ideas of humanity generally agree. An attempt was also made to do justice to the definitive decision which was made in Christ. He is the focal point and terminus of history. He is the confirmation of the deity of God. God can and will never be different than the God who raised Jesus of Nazareth, the crucified, from the dead and gave him a name that is above every name, the holy name (Phil. 2:9). An attempt was also made to do justice to the reality of the experiences of people living today and yesterday in suffering and guilt. If God is the God of the world, then the entire world process has to be included in a theological concept, not only as a moment in the present but together with the whole of history. If this world is God's world then all things, to the remotest corners of the universe, are related to God. Nothing can be excluded from the purview of theology. Nothing is irrelevant. An attempt has also been made to do justice to the open situation which is history. The journey continues. That which is still to come is of essential importance for the interpretation of what was. One can even say that the future will confirm or invalidate what has been. Not until history has been concluded can the definitive conclusions be drawn. Till that time we must keep the enterprise open, even the theological enterprise. Theological, that is, referring to our discourse about God. Also, as far as God is concerned, history remains open for as long as he acts. The Father is working still, says the Son (John 5:17). Therefore he works also. The Spirit is working still; through him the Father and the Son are at work. Neither for God nor for the world has rest come. As long as God continues to act, all sorts of things can happen. As long as his way continues and involves

315

acting humans, there will regularly be surprises. They flow from the abundance of divine possibilities. But the core of all surprises has already been given in Jesus Christ: God is the Savior of the world.

My theological design is an attempt to do justice to as many data as possible. Scriptural data play a key role in that attempt precisely because of the decisive place of Jesus Christ. But the faithful reading of Scripture, with one's ears open, teaches us to view the way of God with the world as more fascinating and variable than would be the case if it had all come together in a single point. The design offered here is not absolutely new, but rather is a collage of a variety of other designs. I have borrowed insights from Augustine, Calvin, Barth, van Ruler, Moltmann, and Pannenberg; and other people undoubtedly see still other connections. One theologian furnished a snippet; another provided the vague contours of the collage. But that is how theology works. One does not start from the ground up; one tries rather to build on what others have put into our hands.

21. PRAYER AND ARGUMENT

CALLING INTO PLAY EVERYTHING THAT IS IN THE WORLD, THE SPIRIT GOES his way searching toward the final fulfillment of the world, a world which is at the same time proof of divine faithfulness. Everything is called into play, not only all that exists in the way of possibilities in the world but also all that exists in the way of possibilities in God. The full deity of God is at work in the Spirit. As divine action the Spirit's action is open action. Something really happens; real choices are made. At the same time there is the decisive choice of God in Christ: the choice of grace, salvation, faithfulness. The Spirit possesses all the freedom of God; it is, however, the freedom in which the Spirit also chose Jesus Christ and so his own deity. Christ, when he was born, was "conceived by the Holy Spirit." When he was raised it was by the power of the Holy Spirit who is Lord and who makes alive. Accordingly, the Spirit is involved to the full extent in the redemption in Jesus Christ. At the same time he is the one sent to make the work of Jesus Christ, God's choice for mankind, known to the world. When the Spirit is sent at Pentecost, that occurs not against the Spirit's grain and will, as if he is a slave of the Father or Christ, but in the fullness of his divine freedom. He who brought the Son into the world, who as the power of God called him into life, with the same power and by his own divine choice goes into the world. The choice of Jesus Christ is his own. The way of the kingdom of God is his own. Consequently, it is impossible to play the Spirit and Christ off against each other. They are not opposed to each other; both are fully involved in the one divine work for which both have chosen and in which from the earliest beginnings both have cooperated. Nor, therefore, is the Spirit an appendage of the Son, appearing on the scene later; he is as much active in the sending of the Son as the Son is active in the sending of the Spirit.

Accordingly, the choice of God in Christ is as much the Spirit's choice as that of the Father and the Son. In this manner, from this point on, he wants to be God, gracious and saving. That is how God is in heaven and also on earth. This, and no other way, is how the Spirit is God. The goal of the way of the Spirit is fixed, not on account of an external cause but on account of the essence of his own divine heart. The Spirit is the Comforter. He is the divine power who gives form to and realizes the grace of God, salvation from guilt and sin, the liberation from diseases, the conquest of death in the world. He is the driving force who transforms the world to the level of Christ, and who informs us of that fact. God's choice is not a hidden choice, but one that is communicated to humans. We *know* God wills our salvation. We *know* he wills to grant us eternal life. We *know* God loves us. As we saw in preceding sections, we have to say at the same time that God does this in a constantly varying way. It is not a straight line but a zigzag course which the Spirit travels in his search. On the one hand the decision has been made; on the other the realization of salvation is an open process in which the Spirit acts. We are caught up squarely in the middle of it. On the one hand the decision has been made known to us; on the other, its realization takes place in our existence searchingly, by way of building and breaking down, plucking up and planting again. The sequence is often absolutely unclear. That which is broken down is not always built up again. What seemed to us to be a plant that could grow toward the kingdom is plucked up and in its place comes a growth we cannot fathom. Thus history, both as the history of the individual and as the history of the world, lurches forward. Now one could say, "This history is in God's hands; we simply have to leave it there. We take things as they come. There is every reason for us to do this, for in Christ God has decided upon the salvation of the world. Having heard the gospel of Christ we can only receive the way of God as the expression of his love."

If we say that, however, we are forgetting two things. In the first place, we are ignoring that the way of God by the power of the Spirit is an open one. The process is still fully in progress. It is the way of Christ, the way that is *now* being realized via the acting Spirit of the electing

317

God, not via the computer. History has not been concluded. In the second place we are losing sight of the fact that we ourselves are part of it. We are the work of God's hands by the Spirit. We have been informed for a purpose. Things are not being realized apart from us; on the contrary, we ourselves are involved. We have been willed by God. We, together with our capacity to speak and to choose, are the ones to whom God proves his faithfulness. That means no less than the fact that we ourselves may think and talk as partners of God about the realization of the kingdom of God. If humans may not join in the dialogue, then the faithfulness of God for which he decided in Jesus Christ is no longer faithfulness to humans. For God created us thinking and talking human beings. If a human can no longer think, choose, and talk, she is robbed of her humanity, whereas God's goal is precisely to save that humanity. If humans are not involved in the realization of salvation as thinking beings, they are not involved as humans. If we, with everything we are, remain uninvolved in salvation, we are not being saved in our true humanity; and then God is unfaithful to the work of his hands after all. Consequently, the humanity of humans involved in the realization of the kingdom serves to ground the deity of God. That is not because man opted for this, but because God's own choice from the beginning was for the humanness of human beings. God opted for this human being. And the consistency of his choice is his faithfulness to this human being.

Accordingly, humans either have been involved in realizing the kingdom as thinking, talking beings, or they have been uninvolved. We are partners in thinking and talking about it. The relationship between God and man is not simply that of giver and receiver. Man is not purely passive. We are permitted to be something for God because God has willed it. The Spirit effects the coming of the kingdom through speaking, thinking human beings. To think and talk as partners is to think and talk first of all as partners of God. There is reciprocity, as van Ruler put it. To "talk with" is not necessarily to "repeat after," as though in everything we would have to agree with God. We talk and think *together* with him about the realization of his faithfulness to us; and if we are not in conscious inward agreement with him, it is not faithfulness to us but to a projection of us.

Van Ruler views reciprocity as the middle course between autonomy and heteronomy. It is theonomous reciprocity,[4] a divine initiative but at the same time genuinely reciprocal. The Spirit enters into the whole of our physical existence, our history. Covenant history embraces "both babies and states" (p. 31). If human

---

4. Van Ruler, *Theologisch Werk*, vol. 6, p. 35.

beings can totally participate in it that means "that pneumatology culminates in the great thesis that in the Spirit the theodicy begins to dawn on humans" (p. 35). Now already we can meaningfully think along with God about the way of God, though we are not yet in the eschatological fullness to which the Spirit is leading us.

When van Ruler excludes from this reciprocity the moment of regeneration and says of it that then "for a moment we are in the hands of God" (p. 37), he is not only not consistent, but counterposes the Spirit and man in a way which fails to do justice to the fact that the Spirit is the sustaining ground of all we think and are. In the Spirit God and man are not competitors. The Spirit works through humans. Van Ruler in fact sees a similar competitive relationship between man and the Spirit in the entire history of salvation when he writes that the indwelling of the Spirit, "like all sharing of the same dwelling is accompanied by conflict."[5]

To think and talk together with God is to *pray*. To pray is not to plunge mystically down into the eternal deity where we feel secure. For then we are giving up our humanity as thinking, acting human beings. One might still be able to say, "I can choose to give up my own willing and thinking and plunge into blessed nothingness." In the first place, however, in the Christian faith this "blessed nothingness" can never be separated from Jesus Christ. In any case, in this context mystical immersion would be mystical immersion in Christ, in that God who in Christ extended his grace. I will not say that this is at all times illegitimate. Mysticism also is a form of being Christian. But it is always a temporary one. It is the form of rest. One can be so exhausted from fighting, thinking, and talking that some respite is needed. Then a human being may momentarily immerse himself in the love of God. There can be a time of total surrender to him who has accomplished all in my place, for whom I need not do anything anymore and in whose all-embracing love I may let myself go. But it cannot be for longer than a moment.

For God-in-Christ is not the serenity of eternal silence, the *sige* of Gnosticism, but the electing, acting, and speaking God. Christ is not silence; he is the Word. Accordingly, the most intense union with Christ is the listening union in which God's choice enters and penetrates our deepest self. We are silent not just to experience the silence but to listen to the Word of God. On account of its peculiar origins Christian mysticism is not suited to immersion in nothingness. For surrender to perfect grace has its basis in the hearing of the Word as the proclamation of grace, and in the action of the sacrament as an act of fellowship. And if in union with Christ we listen to the Word of God, the idea is not to let it pass over our heads but to let it be the Good News we pass on. In that way we are

5. Ibid., vol. 1, p. 185.

the people God intended. God did not create man for silence; he created him to speak. God is not the God of silence but of history, a history in which something needs to happen. It is *his* history; it is also *our* history. He has a goal for which he works and we are involved. If we opt for pure passivity, we are not opting for the human being for whom God opted. Then we are ultimately not choosing for the *human* being, but for escape from our humanity. However, that is precisely what God has not willed. He did not run from humanity but opted for it to the end, right into death.

Accordingly, human prayer—and Christian prayer cannot be other than human—in its deepest form is not the silence of immersion in Christ but consciously formulated prayer. Knowing of God's choice in Jesus Christ, prayer is a conscious choice for the coming kingdom. That then is the simplest prayer of the human who has heard the gospel: "Your kingdom come." If God is active in bringing in his kingdom, we are allowed to choose with him for that kingdom. We have come to agreement with him. We consent to it and join him in wanting it. "Let your kingdom come." On the one hand, that is the passive consent in which we express agreement with the coming of the kingdom. That is the beginning of Christian prayer: we agree with God's choice to save the world. That is the basis of our being Christians. We may know ourselves to be a part of that choice. But the kingdom of God antecedes the individual and the individual's consent to his salvation is consent to the kingdom of God in Christ. In other words, the acknowledgment of Jesus as Lord is the beginning of faith. And the beginning of prayer is the declaration of agreement with God. However, the petition "Your kingdom come" is not only passive consent; it is also an active desire. It is to ask God to apply all his divine power to the realization of the kingdom. It is to ask for the Spirit that he may transform the world in accordance with the image of Jesus Christ. In Christian prayer it is not only the Christian who is prodded by the admonishing Spirit, but also God himself. And God can be prodded because man is someone other than God—a real partner.

Meanwhile, Christians give further definition to the petition, "Your kingdom come." They reflect on what that kingdom will look like. It is the kingdom of Jesus Christ who forgives sin, heals the sick, redeems people from their misery, and extends the hand of fellowship to the outcast. Every illness is a sign that the kingdom has not yet been realized. Every unforgiven sin blocks the path of total acceptance. Every dead person is a sign of the presence of the last unconquered enemy. Consequently, the church prays for the healing of the sick. Let the power of the Spirit overcome the powers of darkness. Consequently, the Christian church prays for the forgiveness of sins. Let the reconciling work of the Spirit clear away the barriers standing in the way of love. In that way the simplest prayer of the individual believer becomes a cry for the kingdom. For as long as someone is still living in brokenness, with soul and body in pain, God's purpose in Christ has not been realized.

Also, a non-Christian's call for liberation is a cry for the coming kingdom, touched by the same longing for wholeness which God chose in his faithfulness to Jesus Christ. If the Spirit wants to realize the kingdom of God, he will also have to take this prayer with him. Thus, the praying human formulates the path of the kingdom. By the Spirit and for the Spirit he formulates the choice that has to be made. In the name of Jesus prayer is not empty anymore. It is the decisive choice for the kingdom. The prayer will have to be realized, or the kingdom will not be realized. As long as there is one sick person left or one sin left unreconciled, the kingdom is incomplete, and as such it is not the kingdom of *God*. Where people articulate their distress and needs they cry out for the realization of the kingdom of God and show the way to the Spirit.

But people are limited. There is good reason why the realization of the kingdom is a divine work requiring the involvement of the Spirit of God himself. Humans may make their contribution, but they do not see everything that is being contributed. I do see my own pain and that of a small circle around me, but not the pain of others, which is equally a cry for the coming kingdom. Consequently, prayers are often contradictory. They often have the character of the saying, "One man's meat is another man's poison." But even if all human beings were to have one common desire, even that would not be the all-encompassing prayer for the kingdom. For that exceeds the capacity of humans. The whole of creation is involved in it, as Romans 8:19-23 so brilliantly describes it. All of creation is the work of God, a work that embraces more than humans. Together with the animals and the flowers, the earth and the stars, and all that exists between heaven and earth of which our wisdom has never dreamed, it is the work of God. For that reason they are all involved in the kingdom of God. And God himself is involved. Not only do we have to come to agree with God; in the realization of his kingdom God must also arrive at agreement with us. When we reflect on this, we also realize that our prayer is extremely limited. On the one hand. it embraces everything: unless our cry for help is heard the kingdom will not be. On the other hand, it is a drop in the bucket or less in the sea of the nations encompassed by the Spirit. We do not know how to pray as we ought (Rom. 8:26). That does not mean we can stop praying since it is not relevant anyway. It is just as relevant as the petition "thy kingdom come." But it must be incorporated in the motley commingling of all the prayers that rise from the whole of creation, which only the Spirit can survey. Only he knows all things.

And the Spirit does not do all things at once. His will is to realize the kingdom; he prays with and for us "with sighs too deep for words" (Rom. 8:26). The longing of creation is his own. But he does not do everything at once. He works in the way of history, in the manner of process. That also implies that the Spirit has to prioritize. On the road of the kingdom one person will sometimes have to wait for another. The Spirit has time. We must sometimes also learn to have time. That belongs to the way of the kingdom. We have to wait for the other oppressed people. We cannot enter the kingdom and meanwhile forget the others. All the saints, even those who died a martyr's death, cry "how long?" (Rev. 6:10). A time will come, sooner or later, when we have to wait for others. We can only celebrate the kingdom together. And my advantage could very well be at the expense of someone else, and thus at the expense of the kingdom and ultimately of my own. In the realization that accords with the Spirit the community and the individual can never be separated. God aims at all in their commonality and their individuality. We may utter our prayers—the distress that is known to us—knowing that only salvation from that distress can be the will of God in Christ, but we have to add "Thy will be done," as Jesus did in his agony in Gethsemane (Matt. 26:39). That is not a trick to undo the force of the prayer. This prayer is a genuine communication to God that in the realization of his kingdom he must take this distress into account; at the same time it is the acknowledgment that the manner in which he must resolve this can only be fully clear to the Spirit. I do not want to be saved at the expense of another, at the expense of the whole of creation, or ultimately at the expense of God himself.

To pray is reverently to ask God to take account of our pain and distress. As children we approach him who is our Father and ask for his saving presence. In the depths of our distress we say that we are almost at the end of our rope, and we ask for a sign of his grace. With eager longing we look for light in the darkness. But the Christian always prays in fellowship with the entire world. Intercession for each other is rooted in a deep sense of being united on the road of the kingdom. When we pray we cannot just pray for ourselves. Therefore we ask that God may be savingly present to all. And the more the church is united by mutual intercession, the more the church becomes the interpreter of the one prayer for the world—the more our prayer will approximate the sighing of the Spirit who is at work realizing the kingdom. The more in our prayers we are mindful of the other, the more we are speaking in the Spirit of the kingdom.

322

However, when we pray "Thy will be done" we do not merely mention to God the distress we feel and then leave it to him. We may really think and pray as his partners. We know of Jesus Christ, of salvation, wholeness, and love. We are involved in it. Accordingly, it will have to become clear to us. We shall have to come to agreement with God. We must convince him or he must convince us that the way the Spirit is going in history is the right way. Let me cite a pair of examples from the Bible. From the Old Testament, both are testimonies to the awesome freedom and boldness with which people may relate to God. They speak of divine justice, of a divine will, and divine decisions. And they want, even demand, that human reality and what humans experience shall be in accord with them. If these examples already occur in the Old Testament as a way of relating to God, how much more reason do we have in Christ to go to God with all boldness, knowing of his justice, his will, and his firm decision in Christ.

The first example is the dialogue between Moses and God in Exodus 32 and 33. The Israelites have made the golden calf and God is very angry. These chapters brilliantly convey God's dynamic way through history and the role a human can play in it. God liberated Israel from Egypt. The opening statement of the decalogue solemnly intones, "I am the Lord your God, who brought you out of the land of Egypt, out of the house of bondage" (Exod. 20:2). At the very beginning of the liberation, when God called Moses, he referred to "my people" (Exod. 3:7). Israel was God's people and Moses must serve God in liberating the people. But now Israel has sinned. God is angry and the whole story is reversed. "And the Lord said to Moses, 'Go down; for your people whom you brought up out of the land of Egypt, have corrupted themselves'" (Exod. 32:7). The God of whom Exodus speaks is certainly no "independent being" (ens independens). Not only do humans evoke reactions in him, but even the way he thinks about the relationship he has with Israel and Moses is determined by human action. All of a sudden the enterprise is no longer a matter of God's initiative and God's people, but of Moses' initiative and Moses' people. Instead of the powerful God who by his superior might brings out and liberates his people, he is the God who will only go with Moses under certain conditions, just as at one time Moses would only go with God under pressure and under certain conditions. The whole enterprise is now put on Moses' back again. God not only changes his plans but even places his earlier action in another light. God's anger reaches the point where he wants to destroy Israel. The God who once chose Israel as his people now denies his election (it is now "your people"!) and wants to annihilate the people to whom he promised his everlasting faithfulness (32:10).

The most exciting part of Exodus 32 and 33, however, is still coming. For God does not simply proceed to destroy Israel. One would think that once he has made up his own independent divine mind he not only would be able to do it, but that at that very moment it would be effected. But that is not what happens. God first has to tell Moses, "Now therefore let me alone, that my wrath may burn hot against them and I may consume them" (32:10). Moses has in his hands the readiness of God's wrath. Mind you, the divine decision lies in the hands of a human. Then follows Moses' reaction. Moses says, "You cannot do that, God. You cannot destroy your own people." He advances arguments. In the first place, Moses puts the matter in proportion: they are God's people, not his; he did not bring them out of Egypt, but God himself did it with great power and a mighty hand (v. 11). It was God's own plan— he must not now change his mind. In the second place, God cannot do it on account of the Egyptians. They would only stand by laughing if Israel now "went down the drain." They would say, "With evil intent did he bring them forth, to slay them in the mountains, and to consume them from the face of the earth" (v. 12). In the third place, God cannot destroy Israel on account of the fathers: "Remember Abraham, Isaac, and Israel, thy servants, to whom thou didst swear by thine own self, and didst say to them, 'I will multiply your descendants as the stars of heaven, and all this land that I have promised I will give to your descendants, and they shall inherit it for ever.'" God is "stuck" with his own promise. If he should go back on it, his deity would not mean anything. Moses argues as a man argues with a friend who is about to make a totally irresponsible decision. And then comes God's reaction: ("Moses, actually you are right; this is not the way to go; my apologies for what I said a minute ago.") "And the Lord repented of the evil which he thought to do to his people" (v. 14).

That does not mean the issue is now closed. For Moses it is not. He is furious not at God, but at the people. The rescuing advocate also proves to be the hard judge—in the name of God. Apparently God and Moses are in total agreement that an example has to be set. To the Levites Moses says, "Thus says the Lord God of Israel, 'Put every man his sword on his side, and go to and fro from gate to gate throughout the camp, and slay every man his brother, and every man his companion, and every man his neighbor'" (v. 27). But even then the matter is not over. God is still angry. He no longer wants to go up with the Israelites; he only wants to send along his angel (v. 34). The angel here serves as a sign of distance. God does not abandon his people, but at the same time the earlier closeness when he was in their midst with his own "face" is gone. God sends a messenger but no longer shows his face. That is how Exodus 33 starts out. Impressed by this decision of God, the people mourned (v. 4). But it is for their own protection that the Lord is no longer willing to dwell among them. If the arguments of Moses are correct (and they proved to be convincing to God!) then God had better stay at a distance. "If for a single moment I should go up among you, I would consume you" (v. 5). But God does want to think about the matter some more: "So now put off your ornaments from you, that I may know what to do with you" (v. 5).

A conversation, initiated by Moses, now follows between him and God: "Moses said to the Lord, 'See, thou sayest to me, "Bring up this people"; but thou hast not let me know whom thou wilt send with me. Yet thou hast said, "I know you by name, and you have also found favor in my sight." Now therefore, I pray thee, if I have found favor in thy sight, show me now thy ways, that I may know thee and find favor in thy sight. Consider too that this nation is thy people' " (vv. 12, 13). Moses wants to know where he stands. If God is really gracious, he cannot be halfhearted in his commitment to Israel and to Moses. Then comes God's question (in the author's version): "Do you want me to go with you, to put your mind at rest?" (v. 14). Moses here is the assertive and God the questioning one. Moses says that indeed God's presence must go with them. The presence of God in Israel is his election; only therein is his election made real (v. 16). Again God agrees with Moses: "This very thing that you have spoken I will do; for you have found favor in my sight, and I know you by name" (v. 17). Moses is here in conversation with God; he is a human who argues with God; a human who persuades God to change his mind and points a way for God to go, not in some minor issue, but in the matter of God's choice for Israel as a channel of blessing to the nations. If God is a seeking God, if he is a living God, if God is a God of human beings, then a human who holds God to his own actions, to his own promises, and to his own dignity, is capable of great things. About the power of prayer James has this to say: "Elijah was a man of like nature with ourselves and he prayed fervently that it might not rain, and for three years and six months it did not rain on the earth. Then he prayed again and the heaven gave rain, and the earth brought forth its fruit" (James 5:17f.). If Moses already could speak as he did—with only the election of Abraham and the liberation from Egypt behind him— how much more reason is there for Christians—who confess that God has raised Christ from the dead and that we are God's children in him—to speak with God in this fashion. We are in a later phase. Now one can comment that it is after all not just anybody who is praying here: it is Moses. Does not Moses occupy a very special position? The text in James indicates the precise opposite: "Elijah was a man of like nature with ourselves." In Israel Moses and Elijah were the two bearers of the covenant. Elijah was almost messianic, the forerunner of the kingdom. When *he* prays, it can really be effective! Says James, "He was like the rest of us." But at least he prayed. God's reaction depends not on the fact that Elijah prayed, but on whether a human being prays and on what arguments this person has. If that is true of Elijah, there is no reason to accord special status to Moses.

Another objection may arise from the belief that Exodus 32 and 33 represent primitive anthropomorphic discourse about God. We, by contrast, cannot speak about God like that anymore. Quite apart from what I remarked earlier about the relationship between God's being and his revelation, it is particularly true for Exodus 32 and 33 that this thesis is incorrect. The passage very much reflects the glory of God. God is the Holy One, the Wholly Other. When Moses asks to be allowed to see the glory of God, God refuses. "Man shall not see me and live" (Exod. 33:20). God is the Holy One who *consumes* those who oppose him (Exod. 33:5), the one before whom no man can stand. Even the radiance of God's glory is so intense that its reflection blinds people (33:23; 34:30). The divine glory is inaccessible. And the face of God is too exalted for human beings. But this face will go before Israel. And a human can still speak to this holy God. With this unapproachable and holy God he may deal, and this invisible and glorious one allows himself to be convinced by a human, and shown the way by a man.

One who lives with the God of Israel does not have to resign himself to the dark clouds which are gathering over his head or on the horizon of the world. One may point God to his promises. One can point out to him his dignity and standing. One can refer him to what he himself began with us. If he has begun, in the name of Jesus, to call people to himself, then he must not all at once abandon them. One can negotiate with God, pleading for others, pleading for oneself, and yes, pleading for God himself. People are more likely to be too reserved and reticent before God than too bold. People fear his holiness or underestimate the importance of their own prayer, perhaps because they themselves do not believe in it (James 1:5-8). In situations of guilt and suffering we are not called to be passive, but to call on God to give signs of the coming kingdom. We can refer him to his own choice in Christ, to the healing of the sick, to his power to forgive sins, to his victory over death. If God wants to confirm his choice in Christ, he has to verify it. Sometimes God allows himself to be persuaded by people, agreeing with their arguments or proposals.

That is not only the case with Moses, whose intercession was pivotal, but also in the case of Hezekiah, who prayed for his own healing.

The prophet had already told him in the name of the Lord to set his affairs in order because he was going to die (Isa. 38:1). But after Hezekiah prayed and wept, the oracle was revoked (vv. 2-5). God even responded positively to the very demanding proposals of Jabez. "Jabez was more honorable than his brothers; and his mother called his name Jabez, saying, 'Because I bore him in pain.' Jabez called on the God of Israel, saying, 'Oh that thou wouldst bless me and enlarge my border, and that thy hand might be with me, and that thou wouldst keep me from harm so that it might not hurt me!' And God granted what he asked" (1 Chron. 4:9f.). Jabez does, to be sure, talk very much to his own advantage. His prayer does not seem to be a model for how to pray to Israel's God. Beyond this we know nothing about Jabez, but in these few verses the author of 1 Chronicles shows us how God may react to people. And he apparently finds this prayer, plus its answer, so important that he is prepared to interrupt his summary (dull to us but essential to him) of the genealogical record to include it.

In the examples cited above, God let himself be persuaded by humans of the rightness of their cause. But the reverse also occurs. The dialogue between humans and God is not one-sided, always coming down on man's side. There is genuine reciprocity. God initiates an action; a human has a voice in it, but is merely one of the partners. He is not the only one to speak. The actual decision is even made by God. The reciprocity, as van Ruler said, is theonomous. And sometimes God decides that the human petitioner is wrong, or at least that he should keep his mouth shut from that point on. After an incident at Meribah, where Moses failed to demonstrate to God the faithfulness he requires, God decided that Moses might not bring the people into the promised land (Num. 20:12). Deuteronomy relates that Moses nevertheless begged God to be allowed to go to Canaan: "Let me go over, I pray, and see the good land beyond the Jordan, that goodly hill country, and Lebanon" (Deut. 3:25). These are very moving words by which Moses, the great man, as a child asked God for a favor. But all at once God is relentless. He "would not hearken to me." He even forbade Moses to bring it up again: "Let it suffice you; speak no more to me of this matter" (v. 26).

The second example, one I wish to discuss at somewhat greater length, is that of Job. Job had to endure much. He lost his livestock; he lost his children; and his wife does not agree with his willingness to bear all this and to remain faithful to God (2:9). Then his friends come in order to comfort him. These friends are often pictured as people who have only come to find fault with Job, people who are hard and cold. But that is not true to the story. To start with, they kept silent for seven days and could only weep (2:12f.). In the face of great suffering one does better to keep silent. And they do so for seven days, the period of fullness. When they finally open their mouths they say what pastors have said to the grieving in every age: "I would put it in the hands of God, Job." "As for me, I would seek God, and to God would I commit my cause; . . . Behold, happy is the man whom God reproves; therefore despise not the chastening of the Almighty. For he wounds, but he binds up; he smites, but his hands heal" (5:8, 17f.).

Only after Job begins to protest, saying that they do not at all understand, and that God is treating him unfairly, do they get irritated and say it is no wonder that God punishes him. If Job has the nerve to have such a big mouth against God and to lodge accusations against the Holy One, he is not at all the pious man they always took him to be. Out of Job's own mouth he stands condemned: the punishment is just. But Job maintains that God is treating him unfairly. "I was at ease, and he broke me asunder; he seized me by the neck and dashed me to pieces; he set me up as his target, . . . although there is no violence in my hands, and my prayer is pure" (16:12, 17). His friends fail to understand and God treats him unjustly.

Still, Job continues to make his appeal to God. "Even now, behold, my witness is in heaven, and he that vouches for me is on high. My friends scorn me; my eye pours out tears to God, that he would maintain the right of a man with God, like that of a man with his neighbor" (16:19-21). God must first settle things with himself. God must do justice to man in the courtroom where man confronts him. First, things have to be put in order in heaven for the way God is now acting—which is misgovernment. If God is truly God, if he is true and just, he must first come to terms with himself. And if he does that, affairs on earth will also become clearer; then justice can be done there too. In the book of Job the man who is truly faithful to God is not the passive human being, nor one who defends God, but one who calls God to account. If things on earth are such a mess that the innocent suffer, and on top of that are then faulted, then God's government is all wrong. No pious words can help. Job's faithfulness consists in the fact that he does not renounce God, but wants to battle the issue out with God. To the very end God is important to him. If God does not correct everything that has happened, then an injustice has been done not only to Job; then God himself is finished. For the individual act of renouncing God does not help in any way to alleviate suffering in the world. Nor does it help to justify the ways of God. The only one who can set matters straight is God himself. That is Job's appeal—"as God lives, who has taken away my right, and the Almighty, who has made my soul bitter" (27:2). God is not fair—it is the wicked who deserve to be punished (27:13-23). But now God punishes the righteous; for if God were really just he would acknowledge Job's innocence. "Let me be weighed in a just balance, and let God know my integrity" (31:6). God is not fair; he is guilty of misgovernment. That is Job's position. Is it any wonder his friends are all down on him? Is God not always right in the course he follows, even though we do not understand anything of it?

God's answer is not unambiguous. On the one hand, he says to Job, "Just what do you want? Who will fathom what I am doing? I am the mighty God who created all things; I made the large beasts, the monsters that inspire fear in man, crocodiles and hippopotami, Leviathan and Behemoth, the symbolic representatives of chaos. But I have raised them and I control them. The stars follow the course I have set for them and I call them by name. I am the mighty God—how would you, puny man, be able to understand me?" (Job 38–41). God summons Job to show what he can do if he thinks he knows so much (40:2-9). Finally, Job has to acknowledge that God is right. He yields. "I know that thou canst do all things, and that no purpose of thine can be thwarted. . . . Therefore I have uttered what I did not understand, things too wonderful for me, which I did not know . . . therefore I despise myself, and repent in dust and ashes" (42:2, 3b, 6). In his incomprehensible freedom God has approached Job, and Job admits that God is greater than he. And that is well. "I had heard of thee by the hearing of the ear, but now my eye sees thee" (42:5). Job has been persuaded by God and admits God is right. He had not understood God. But the narrator at the same time adds that Job has understood God better than his friends. They had not spoken of God what is right, as Job did (42:7). Consequently, God's anger is kindled against them. One who enters a dispute with God does more justice to him than one who a priori endorses his policies. A human has to battle things out with God. That person will get an answer even if God does not prove him right. Only that man can be convinced and see God. God does not get angry with him, though there are peals of thunder when he speaks (38:1; 40:6). God, however, does get angry over the people who passively submit to his rule.

The story which frames the dialogues comes down even more firmly on Job's side. Job the righteous man is the victim of a wager made in heaven. Is Job wrong when he calls this misgovernment? Accordingly, the book ends with the restoration of Job's earlier happiness. The Lord gives Job double what he had before. Double restitution is the rule for things taken wrongfully (Exod. 22:1-9). Job did not wrong God when he said God wronged him. His only fault was his failure to recognize the greatness and freedom of God. God is a more majestic mystery than the unsearchable wisdom, the understanding of the true meaning of things, of which Job had spoken in chapter 28. Prayer and argument belong to the believer's association with God. Sometimes God is persuaded, and sometimes man. Sometimes God bluntly says "no," as he did to Moses.

Now one can say that in Jesus this has all been summed up. He is the innocent, righteous sufferer; he is the intercessor and mediator; he is the man who calls God to account: "Why have You forsaken me?" He became convinced, so that he could die with the words of the pious on his lips: "Father, into thy hands I commit my spirit" (Luke 23:46). In Christ we may therefore securely rest in God. With our whole existence we have been incorporated in Jesus. He has taken over for us all our questions and sorrow, our innocence and our guilt. We no longer have to fight the battle of Moses and of Job; Jesus has done that, and we may rest in his work.

It is a question, however, whether by saying that we do not arrive at the position of Job's friends. Things are not that smooth—even after the death and resurrection of Christ. Paul made a plea similar to that of Moses in Deuteronomy 3. From the Lord he had received a thorn in the flesh, a messenger of Satan to buffet him (2 Cor. 12:7). We do not know the nature of what troubled him; in any case it was a great burden to Paul. He writes, "Three times I besought the Lord about this, that it should leave me" (v. 8). But, like Moses, Paul is rebuffed: "He said to me, 'My grace is sufficient for you, for my power is made perfect in weakness'" (v. 9). By way of the martyrs beneath the altars, the persecuted church of Revelation asks how long it will still be before the Lord will set things in order (Rev. 6:10). But the answer is that the church has to wait. The divine answer adds that the wait will be for a short while (v. 11). But what is a short while for God may seem a long time to people. Furthermore, after Easter the righteous remain in tension. One may even say that after the resurrection of Christ that tension has increased. If God has made a definitive choice and has proven his power in the conquest of death, why then do we not at all notice the realization? If God's intent is to be a God of liberation, and he has the power to liberate, then does he do justice to the world when he lets it perish in misery, and to the believer when he lets him suffer? If we take God seriously, we are only doing justice to him if we call him to account. In the pastorate one often hears it said, "Fortunately I am not rebellious, pastor." The opinion of many Christians is that to be rebellious in suffering is a great sin. The non-rebellious is fortunate, because then as a sufferer he experiences some peace amidst suffering. One cannot always process everything down to the depths. But not to be rebellious can also mean one is afraid to be rebellious, because one thinks it is impermissible. Then this remark to the pastor serves to secure oneself against the harsh God who has already beaten a person almost senseless. The examples of Job and Moses, however, and of so many others in the Bible, can teach us that it is not a sin to be rebellious, but is instead an open road to God. We are permitted to call God to account over suffering, our own and that of others.

One who acquiesces in the way the world runs fails to do justice to the choice God made in Jesus Christ. If Christ Jesus is the decisive way in which God wills to reveal himself, then it is important, as it was for Job, to call this God to witness against himself as the God who allows the world to suffer, and who brought sorrow into one's life. To dispute with God, far from being inappropriate for a Christian, rather becomes him because he thereby shows he is taking God with all seriousness. If in our dispute with God we are hindered because we are conscious of the sin of the world and of our own guilt before God, we must in the first place call to mind the dispute of Isaiah: "O Lord, why dost thou make us err from thy ways and harden our heart, so that we fear thee not?" (Isa. 63:17). If God is indeed the mighty liberator, why then does he not liberate us from the power of sin? Another way is that of Moses, that of intercession. Intercession is not only a matter of making deeply reverent requests. To intercede with God is to put him on the spot on the grounds of his faithfulness. In Jesus Christ we have better arguments than Moses.

One who enters into dialogue with God can sometimes persuade God. Another time a person is persuaded by the Spirit of God, perhaps not in thunder and storm as Job was, but certainly by the power of the same Spirit. Sometimes, too, the answer remains open. Then a blunt "no" follows, or no answer comes at all. God's ultimate secret was not disclosed to Job. Moses and God are not equals. The saints beneath the altar still have to wait. The prayers of innumerable people remain unanswered. Many of our prayers resemble our conversations: they end without agreement or even without a clear conclusion. We have not been able to persuade God to listen to us and God has not persuaded us that the way he took with us was the best. The verdict on all the conversations between God and humans is still out. The future remains open. But it can only remain open if people continue to think and talk with God as his partners-in-dialogue. Those who talk with God are certainly not yes-men. Even less are they wheedlers. They hold God to the fact that in Christ he chose to be a God of humans.

In our generation the experience of many Christians is that no answer came. We are living with an absent God. That is no reason to stop praying. It is no reason to renounce the faith. To renounce the faith is not merely a choice which concerns a human personally. It is also an act of renouncing hope for the world. If we view the world as absolutely

331

devoid of God, a place in which God plays no role at all, then the world is hopelessly lost, doomed to disappear in a final catastrophe. The only hope for the world is God in Jesus Christ. If the world in no shape or form shows the signs of the presence of this God, then we must be radical: either God had better demonstrate who he is—and how long do we have to wait?—or the world is lost. What has been said here of the world as a whole applies equally to the individual. Every instance of suffering is a breach in the kingdom—even for the suffering of an individual one can call God to account. And the individual can battle it out with God, as Job did. For one single individual concerns all and everything.

22. PARTICIPATION WITH GOD

HUMANS MAY THINK AND TALK AS PARTNERS OF GOD ABOUT THE ROUTE HE is taking to his kingdom. But that is not all. For they can be much more actively involved in the coming of the kingdom. We already saw that the Spirit does not act "over the world's head," but employs all the potentials of what God began in the world, even the human potentials. Humans are not only thinking, talking beings; they are also acting beings. To involve a human is to involve an acting human, who can perform deeds which mark the road to the kingdom.

In Jesus Christ God revealed himself definitively as a God of love and grace. He healed the sick; he received the outcasts of society; he forgave sins; he saved people from death. When people are taken up into the process by which the kingdom of God is realized, they begin to act jointly with God. Humans perform deeds of love and grace. A Christian is called to do acts of mercy. Not only are Christians called to do them; they also do them. If the mercy of God is not realized in human deeds, it is not realized at all. Then that mercy remains an airy abstraction instead of being realized in this world, a world destined to be the kingdom of God. Not only are Christians called to perform acts of mercy; *all* humans are called in Jesus Christ to perform acts of mercy, for the kingdom of God in Jesus Christ is valid for the entire world. Accordingly, the signs of the kingdom are not reserved for Christians. Every sign of love, every act of grace, is a step on the way to salvation, a deed of the Spirit. The Spirit is not boxed in by the church.

Some human acts are clearly recognizable as acts inspired by the Spirit of Christ. Where humans sacrifice themselves for others in his name, there one sees rays of the dawn of the kingdom. People who show compassion toward society's outcasts are following Jesus. People who devote their energies to the healing of the sick are erecting signs of the kingdom where there is no sickness. People who search for peace among the nations are followers of the peaceable kingdom. People who in the name of Jesus refuse to bow before this world's powers are erecting a visible sign that Christ is Lord—even though they themselves are thrown to the lions.

People can work together with God in the direction of the kingdom in many different ways. But matters are not always very clear, certainly when it concerns method. One can search for the road to peace, but the problem comes with the question how best to serve the cause of peace. Must we maintain a balance of power, demonstrate for the elimination of nuclear weapons from the world, or only preach and refuse to join the arms race? Though the goal can be clear, the road to the goal is uncertain. One sometimes has to grope one's way to the kingdom. In this man proves to be a real partner of the Spirit. The Spirit also goes his way searching. He acts and chooses in an open situation. Called to a role in that process, humans are in the same position. We are on the way to the kingdom as searchers in the manner of trial and error.

Now as humans we are not alone in that process—we have each other. Primarily, that means we can consult with one another. Together we can discuss what the best way is. No person can find the way alone, because it is the way in which all are involved. We either travel that road together or we do not travel. Since people are never all in agreement (the contrary is rather the case) and history continues, decisions are continually made and actions performed which do not accord with each other, or are even contradictory. On the one hand, this hinders the progress of the kingdom. On the other hand, it is a good thing: the differing choices correct each other and prevent one choice, possibly a wrong choice, from prevailing. That is the second advantage of the fact that people are not alone. The trial-and-error character of the process is maintained, and error is not the definitive end. For no single act is totally in accord with the standards of the kingdom of Jesus Christ. As long as the kingdom is not fully realized, every act carries within it something of the old structures of the world. One could prematurely force a decision by endorsing the idea that on the one hand there are deeds of perfect grace and of sacrificial love, and on the other deeds of violence and egoism. The first are the deeds that perfectly fit into the kingdom of Christ. They belong in the category of the new man in a new creation. The others reinforce the earthly structures, earthly power; they belong to the old regime that has passed away in Christ. This contrast plays a role especially in political discussion, not the least in questions concerning armaments.

The contrast, however, is unreal. In the first place, Christ is not Lord in isolation, but Lord and Savior of the world. Christology by itself is no Christology. True Christology always mirrors the God who is oriented to the world. Hence, Christian ethics does not exist in isolation either. It is always the ethics of a kingdom breaking into the world. Accordingly, every Christian makes use in every decision of earthly structures. He eats his daily bread which he receives only within the structures of earthly society. Even when he speaks about Christ, he speaks in words belonging to the language of a certain people and a certain social group. When he seeks to bring about change, he does that with the normal psychological methods of persuasion. When people in the West strive for a free society, they do it with the ordinary weapons of deterrence. The preservation of the free West occurs via the technology of arms and the structure of a balance of power. A person who, like myself, disagrees with this in any case cannot accuse others of using earthly power structures. For one who decides to go out to demonstrate also uses power structures—e.g., those of psychological, social, and political persuasion—exerting influence via the effect which a demonstration has on people. Even one who, though he rejects the method of demonstration, simply argues in support of his choice does something to influence people.

Accordingly, everyone in any action makes use of earthly structures. And in ethics the choice is not whether one follows a purely Christian lifestyle or makes concessions to the existing ordinances and powers. In the first place, as long as one is on earth, one cannot live a purely Christian life; and in the second place, Christianity's goal is not to be purely Christian but to preserve God's creation. The question is not *whether* one makes use of earthly possibilities, techniques, and means of exercising power and influence; it is rather a question which techniques one employs and how one employs them. That is what makes ethical choices so exciting. If in South Africa one seeks a just society for all, one has to make decisions. One can employ the tactic of speech, or that of passive resistance, or that of violence. With respect to those who carry weapons one can say they are not in accord with the high standards of Jesus Christ. True, they are not. They get their hands dirty. They burden themselves with guilt the moment blood clings to their hands. And they do not reach the goal. The truth is still that those who take the sword will perish by the sword. But if one does not engage in armed resistance, people will continue even longer to suffer under an unjust regime. Then too blood, the blood of the righteous, will flow. Then when families continue to be ripped apart people suffer even longer. Then too one has burdened himself with guilt. Whichever choice one makes, one cannot escape being guilty.

No one who makes ethical decisions can escape getting his hands dirty. That is the case in political ethics and it is the case in social ethics. Wherever people make decisions and proceed to act (and not to act is also an act), they employ methods and make choices which are out of tune with the decisions of God in Jesus Christ. There is not a single fixed rule which is applicable as an invariable command in all situations, including the commandments of the Decalogue. Shiphrah and Puah cheerfully told a pack of lies to Pharaoh and did so correctly (Exod. 1:18-21). Ehud, in a confidential conversation with the occupying dictator Eglon, king of Moab, ran a sword into his fat body (Judg. 3:12-30). Tamar degraded herself by playing the prostitute (Gen. 38). Each act must always be placed in the context of the totality of possibilities and responsibilities which people have. In that connection one must not be afraid to make his hands dirty. The Spirit is not either. He too makes use of everything that is in the world. People who live in the Spirit continually besmirch themselves. But that was God's own choice when he began to save *this* world, the world he started.

But if everyone makes his hands dirty and burdens himself with guilt as he acts, must not we draw the conclusion that choice does not matter, all the more true because human decisions are so limited, and one person's decision needs the decision of another to correct it or to avoid one-sidedness? In other words, "Is it possible to have ethics?" Ethics, after all, requires a critical standard by which actions can be measured. If a human action can only be judged by the action of another, we end up in boundless relativism and find ourselves in ethical quicksand. If every human action makes use of methods which are beneath the standards of the kingdom, and therefore renders the human actor guilty, is not every ethical act negative, and is it not therefore utopian to speak of ethical action?

It is undoubtedly true that there is no absolute ethics. But that is not to say there is no absolute norm. It does not consist, however, in some legal rule, but is the kingdom itself; but then not everything that is beneath the standard of Christ is to be rejected. Indeed, in that absolute sense no ethical action is possible. The Spirit does not lift us above the earth and its history. The issue in ethics is whether a given choice is relatively more or less serviceable to the attainment of the goal, that is, the kingdom of God. Christian ethics is the ethics of orientation to the kingdom. That is to say, in choices for Christian action the criterion is whether by them the kingdom is advanced. And that is always a relative choice. No single human act ever realizes the kingdom once and for all.

Every act advances it more or less. And if the kingdom applies to humanity as a whole, then Christian ethics does not just apply to the actions of Christians: every human act is subject to the criterion of whether it advances the kingdom.

Accordingly, human action can be measured by a criterion. That means one must be able to justify one's actions. Human action may be relative, but it can be assessed. One must be able to be up front with one's choices, and show how they can be serviceable to the coming kingdom. One who cannot do that has acted unethically. However, since no choice ever brings in the kingdom absolutely, no action is ever totally defensible. Something always remains uncovered. The converse, however, is more important: because no human action ever totally blocks the advance of the kingdom, it is always possible to find something good in it. Accordingly, it is very important that Christian ethics be a relative ethics: one has to weigh the different alternatives. When one makes a choice, it is not relevant to say something good in it is good (this will undoubtedly be true); the question is whether or not there was a better choice. No matter how good the choice that was made, if there was a better choice, it was the wrong choice. And conversely, no matter how far a given choice was beneath the standard of Jesus Christ, if there was no better choice, it was the correct choice.

If the kingdom of God is the goal of human action, then we have been given a number of criteria which have priority in ethics. The kingdom is the kingdom of God which saves the world. By that token every choice which is contemptuous of the earth is judged. In Jesus Christ God is a God of human beings. Therefore every choice which takes no account of human society is to be rejected. In Jesus Christ God is Lord over all; his salvation is intended for all. Therefore, every choice which advances the well-being of one group, nation, or social class, while leaving others behind on the road to salvation and wholeness, is wrong. Every choice which does not start with those who are farthest behind on the road to this wholeness is a wrong choice. Now human existence has many aspects: economic, social, psychological, political, etc. It may be that some are ahead in one dimension and others in another. One is rich in one thing, another in some other. Everyone will have to share his kind of riches with his neighbor, thus serving one another on the way to the righteousness of the kingdom. For that matter, wealth in only one dimension of life tends to break up and disorganize human existence. For not only the whole of humanity belongs to the kingdom, but also the whole man. A choice which only serves one's economic advantage at the expense of other aspects of human existence is as censurable as a choice which only serves the national interest and leaves other nations behind (as a rule, for that matter, these two choices go together). But the same is true for a choice which only serves the religious life.

On account of the relativity of the available choices, it is often hard to make out which of them would serve the kingdom of God, the more so since the structures of human society (to say nothing of the totality of the world, let alone the cosmos) are so complex that all aspects cannot possibly be surveyed. But the inescapable choice is that of God in Jesus Christ. There is the promise of the kingdom which Jesus proclaimed in word and deed. By that standard we can measure our own deeds, and our collective deeds. It is possible to make a judgment about human actions. Humans as choosing beings can act judgingly in relation to each other, something structured in an ordered society in a judicial power.

But Christian ethics will demand from a judicial power that it judge in accord with the measure in which the kingdom is advanced. That is always a choice for man, because the kingdom of God is for man. When the judicial power is confronted with this demand, that means that the legislature must be required to pass the legislation that will make this possible. Since the legislature is not its own norm and the state is not autonomous, every individual human can subject the state to criticism. This criticism can be so serious that the choice for what will be most serviceable to the kingdom may at times turn out to be in the style of Ehud. But also, that choice is not autonomous but itself is to be measured by the coming of the kingdom; hence it is open to criticism. Ehud may call Eglon to account, but Ehud himself must be called to account. The process of acting and giving account for the action remains an open process as long as people act. Even the assessment is again a new choice which is subject to criticism. As long as the final judgment has not been rendered, even human judgment remains a process of searching. Soon every man's work comes under judgment, says Paul; then it will be manifest whether it was gold, silver, precious stones, wood, hay, or stubble (1 Cor. 3:12). Till then the definitive judgment has to be delayed. That does not mean, however, that on the open road to the kingdom we, as humans who act together with God, may and must not for the time being pronounce a provisional and relative judgment.

For that matter, humans do not judge by themselves. Man judges because he has been called into play by the Spirit who judges. The Spirit who realizes the kingdom himself subjects the world to judgment, unmasking unrighteousness. He is the Spirit who burns like fire (Acts 2:3; Isa. 4:4) and convinces the world of sin and of righteousness and of judgment (John 16:8). The Spirit who witnesses to Jesus Christ continually subjects both the church and the world to criticism. That criticism may be that the church is lukewarm (Rev. 3:15f.), or that it has left its first love (Rev. 2:4). The criticism may be that Rome with its religious ambitions and dictatorial power is a beast whose rule was derived from the devil (Rev. 13). That criticism comes out when Ananias and Sapphira drop dead on account of their deception (Acts 5:1-11). In the proclamation of Jesus Christ the church and the world are continually placed under criticism. Wherever the Word opens up people are confronted with judgment over their lives. By the absolute norm of the kingdom the judgment is always negative; people always fall short. By the relative norm of the kingdom-in-process-of-realization, it is an exhortation to examine oneself and one another to see if our deeds are deeds of the Spirit of Christ.

The Spirit of Christ subjects the world to criticism. But in the process he at the same time subjects himself to criticism. For the world does not exist or run apart from the power of God who is himself the Spirit. He is the driving force of the world and its history. In his judgment of the world the Spirit also judges himself. By that statement we have plumbed the depths of Job's appeal. God is called to render judgment over God himself and therein lies the basis for judgment over people (Job 16:19-21). This means that the last judgment is not only a judgment of God concerning people, but also a judgment concerning God himself. The great tension in the last judgment consists in the verdict of the Father and the Son on the work of the Spirit whom they have sent, just as the great tension of Golgotha and Easter lay in the verdict of the Father and the Son on the work of the Son whom they had sent. In the verdict on the work of the Spirit lies the salvation or non-salvation of the world. Therein lies also the verdict on the deity of God. The *laus Dei* (praise of God) and the *salus populi* (salvation of the people) are inseparably bound up with each other.

23. A New Heaven and a New Earth

What then shall we say to this? If God is for us, who is against us? He who did not spare his own Son but gave him up for us all, will he not also give us all things with him? Who shall bring any charge against God's elect? It is God who justifies; who is to condemn? Is it Christ Jesus, who died, yes, who was raised from the dead, who is at the right hand of God, who indeed intercedes for us? Who shall separate us from the love of Christ? Shall tribulation, or distress, or persecution, or famine, or nakedness, or peril, or sword? As it is written, "For thy sake we are being killed all the day long; we are regarded as sheep to be slaughtered." No, in all these things we are more than conquerors through him who loved us. For I am sure that neither death, nor life, nor angels, nor principalities, nor things present, nor things to come, nor powers, nor height, nor depth, nor anything else in all creation, will be able to separate us from the love of God in Christ Jesus our Lord. (Rom. 8:31-39)

The verdict of the last judgment lies in the future. It will be a real judgment, which means one cannot tell in advance what the verdict will be. On the occasion of the last judgment God will render his verdict on the course of history. If the last judgment is an open matter, we cannot yet make any definitive statements about it. Eschatological assertions are, in a double sense, assertions of faith. In the first place, *everything* we say about God and the world is based on the faith that God exists and has a relationship with the world. But given that faith, and reflecting on the history of God's action in the past right up until the present, we can make relatively certain statements. Specifically, in light of God's choice in Jesus Christ we can, looking back, say who and what God is. There exists a point in history where a verdict was rendered. We have been left extensive testimony of events in the first century which, in accord with their theological meaning, contain data on which we can build. Christologically we operate, within the circle of the Christian faith, with certainties from the past. Eschatologically, however, we work with the uncertainties of the future. The way of the Spirit is an open one. There is real divine action based on real choices. On the *dies irae* (day of wrath) a real verdict will be rendered. When the Christian community says positive things about the future, it is not based on information about the future it has at its disposal. If that were the case the work of the Spirit would shrivel up, the Spirit would be stripped of his divine character, and the last judgment would no longer be a divine judgment. If now already we can say how the verdict will turn out, God no longer has to judge. When the Christian church makes a statement about the judgment, it is rooted in the confidence that God will confirm his choice in Jesus Christ, not on a future process which the church can understand in advance. Eschatological certainties are christologically-based certainties. But pneumatologically, in the sense of realization, nothing can be said about the eschaton with certainty. In that sense the future lies completely open. Everything we can say about the eschaton is based on the trust that God, in a decisive future, will confirm his choice in Christ, which is why we have prefaced this section with the conclusion of Romans 8.

In Romans 8 (vv. 18-30) Paul says that the creation waits with eager longing for the revelation of the children of God. But the Christian community also awaits with eager longing the realization of the deliverance (v. 23) which is given in Christ and in which the Spirit causes us to share (v. 2). Together with the whole creation we long for the glorification to come. In this process we searchingly hope and pray, not knowing how to pray as we ought (v. 26). Now we see in a mirror dimly (1 Cor. 13:12), waiting until we know as we are known. In this process of searching expectation we are not alone. The Spirit himself intercedes for us with sighs too deep for words (Rom. 8:36). He is at our side helping.

Romans 8:26 uses the word *sunantilambano* for this. In such a double composite the prepositions have a more highly charged meaning than in a single composite. *Sun* and *anti* refer to a form of joint action in which commonality as well as duality and distance emerge. In the story of Mary and Martha, where the word also occurs (Luke 10:40), its use is quite characteristic. Mary must come and help Martha; she must "also give a hand."

Both the church and the Spirit eagerly await glorification. Revelation says the same thing in pictorial language: "The Spirit and the Bride say, 'Come'" (Rev. 22:17). This is their cry in a world which shakes under the thudding hooves of the beasts from the abyss, a world which groans under the suffering of the present aeon (Rom. 8:18). The words of Romans 8:31-39 are sounded against this background. The certainty of the future lies in God who loves us in Christ, no matter what powers are at work. Our confidence is that he will fulfil the promise of glorification. This confidence is not just an arbitrary opinion or wishful thinking. In several ways it rises above that:

1. In his actions God has already shown consistency. We have before us the history of his action in which over and over he opted for human beings. This was confirmed in Jesus Christ to whom God, through death, proved his faithfulness and in whom he opted for humans to the end. This history gives us hope that God will not now, at the very last moment, put an end to the world. The choice of God in Jesus Christ gives us confidence—confidence that is not misplaced—that God will confirm his work. Says Romans 8: "He who did not spare his own Son but gave him up for us all, will he not also give us all things with him?" (v. 32). In Christ it has become apparent that God is *for* us (v. 31). If God who has proved to be mighty has chosen for us, then it is inconceivable there could be powers able to block the realization of his choice. On the basis of God's choice in the past, and his past deeds, we may have a well-founded expectation that glorification will follow.

2. This christological argument is further developed in the idea that

Christians still have before them the destination which Christ already attained. There is an analogy, even a parallel, between his way and ours. He has entered glory; our hope is to follow him in that. But he attained glory through suffering and even death. It is to be expected, therefore, that our way too will pass through suffering. Is not the moment we enter the darkness of death the guarantee that we shall follow him who rose from the dead? As ground for our eager expectation, Romans 8:17 mentions that if we have suffered with Christ we shall also be glorified with him. We die with Christ in order to rise with him. We travel the road of suffering with him in the expectation that the way of suffering will be for us the way of glorification with him. If the world suffers and believers groan together with the whole creation, that is no reason to despair of the coming glorification. On the contrary, it is a sign of hope. It points to the close tie between Christ and the creation. Our suffering—in illness, grief, or loneliness—points to the close tie between us and our Lord. Suffering strengthens the consciousness that we are united with Christ and will also follow him the rest of the way, the way of glorification. Suffering in the present aeon makes clear that *essentially* we do not belong to this aeon but to the aeon of him who died to the present aeon. Where amidst the suffering of the world people are conscious of this relationship to Christ, there the longing for glorification grows all the more. The saints say, "How long, O Lord?"

3. Among all the acts of God belongs the act of giving me faith in Christ. In the course of the Spirit's movement via tradition, I too have been reached. Thus God has clearly chosen for me. Not only did he will to choose me, he also made the choice effectual. The gospel has been made known to me and become familiar to me. I have accepted it. If by the Holy Spirit God has confirmed to me his decisive choice in Christ, then I have good grounds for assuming that after this he will still and to the very end validate the choice. The perseverance of the saints is not a remarkably static conception of eternal salvation; it flows forth from hearing the gospel as the way of the Spirit in the world.

4. The Spirit who realizes salvation in Christ is not an isolated given. He is not another God: he is the Spirit of Christ, the divine Spirit. His sighs are not sighs in the dark; his sighs are in accord with the will of God, rooted in the choice of the God who causes all things to work together for good, who elects and predestines men to be conformed to the image of his Son. Therefore he also called, and the purpose of the calling is to glorify (Rom. 8:27-30). The Spirit knows the goal for which he is working. As God, and along with God, he knows of the resurrection and glorification of Christ as his choice for the world. Consequently the Spirit is not only a helper, not even only a divine helper, but also the

guarantee (2 Cor. 1:22; 5:5; Eph. 1:14), the first fruits (Rom. 8:23). Just as Christ is the firstfruits of the kingdom of God (1 Cor. 15:20, 23), so his Spirit is the firstfruits in our lives, the beginning of the future. If he leads us to judgment and Christ is the judge, then the verdict cannot be an arbitrary one. If the Spirit is the Paraclete, the one called to be at our side as helper, then we can look forward to the future with confidence.

5. The relationship the Spirit forges between Christ and his church is not only one of reflection upon the acts of God, with the attendant conclusion being a reasonable certainty that God will continue to act as before. It is not merely a rational relationship, but rather a relationship of the whole person. We are in Christ and Christ is in us. With our whole existence we are woven together with Christ. It is a relationship of love without distance. In that relationship it is inconceivable that there would be a glory for Christ in which we could not share. If we were not to receive the glory, it would mean the downfall of Christ who dwells in us by the Spirit. It is the denial of his glory. Then, too, a negative judgment about the human being in Christ implies a negative judgment about the faithfulness of God and hence about God's deity. Then God would again recede behind Easter, the day he definitively demonstrated his divine faithfulness.

Accordingly, eschatology has a Christological foundation: Certainty is based in Christ. Also, it is pneumatologically confirmed insofar as the Spirit as Christ's Spirit has united us to him. At the same time this certainty is pneumatologically open insofar as the realization still has to occur and the Spirit continues to act. It is also open insofar as the judgment as a divine decision is an open judgment. This means that no assertions can be made about the eschaton other than christological ones. All answers arising from questions concerning the realization of the kingdom by the Spirit have to remain open. We wish to begin with this pneumatological openness in order subsequently to focus on the christological certainty.

The first question arising in this framework concerns the relationship between the continuity of history and the discontinuity of the last judgment. It is not correct to treat this relationship as a polarity between human action and divine action. Also, if the kingdom is an extension of history, it is the result of God's action. If one were to deny that, one would deny the deity of the Spirit. It is certain that the kingdom is the fulfillment of this history in which we humans live and in which Jesus Christ had his place. History and eschaton are not opposites. It is also certain that the eschaton is an act of God, as part of the divine verdict in the final judgment, in which the world arrives at its final destination. It is the decisive action of God in the interest of *this* world. But the question whether this will be achieved via an evolutionary or via a revolutionary method has to remain open. That depends on a future decision of God.

A second question linked with eschatology concerns the *apokatastasis panton* (the restoration of all things and all mankind). In Christ God has demonstrated once and for all that he opts for humans. He is faithful to what his hands have begun. But we have also said that the Holy Spirit realizes this choice in everything God began. The whole world is taken up into the way of the kingdom. It is also natural, then, to conclude that all things will also share in the coming glorification. Yet this conclusion comes a trifle too fast. In the first place, though the Spirit does work with all things and all things are taken up into the process, as he acts he repeatedly makes new decisions. We do not know how things will turn out in the end. If we thought we knew, we would be calculating eventualities ahead of the Spirit's action. Add to this the conclusion that the *apokatastasis panton* is an anticipation of the last judgment. If we fix the divine decision in advance it will no longer be a divine judgment. In the interest of the freedom of God Barth rightly rejected the inference of the *apokatastasis* from Christology. For the same reason we cannot infer the *apokatastasis* from pneumatology.

The New Testament repeatedly refers to a negative judgment over people. In the parable a distinction is made between sheep and goats (Matt. 25:33). According to the Apocalypse the devil and his angels, together with notorious sinners, are cast into a lake of fire and brimstone. As for the cowardly, the faithless, the polluted, murderers, fornicators, sorcerers, idolators, and liars, they will not enter the New Jerusalem (Rev. 20:10; 21:8). From the beginning the message of the church contained clear elements of warning that the future of human beings can be twofold.

It is wrong, however, to draw a line from this to a future situation— as though those elements of the message were descriptive of a future state. The message is a moment in the process of the Spirit in which everything—the darkness, the downfall and decline, and the wrath of God—plays a role on the road to judgment. It is a history charged with the tension of the two roads by which choices can be made. But the question remains as to what the definitive state of affairs will be. One can just as easily find elements in the message which from the beginning point to the all-encompassing significance of Christ and his salvation. The whole creation awaits the revealing of the children of God (Rom. 8:19-22). Christ is the cosmic Christ in whom all things are created, which especially the letters to the Ephesians and Colossians proclaim. God desires all men to be saved (1 Tim. 2:4).

Meanwhile, the above does mean that in the present dispensation

343

the message of the church, which goes its way searching and choosing, has to contain the elements of the two ways. "In the way of the Spirit" our choices are of decisive importance: they are of value for all eternity. Without the preaching of the two ways the Christian message loses its urgency and misses its function as a message of the kingdom-in-process-of-realization. At the same time, if it is not rooted in God's decisive choice for human beings in Jesus Christ it lacks power.

One development of the theory of *apokatastasis* can be that suffering and even death are included in the eschaton in the sense that suffering is accepted and has therefore lost its sting. When Christ is glorified, he is glorified as the sufferer who accepted suffering and death. Death is an enemy as long as one does not accept it, but the moment one does it is a brother, given the unlimited possibilities of God. When people resignedly put all things in the hands of God there is no more suffering. Absolute obedience, which is also inwardly complete, is absolute freedom. Where heteronomy and autonomy coincide there is theonomy, the unity of all being. When my finitude recognizes itself in the totality of being and my limited situation finds its roots in the all-encompassing essence of existence I am no longer estranged.[6]

An objection to this view is that the New Testament texts speak of victory over death, of a glory which does not consist in acceptance of suffering, but is the opposite of suffering. One could perhaps interpret this terminology as an attempt in cultic language to express the inexpressible, though that requires an enormous hermeneutic shift. A stronger objection is that it robs history of its meaning. If the eschaton consists of the acceptance of all that is, even of that which has been thought to be, then ultimately no choice has been made. Then God has made no decisions in history, not even decisions which are of definitive importance to God, like the choice between good and evil. The idea that God makes a choice, which is the basis of a real Christology, can never be fitted into a model based on the conquest of the existential alienation which flows from unaccepted creaturely finitude, any more than it can be squared with the notion that God is merely the ground of being, being itself, as Tillich says.

If the realization of the kingdom is the work of the Spirit which has not yet been concluded, then no assertions at all can be made about the details of the kingdom. If on the large issue of the *apokatastasis* the answer has to remain open, then all other answers have to remain even much

6. This idea can be found in Paul Tillich's *Systematic Theology* vol. 1, pp. 163-66. Heteronomy, like autonomy, entails alienation. In revelation this alienation is overcome. Christ by his perfect self-offering brought to light victory over alienation (vol. 2, pp. 144-45).

more open. How things will be in the kingdom can only be rendered in imagery. It is the kingdom which lies in the future; no human has that kingdom at his fingertips, not even cognitively. That kingdom will be the product of divine action and is for that reason alone beyond our human capacity to conceive. It is "what no eye has seen, nor ear heard, nor the heart of man conceived" (1 Cor. 2:9). When the subject is the kingdom, all one says about it is said in order not to be silent, in evocative images which may easily contradict each other in factual content while reference is still to the same object. Every culture has its own imagery. In the wealthy Jerusalem of the early days of Isaiah, the image was of an idyllic country life (Isa. 11:6-9). Amidst the poverty of the great city of Ephesus of the days of Revelation, it was the city with streets of gold and gates of pearl (Rev. 21:18-21). In Revelation we read that the New Jerusalem has a strong wall with twelve foundations and twelve gates; behind that wall people can live in safety (Rev. 21:12-14). At the same time we are told that the gates are never shut because there will be no thieves or robbers (Rev. 21:25-27). A man about to start measuring the ground to lay out the walls of the city is stopped because he has failed to understand what the New Jerusalem will be: a city inhabited as villages without walls. In the messianic kingdom there is nothing from which one has to protect oneself behind walls (Zech. 2:1-5). The motives are the same in each case: security is the object, but the images are contradictory.

One can speak about the kingdom in apocalyptic images. One has to remember, however, that they are images, which should prompt us to be very sober. It is enough to refer to the glories of the coming kingdom with one or more pithy images. It is not desirable to indulge oneself in elaborate apocalyptic fantasies of an earthly paradise. The same applies to a spiritual paradise. It would be decidedly wrong if one were to regard these fantasies as an ontological description of the new earth. One who uses the images of the Old and New Testament to that end has misconstrued their eschatological character.

To speak about the kingdom is to speak by way of analogy. In the New Testament that truth is expressed in the concepts of the "new heaven and the new earth." On the one hand there is identity: the reference is to heaven and earth. At the same time the adjective "new" indicates the character of the other reality which can only be approached analogically. The notion of "newness" pervades the New Testament, as a term indicating the analogical character of discourse about the future.

Pneumatologically, therefore, we face the eschaton in an open situation. We can only speak about the kingdom, realized and coming, as an unfinished process which can in no way be apprehended. It is to be expected. We can hope, look forward to, pray, sigh, and work, but it is not at our disposal. The certainties we have are based on the decisive turn of events which occurred in Christ. They are certainties *per analogiam*, by faith: because God in Christ chose in favor of humanity. The well-founded expectation is that in the future he will also choose for humanity. Within this *analogia fidei*, however, there is also an *analogia entis*. The structure of Christ's being corresponds to that of the world in the kingdom of God. It is an analogy, which indicates both similarity and difference. Consequently, from within the analogy to Christ one can only suggest a basic structure. He is the head; we are the members. Still, we are the members of him who came into the world. As they are realized, the essential structures of God's choice are not alien to us. They touch the essentials of our existence. The primary reality is that in Jesus Christ death has been overcome. In that reality God's verdict on the world has become public. The resurrection of Christ is the salvation of the world, the core of the good news. Liberation from death is also the central reality of the kingdom of God. In other words, the kingdom is eternal life. But deliverance from death is also deliverance from fear. "Finitude in awareness is anxiety" said Tillich.[7] Where death no longer reigns, the primal anxiety which pervades human existence is gone. In the wake of death a series of other enemies follow: sickness, sorrow, alienation. With the disappearance of death they have been deprived of power. Characteristic for the messianic signs of the coming kingdom, accordingly, is victory over the powers.

At the same time the resurrection of Christ is the resurrection of the crucified, of him who identified with prostitutes and publicans, Samaritans, Phoenicians, and Syrians. He is the savior of sinners and pagans. In Christ's resurrection God placed himself on the side of sinners and pagans. Consequently, his kingdom bears the stamp of the forgiveness of sins and the acceptance of all. The new existence is ruled by forgiven guilt and broken-down walls of separation. Hence, the kingdom of God is the realm of freedom in which people may live without fear. For anxiety is not only the awareness of finitude; it is also the awareness of guilt. However, where guilt has been removed people may live together as brothers and sisters.

The fundamental data of the kingdom under Christ's rule are no other than those mentioned in the Apostles' Creed: the communion of saints, the forgiveness of sins, the resurrection of the body, and eternal life, as realizations of the way the Spirit travels with the church. Where the church, in the Spirit as firstfruits, already participates in the kingdom,

---

7. Tillich, *Systematic Theology* vol. 1, p. 212.

it participates as communion of saints in forgiveness, and in the resurrection of Christ it already participates in eternal life.

However, there is in addition to the forgiveness of sins and eternal life a third fundamental datum, which is implicit in the Apostles' Creed. It is the certainty of the kingdom or, in other words, the irreversibility of the process, implied in the confession that Jesus Christ is the Son of God, and in the trinitarian framework in which the Spirit is mentioned. The kingdom is the result of divine deeds. The Apostles' Creed tells us who God is and what God does. God's acts issue in eternal life. It is a divine choice, one he never reverses. God cannot ever ignore or pass by Jesus Christ, we said. Nor can he ever pass by the coming kingdom once the Spirit has realized it. And in his last judgment he has pronounced his definitive "yes" (*that* he will do this we believe on the basis of his "yes" to Christ on Easter morning). Accordingly, the kingdom is above the ambivalence of the choice by which the history of this world is driven forward. Where the final choice has been made once and for all, no other choice can possibly be made anymore. Then the ambivalence between good and evil, between doing a thing and not doing it, is gone. There the incentive to action is also gone, for action is the effect of the choice for something other than what is. The kingdom is the realm of rest, which is different from quiet. It is the rest of the joy over what has been accomplished. In the kingdom the history of the world is not thrown out as garbage. It is carried along in the hearts of people who recognize in this history the triune God, who linked his own history to theirs and *in that way alone* willed to be God. Then, with unspeakable joy, humans can say about God's way through history, "It is very good." In the eschaton humans will join God in judging. If *they* are not agreed that it is good, it is not good. If they still have complaints, the kingdom is not the kingdom of peace and consequently not the kingdom of God. The saints will judge the world (1 Cor. 6:2). But if they judge the world, they are also judging the God of the world. If in the last judgment God will justify the world, the world will justify God.

Where the fear of death is gone, where anxiety over guilt is gone, where the ambivalence of choice is gone, there is freedom. The outcome is a completely new society. The kingdom of God is the new earth. Living in *this* world, with its transience, guilt, and insecurity, we can even now speak *per analogiam* about the future, *our* future. We shall constantly have to use the adjective "new." We are a new creation, there is a New Jerusalem, and we shall live on a new earth.

We would be unfaithful to the character of this book, however, if we should fail to end with the remark that a new heaven is also on the way. God and human beings are jointly involved in history. God initiated it, choosing for man. God and man jointly went their strange zigzag way.

In Jesus Christ God chose once and for all to be a God of humans; and in the Spirit of Christ, which is in the spirit of his choice in Christ, he chose to involve humans in that way. He is a God of human beings. His history is the history of man; the history of man is his history. If in the new aeon people will live on a new earth, about which we can now only speak analogically in relation to the old aeon, then God will dwell in a new heaven, about which we can now only speak analogically in relation to his earlier deeds.

Revelation 21:1 reads, "Then I saw a new heaven and a new earth; for the first heaven and the first earth had passed away, and the sea was no more." In the apocalyptic thinking of Revelation earthly events are prepared for in heavenly events. Earthly conflict mirrors heavenly conflict. Accordingly, a new and peaceful earth is possible only with a new and peaceful heaven. In the old heaven there was continual conflict between good and bad angels. Michael and the dragon fought their battles. Now heavenly beings serve to indicate the distance between God and the world. God's involvement is not direct but indirect. When God dwells with man on a new earth, there is really no room anymore for angels, any more than there is room for the Torah and the temple. The awesome distance is superfluous. Angels have completed their time of service and can leave. U. Wilckens believes this is made explicit in 1 Corinthians 15:24.[8] In my opinion the reference there is especially to the powers which are hostile to the kingdom. These are annihilated by Christ. The image is comparable to that of Revelation where Satan is thrown into the lake of fire and brimstone. Revelation 21:1 says this with the words, "and the sea was no more." From ancient times the sea was a power hostile to God's creation and the place from which came the beast which rebelled against God (Rev. 13:1). But this source of evil powers has dried up. So one may also ask whether angels as a good power will not be superannuated when evil powers are denied a place in heaven and the sea is no more. If so, talk of good angels then becomes redundant. It is striking that the book of Revelation which is full of angels does not say a word about them in its vision of the peaceable kingdom. In God's dwelling with people as that is pictured in Revelation 21 and 22 angels can only be in the way.

Heaven is not only the abode of heavenly beings; it even designates God. When a new heaven comes, God himself is renewed in his relationship to people and himself. The tension in apocalyptic goes to the limit. Heaven and earth, God and people, are moved by it. And heaven and earth, God and people, arrive at victory and glory.

When people live on a new earth and under a new heaven, it is a new relationship. Both God and man then stand in a new relationship.

8. Ulrich Wilckens, *Der Brief an die Römer*, vol. 2 (Zurich: Benziger Verlag, 1980), p. 153.

If it is granted to man to live in a relationship of extreme closeness to God, then God lives in a relationship of extreme closeness to man. "And I saw no temple in the city, for its temple is the Lord God the Almighty and the Lamb. And the city has no need of sun or moon to shine upon it, for the glory of God is its light, and its lamp is the Lamb" (Rev. 21:22f.). When God is all and in all (1 Cor. 15:28), that is not only a human fulfillment in his being confirmed by God, but also the fulfillment of God as the one of whom and by whom all things exist (Rom. 11:36). The joy of humans is accompanied by the joy of God. Where the tears are wiped away from human faces there also the tears of the divine face disappear. When suffering humans rise in glory, they are united with the crucified God who sees his glory made full. When the sighs of the suffering humanity of the present age are transformed into the praises of love, then the sighs of the Spirit (too deep for words!) cease; for then the Spirit, himself the love of the Father and the Son, sees that love realized in the lives of people.